T0197168

Richard Rhodes

MASTERS OF DEATH

Richard Rhodes is the author of nineteen books. His *The Making of the Atomic Bomb* won a Pulitzer Prize, a National Book Award, and a National Book Critics Circle Award. He has received Guggenheim, Ford Foundation, MacArthur Foundation, National Endowment for the Arts, and Alfred P. Sloan Foundation fellowships, and lectures frequently to college and professional audiences. Rhodes and his wife live in California.

MASTERS OF DEATH

THE SS-EINSATZGRUPPEN
AND THE INVENTION OF THE HOLOCAUST

Richard Rhodes

VINTAGE BOOKS
A DIVISION OF RANDOM HOUSE INC.
NEW YORK

FIRST VINTAGE BOOKS EDITION, AUGUST 2003

Copyright © 2002 by Richard Rhodes

The Library of Congress has cataloged the Knopf edition as follows:
Rhodes, Richard.
Masters of Death: The SS-Einsatzgruppen and the invention of the
Holocaust / Richard Rhodes.
p. cm.
ISBN 0-375-40900-9 (alk. paper)
1. Holocaust, Jewish (1939–1945)—Poland.   2. Holocaust,
Jewish (1939–1945)—Soviet Union.   3. Nationalsozialistische
Deutsche Arbeiter-Partei. Schutzstaffel. Sicherheitsdienst.
4. World War, 1939–1945—Secret service—Germany.
5. Germany—History—1933–1945.
I. Title.
D804.3 .R53   2002
940.52'18—dc21
2001038898

Vintage ISBN: 978-0-375-70822-0

Author photograph © Marion Ettlinger
Book design by Peter A. Andersen
Maps by Mark Stein Studios

www.vintagebooks.com

146119709

For Laurie Anne Pearlman and Ervin Staub

Death is a master from Germany
　　his eyes are blue
He strikes you with leaden bullets
　　his aim is true
　　　　PAUL CELAN, *Todesfuge*

CONTENTS

Photographs follow page 146.

On the grounds of a commercial rose nursery in Vinnitsa, a town in western Ukraine, two long, grassy beds and a smaller, square bed beside them have been set off with white wrought-iron fences and marked with stone memorials. A Ukrainian historian, Faina Vinokurova—a warm, buxom woman with red hair and commanding presence—led me to this place of sunlight and roses on a June day not long ago. As we stepped around the wooden driveway gate onto the nursery grounds, Ms. Vinokurova's shoulders slumped and her face filled with immeasurable sadness. The long beds had been killing pits, she explained. Four thousand people, Ukrainian Jews, had been murdered there on 16 April 1942. We went over to the smaller bed. It had been a killing pit as well; it held the remains of a thousand murdered children.

Vinnitsa was the last killing site I visited to walk the ground where the events described in this book took place. I had started in Warsaw two weeks earlier, had toured what remained of the death camps at Treblinka, Majdanek and Auschwitz-Birkenau, and then had moved on to places with names less well known: in Lithuania, the Ninth Fort and Ponary; in Belarus, Katyn and Maly Trostinets; in Ukraine, unnamed sites in Uman and Zhitomir, as well as the nursery beds in Vinnitsa. One site I visited almost everyone has heard of: Babi Yar, a ravine in Kiev, where in September 1941 a killing squad led by a tall, mean, drunken former architect named Paul Blobel murdered thirty-four thousand people in two days.

But there were dozens of Babi Yars. Hundreds of killing sites mark massacres from Tallinn on the Baltic Sea in Estonia southward to Odessa on the Black Sea in Ukraine. They were the work of special task forces—in German, Einsatzgruppen—organized by SS-Reichsführer Heinrich Himmler and his second-in-command, Reinhard Heydrich, to follow behind the German army as it advanced into eastern Poland and the western districts of the Soviet Union beginning in late June 1941. The ostensible purpose of the Einsatzgruppen was to secure the rear areas from "partisans" and saboteurs. In fact, their assignment was to murder Jews, not indirectly by herding them into gas chambers but directly, by shooting them into antitank ditches, natural ravines or pits freshly dug by Russian prisoners of war.

The story of the Einsatzgruppen is almost unrelievedly grim, which is perhaps why it has hardly been told. You may well ask why you should submit yourself to the experience of reading about such events. I asked myself the same question, and asked it again more than once as I researched and wrote this book. One answer is that it is impossible to understand how the Holocaust unfolded without knowing this part of the story, because the Einsatzgruppen massacres preceded the invention of the death camps and significantly influenced their development.

Another answer is that the Einsatzgruppen story offers insights into a fundamental Holocaust question: What made it possible for men, some of them "ordinary men," to kill so many people so ruthlessly? As a guide to that question, I have drawn on the research of criminologist Lonnie Athens, which I reported in my previous book *Why They Kill*. Athens identifies experiences of violent socialization as the fundamental cause of violent criminality, and certainly the violence of the Einsatzgruppen, directed without provocation against unarmed victims, was criminal. I review Athens's violent-socialization model of violence development in Chapter 2 and integrate it with its institutional equivalent, which is military and police training and experience.

But the answer that made the most sense to me personally came to me when I remembered the anger that had pushed through the sadness I felt walking among the mass graves in Vinnitsa with Faina Vinokurova: that these victims herded to their deaths deserved written witness, victims who hardly had time to say farewell to the loved ones beside them as they descended into those long graves, victims whose children were torn from their arms, victims who left little record behind. The least I could do, it seemed to me, was work out a narrative of Einsatzgruppen crimes, and if reading about those crimes was painful, it did not even remotely compare to what the victims went through.

PART ONE

THE WAR IN THE EAST

ONE

Eastward from Pretzsch

In the spring of 1941 a police academy in Pretzsch, a town on the Elbe River about fifty miles southwest of Berlin, became the site of a sinister assembly. Several thousand men from the ranks of the SS—the Nazi Party's Schutzstaffel, or defense echelon, a police and security service that answered directly to Adolf Hitler and operated outside the constraints of German law—were ordered to report to Pretzsch for training and assignment. They were not told what their assignment would be, but their commonalities offered a clue: many of them had served in SS detachments in Poland, which Germany had invaded and occupied in 1939, and preference was given to men who spoke Russian.

Assignment to Pretzsch emptied the SS leadership school in Berlin-Charlottenburg and depleted the professional examination course of an SS criminal division. It drew in lower- and middle-ranking officers of the Security Police (the Gestapo and the criminal police), some of them passed on gratefully by their home regiments because they were considered too wild. The Waffen-SS, the small but growing SS army, contributed enlisted men. High-ranking bureaucrats within the shadowy Reich Security Main Office,* an internal SS security agency, were posted to Pretzsch as well. They had been handpicked for leadership positions by Obergruppenführer† Reinhard Heydrich, the head of the RSHA and the second most powerful man in the SS, and his superior Heinrich Himmler, the Reichsführer-SS.‡ Most of these handpicked leaders were lawyers, and a few were physicians or educators; most had earned doctoral degrees. Among the more exotic specimens were Otto Ohlendorf, a handsome but argumentative young economist who had fallen into disfavor with Himmler; Paul Blobel, a rawboned, highstrung, frequently drunken architect; Arthur Nebe, a former vice squad detective and Gestapo head who had enthusiastically volunteered; and Karl Jäger, a brutal fifty-three-year-old secret police commander. A reserve battalion

---

*The Reichssicherheitshauptampt, abbreviated RSHA.
†Lieutenant General.
‡SS National Leader, a title unique to Himmler.

4 THE WAR IN THE EAST

of the regular German Order Police (uniformed urban, rural and municipal police) completed the Pretzsch roster.

Soon the men learned that they would be assigned to an Einsatzgruppe—a task force. Einsatz units—groups and commandos—had followed the German army into Austria, Czechoslovakia and Poland when Germany had invaded those countries successively in 1938 and 1939. Einsatzgruppen secured occupied territories in advance of civilian administrators. They confiscated weapons and gathered incriminating documents, tracked down and arrested people the SS considered politically unreliable—and systematically murdered the occupied country's political, educational, religious and intellectual leadership. Since Germany had concluded a nonaggression pact with the Soviet Union in August 1939, many of the candidates at Pretzsch assumed they would be assigned to follow the Wehrmacht into England. Some of them had previously trained to just that end.

By the spring of 1941, Poland had already been decapitated. Albert Speer, Hitler's architect and later his munitions and armament minister, remembered that on the night of 21 August 1939, when news of Josef Stalin's agreement to the nonaggression pact had settled Hitler's decision to invade Poland, the Führer and his entourage had drifted out onto the terrace of his mountain retreat on the Obersalzberg to watch a rare display of northern lights vermilioning the mountain across the valley. "The last act of *Götterdämmerung* could not have been more effectively staged," Speer writes. "The same red light bathed our faces and our hands. The display produced a curiously pensive mood among us. Abruptly turning to one of his military adjutants, Hitler said: 'Looks like a great deal of blood. This time we won't bring it off without violence.' "

The next day the Führer belabored the generals and field marshals of the Wehrmacht for hours with an impassioned harangue. He told them Germany needed room to expand and as a buffer against the Russians. Therefore he meant not merely to occupy Poland but also to destroy it; in its place a new German eastern frontier would arise. "The idea of treating war as anything other than the harshest means of settling questions of very existence is ridiculous," he challenged the army commanders. "Every war costs blood, and the smell of blood arouses in man all the instincts which have lain within us since the beginning of the world: deeds of violence, the intoxication of murder, and many other things. Everything else is empty babble. A humane war exists only in bloodless brains." A field marshal who attended the conference reported Hitler warning them "that he would proceed against the Poles after the end of the campaign with relentless vigor. Things would happen which would not be to the taste of the German generals." The field marshal understood the warning to mean "the destruction of the Polish intelligentsia, in particular the priesthood, by the SS."

When Germany had attacked Poland on 1 September 1939, beginning the Second World War in Europe, five Einsatzgruppen that Heydrich had organized followed behind the five invading Wehrmacht armies, each group subdivided into four Einsatzkommandos of 100 to 150 men. These advance cadres were augmented with Order Police battalions, Totenkopf* concentration-camp guard regiments and Waffen-SS, producing a combined SS force approaching twenty thousand men. The commander of one of the Polish Einsatzgruppen in 1939, Bruno Streckenbach, would become the head of SS personnel responsible for recruiting the new Einsatzgruppen forming at Pretzsch in May 1941.

Himmler's SS was famously thorough. Heydrich, a tall, horse-faced, sneering former naval officer whom even his own subordinates called "the blond beast," had started his career organizing elaborate card indexes on Nazi Party enemies, a system Hitler had instituted in the early days of the party to keep tabs on his own supporters. If the Einsatzgruppen in Poland followed standard SS practice, the lists Heydrich's staff compiled of Polish enemies would serve them well. An SS officer on a later mission to the Caucasus describes how the system worked:

> As a group leader I was sent supplementary documentation. By far the most valuable was a slim little book, part of a limited, numbered edition, which I never let out of my sight. The typeface was tiny, I remember, and the paper was extra thin, in order to pack the most information into the smallest possible space. . . . It consisted of a series of lists, including the names of every active member of the Communist party in the Caucasus, all the nonparty intelligentsia, and listings of scholars, teachers, writers and journalists, priests, public officials, upwardly mobile peasants, and the most prominent industrialists and bankers. [It contained] addresses *and* telephone numbers. . . . And that wasn't all. There were additional listings of relatives and friends, in case any subversive scum tried to hide, plus physical descriptions, and in some cases photographs. You can imagine what the size of that book would have been if it had been printed normally.

All these categories of people in Poland, and the Polish nobility as well, were marked for murder. During the first weeks after the invasion,

*Death's-Head.

while the Wehrmacht still controlled the occupied areas, a historian of the Polish experience summarizes, "531 towns and villages were burned; the provinces of Lodz and Warsaw suffered the heaviest losses. Various branches of the army and police [i.e., Himmler's legions] carried out 714 [mass] executions, which took the lives of 16,376 people, most of whom were Polish Christians. The Wehrmacht committed approximately 60 percent of these crimes, with the police responsible for the remainder." The historian cites an Englishwoman's eyewitness account of executions in the Polish town of Bydgoszcz:

> The first victims of the campaign were a number of Boy Scouts, from twelve to sixteen years of age, who were set up in the marketplace against a wall and shot. No reason was given. A devoted priest who rushed to administer the Last Sacrament was shot too. He received five wounds. A Pole said afterwards that the sight of those children lying dead was the most piteous of all the horrors he saw. That week the murders continued. Thirty-four of the leading tradespeople and merchants of the town were shot, and many other leading citizens. The square was surrounded by troops with machine-guns.

Three weeks after invading Poland, the Wehrmacht washed its hands of further responsibility for the decapitation, leaving the field to the specialists of the SS. Heydrich met with Quartermaster General Eduard Wagner to agree on an SS "cleanup once and for all" of "Jews, intelligentsia, clergy, nobility." Heydrich then wrote the Einsatzgruppen commanders specifically concerning the "Jewish question in the occupied territory." Cautioning strict secrecy, he distinguished between "the ultimate aim (which will take some time [to accomplish])," and "interim measures (which can be carried out within a shorter period of time)." In the short term, Jews living in territories in western Poland scheduled to be annexed to Germany were to be "cleared" by shipping them eastward; Jews in the remainder of Poland were to be concentrated into ghettos in towns with good railroad connections. Heydrich's letter did not specify what measures the "ultimate aim" would require. Long after the war, when Adolf Eichmann saw this 1939 document, he concluded that it embodied the "basic conception" of "the order concerning the physical extermination of the Jews" of the occupied territories. Large numbers of Polish Jews were murdered in any case, because they were politically suspect for reasons other than their religion; at this early point in time, Heydrich was basically assigning his Einsatzgruppen the transitional task of bringing the Jewish population of Poland under SS control.

An incident in the town of Wloclawek during the last week of September was unusual only in its conflict between authorities. A Totenkopf unit had arrested eight hundred Jewish men. Some of them had been *"auf der Flucht erschossen"*—"shot while trying to escape"—a standard euphemism for extrajudicial killing in the concentration camps guarded by Totenkopf regiments. The SS unit leader had planned to arrest every Jewish male in town, but the local Wehrmacht commander had over-ruled him. "They will all be shot in any case," the SS leader had countered. In his innocence the commander had responded, "The Führer can hardly intend us to shoot all the Jews!" Warsaw fell on 28 September 1939, and the day before, Heydrich could already report that "of the Polish leadership, there remained in the occupied area at most 3 percent."

SS brutality in Poland descended to unadorned slaughter in October, when Himmler extended executions to the mentally and physically disabled. The so-called euthanasia program was just beginning in Germany, to be directed initially against children, but the first SS killings preceded any euthanasia murders. The SS's victims were German, removed from hospitals and nursing homes in the Prussian province of Pomerania and transported by train across the border into occupied Poland. The euthanasia program in Germany had to proceed by stealth, but occupied territory was no-man's-land, beyond German law and public scrutiny. Just as it would be easier to murder Jews in the subjugated lands east of Germany, so it was easier to murder the disabled there, including German citizens.

A large SS regiment had been resident in the Free City of Danzig before the war, commanded by SS Sturmbannführer* Kurt Eimann. Eimann recruited several thousand members of the regiment into an auxiliary police unit that bore his name. Late in October 1939, the Pomeranian disabled were crowded into cattle cars and shipped into occupied Poland. The Eimann Battalion met the train at the railroad station in the town of Neustadt. In a nearby forest, Polish political prisoners labored to dig killing pits to serve as mass graves. Trucks delivered the disabled to the forest. The first victim was a woman about fifty years old; Eimann personally dispatched her with a *Genickschuss*, a shot in the neck from behind at the point where the spinal cord enters the skull. Historian Henry Friedlander quotes from postwar trial testimony: "In front of the pit [Eimann] shot the woman through the base of the skull. The woman, who had walked in front of him without suspecting anything, was instantaneously killed and fell into the pit." During November 1939, further victims were transported from Danzig, filling the Neustadt pits with some 3,500 bodies. To eliminate witnesses, Eimann had the political prisoners who dug the pits murdered and the pits covered with dirt.

*Major.

Friedlander found that essentially all the disabled in the Polish districts annexed to the Third Reich were shot into mass graves: 1,172 psychiatric patients in Tiegenhof beginning on 7 December 1939, for example; 420 psychiatric patients from the hospital in Chelm, near Lublin, on 12 January 1940. A Sonderkommando* formed of German security police from Posen and Lodz by an Einsatzgruppe leader, Herbert Lange, used moving vans fitted with tanks of pure carbon monoxide to murder patients throughout a former Polish province that was annexed to Germany as Wartheland. "After killing handicapped patients in 1940," Friedlander adds, "the [Lange commando] possibly also killed Jews in the small villages of the Wartheland with these early gas vans." "Little by little we were taught all these things," Eichmann would explain without apology. "We grew into them."

A secret annex to Germany's nonaggression pact with the Soviet Union had divided Poland between the two powers. To claim Russia's share of the spoils, the Red Army had invaded Poland from the east on 17 September 1939. Hitler assigned Himmler the work of expelling eastward more than eight million non-Germans from what had been western Poland and moving ethnic Germans westward out of the Soviet-occupied Baltic states to settle in their place. To launch the grandiose winnowing, Himmler ordered Eichmann to organize transportation for a half million Jews and another half million Gentile Poles. "I had to set up guidelines for implementation," Eichmann recalled, "because those were the *Reichsführer*'s orders. For instance, he said, 'No one is to take any more with him than the Germans who were driven out by the French.' After the First World War, he meant, from Alsace-Lorraine, or later from the Rhineland and the Ruhr. I had to find out; at that time, fifty kilos of luggage were allowed [per person]." Himmler issued his expulsion order on 30 October 1939, setting February 1940 as a deadline. After 15 November 1939, the entire railway network of the area of occupied Poland that the Germans had named the General Government—central and southern Poland—was reserved for resettlement transports. Trainloads of Jewish and Gentile Poles began moving east in December. The victims were dumped in the General Government in the middle of Polish winter with no provision for food or shelter. An uncounted number died of exposure or starved, results that led the newly appointed and histrionic head of the General Government, Hans Frank, formerly Hitler's personal lawyer, to declare in a public speech, "What a pleasure,

Sonder means "special."

finally to be able to tackle the Jewish race physically. The more that die, the better." Himmler himself alluded to the devastating consequences of resettlement in a speech the following autumn to one of his battalions, bragging that Poland had been the place

> where, in a temperature forty degrees below zero, we had to drag away thousands, tens of thousands, hundreds of thousands—where we had to have the hardness—you should listen to this, but forget it again at once—to shoot thousands of leading Poles, where we had to have the hardness, otherwise it would have rebounded on us later. In many cases it is much easier to go into battle with a company of infantry than it is to suppress an obstructive population of low culture or to carry out executions or drag people away.

"It's enough to make your hair stand up," the Nazi propagandist Hans Fritzsche would remark after the war, "the childish way these philosophic dilettantes played around with populations as if they were playing checkers."

The transfer of populations foundered as the demands of war production exposed the recklessness of deporting useful manpower, but mass executions of Poles and Jews continued in the General Government; more than one hundred such executions were carried out in the last months of 1939, accounting for at least six thousand lives.

Although the Wehrmacht had conducted mass executions while it was still fighting to subdue Poland, before the fall of Warsaw, those slaughters in its eyes had been disciplined and justified. In contrast, the army leadership was disturbed by the excesses of the Einsatzgruppen in Poland. It was not the victims' suffering that disturbed the military leaders; they were hardly concerned with the victims. Rather, they were concerned with arousing Polish resistance and with the effect of the killings on the character and morale not only of Wehrmacht soldiers but even of the German nation. The most detailed assessment that survives, a memorandum by Eastern Territories Commander Johannes Blaskowitz, is bluntly prophetic:

> It is wholly misguided to slaughter a few ten thousand Jews and Poles as is happening at the moment; for this will neither destroy the idea of a Polish state in the eyes of the mass of the population, nor do away with the Jews. On the contrary, the way in which the slaughter is being carried out is extremely damaging, complicates the problems and makes them much more dangerous than they would have been if premeditated and purposeful action were taken. . . .

It is hard to imagine there can be more effective material in the entire world than that which is being delivered into the hands of enemy propaganda. . . .

The effects on the Wehrmacht hardly need to be mentioned. It is forced passively to stand by and watch these crimes being committed. . . .

The worst damage affecting Germans which has developed as a result of the present conditions, however, is the tremendous brutalization and moral depravity which is spreading rapidly among precious German manpower like an epidemic.

If high officials of the SS and the police demand and openly praise acts of violence and brutality, then before long only the brutal will rule. It is surprising how quickly such people join forces with those of weak character in order, as is currently happening in Poland, to give rein to their bestial and pathological instincts. . . . They clearly feel they are being given official authorization and that they are thus justified to commit any kind of cruel act.

Descriptions of cruel deportations and drunken massacres were couriered back to Berlin and compiled into a dossier of accusations against the SS, and on 24 January 1940 Himmler took tea with Walther von Brauchitsch, the Commander in Chief East, to negotiate a truce.

No record of the meeting survives, but the excuses Himmler offered von Brauchitsch probably crept into a speech he gave a few weeks later:

Obviously it is possible in the east with the trains—but not only the evacuation trains—that a train freezes up and the people freeze. That is possible, that happens unfortunately with Germans as well. You simply cannot do anything to prevent it if they travel from Lodz to Warsaw and the train remains standing ten hours on the track. You cannot blame the train or anyone. That is just the climate. It is regrettable for Germans, it is regrettable for Poles, if you like it is even regrettable for Jews—if anyone wants to pity them. But it is neither intended, nor is it preventable. I consider it wrong to make a great *Lamento* about it.

To those who said it was cruel to march Poles off from their houses with little notice, Himmler went on, "may I kindly remind them that in 1919 our Germans were driven on a punishment trek across the bridges with thirty kilograms of luggage. . . . We have really no need to be crueller [than the French occupation forces were]; however, we do not need either to play the great, wild, dumb German here. Therefore we do not need to get excited about it."

Discipline was the issue, Himmler agreed, not excess:

> I will in no way deny that in the East—it is very well known to me—
> this or that excess occurred, where there was boozing, where people
> were shot drunkenly, people who would perhaps have been among
> those shot in any case, who however should not have been shot by
> people boozing—where looting occurred in the whole East, at times
> in a way, I must say, such as I had not imagined possible, by every
> possible office, by all possible people in all possible uniforms. But one
> does not excite oneself unnecessarily over that. In my view one has to
> grasp the nettle. . . . The question is merely whether you shoulder the
> load or you don't shoulder the load.

But excuses were unlikely to placate a Wehrmacht commander in
chief, and Himmler went on to counter the army's criticism by framing
the SS actions as antiresistance measures and by invoking superior
authority. He sketched this perspective in notes in his own hand for a
speech he made in March 1940 to the supreme army commanders:"Executions of all potential leaders of resistance. Very hard, but necessary.
Have seen to it personally. . . . No underhand cruelties. . . . Severe penal-
ties when necessary. . . . Dirty linen to be washed at home. . . . We must
stay hard, our responsibility to God. . . . A million workslaves and how
to deal with them." And the appeal to authority, reported by an aide of
von Brauchitsch's who was present at the meeting:"With wagging pince-
nez and a dark expression on his common face [Himmler] had said he
had been charged by the Führer to take care that the Poles could not rise
again. Therefore extermination policy."

The three-week course at Pretzsch in June 1941 involved only minimal
training. Bruno Streckenbach, one man remembered, told the new Einsatzgruppen "that this was a war assignment which would be concluded
by December at the latest." Another recalled hearing from Stahlecker,
the newly appointed chief of Einsatzgruppe A, that "we would be putting down resistance behind the troop lines, protecting and pacifying the
rear army area (the word 'pacify' was used very frequently) and hence
keeping the area behind the front clear. . . . Stahlecker also told us we
would have to conquer our weaker selves and that what was needed
were tough men who understood how to carry out orders. He also said to
us that anyone who thought that he would not be able to withstand the
stresses and psychological strains that lay ahead could report to him
immediately afterwards." The men sat through familiar lectures on
honor and duty and the subhuman nature of the people they would be

asked to corral. They conducted "terrain exercises," which one of them dismissed as "games of hide and seek." The military training, another remembered, "was very brief. It was limited to firing of weapons. The men and the NCOs had the opportunity to go on a range and fire their weapons. At that time no intensive military training was possible, because the physical condition of the men didn't permit this in most cases; . . . all the men intended to be sent to an *Einsatz* were inoculated, and the results of this inoculation brought fever and weakness in its wake, so that military training was not possible." Nor, evidently, was it necessary for accomplishing the work the Einsatzgruppen would do.

Only near the end of their time in Pretzsch, a few days before they would march, did the men learn where they were going: Russia. The Third Reich was preparing a surprise attack against the Soviet Union, Operation Barbarossa, scheduled to begin on 22 June 1941. Behind the Wehrmacht as it invaded the U.S.S.R. from the west would follow four Einsatzgruppen. Einsatzgruppe A, under forty-year-old SS-Brigadeführer* Stahlecker, attached to Army Group North, would operate in the former Baltic states of Estonia, Latvia and Lithuania. Einsatzgruppe B, under forty-six-year-old SS-Brigadeführer Arthur Nebe, attached to Army Group Center, would "pacify" Byelorussia. Einsatzgruppe C, under forty-nine-year-old SS-Brigadeführer Dr. Otto Rasch, attached to Army Group South, would sweep northern and central Ukraine. Einsatzgruppe D, under thirty-four-year-old SS-Standartenführer† Otto Ohlendorf, attached to Eleventh Army, would operate in southwestern Ukraine (Bessarabia), southern Ukraine, the Crimea and the Caucasus.

The four task forces were further subdivided into a total of sixteen Sonderkommandos and Einsatzkommandos, the real operational units of the formations, answerable to the task force leaders but functionally independent. Blobel, for example, led Sonderkommando 4a of Rasch's Einsatzgruppe C, operating through the Ukraine to Kiev and beyond; Jäger, the brutal, walrus-mustached secret policeman, led Einsatzkommando 3 of Stahlecker's Einsatzgruppe A, operating throughout Lithuania.

Einsatzgruppe A, the largest of the four task forces, counted 990 personnel (divided into two Sonderkommandos and two Einsatzkommandos), including 340 Waffen-SS, 172 motorcycle riders, 18 administrators, 35 Security Service (SD) personnel, 41 Criminal Police, 89 State Police, 87 Auxiliary Police, 133 Order Police, 13 female secretaries and clerks, 51

---

*Brigadier General.
†Colonel.

interpreters, 3 teletype operators and 8 radio operators. Ohlendorf, whose Einsatzgruppe D, with a roll call of about 500, was the smallest of the four (but was subdivided into four Sonderkommandos and one Einsatzkommando), would testify that his task force "had 180 vehicles. . . . This large number of [trucks] shows that the *Einsatzgruppe* was fully motorized. The *Waffen*-SS . . . were equipped with automatic rifles. The others either had rifles or automatic rifles. I believe that is about the total equipment." The fact that the Einsatzgruppen were fully motorized is significant: the Wehrmacht itself was only partly motorized in June 1941, with much of its artillery still horse-drawn. Himmler intended his Einsatzgruppen to succeed and made sure the units were properly outfitted.

No detailed record of Einsatzgruppen equipment has survived, but a military historian, French L. MacLean, offers a speculative list derived from standard German military practice. Basing his estimates on Einsatzgruppe A, MacLean puts the total number of vehicles per group at about 160, of which sixteen would have been motorcycles, some with sidecars. Another sixteen would have been staff cars, MacLean estimates, "leaving some 128 as cargo and troop-carrying trucks—most likely Opel 'Blitz' 3-ton types. . . . Some 63 trucks would have been used to transport *Einsatzgruppe* soldiers; 50 others would have been remaining to haul required supplies."

The four Einsatzkommandos of Einsatzgruppe A and the headquarters staff would have been issued field radios and possibly teletype machines for communication; radio messages that the British intercepted provide documentary evidence of Einsatzgruppen crimes. For electricity, MacLean notes, the units would each have had at least one mobile generator, "most commonly a large 507-pound two-cylinder variety." There is no mention among eyewitness accounts of earth-moving equipment such as bulldozers; MacLean issues each Einsatzkommando at least forty shovels for digging mass graves, and possibly surveying equipment to record sites. "Each group would have also had a large field range mounted on one of the trucks to provide food for the troops. All elements would have additionally carried their own ammunition, cold-weather heating stoves, medium-size tents, portable field desks and chairs, spare parts for vehicles, light sets, cooking and serving utensils, arms room supplies, a few days' worth of rations and water, gas and petroleum products for the vehicles, and sundry other items required for living in the field." Weapons, MacLean proposes, would have included Luger, Mauser Model 1910 and Walther P-38 pistols for officers and Mauser Kar 98b rifles for enlisted men. Machine pistols ("Bergmann 9mm Model 35/Is or MP 38s") were commonly used by both officers and enlisted men. Machine guns would control perimeters; hand grenades would flush victims from hideouts. There was no need for large arms, MacLean concludes: "The mission of the *Einsatzkommando,* after all, was execution, not combat."

This time around, the Reichsführer-SS wanted no Wehrmacht complaints about his Einsatzgruppen operations; with Hitler's support he saw to it that the military signed off in advance. Hitler himself dictated the necessary paragraph in the formal "Instructions on Special Matters Attached to Directive No. 21 (Barbarossa)," which Field Marshal Wilhelm Keitel, chief of the Armed Forces High Command, issued on 13 March 1941:

> Within the field of operations of the army, in order to prepare the political and administrative organization, the *Reichsführer-SS* assumes on behalf of the Führer special tasks which arise from the necessity finally to settle the conflict between two opposing political systems. Within the framework of these duties the *Reichsführer-SS* acts independently and on his own responsibility.

The "two opposing political systems" were Bolshevism, which Hitler and his Nazi leadership believed to be a Jewish conspiracy, and National Socialism.

Negotiating the details of this order, Army Quartermaster Wagner and Heydrich agreed on 26 March 1941 that Heydrich's task forces were "authorized within the frame of their assignment to carry out on their own responsibility executive measures concerning the civilian population." "Special tasks" and "executive measures" were SS euphemisms for mass murder. By ceding to Himmler's organization independent authority over civilians in the territories it would occupy upon the commencement of Barbarossa, the Wehrmacht was knowingly colluding in atrocity.

It did so partly because it accepted Hitler's argument that "Jewish" Bolshevism was a fundamental threat to the German state, if not to civilization itself—and partly because Hitler bought it off with medals and promotions. A general attending a March 1941 speech to several hundred Barbarossa commanding officers and chiefs of staff heard Hitler invoke a "clash between two ideologies." Bolshevism, the Führer claimed, was "the equivalent of social delinquency. Communism is a tremendous danger for the future. We must get away from the point of view of soldierly comradeship [between opposing armies]. The Communist is from first to last no comrade. It is a war of extermination." To be exterminated were "Bolshevik commissars and the Communist intelligentsia. . . . Commissars and the NKVD [i.e., Soviet secret police] people are criminals and must be treated as such."

The political purges of the previous decade in the U.S.S.R. gave weight to Hitler's assertions; the German military was keenly aware that the NKVD purges had decimated the ranks of Red Army officers. "Out of eighty members of the 1934 Military Soviet," writes Barbarossa historian Alan Clark, "only five were left in September 1938. All eleven Deputy Commissars for Defense were eliminated. Every commander of a military district . . . had been executed by the summer of 1938. Thirteen out of fifteen army commanders, fifty-seven out of eighty-five corps commanders, 110 out of 195 divisional commanders, 220 out of 406 brigade commanders, were executed. But the greatest numerical loss was borne in the Soviet officer corps from the rank of colonel downward and extending to company commander level." From the point of view of a German officer, it would not be wise to lose the war.

The final components of Wehrmacht capitulation to SS operations in the war zone were assembled in further negotiations in May 1941 between Quartermaster Wagner and Walter Schellenberg, the polished, diplomatic SS officer who directed the counterespionage section of Heydrich's RSHA. The Einsatzgruppen, Wagner had agreed, would operate even in the front-line areas (under Wehrmacht supervision) as well as completely independently behind the lines, with logistic support—quarters, fuel, rations—from the army. "This is the first time these special units will have been engaged at the front," Heydrich had emphasized when he briefed Schellenberg conspiratorially before the negotiations began; "every one of their members will have the opportunity to prove himself and to earn a decoration. This should finally dispel the false impression that the staff of the executive departments are cowards who have got themselves safe posts out of the fighting line. This is extremely important, because it will strengthen our position in relation to the Wehrmacht." If the Einsatzgruppen were ideological vanguards, they would also be instruments of bureaucratic infighting—of which Heydrich was a master.

Further support for the Einsatzgruppen came on 6 June 1941, when the army high command (OKH, Oberkommando des Heeres) issued its Commissar Order. Written distribution of this notorious order was confined to a few senior officers, who passed it along orally to their subordinates. The Communist political commissars, in the OKH's eyes, were "bearers of the Jewish-Bolshevik worldview" within the Red Army and the "initiators of barbaric, Asiatic methods of combat." They could be expected to visit special cruelty upon German POWs, the Commissar Order asserted, and should therefore be shot on capture. Other Soviet functionaries could be sorted into those who were active opponents of Germany (also to be shot on capture) and those who were not (who might be spared). Doubtful cases were to be handed over to the Einsatzgruppen. With the Commissar Order, Keitel asserted in a postwar deposition, Hitler was clearing the way "for Himmler to become, alongside the Wehrmacht, a key factor in the conduct of the war in the East. The justification for this move was sought in the claim that the Soviet government had not ratified the 'Hague Agreement' of 1907 or the Geneva accords and had intentionally set itself above the conventions of international law; their breach relieved us of our corresponding obligations."

On 17 June 1941, a day or two after Streckenbach told the men in Pretzsch about Barbarossa, Heydrich ordered the chiefs of the Einsatzgruppen and their commandos to Berlin, to RSHA headquarters at No. 8 Prinz Albrechtstrasse, where he briefed them further on their impending mission. Erwin Schulz, who had led an Einsatzkommando in Czechoslovakia in 1938 and who had just been appointed to lead Einsatzkommando 5 (EG C), remembered Heydrich using many of the same arguments Hitler had used with the Wehrmacht leadership. "The fight which would soon take place would be the hardest and most bitter the German people have ever gone through," Schulz testified Heydrich told them. "In the fight to come not only were people fighting against other people, but for the first time ideology was fighting against another ideology. . . . He explained that Bolshevism would not stop from using every means of fighting, as Lenin had already written; emphasizing in particular the part the partisans were to play, which Lenin and others had written about, and this could not be misunderstood. [He said] that everyone should be sure to understand that in this fight Jews would definitely take their part, and that in this fight everything was set at stake, and the side which gave in would be . . . overcome. For that reason all measures had to be taken against the Jews in particular. The experience in Poland had shown this."

Schulz emphasized in this postwar testimony, however, that neither in Berlin nor in Pretzsch had Heydrich and Streckenbach mentioned either the Commissar Order or the extermination of the Jews. At the outset of Barbarossa, at least, the work of the new Einsatzgruppen would be similar to the work of the Einsatzgruppen in Austria, Czechoslovakia and Poland—brutal enough work at that. Heydrich ordered four categories of enemies executed: "[1] All officials of the Comintern* (most of these will certainly be career politicians); [2] officials of senior and middle rank and 'extremists' in the [Communist] Party, the Central

*The Communist International, the international organization of the Communist Party.

Committee, and the provincial and district committees; [3] the people's commissars; [4] Jews in the service of the party or the government; [as well as] other extremist elements (saboteurs, propagandists, snipers, assassins, agitators, etc.)." Heydrich also told the Einsatzgruppen leaders to secretly encourage and not to interfere with "any purges that may be initiated by anti-Communist or anti-Jewish elements in the newly occupied territories." Which meant that Jews who were not "in the service of the party or the government" were targeted from the outset; if the SS was not yet prepared to be seen murdering large numbers of Jews without at least minimal "political" justification, it was charged with the responsibility of organizing others to do so. ("The aim of *Einsatzkommando* 2 from the beginning," commando leader Rudolf Lange would report from Latvia in January 1942, "was a radical solution of the Jewish problem through the execution of all Jews.")

The SS probably approached mass murder cautiously because of its past conflicts with the Wehrmacht; it needed first to assess whether the army on the scene would support and ignore the SS's performance of its murderous "special tasks" in the occupied territories as the high command in Berlin had agreed to do. And in any case, as Streckenbach had informed the new Einsatzgruppen in Pretzsch, Russia was expected to be defeated by December. For now, elimination of the "Jewish-Bolshevik" leadership and intelligentsia; after the quick victory, there would be time to deal with the rest of the Eastern Jews.

But not only the Jews. A more grandiose vision than revenge against the Jews drove the Nazi elite. Himmler had refurbished a Saxon castle, Wewelsburg, for his SS leadership, which he considered "a knightly Order." Sited on a bluff of the Alme River near Paderborn in western Germany, it looked out grandly across the Westphalian plain. One week before Barbarossa, the Reichsführer-SS assembled his top SS and police leadership at Wewelsburg for a three-day meeting. Heydrich attended; so did Heydrich's stern, balding rival Kurt Daluege, the chief of the Order Police, and the Higher SS and Police Leaders Himmler had designated to assume civilian control of the occupied Soviet territories once the Wehrmacht moved on. Speaking to the assembled Gruppenführers* in their elegant black uniforms, Himmler repeated Hitler's arguments about an ultimate contest between ideologies and the necessity of seizing new living space—*Lebensraum*—for the Fatherland. He then put a number on what that seizure would mean. "It is a question of existence," he said, "thus it will be a racial struggle of pitiless severity, in the course of which 20 to 30 million Slavs and Jews will perish through military

---

*Major Generals

actions and crises of food supply." In Himmler's vision, the Nazi plan for *Lebensraum* meant clearing the Soviet Union of its indigenous population all the way to the Urals through war, murder, enslavement and deliberate starvation.

Heydrich inspected his troops immediately before they moved out. "On that day of inspection," Erwin Schulz recalled, the Einsatzgruppen commandos "were gathered together on the marching field . . . and lined up in the open square." Heydrich hurried his walk through the ranks; a rainstorm was coming that might ground his plane and he needed to return to Berlin. "And then the inspection took place by Heydrich," Schulz concludes, "and after the inspection they marched out of this place down the road." No more sinister phalanx was ever loosed on the world.

TWO

Vicious Circles

The Third Reich was built on violence. It governed with violence, dominated Europe with violence and provoked a violent response that finally destroyed it. The scale of its use of violence, not only its anti-Semitism, distinguishes it from other contemporary governments and regimes. Anti-Semitism had a long history in the West and pervaded European society. The Jews of the Diaspora had migrated to Poland and western Russia in the first place because Christian anti-Semitism had driven them out of western Europe in the fourteenth and fifteenth centuries. Millions of copies of the widely translated, bogus *Protocols of the Elders of Zion,* supposedly a transcription of a secret Jewish council's plans to subvert legitimate governments and take over the world, were sold internationally in the 1920s and 1930s; Henry Ford took the forgery as literally as Adolf Hitler did. Hitler cherished a fanatic hatred of the Jews, whom he believed to be his regime's most dangerous enemies, and he put the highest priority on their elimination, but he intended to enslave and destroy with privation the far more numerous Slavic peoples as well, as Himmler's words at Wewelsburg confirm.

The control of violence is a fundamental responsibility of government. Governments control violence by monopolizing it. They authorize military and police forces to use violence but deem criminal any other individual or institutional use. From this basic division, which evolved across five centuries in the West as governments enlarged and centralized, the common belief has emerged that government violence is rational (or at least deliberate and intentional), while private violence is irrational, aberrant, the product of psychopathology rather than deliberate intention. In fact, violence is violence, whether public or private, official or unofficial, legal or illegal, good or bad. Violence is an instrumentality, not a psychopathology or a character disorder. Violence is a means to an end—domination and control—one of many possible means. Since its essence is injury, its efficacy in the long term is marginal, but its short-term advantages are obvious.

To say that governments monopolize violence is to imply that violence is a commodity that can be collected and stored. Violence is a behavior. As such, it resides in individuals, people who have experienced it and out of that experience learned to produce it more or less on demand. Weapons enter the picture as tools violent people may or may not use to amplify their violence production. Governments monopolize violence by authorizing some of their citizens to use violence in circumstances deemed legal and official. These citizens may have come to their official duties already experienced with violence, or they may gain their violent experience through official training. However they learn to use violence, even these violent officials are authorized to do so only under specific circumstances, and if they use violence under unauthorized circumstances, such acts are deemed criminal. Police brutality and military atrocity, for example, are two categories of criminal violence. The violence that police and military apply illegally—against noncombatants, for example, or against citizens who have not committed a crime or are not resisting arrest—is similar to the violence they use officially. Ironically, such illegal but otherwise comparable acts by violent officials are often characterized as "irrational" or "crazy."

Many theories have been proposed to explain violent behavior, including loss of control, involuntary impulse, unconscious motivation, lack of conscience, character disorders, genetic inheritance or neurological damage. Some of these theories are anecdotal, based on an observer's interpretation of a violent actor's intentions. Others derive from statistical correlational studies, which by definition do not reveal causal relationships but merely identify qualities that may be associated in some way with violent behavior. That people become violent because they have low self-esteem, for example, is a widely accepted theory that minimal interaction with violent people, including violent professionals, quickly disconfirms: violent people usually have overweeningly high self-esteem verging on egomania, because they are confident of their ability to handle conflict and because other people, fearing them, show them great deference. Not all sociopaths are violent; not all violent people have neurological damage; unconscious motivation is by definition unprovable; and any theory of violence development that fails to account for official violent behavior as well as criminal is incomplete.

In his history *Hitler's Willing Executioners*, the young Holocaust scholar Daniel Jonah Goldhagen ascribes Nazi mass murder to what he calls "eliminationist anti-Semitism," which he defines as "the belief that Jewish influence, by nature destructive, must be eliminated irrevocably from society." Besides being tautological—because it includes the effect (elimination) in the cause ("eliminationist anti-Semitism")—Goldhagen's theory fails to explain the Third Reich's fervor for murdering not only Jews but also Slavs, Gypsies, homosexuals and the disabled.

It assumes that violence is essentially an overflow phenomenon, so that when too much of some volatile substance has accumulated in an individual or a society (in this case anti-Semitism), it will overflow in the form of violent behavior; as Goldhagen writes naively and again tautologically, "People must be motivated to kill others, or else they would not do so." In fact, motivation is not sufficient by itself to produce serious violence; people must also have undergone prior violent experiences: they must have *learned* to be violent and must have come to identify themselves as violent. Otherwise their intense hatreds will emerge as ugly but nonviolent behaviors, such as expressions of contempt, denunciations, discrimination, ostracism—exactly the sort of behaviors that the rest of twentieth-century Europe, and Germany before Hitler, demonstrated toward the Jews. As several critics have noted, Goldhagen's theory that eliminationist anti-Semitism explains the Holocaust also isolates the most destructive genocide of the twentieth century as a unique event (in Goldhagen's formulation, "a radical break with everything known in human history"), disconnected from the other genocides of the age, when in fact other genocides—of the Armenians, for example, or of the Tutsi in Rwanda—resemble the Holocaust in etiology if not in scale even though anti-Semitism played no part in their occurrence. There is much of value in Goldhagen's book, but the evidence, including the evidence he cites, does not support a theory that ideology *causes* violent behavior, though it may well be used to justify it.

One theory that accounts for violent officials as well as violent criminals and is based on causal rather than correlational evidence is the violent-socialization theory of the American criminologist Lonnie Athens. Using the method of universals formulated by the Scottish philosopher David Hume, which identifies cause and effect retrospectively (and therefore always provisionally) by discovering the unique attributes of an exemplary population, Athens interviewed incarcerated violent criminals and isolated from their narratives the minimum sequence of violent social experiences that they *all* had in common, a sequence that he found to be missing or incomplete in people with experience of violence who had not committed serious violent acts.

Athens did not study violent officials. Some violent officials (notably police) are self-selected and come to their profession already experienced with violence, as many of the Einsatzgruppen did. For those officials who acquire their violent skills in official training, there are clear parallels between their training experiences and the four-stage developmental process that Athens identified in the backgrounds of violent criminals. Since violence, official or private, is learned through violent experience, such parallels are to be expected and should not be surprising. If Athens's violent socialization model is correct, however, there should also be significant *differences* between the formal programs of training of violent officials and the informal violent socialization process, because violent criminals use violence in situations where violent officials are constrained. Such differences do emerge on analysis, and Athens's theory explains them. None of the other theories of violence development passes this crucial test.

The violent socialization process, Athens found, divides into four stages, which he calls (1) brutalization; (2) belligerency; (3) violent performances; (4) virulency. The stages are sequential: each stage has to be fully experienced before the subject advances to the next one, a process that can occur cataclysmically in a short period of time or across a period of years. Brutalization is inflicted on novices and is thus involuntary, but passage through the three later stages results from *decisions* the subject makes. So people become violent by choice, not by chance. Their choices may be constrained by their circumstances, but they are never the only possible choices available. (Many people brutalized in childhood, for example, do not become violent adults. They make other choices that lead to nonviolent outcomes.) And once a subject has completed violent socialization and has become dangerously violent, Athens found, each act of violence he perpetrates is a further deliberate choice, not merely an automatic reaction or a loss of control. Which means that people who use violence against other people choose to do so and are therefore responsible for their acts. That violence is a choice rather than a compulsion or a release is taken for granted in the military and among police; the concept has been obscured where private violence is concerned simply because such violence has become deviant in modern civilized society, relatively uncommon and unfamiliar. Criminal law, however, drawing on centuries of common experience, is founded on the presumption that violent acts are deliberate.

Distinctions such as these are important for assessing the responsibility of Einsatzgruppen personnel for the atrocities they committed.

Brutalization, the first stage of violent socialization, Athens found to consist of three distinct but related significant experiences that might occur in any order and at differing times and places: (a) violent subjugation (an authority figure from one of the novice's primary groups uses violence or the threat of violence to force the novice to submit to his authority by showing obedience and respect); (b) personal horrification (the novice witnesses people close to him undergoing violent subjugation); (c) violent coaching (to prompt violent conduct, people whom the novice perceives to be or to have been authentically violent instruct the novice in how to conduct himself when confronted with conflict, emphasizing that he has an inescapable personal responsibility to physically attack people who provoke him).

Many people today identify these three conjoined experiences with child abuse, but they have been the common lot of children throughout most of human history and continue to be the common lot of children in much of the world today: domination with violence or the threat of violence by parents, adult relatives and older siblings; witnessing the domination of mothers and siblings; coaching, especially of boys, that physical violence is an expected and appropriate way to settle disputes. Certainly brutalization was the common lot of most children in Germany at the beginning of the twentieth century. It is also the standard boot camp experience of military recruits: real or threatened violent subjugation by drill instructors, witnessing drill instructors similarly subjugating barracksmates, coaching in combat responsibilities. Military training imposes on recruits both violent coaching in Athens's sense and specific instruction in weapons and tactics, and brutalization may continue beyond basic training. "Harsh military discipline had a long tradition in Germany," the historian Omer Bartov reports in *Hitler's Army*. ". . . The strict obedience demanded from the troops, and the draconian punishments meted to offenders, doubtlessly played a major role in maintaining unit cohesion under the most adverse combat conditions." SS training as Himmler organized it was known for its brutality; training in the Totenkopf divisions that supplied guards for concentration camps was even more brutal. Even ordinary police training before the war in German-speaking Europe was brutalizing: Fritz Stangl, later to be commandant of the death camp at Treblinka, told writer Gitta Sereny of his police academy experience in Austria, "They called it the 'Vienna School.' . . . They were a sadistic lot. They drilled the feeling into us that everyone was against us: that all men were rotten."

Brutalization "is an odious and traumatic experience," Athens observes. It leaves the novice shaken, "dejected by the events that have transpired in his life," deeply troubled and confused. "Why did all this happen to me?" he begins to ask himself. The onset of this emotional turbulence signals the beginning of the second stage of violent socialization, belligerency.

Like other social traumas people suffer in life that expose them to challenges their previous experience has not prepared them to master—serious illness, a natural disaster, physical disfigurement, the death of a loved one—the trauma of brutalization shatters the novice's identity. Breaking down a recruit's identity is the purpose of military basic training, of course, part of an institutional process that military organizations have evolved by trial and error over hundreds of years to turn a civilian into a soldier.

Moving into belligerency, the novice questions his previous values, which failed to encompass brutalization. Brooding over his brutalization experiences, he comes to focus on his personal performance and responsibility, finally identifying the specific question he has to answer: What can I do to stop other people from violently subjugating me and people I value? Expressed differently, his problem is to find a way to reorganize himself into someone who can successfully survive further encounters with the kind of traumatic experience that has shattered his former identity.

When people have undergone social trauma and fragmentation, they seek guidance from others who have successfully overcome comparable experiences. The belligerent subject has a fund of advice at hand on how to deal with violent subjugation—the stories and ridicule and threats and harangues of his violent coaches—and now, abruptly, he realizes that their advice makes sense. "It is *as if* the subject had earlier been partially deaf," Athens writes, "and has only now heard what his coach has been telling him all along: resorting to violence is sometimes necessary in this world."

Struck by his insight, which takes on the force of a personal revelation, and convinced of its correctness, the belligerent subject now "firmly resolves to resort to violence in his future relations with people." This first violent resolution—resolving to seriously injure or even kill someone should the circumstances arise—is a landmark in the subject's life, but it is still strongly qualified. "The subject is prepared to resort to potentially lethal violence," Athens explains, "but only if he deems it absolutely necessary for the well-being of his body and mind and if he believes he has some chance of success." That is, he resolves to use violence—but only defensively, to protect himself or the people he values against imminent danger or at least purposeful and cruel antagonism. Why these qualifications? Because personally attacking someone with serious violent intent involves risking serious injury, even death. No one confronts such risks lightly, not even seasoned police officers or combat soldiers.

In making this mitigated violent resolution, the subject moves from belligerency, stage two of violent socialization, to stage three: violent performances. Given the right circumstances, he undertakes to use serious violence against someone who has seriously provoked him. A subject can win or lose such a violent confrontation, or the fight can result in a draw. Defeat, especially repeated major defeats, may lead him to question the wisdom of his violent resolution, to decide he has little aptitude for violence and to resign himself to nonviolence. Then his resolution may wither away, or the still-fragile new identity he has been trying to construct may shatter as his old identity shattered, leaving him once again fragmented and derelict. Suicide and violence are inversely correlated in specific populations, for example, suggesting that suicide is an alternative outcome to resolving the conflicts that brutalization presents. A few Einsatzgruppen personnel made that choice, as did, of course, a much larger number of Jewish victims.

But success with defensive violence marks a turning point in the subject's violence development. He has proven his resolve, which gives him great personal satisfaction. He has also answered the painful question he identified during the belligerency stage of how to protect himself and the people he values from violent subjugation. Stage three of violent socialization appears in fact to be relatively stable; many people who have been violently socialized to this point stop here and move no further, remaining prepared throughout their lives to use serious violence only when physically threatened or seriously antagonized—in Athens's terminology, marginally violent. Modern Western societies are composed of mixed populations of pacifist and marginally violent people: people who are not prepared to use serious violence even if physically threatened or seriously antagonized and people who are. Neither population considers itself to be violent, since its violence, if any, is essentially defensive. Modern Western societies also, of course, include small populations of fully violent people, a deviant minority that law enforcement agencies work to restrain.

Institutional violence training is designed to socialize officials to the point of defensive violent performances—that is, to make them marginally violent—but to block further violence development. Police and soldiers are violently socialized to this third stage to prepare them to control and protect the rest of us. Many remain marginally violent throughout their careers. But stage three can be a slippery slope, since it already encompasses the majority of the violent experiences necessary to become fully, malefically violent. All that is missing is social reinforcement of a violent identity and a widening resolution to use violence.

Those final components of violent socialization constitute stage four, virulency. However personally satisfied a violent performer may be with his defensive victories, they will not change his fundamental view of himself—his self-conception, his identity—unless other people acknowledge them and demonstrate their full significance to him by their actions. When people learn of a successful violent performance by someone whom they previously judged not to be violent, they act differently toward him: they begin treating him as if he were dangerous. "They act toward him much more cautiously," Athens writes, "taking particular pains not to offend or provoke him in any way. . . . For the first time, the subject keenly senses genuine trepidation when he approaches people." These heady experiences of violent notoriety, especially when combined with his painful memories of feeling powerless and inadequate during brutalization and belligerency, encourage the subject to believe that violence works, that he has discovered a way not only to reliably protect himself from the violent oppression of others but also to dominate other people just as he was once dominated. At which point, Athens found, "the subject makes a new violence resolution which far surpasses the one [he] made before. . . . He now firmly resolves to attack people physically with the serious intention of gravely harming or even killing them for the slightest or no provocation whatsoever. . . . In making this later violent resolution, the subject has completely switched his stance from a more or less defensive posture to a decidedly offensive one."

With this final resolution to use violence *offensively,* the subject's violent socialization is complete. Someone who is prepared to use serious physical violence against victims who provoke him minimally or not at all is clearly a dangerous person; such acts are felonious in modern societies regardless of their perpetrator's official status.

Athens's evidence that violent socialization was the common denominator among the violent criminals he studied strongly supports his contention that it is the cause of violent criminality. The clear parallels between violent socialization, which Athens discovered in the common past of violent criminals, and military combat training, which has evolved by trial and error across the centuries, demonstrate prima facie that a truncated form of violent socialization has been adapted by military institutions to convert recruits into capable violent professionals.

Militaries limit violence in much the same way entire societies limit violence: by instituting and maintaining both formal and informal social controls. Military law, for example, distinguishes legal and acceptable killing of enemy combatants from illegal and unacceptable killing of enemy prisoners, mutilating enemy dead, torturing prisoners or raping, battering or killing noncombatants. Unacceptable violence is punishable under military law much as unacceptable violence is punishable under civilian law.

Social trepidation and violent notoriety in military organizations are organized, constrained and parceled out in mandated rituals of rank deference—speaking when spoken to, standing at attention, saluting, calling officers "sir," giving or receiving obligatory orders—which not only recall the hierarchical chain of command but also formalize the different degrees of military (by implication, violent) experience. Badges and medals, which civilians sometimes find mysterious or even quaint, are potent and awe-inspiring emblems of honorable violent performance. Formal and informal evocations of military honor and pride delimit the boundaries of acceptable violent behavior. Social stigmatizing and shunning can have lethal consequences under combat conditions and are therefore powerful social controls when directed against soldiers who use violence malefically. Distancing—mechanically (killing at a distance with artillery or bombs) or organizationally (multiple executioners shooting at the same time)—also effectively limits socialization beyond defensive violence.

Constraining soldiers to defensive violence is important to militaries for reasons more immediately practical than simply conforming to treaty obligations limiting military violence: soldiers whose experiences and choices have carried them through virulency to criminal maleficence are subversive of military discipline and dangerous not only to the enemy but also to their own ranks, particularly to the superiors who order them into harm's way. Bartov describes the development of just such complications in the Wehrmacht after Barbarossa:

> Within the ranks of the army, breaches of combat discipline were punished with unprecedented harshness and contempt for life; conversely, soldiers were ordered to commit "official" and "organized" acts of murder and destruction against enemy civilians, POWs and property; and, as a consequence of the legalization of criminality, the troops soon resorted to "wild" requisitions and indiscriminate shootings explicitly forbidden by their commanders. In stark contradiction to the harsh combat discipline, however, the troops were rarely punished for unauthorized crimes against the enemy, both because of their commanders' underlying sympathy with such actions, and because they constituted a convenient safety valve for venting the men's anger and frustration caused by the rigid discipline demanded from the men and by the increasingly heavy cost and hopelessness of the war. Thus a vicious circle was created whereby the perversion of discipline bred increasing barbarism, which in turn further brutalized discipline.

Athens's violent-socialization model supplies an evidence-based instrument through which to view the Third Reich, and specifically the Einsatzgruppen, that may help to illuminate their history and thus the history of the Holocaust.

. . .

When Field Marshal and Reich President Paul von Hindenburg, a giant with a *basso profundo* voice, invited Adolf Hitler to assume the chancellorship of Germany on 30 January 1933, the new Führer installed a government of criminals and radicalized former soldiers, including convicted assassins such as Nazi Party official Martin Bormann and future Auschwitz commandant Rudolf Höss. Nearly thirty percent of Nazi Party members had a strong militaristic background, many of them as irregulars fighting in the streets as members of the Freikorps, which were responsible for nearly four hundred political assassinations in the postwar years of turmoil.

Hitler himself had been imprisoned at Landsberg in 1924 for high treason for his part in the Munich Beer Hall Putsch, which included firing into the air to take command of a crowd and holding hostages at gunpoint. Before that, in 1921, he and two other party leaders had rushed a speaking platform and assaulted a Bavarian monarchist speaker with clubs and chairs. Since the three men's bodyguards had joined in the assault—a total of six men surrounding the victim, Otto Ballerstedt—the extent of Hitler's personal participation is unclear. Neither incident can be characterized as a successful violent performance, and there is no other evidence that Hitler was personally violent, however many millions he would later order killed. He served for four years as a courier in the German army in the First World War, but "despite his habits of exaggeration and self-inflation," writes biographer George Victor, "despite being in fifty battles, he took no personal credit for any killing." Hitler apparently never moved past the violent performances stage of violent socialization, and continued to exhibit features of belligerency, including psychological disorganization, remembered humiliation, contempt for traditional institutions and fantasies of violent revenge. Throughout his life he remained locked in a personal struggle with his previous brutalization, a trauma that ordering others to kill could temporarily assuage but never resolve. He claimed to be inhibited from using violence himself by his middle-class morality. Danzig politician Hermann Rauschning, who knew Hitler personally, sensed his unresolved belligerency and understood that it made him more dangerous than he might have been had he been personally violent:

> Everyone who knew Hitler during the early years of struggle knows that he has by nature an easily moved and unmistakably sentimental temperament, with a tendency towards emotionalism and romanticism. His convulsions of weeping in all emotional crises are by no means merely a matter of nerves. . . . For this very reason, *there lies behind Hitler's emphasis on brutality and ruthlessness the desolation of*

a forced and artificial inhumanity, not the amorality of the genuine brute, which has after all something of the power of a natural force. Nevertheless, in the harshness and unexampled cynicism of Hitler there is something more than the repressed effect of a hypersensitiveness which has handicapped its bearer. *It is the urge to reprisal and vengeance,* a truly Russian nihilistic feeling. [Emphases added.]

Hitler's childhood brutalization is incontrovertible, although his biographers have been curiously reluctant to acknowledge it. Their reluctance may stem from unwillingness to be seen "psychoanalyzing" so large and destructive a historical figure. Psychoanalysis may be left to the analysts, but reporting a subject's well-authenticated social experiences is a biographer's first responsibility.

Adolf Hitler's father Alois was an Austrian customs official who had worked his way up from the peasantry. Adolf's mother Klara, twenty-three years younger than her husband, had been a servant in Alois's house during his second wife's last illness. The three children she bore Alois prior to Adolf had died of diphtheria within days of each other in the summer of 1887; Adolf was born on 20 April 1889. A fellow customs official and neighbors characterized Hitler's father as harsh, "unsympathetic," "inaccessible," "hard to work with"; even one of Alois's friends commented that "his wife had nothing to smile about."

Adolf's older stepbrother Alois Jr., who left home at fourteen to escape his father's violent subjugation, never forgot the severe beatings he received. His son William Patrick Hitler told American investigators that "Alois Sr. frequently beat [Alois Jr.] unmercifully with a hippopotamus whip. He demanded the utmost obedience . . . every transgression was another excuse for a whipping." Alois Jr.'s first wife Brigid added that Adolf's father had been a man of "a very violent temper" who "often beat the dog until the dog would . . . wet the floor. He often beat the children, and on occasion . . . his wife Klara." Adolf's younger sister Paula (born in 1896) told the biographer John Toland, "It was my brother Adolf who especially provoked my father to extreme harshness and who got his due measure of beatings every day."

Hitler himself bragged to one of his secretaries that after reading about Indian stoicism in the Wild West novels he consumed as a boy, he had "resolved not to make a sound the next time my father whipped me. And when the time came—I still can remember my frightened mother standing outside the door—I silently counted the blows. My mother thought I had gone crazy when I beamed proudly and said, 'Father hit me thirty-two times!' " To dinner guests in Berlin, Albert Speer reports, "Hitler repeatedly talked about his youth, emphasizing the strictness of his upbringing. 'My father often dealt me hard blows. Moreover, I think that was necessary and helped me.' " Both Alois Jr. and Adolf were choked or beaten unconscious by their father for major truancies: in Alois Jr.'s case, for skipping school for three days to build a toy boat; in Adolf's, for running away from home at the age of ten or eleven to escape his brutal father.

Hitler moved into rebellious belligerency when he was eleven, after his attempt to run away from home. His excellent schoolwork abruptly deteriorated. He began reading his Wild West books in school, carried a Bowie knife and a hatchet and earned from his teachers such labels as "solitary," "resentful," "sullen" and "uncooperative." Nor did his father's abrupt death early in 1903 relieve his conflict. His principal teacher in middle school corroborated his belligerency in testimony at his 1924 putsch trial:

> Hitler was gifted, one-sided, uncontrolled, and was known to be stubborn, inconsiderate, righteous and irate; it was difficult for him to fit into the school milieu. He also was not diligent, because otherwise, with his talent, he would have been more successful. . . . Instructions and admonitions were received with undisguised irritation; from his schoolmates he demanded unconditional submission, like the Führer role, and was inclined to pranks.

But without success at violent performances, Adolf was stuck in transition between identities. His fantasies settled on military glory after he read an account of the Franco-Prussian War. "It was not long before the great historic struggle had become my greatest inner experience," he wrote in *Mein Kampf.* "From then on I became more and more enthusiastic about everything that was in any way connected with war or, for that matter, with soldiering." He was already practicing public speaking, however—improvising orations for his close friend August Kubizek "accompanied by vivid gestures"—and at fifteen, Kubizek reports, he was already "a pronounced anti-Semite."

After his mother died of breast cancer late in 1907, Adolf, now eighteen, moved to Vienna, where he hoped to study architecture but was rejected for admission to the Academy of Arts. He blamed that rejection on the Jews. "In Vienna I learnt to hate the Jews," he told newspaper editor Richard Breitling in 1931. ". . . I really wanted to be an architect. The Vienna Jews knew how to stop that. They were wrong because now they have a politician on their hands." Failing to resolve the conflicts of brutalization leads to breakdown, and Hitler sank into depression and disorder in Vienna, where for six years he lived a life of impoverished semi-homelessness. "This pathological, evil-smelling world of envy, spite and egotism," writes Joachim Fest, "where everyone was on edge for a chance to scramble upwards and only ruthlessness guaranteed escape, became for the next few years Hitler's home and formative background. Here his idea of mankind and his picture of society were molded; here he received his first political impressions and asked his first political questions, to which he responded with the growing resentment, the hate and impotence of the outcast." Hitler acknowledged the importance of his Vienna years: "At that time I formed an image of the world and a *Weltanschauung*," he wrote in *Mein Kampf,* "which became the granite foundation for my actions. I have had to add but little to that which I learned then and I have had to change nothing. . . . [Vienna] was and remained for me the hardest, but also the most thorough, school of my life."

The Great War spared him further humiliation, and when he joined the Bavarian infantry in August 1914, he greeted it ecstatically: "To me, those hours seemed like release from the painful feelings of youth. I am not ashamed to admit even today that, gripped by wild enthusiasm, I fell to my knees and thanked Heaven from an overflowing heart for granting me the good fortune of being allowed to live at this time. . . . I knew that my place would then be where my inner voice directed me." Hitler's socialization had been excruciatingly prolonged by his failure either to succeed at violent performances or to find some nonviolent alternative. In fantasy he had identified military service as a way forward, and now suddenly a great world war intervened to allow him to test that possibility.

Between 1914 and 1916 he served at Ypres, Flanders, Neuve Chapelle, Flanders, La Bassée, Arras and Flanders again. As a courier, he carried messages from regimental headquarters back and forth to the front lines. "The orders he carried set battalions in motion," observes Nuremberg Trial psychiatrist G. M. Gilbert, "started artillery barrages, or sent further orders down the line to hold ground regardless of losses." Gilbert suspects these experiences provided Hitler with "a vicarious identification with authority." Hitler's identification was more than vicarious; his experiences as a courier revealed to him both the power and the refuge of delegated violence, of which he was the channel. He saw plain soldiers killed by the hundreds and thousands, and officers too, but the senior officers at regimental headquarters who ordered the violence directed and surveyed the carnage from safety, just as he would do as Führer from his safe bunkers dug in well behind the lines.

He loved soldiering and thought of himself as indestructible, but by 1915 what he called in a postcard home "the everlasting artillery fire" had traumatized him as it traumatized everyone else. In *Mein Kampf* he claimed he pulled himself together:

Thus it went on, year after year, but the romance of battle had made way for horror. The enthusiasm gradually cooled off, and exuberant joy was stifled by mortal fear. The time had come when every one of us had to struggle between the instinct of self-preservation and the call of duty. I, too, was not spared by this struggle. Whenever Death was on the hunt, a vague something tried to revolt, and strove to represent itself to the weak body as reason, yet it was only cowardice which in such disguise tried to ensnare the individual. A grave tugging and warning then set in and often it was only the last remnant of conscience which decided the issue. Yet the more this admonished one to caution, the louder and more insistent its lures, the sharper resistance to it grew, until finally, after a long inner struggle, the sense of duty carried the day. In my case, this issue had been decided by the winter of 1915–16. At last my will was undisputed master. If in the first days I went over the top with rejoicing and laughter, I was now calm and determined. And this was enduring. Now Fate could bring on the ultimate tests without my nerves shattering or my reason failing.

Ever after, he could produce a five-minute running imitation of an artillery barrage, reproducing all the different sounds the deadly shells made as they tumbled through the air. But his nerves did finally shatter. He was wounded in the left thigh by shrapnel on the Somme in October 1916, recuperated in a hospital, returned to duty, served in Flanders, on the Marne, in Champagne and back in Flanders in 1917 and 1918. In October 1918 he was gassed at La Montagne—Fest confirms the injury from Hitler's war record—and may also have suffered combat trauma after being buried by a shell blast. The mustard gas temporarily blinded him and he was sent to a hospital in Pasewalk, north of Berlin, for treatment. Several weeks later he was beginning to see again—"distinguishing the broad outlines of the things about me," he says in *Mein Kampf*—when "the monstrous thing happened." The monstrous thing was the collapse of Germany, army and navy mutinies, Socialist coups and the declaration of the Weimar Republic, for Hitler "the greatest villainy of the century." The war had ended in defeat. When a chaplain came to the hospital and explained what that defeat would mean, Hitler took it personally. He could hardly take defeat otherwise, since soldiering had given him a chance to try on a stable identity:

> The old gentleman . . . began to tell us that we must now end the long War, yes, that now that it was lost and we were throwing ourselves upon the mercy of the victors, our fatherland would for the future be exposed to dire oppression, that the armistice should be accepted with confidence in the magnanimity of our previous enemies—I could

stand it no longer. It became impossible for me to sit still one minute more. Again everything went black before my eyes.

"Do you know that I once was blind?" Hitler shouted at Richard Breitling during his 1931 interview. "In November 1918," he went on, "when the Reds were laying Germany waste, I was in a military hospital, blinded. That was when I began to see." Some biographers have interpreted these ambiguous statements to mean that Hitler suffered a second, hysterical blindness at Pasewalk when he heard of the German collapse. Of more significance is a claim he repeatedly made later—most credibly in a conversation with Hearst journalist Karl von Wiegand three or four years after the war—that he conceived his political calling at Pasewalk. Von Wiegand said Hitler told him about his gas injury in 1921 or 1922 and added, "As I lay there, it came over me that I would liberate the German people and make Germany great." Ordering others to commit acts of heinous violence on his behalf became for Adolf Hitler a substitute for using personal violence himself.

None of this personal history would be relevant if Hitler had gone on to live a minor life, but his personal struggle colored and shaped the political party he founded and the subsequent Nazi state. "At its roots," Fest confirms, "National Socialist ideology contained only one tangible idea: the idea of struggle. This determined the classifications, the values and the terminology both of the early movement and of the Third Reich. It not only gave Hitler's written confession of faith [i.e., *Mein Kampf*] its purposeful title but also so deeply marked the content and tone of the book that at times even the idea of race, the other cornerstone of National Socialist ideology, had to take second place."

Hitler's struggle with identity and with dominance resonated with the millions of Germans, particularly ex-soldiers, who had been impoverished, humiliated and declassed by the Great War, writes sociologist Eric Wolf:

> World War I brought a new kind of warfare. . . . Massed battles, fought across a labyrinth of trenches, devoured lives by the hundreds of thousands. It was for many a liminal experience [i.e., they crossed a threshold] . . . which separated them from ordinary life, shattered their customary ego structure, and reintegrated the initiates into the primary group of fellow soldiers. This sequence of breakdown and reemergence gave rise to the syndrome of the returning veteran who found himself unable to relate to the people at home. In the wake of German defeat, many continued to fight on, notably against the revolutionary Red Guards in the Baltic countries. Some 200,000 veterans joined the armed bands of the postwar *Freikorps* and became

subsidized strong men for right-wing causes during the Weimar
Republic, until they were absorbed into the [Nazi] movement. "These
people told us the war was over," said the future SA leader Friedrich
Wilhelm Heinz. "That was a laugh: we ourselves were the war."

"It is nonsense to explain Hitler's triumph by age-old German tendencies or trends in German intellectual thought," writes sociologist
Peter Merkl, seconding Wolf. "World War I was the major turning point
in German political development; its consequences doomed the Weimar
Republic and set the stage for the success of Adolf Hitler."

During the war Hitler had identified the enemy as "foreign influ-
ences" and "domestic internationalism"—that is, Marxist ideology,
Communism. But even immediately after the war, though certainly a
vicious anti-Semite, he still had not linked the Communists definitively
with the Jews. In a guide to army instruction on "the danger of Jewry"
that he wrote in September 1919, he called the Jews "a racial tuberculosis of the peoples" but argued for an "anti-Semitism of reason," which
"must lead to the systematic combatting and elimination of Jewish privileges," with its "ultimate goal . . . the implacable removal of the Jews."

Defeat in war was followed by widespread German suffering. "The
effects of the inflation," writes historian Anna Bramwell, "were to render fixed incomes and pensions valueless, to bankrupt many creditors,
and to interfere with internal trade. This, together with the effects of the
wartime blockade, had meant years of hunger and sickness. In 1919, 90
percent of all hospital beds were occupied by [tuberculosis] cases.
British observers in Germany such as [John Maynard] Keynes commented on the starving children, their faces yellowed by shortages of
fats. One striking feature of photographs of German crowds in the
1920s . . . is the gaunt faces." The Depression, when seven million Germans were unemployed, finished the job. Humiliation, hyperinflation,
hunger, unemployment encouraged messianic agitators such as Hitler.

Hitler "welcomed the misery," writes one analyst, ". . . declaring the
need for pride, will, defiance, and 'hate, hate, and again hate!' " He soon
realized, however, that his all-encompassing hatreds were confusing and
began to narrow them down. He wanted to hang all the Jews in Germany, he told several interviewers fiercely, and leave them hanging until
they stank, "as long as the principles of hygiene permit." But he also
talked calmly of deliberately searching for "the right kind of victim . . .
especially one against whom the struggle would make sense, materially
speaking," and coming to the conclusion "that a campaign against the
Jews would be as popular as it would be successful. . . . They are totally
defenseless, and no one will stand up to protect them." At another time

he added, "Experience teaches us that after every catastrophe a scapegoat is found."

As his allusion to scapegoating implies, Hitler's dazzling rise to
power, and the charismatic authority his millions of followers ceded to
him, derive directly from the religion-like structure of his politics;
National Socialism as Hitler organized it was essentially a religious cult.
René Girard, a French anthropologist, has proposed that religions arise
in times of great social conflict when the community drains its violence
into a chosen scapegoat; his summary of the process could be a summary
of the rise and triumph of Nazism:

> Suddenly the opposition of everyone against everyone else is replaced
> by the opposition of all against one. Where previously there had been
> a chaotic ensemble of particular conflicts, there is now the simplicity of
> a single conflict: the entire community on one side, and on the other,
> the victim. The nature of this sacrificial resolution is not difficult to
> comprehend; the community finds itself unified once more at the
> expense of a victim who is not only incapable of self-defense but is
> also unable to provoke any reaction of vengeance; the immolation of
> such a victim would never create fresh conflict or augment the crisis,
> since the victim has unified the community in its opposition. The
> sacrifice is simply another act of violence, one that is added to a
> succession of others; but it is the final act of violence, the last word.

And this scapegoating process not only worked for a significant part,
perhaps a majority, of the German public, it also worked personally for
Hitler himself. From scattershot contempt for a wide range of persons,
concepts and organizations, he began to discover Jews everywhere
working devilishly behind the scenes. "The revolution of 1918 and the
entire Weimar Republic were Jewish," historian Eberhard Jäckel paraphrases Hitler's universalizing of Jewish influence: "Marxism and the
Soviet 'dictatorship of blood' and, of course, high finance . . . were Jewish; the political parties of the Left were 'mercenaries of Jewry'; and,
finally, democracy, parliaments, majority rule and the League of Nations
were all Jewish as well."

The idea of a war of conquest against the Soviet Union surfaced in
Hitler's thinking in 1924. He linked Bolshevism with a Jewish "international conspiracy" finally definitively in *Mein Kampf,* written in Landsberg Prison between April and December 1924 and published in two
volumes beginning in June 1925. Jäckel finds "four new aspects of Hit-
lerian antisemitism" in Hitler's book: "its increased significance to Hitler
himself; a new universalist-missionary element; its linkup with [Hitler's]
outline of foreign policy; and, finally and above all else, an enormous

radicalization of the intended measures [against the Jews]." The elimination of the Jews, Jäckel adds, "had now turned into their extinction and extermination; indeed, it had become quite openly an advocacy of their physical liquidation, of murder."

The result for the half-million Jews of Germany, once Hitler took power and installed his Third Reich, was gradually escalating oppression as the Nuremberg Laws systematically abrogated the rights of Jewish citizens and government policy drove them to emigrate (after forfeiting their assets). Paradoxically, the first mass-murder operation of the Nazi regime was the purging of Hitler's own paramilitary army, the SA brownshirts—the Röhm Purge of June 1934, when Himmler's SS forces hunted down and murdered more than two hundred of Hitler's and Hermann Göring's political enemies.

"Associates of Hitler," Victor writes, "said the arrests after the Reichstag fire, the Röhm purge, and the anti-Semitic measures of the 1930s were experiments. They served to condition him to escalating aggression, to condition his followers and the nation for the mass destruction to come, and to find out how far he could go." Certainly Hitler's murderous escalations in the 1930s tested the German public's and the world's tolerance for Nazi violence and atrocity. "Conditioning," however, implying that Hitler was hardening himself, is inaccurate; in fact his level of violent socialization never changed until the end of his life, when he shot his new bride Eva Braun in the last days of the war before committing suicide. "The final aim of our policy is crystal clear to all of us," Hitler told his party leadership in 1937, speaking of his plans for the Jews. "All that concerns me is never to take a step that I might later have to retrace and never to take a step that could damage us in any way. You must understand that I always go as far as I dare and never further." What was the final aim that was crystal clear? In 1935, in a private conversation that an adjutant wrote down—a handwritten note survives—Hitler told his closest colleagues, "Out with them from all the professions and into the ghetto with them; fence them in somewhere where they can perish as they deserve while the German people look on, the way people stare at wild animals."

Violence begot violence. The concentration camps multiplied. When Germany absorbed Austria in March 1938, political opponents were murdered by Einsatzgruppen-like cadres and Jews were arrested en masse and deported to German concentration camps. The first synagogue was burned in Germany in June 1938, after which more than two thousand German Jewish citizens were arrested and confined. At Evian, on the French shore of Lake Geneva, in July 1938 thirty-three nations and thirty-nine private organizations gathered at President Franklin

Roosevelt's request to consider facilitating emigration of political refugees from Germany and Austria, but with the exception of Denmark and Holland, none of the nations was prepared to change its quota and accept more Jews. In October German troops invaded Czechoslovakia. That month Germany expelled twenty thousand Polish Jews as well, and Kristallnacht followed in November.

"We are going to destroy the Jews," Hitler bluntly told the Czech Foreign Minister, Frantisek Chvalkovsky, on 21 January 1939. "They are not going to get away with what they did on 9 November 1918. The day of reckoning has come."

And so in June 1941 the Einsatzgruppen rolled out eastward.

THREE

Barbarossa

Sunday morning, 22 June 1941, the Wehrmacht struck east, opening a war against the Soviet Union that would consume forty million lives. A German officer, Siegfried Knappe, shouting in the morning darkness, heard "the crack of rifle shots, the short bursts of machine guns and the shattering crashes of hand grenades. The rifle fire sounded like the clattering of metal-wheeled carts moving fast over cobblestone streets." Some Wehrmacht units, surprising border garrisons that offered only confused resistance, advanced thirty miles into Soviet-occupied Polish territory on that first long day. "Polish civilians in a church service applauded us," Knappe reported of passing through Bialystok, ninety miles northwest of Warsaw; "they were very happy because they had not been permitted to conduct church services under the Russians and they felt liberated."

In the next days the Einsatzgruppen followed. Bristling with Mausers and machine pistols in their trucks and cars, they fanned out across Poland northeastward toward the Latvian port city of Riga on the Baltic and the old Lithuanian cities of Kaunas and Vilnius, eastward into Byelorussia toward Minsk on the post road to Moscow, southeastward toward Rovno and Lvov, Tarnopol and Kamenets-Podolsky in the western Ukraine. Ahead of the German forces, an eyewitness on the highway to Minsk recalls, "people were fleeing eastward in panic, on foot, to look for a place to hide from the onrushing enemy. The highway was jammed with demolished trucks, smashed cannon, discarded machine guns. Now and again, aircraft with the Nazi emblem swooped over this pile of assorted weapons. They flew so low that we could see the mocking, contemptuous faces of the flying German thugs. They made one foray after another, 'playfully' firing their machine guns into groups of terror-stricken people on the road, mostly women holding children by the hand or in their arms." Already in the border towns local squads of police and SS were rounding up people to be shot on orders from the Gestapo in Berlin.

When forward units of the German Army occupied Kaunas in central Lithuania on 23 June 1941, a small advance detachment of Einsatzgruppe A entered the city with them and set to work immediately organizing "spontaneous" attacks against Jews. The town of stone buildings and chinked-log wooden houses at the junction of the Neris and Nemunas Rivers counted 35,000 Jews among its population of 120,000 people. Also known as Kovno, Kaunas had served as the Lithuanian capital under Soviet domination, and the occupying forces found four large groups of armed Lithuanian nationalists competing to help them harry the retreating Soviet garrison.

Within a day or two of the occupation, several enlisted men in a bakers' company of the Wehrmacht Sixteenth Army encountered what was probably the first pogrom in Kaunas when they joined "a crowd of people gathered in a square somewhere in the center of the town."

"We were quartered in an old Russian barracks," a sergeant recalled, "and immediately started to make bread for the troops. I think it must have been one day after we had arrived in Kovno that I was informed by a driver in my unit that Jews were being beaten to death in a nearby square. Upon hearing this I went to the said square [with] other members of our unit." On the cobbled square, lined with houses and opening onto a park, the sergeant "saw civilians, some in shirtsleeves . . . beating other civilians to death with iron bars." He heard someone say that "these were Jews who had swindled the Lithuanians before the Germans had arrived." The bystanders were mostly German soldiers. The sergeant questioned those nearest him, who told him that "the victims were being beaten to satisfy a personal desire for vengeance." His account continues:

> When I reached the square there were about fifteen to twenty bodies lying there. These were then cleared away by the Lithuanians and the pools of blood were washed away with water from a hose. . . . I saw the Lithuanians take hold of the bodies by their hands and legs and drag them away. Afterwards another group of offenders was herded and pushed onto the square and without further ado simply beaten to death by the civilians armed with iron bars. I watched as a group of offenders were beaten to death and then had to look away because I could not watch any longer. These actions seemed extremely cruel and brutal. . . . The Lithuanian civilians could be heard shouting out their approval and goading the men on.

A bakers' company grenadier remembered asking a medical-corps sergeant beside him "why these people were being beaten to death in such a cruel manner." The sergeant told him that they "were all Jews who had been apprehended by Lithuanians in the city and had been brought to this square. The killings were carried out by recently released

POLAND DIVIDED, 1940

〰〰〰 Polish border
- - - German-Soviet demarcation line

NORWAY

SWEDEN

DENMARK

Baltic Sea

DANZIG

EAST PRUSSIA

GREATER GERMANY

Hamburg

Berlin

Elbe

Munich

Vienna

ITALY

Danube

YUGOSLAVIA

Tallinn
ESTONIA

Riga

LATVIA

Daugavpils

LITHUANIA

Kaunas

Vilnius

Polotsk

Vitebsk

Smolensk

Moscow

SOVIET UNION

Minsk

Mogilev

Bialystok

Baranowicze

Brest-Litovsk

Pinst

Pripet Marshes

Warsaw

Bug

Dnieper

Zhitomir

Kiev

Stalingrad

Lodz

POLAND

GENERAL GOVERNMENT

Lublin

Luck

Rovno

Belaja Cerkov

Berdichev

Kharkov

Krakow

Lvov

Vinnitsa

Uman

Don

Tarnopol

Kamenets-Podolsky

S. Bug

SLOVAKIA

Nikolayev

Kherson

HUNGARY

Budapest

Odessa

Simferopol

ROMANIA

Black Sea

Bucharest

Danube

Volga

| 0 | miles | 250 |
| 0 | kilometers | 400 |

N
W E
S

EINSATZGRUPPEN AREAS OF OPERATION AFTER BARBAROSSA

- - - German-Soviet demarcation line, 1939
→ Path of the Einsatzgruppen, July 1941–1943
—— Front lines, December 1941
☐ Area occupied by German advance

FINLAND

SWEDEN

Tallinn

ESTONIA

Leningrad

LATVIA

Pskov

EINSATZGRUPPE A

Rzhev

Baltic Sea

Riga

Daugavpils

Moscow

Siauliai

LITHUANIA

Polotsk

Vitebsk

EINSATZGRUPPE B

Kaunas

Smolensk

Vilnius

GERMANY

Minsk

Mogilev

Bryansk

Orel

Bialystok

Vistula

Baranowicze

Kursk

Warsaw

Bug

Gomel

SOVIET UNION

Lodz

Brest-Litovsk

Pinsk

Dnieper

Kiev

GENERAL GOVERNMENT

Zhitomir

Kharkov

EINSATZGRUPPE C

Stalingrad

POLAND

Luck

Rovno

Belaja Cerkov

Poltava

Lublin

Vinnitsa

Berdichev

Dnepropetrovsk

EINSATZGRUPPE D

Krakow

Lvov

Uman

Don

SLOVAKIA

Tarnopol

Kamenets-Podolsky

Rostov

Caspian Sea

Cernautsi

S. Bug

Taganrog

Danube

Kherson

Budapest

Sea of Azov

HUNGARY

Odessa

Nikolayev

Krasnodar

Kislovdsk

Simferopol

Black Sea

| 0 | miles | 250 |
| 0 | kilometers | 400 |

N
W E
S

Lithuanian convicts." The SS had released violent criminals from prison, that is, and put them to work murdering Jewish victims to make the "pogrom" look spontaneous. The corporal counted five men wielding crowbars and "about fifteen dead or seriously injured people" collapsed on the cobblestones. Another enlisted man noticed that there were men guarding the square "wearing armbands and [carrying] carbines," and the grenadier identified them as "some members of the Lithuanian 'Freikorps' "—that is, irregulars. The irregulars were feeding victims to the killers, moving in and out of the square "with more Jews who were likewise beaten to death by the convicts." In the ten minutes the grenadier could bear to watch he "witnessed the beating to death of some ten to fifteen Jews." All the victims were men.

A similar scene confronted a colonel who was adjutant to the staff of Army Group North on his arrival in Kaunas on the morning of 27 June 1941. He passed a filling station surrounded by a dense crowd and noticed women in the crowd who had "lifted up their children or stood them on chairs or boxes so that they could see better." He thought he must be witnessing "a victory celebration or some type of sporting event because of the cheering, clapping and laughter that kept breaking out." But when he asked what was happening, he was told that "the 'Death-dealer of Kovno' was at work and that this was where collaborators and traitors were finally meted out their rightful punishment!" He moved closer and witnessed "probably the most frightful event that I had seen during the course of two world wars":

> On the concrete forecourt of the petrol station a blond man of medium height, aged about twenty-five, stood leaning on a wooden club, resting. The club was as thick as his arm and came up to his chest. At his feet lay about fifteen to twenty dead or dying people. Water flowed continuously from a hose washing blood away into the drainage gully. Just a few steps behind this man some twenty men, guarded by armed civilians, stood waiting for their cruel execution in silent submission. In response to a cursory wave the next man stepped forward silently and was then beaten to death with the wooden club in the most bestial manner, each blow accompanied by enthusiastic shouts from the audience.

A military photographer who photographed the scene (and who iden-tified the murder weapon as an iron crowbar) nearly had his camera con-fiscated by a hovering SS officer, indicating just how "spontaneous" these early public massacres were. Bystanders he questioned claimed that the death-dealer's parents "had been taken from their beds two days earlier and immediately shot"—presumably by departing NKVD—

"because they were suspected of being nationalists, and this was the young man's revenge." The death-dealer, the photographer adds, "within three-quarters of an hour . . . had beaten to death the entire group of forty-five to fifty people in this way," after which "the young man put the crowbar to one side, fetched an accordion and went and stood on the mountain of corpses and played the Lithuanian national anthem."

There were other murderers busy at the garage at other times that day. A Gentile Lithuanian, Julius Vainilavicius, described the scene:

> I was returning home after angling. Going past the garage I saw some civilians working there. The Germans were treating them roughly. The Jews were removing [horse] dung with naked hands and putting it into a heap. Yielding to curiosity, I walked into the schoolyard and over the fence kept on watching them. The work being finished, the people were ordered to wash themselves. . . . Here a great massacre began. The Germans and ten to fifteen Lithuanians, who happened to be in the garage at this time, swooped down on the Jews, belaboring them with rifle butts, spades, sticks and crowbars. About fifty people were wounded. They lay on the ground, groaning and crying. Then the water hose was brought and cold water turned onto them. Those who regained consciousness were beaten to death on the spot. After all the Jews were killed, a truck with a group of Jews [i.e., prisoners] came into the yard. They loaded the corpses onto the lorry and drove away. A few minutes later the Germans dispersed the onlookers.

Between these public spectacles, the SS advance detachment organized the Lithuanian irregulars. Einsatzgruppe A leader Stahlecker explained in a follow-up report that "it was not easy at first to set any large-scale anti-Jewish pogrom in motion [in Kaunas]." But the SS found early collaborators in Algirdas Klimaitis, a Lithuanian journalist who led one of the four groups of local irregulars, and a physician, Dr. Zigonys. Under Klimaitis's command, Einsatzgruppe A organized six hundred of the most reliable irregulars into an auxiliary police force; under Zigonys's command, another two hundred. On the night of 25 June 1941, the auxiliaries bombed or set fire to several Kaunas synagogues and burned down sixty houses in the Jewish quarter. That same night they began rounding up Jews, plundering their houses and murdering them— 1,500 victims on the night of 25 June; on succeeding nights another 2,300. The Wehrmacht colonel reports seeing "long columns consisting of some forty to fifty men, women and children, who had been driven out of their homes . . . herded through the streets by armed civilians. . . . I was told that these people were being taken to the city prison. I assume, however, that the route they were taking led directly to their place of execution."

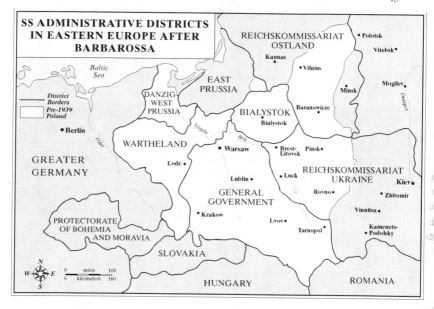

SS ADMINISTRATIVE DISTRICTS
IN EASTERN EUROPE AFTER
BARBAROSSA

"During the last three days," Einsatzkommando 1b reported to Berlin on 30 June 1941, "Lithuanian partisan groups have already killed several thousand Jews."

The Lithuanian auxiliaries justified their arrests and executions by claiming that Jews had been shooting from their windows at the German troops. A Jewish eyewitness, William Mishell, a draftsman in an engineering office, dismisses the accusation as "utterly ridiculous: first of all, the Jews never had arms in Lithuania; and secondly, no German soldiers were present where most of the Jews were being arrested, beaten up and manhandled. Saturday [28 June 1941], the Jewish Sabbath, only made the partisans' zeal higher. Groups of Jews were made to dance in front of jeering crowds and then were beaten in full view of the population, including Germans, but nobody intervened."

From the prison, the victims were marched to a secure facility where their systematic murder could be concealed. Kaunas was ringed with massive forts built by the Czar on the hills above the city prior to World War I and subsequently converted to warehouses or jails. Mishell describes these numbered forts as having "heavy masonry walls . . . topped with barbed wire and observation towers." Bunkered underground barracks and protective earthen berms made the interior compound of a fort "an artificial valley." Into one such valley of death, the Seventh Fort, located in the northeastern suburbs, the auxiliaries drove the crowds of Jewish civilians they had arrested, separating the men from the women and children. "Under heavy blows with the butts of the rifles, we [men] were chased down the slopes into the large hole," a survivor of these early atrocities told Mishell soon after he escaped:

> The entire area was full of humanity. The women and small children, we found out, were locked up in the underground barracks. Here we were now kept for days without even a piece of bread or a drink of water. On top of the slopes were hundreds of Lithuanian partisans with machine guns. Escape was totally impossible. We received strict orders to sit on the ground and not to talk. When somebody moved or was caught talking, the partisans would open automatic fire into the crowd. Not everyone was lucky enough to be killed outright. . . . Many of the wounded were twisting in agony and asking the bandits to kill them, but the bastards would laugh and say, "You were told to keep quiet," but would not shoot, and instead let them die in pain.

There was an artesian well within the Seventh Fort compound, the survivor told Mishell, but they were forbidden to drink from it; people who approached it were shot. Finally, desperate after several days without water, "a group got up and tried to attack the guards. But without guns, weakened by hunger and thirst, they were no match and were mercilessly gunned down by the bandits." The guards gave the survivors some water and bread then, to prevent further mass revolts. After several more days, the stench of the corpses forced the guards to organize a Jewish burial team; when the dead had been removed and buried behind the artesian well, the guards shot the gravediggers.

Later that week, on 4 July 1941, the women and children were led out from the barracks and out of the fort. "They looked terrible," the survivor remembered: "bloody, torn clothes, pale, shaky, barely walking." As soon as the high iron gates closed behind the women and children, "without any warning the guards suddenly opened a murderous fire into the valley [where the men were confined] completely at random, just blanketing the area with bullets, covering the site with dead and injured." Abruptly the shooting stopped. A party of high-ranking Lithuanian army officers had arrived. Their representatives ordered Jewish men who had served in the Lithuanian army to assemble at the gate. The veterans, Mishell's informant among them, were taken to the Kaunas central prison to have their army records checked and to be set free. On 6 July 1941, the men left behind at the Seventh Fort, including

Mishell's father, were murdered. About fifteen hundred people died at the Seventh Fort during the first week of July 1941.

What became of the women and children? The survivor's wife described their ordeal at the fort:

> The women were immediately taken to the underground barracks, where we all lay down on the bare concrete, one on top of the other. For several days we had no food and no water. They would not even let us out. The children were crying and sobbing and were asking their mothers why they were not taking them back home. The weaker women fainted from the thirst and the horrible air. But the nights were even worse than the days. Partisans with flashlights would come in and rob the women of their jewelry. Then others would come and beat up the women because they had nothing to give them any more. A favorite sort of entertainment was to order the women to take off their clothes and dance. When they got sufficiently excited they picked up the more beautiful ones and took them out by force and raped them.

Some of the women the guards raped they then murdered. But the SS was not yet ready to risk the mass killing of women and children. For the time being, dependents who survived their ordeal at the fort were released and returned to Kaunas.

"It was thought a good idea," Stahlecker wrote, summarizing these early Kaunas pogroms a few months later, "for the security police [that is, the SS] not to be seen to be involved, at least not immediately, in these unusually tough measures, which were also bound to attract attention in German circles. The impression had to be created that the local population itself had taken the first steps of its own accord as a natural reaction to decades of oppression by the Jews and the more recent terror exerted by the Communists." Stahlecker's explanation parrots Heydrich's instructions to the Einsatzgruppen commanders before they departed Pretzsch, repeated on 29 June 1941 in a telegram:

> The attempts at self-cleansing on the part of anti-Communist or anti-Semitic elements in the areas to be occupied are not to be hindered. On the contrary, they are to be encouraged, but without leaving traces, so that these local "vigilantes" cannot say later that they were given orders or [offered] political concessions. . . . For obvious reasons, such actions are only possible during the initial period of military occupation.

By his own admission, Stahlecker's Einsatzgruppe organized the early Lithuanian pogroms. Why were locals in the western territories of the Soviet Union willing to do the SS's dirty work? Personal aggrandize-ment and enrichment, long-standing anti-Semitism, private scores to set-tle, jealousy and currying favor for national independence (a forlorn hope) were primary reasons, but "the more recent terror exerted by the Communists" was also a significant factor, especially in Lithuania and the Ukraine, where the SS's pogrom efforts were most successful.

"When Lithuanian and Latvian forces were attached to the execution units," Stahlecker wrote of the areas under his authority, "the first to be chosen were those who had had members of their families and relatives killed or deported by the Russians." The deportations in particular had poisoned Jewish-Gentile relations in Lithuania. Jews were significantly underrepresented in the Lithuanian NKVD, not surprising given Rus-sian anti-Semitism and Communist Party hostility to religion: of 279 Lithuanian NKVD senior officers, 148 were Russians and 111 were eth-nic Lithuanians; the remaining 20 included Jews as well as other nation-alities. One week before Barbarossa, on the night of 14 July, the NKVD had seized and deported to the Russian gulag some 35,000 Lithuanian citizens. Slightly more than half of the deportees were ethnic Lithuani-ans, the other half Jews and Poles, but the Lithuanian nationalists had blamed the deportations on the "Bolshevik" Jews. On the night before Barbarossa, William Mishell and his friend Nahum Shoham had stayed up late discussing the impact of these deportations on the Kaunas Jew-ish community: "Our conversation inevitably turned to the deportations. It worried us, because these deportations had suddenly created enor-mous strains on the Lithuanian society and increased very perceptibly the anti-Semitic feelings."

Despite the deportations, Barbarossa surprised the NKVD, whose jails and prisons in the invaded western territories were crowded with political prisoners. Rather than release their prisoners as they hastened to retreat during the first week of the war, the Soviet secret police had simply slaughtered them. NKVD prisoner executions in the first week after Barbarossa totaled some ten thousand in the western Ukraine and more than nine thousand in Vinnitsa, eastward toward Kiev; comparable numbers of prisoners were executed in eastern Poland, Byelorussia, Lithuania, Latvia and Estonia. These areas had already sustained losses numbering in the hundreds of thousands from the Stalinist purges of 1937–38. "It was not only the numbers of the executed," historian Yury Boshyk writes of the evacuation murders, "but also the manner in which they died that shocked the populace. When the families of the arrested rushed to the prisons after the Soviet evacuation, they were aghast to find bodies so badly mutilated that many could not be identified. It was evident that many of the prisoners had been tortured before death; others were killed en masse." In some cases, cells crowded with prisoners had been dynamited, badly mutilating the remains.

The conquering Germans opened up the prisons and jails and invited the communities to collect their dead, organizing the events to implicate local Jewish citizens in the murders. "Jews were paraded out," historian John-Paul Himka confirms, "forced to clean the corpses and accused of responsibility for the atrocities."

Even though some locals collaborated with the Nazis, neither Heydrich nor Himmler expected to rely for long on pogroms. As Stahlecker would write in his review of the first months of the war, "The Security Police had fundamental orders for cleansing operations aimed at the most comprehensive possible elimination of the Jews." Decapitating the occupied countries and murdering the Jews was the responsibility of the fast-moving Einsatzgruppen and the battalions of Order Police that would follow in larger numbers behind them. At the end of June, eager to determine how the operation was progressing, Heydrich and Himmler set out eastward on an inspection tour.

Like Hitler and Göring, Himmler used an armored train as a traveling command post, named *Heinrich* in his honor. He had followed Hitler to East Prussia in *Heinrich* shortly after the beginning of Barbarossa. When Hitler had moved into his new command bunker Wolfschanze— the Wolf's Lair—dug into a pine forest outside Rastenburg, Himmler had ordered *Heinrich* parked on a railroad siding beside a lake twenty miles away and lived and worked aboard. The train was outfitted with a communications center, a dining car, offices and sleeping cars. People waiting for appointments with the Reichsführer-SS would remember after the war that the dining car was still serving "the good coffee" when only ersatz was available at home. It was from *Heinrich* that the two SS leaders departed on 30 June.

In Augustowo and Grodno, in eastern Poland, they were annoyed to find the Jewish populations still unconfined. Heydrich remedied that oversight the following day with an order that brought killing squads from East Prussia on 3 July 1941. The squads proceeded to murder 316 Jews in Augustowo, including ten women, and the Jewish leadership in Grodno.

Himmler moved on to Bialystok on 8 July 1941, arriving in that medium-sized northeastern Polish city with Higher SS and Police Leader Erich von dem Bach-Zelewski, a large, shrewd Prussian, just after Order Police Battalion 322 had conducted a raid on the Jewish quarter. (A few days earlier in Bialystok, Police Battalion 309 had driven seven hundred Jews into the city's main synagogue, set fire to the building and burned them alive, and Einsatzkommando 9 had conducted mass executions.) Police Battalion 322 had searched Jewish apartments and shops and "requisitioned" property and goods that the Germans claimed had been stolen. It took twenty trucks to carry all the booty to a "booty depot" set up to receive it: "Groceries and luxury wares of all kinds," the police report listed, "leather goods, textiles (coats and rolls of suit material), kitchen appliances and rubber goods," all according to the police "plundered from stores." The battalion executed twenty-one men and one woman who were supposedly "plunderers and fugitives and almost exclusively Jews." They were few in number because only those people who refused to admit that they were "plunderers" were executed.

Himmler inspected the booty depot with Bach-Zelewski and asked about the battalion's duties. He was unhappy with the death toll and ordered more Jews killed. That night, while Himmler and Bach-Zelewski dined with Lieutenant Colonel Max Montua of the Police Regiment Center and the battalion commanders, the police battalions murdered another thousand people.

After the depot inspection, before dinner, Himmler and his subordinates had gone into secret conference. The order that emerged a few days later, on 11 July 1941, signed by Montua and distributed to three police battalions, ratcheted the killing operations one notch higher. It specified, "1. All male Jews between 17–45 years of age convicted of looting are to be executed immediately." Since the battalions conducted neither investigations nor trials, the word "convicted" was a fig leaf, much like the euphemism "shot while trying to escape." Stripped of dissimulation, what the order meant was that from that day forward, any male Jews nominally of military age could be rounded up and murdered without evidence that they had committed any crime.

Increasingly, then, rather than operating behind the scenes promoting pogroms, Germans would be seen organizing and often carrying out mass killings themselves. It followed that such killings could no longer be conducted on garage aprons and in town squares among cheering crowds: "2. The executions are to take place away from cities, villages and traffic routes. The graves are to be leveled to prevent them from becoming places of pilgrimage. I forbid photography and the admittance of spectators. Executions and places of burial are not to be made public."

Himmler's psychological signature clearly marks this early killing order, even beyond the imperious "I forbid" of the second paragraph. The concerns addressed in the third paragraph, and even the language, are Himmler's:

3. Battalion and company leaders are to pay special attention to the pastoral care of the participants in this action. The impressions of the day are to be dispelled through evening gatherings with comrades. In addition, the men are to be instructed regularly on the necessity of this measure, resulting from the political situation.

Montua's order did not reach beyond the Police Battalions, but it signals Himmler's impatience with the body count his killing squads had delivered during the first two weeks of Barbarossa. Other testimony corroborates an increasing application of pressure from Berlin.

Walter Blume, a thirty-five-year-old police colonel with a law doctorate who had been assigned to lead Sonderkommando 7a of Nebe's Einsatzgruppe B, claimed at the trial of the Einsatzgruppen leadership in 1947 that he had worked consistently after leaving Pretzsch to avoid having to carry out mass executions. Whether that claim was true or not (and the Tribunal evidently disbelieved it, since Blume was one of fourteen defendants sentenced to be hanged), his testimony chronicles the initiatives and the troubles of one SS commando on the Eastern front in the early days of the war as it adjusted itself to mass killing.

Sonderkommando 7a advanced first to Vilnius. Shortly after Blume arrived with his commando, he learned that Einsatzkommando 9 of Nebe's group had also turned up in Vilnius. Army Intelligence had denied Blume permission to advance with the Wehrmacht front line. With Vilnius now covered by Einsatzkommando 9, the Sonderkommando leader decided to ignore the Wehrmacht directive, pulled his commando out of the Lithuanian city on 3 July 1941 and headed southeastward toward Minsk:

The road between Vilnius and Minsk made a good impression, good European impression, and was not destroyed. Our vehicles kept their prescribed distance because of [Russian] air attacks. The tempo was set by the slowest truck. We did not take any rest, and therefore we arrived in Minsk on the same day, but very late at night, after it had become dark. The city of Minsk had not been cleared of snipers. Units of the army gave us a place near the theater, where we awaited the next morning. This, then, was the 4th of July 1941. On this day I immediately occupied the most important buildings of the Soviet authorities, especially the Big House of the Soviets with its two to three hundred rooms. It was completely undestroyed and contained most of its materials, especially documents and libraries. My three detachments had their hands full of work in order to safeguard this material.

The next day Nebe turned up in Minsk a day ahead of his staff, called Blume on the carpet and dressed him down for defying the army's directive. Blume countered that his initiative had allowed him to confiscate valuable Soviet documents that might otherwise have been destroyed. When he gave Nebe a long report the following afternoon, the Einsatzgruppe leader was mollified, but then asked Blume why his commando "had not undertaken executions of Jews." Blume claimed he argued that executions "would only cause the Jews to flee and . . . join the partisans. Nebe did not see my point of view. He said it was impossible that he would mention the garrison of a commando in a city in his reports without at the same time reporting about executions of Jews. They expected him, in Berlin, to show activity in this respect, and he would also have to demand that from me."

If Blume in fact resisted, Nebe gave him a direct order:

> He then pointed out that the Jews had set their houses in Minsk on fire when the local combat commander had told them to leave their houses to make them available to Byelorussians who no longer had homes. Nebe had seen these fires on the evening of his arrival. . . . This, he said to me, was an excellent reason for a reprisal action. . . . Nebe now explained to me that he wished, and he ordered, that before I left Minsk a Jewish execution was to take place, namely, as reprisal for the burning of these houses.

Blume then claims to have argued that the officers of two of his three Sonderkommando detachments "were still young and somewhat immature men who had not even received military training and who therefore were not suitable to carry out such an execution. The only officer who was militarily trained was the commanding officer of the third detachment, Obersturmführer* Voltis, who personally was a hard soldierly character." Whereupon Nebe had Voltis sent in, and to humiliate Blume he ignored the normal chain of command and directly ordered the Obersturmführer "to proceed with a reprisal action against the Jews on the next morning before leaving Minsk."

As ordered, Blume testified, Voltis carried out the execution the next morning. Blume claimed to have been "only partly present" to observe it. "As far as I remember it lasted about one to one and a half hours. . . . Ten men at a time would be brought to the execution place. . . . There was [an anti]tank ditch. The ten men were put at that ditch and in a military manner were shot by rifles by the execution commando, which

*First Lieutenant.

included about forty men. Three men always shot at a victim. . . . The number of victims amounted to about fifty to sixty."

After the executions Sonderkommando 7a rolled on:

> How many days we spent on the way towards Polosk I do not exactly remember. At any rate, the roads were partly very bad, and the vehicles had to proceed in second gear almost constantly. When we had reached the fighting troops we were about two days in the front lines until the tanks finally passed through the city. I went into the city with my commando immediately, even before the infantry. Still we arrived too late, for the streets had already been set on fire by the Communist arson units and the NKVD building too was up in flames. . . . This must have been between the 10th and 12th of July. We only spent one day in Polosk. . . . [We] proceeded on the next day in the direction of Vitebsk, which had been captured by the Germans on the 11th of July.

In Vitebsk, northeast of Minsk in eastern Byelorussia and a third of the way to Moscow, Blume assigned Voltis—"who was such an active man," he testified sarcastically—the task of "forming a Jewish Council, registering and marking* the Jews and drafting them for labor service with the army agencies." Blume kept busy preparing reports, but soon enough Nebe called him again to task. "I received a very severe [radio] message from Nebe in which he demanded a detailed report about Vitebsk, and especially about the execution of Jews." At that point Blume simply capitulated. "I therefore gave Voltis the order to prepare a Jewish action [but] limited the order exclusively to able-bodied [Jewish] men. . . . One or two days later in my presence the announced execution was carried out. As far as I remember about eighty able-bodied men were shot in the same manner as they had been shot in Minsk."

Blume had dodged the Minsk executions; this time he was present throughout. "By my presence," he testified, "I wanted to show the men of my execution commando that I would not ask of them any more than I would ask of myself." He watched for two hours as his men murdered eighty unarmed and defenseless human beings, standing them at the edge of a killing pit and shooting them ten at a time; he watched them cry out in agony and crumple and fall, watched dirt scattered over them and the next ten victims marched up to stand where the last ten had stood and be shot in their turn. It affected him:

---

*That is, requiring them to sew yellow stars onto their clothing.

If I am now asked about my inner attitude which I then held, I can only say that it was absolutely split. On the one hand there was the strict order of my superior . . . and as a soldier I had to obey. On the other hand I considered the execution of this order cruel and humanly impossible. My very presence at this execution convinced me of this in a final manner. I still know that I wanted to make the situation easier for my men who were certainly moved by the same feelings. When ten men were shot there was always a pause until the next had been brought in. During these pauses I let my men sit down and rest and I joined them. I still know that I said exactly the following words to them at that time: "As such it is no job for German men and soldiers to shoot defenseless people but the Führer has ordered these shootings because he is convinced that these men otherwise would shoot at us as partisans or would shoot at our comrades and our women and children were also to be protected if we undertake these executions. This we would have to remember when we carry out this order." Furthermore, I tried by talking about neutral subjects to make the difficult spiritual situation easier and to overcome it.

But the "difficult spiritual situation" was not easily overcome, at least not by Blume. "The total impression of this execution of defenseless men," he testified at Nuremberg in 1947, "was shocking. When I came back to my office I was seized by stomach cramps and I had to vomit."

When Blume spoke of conducting the Minsk execution "in a military manner," he meant following the procedure of assigning three men simultaneously to shoot each victim. This seemingly wasteful arrangement, a long-established practice in both military and civilian executions, served important psychological purposes. It was designed to dilute personal responsibility for killing by making indeterminate which executioner's bullet had actually caused the victim's death. Such ambiguity benefited both the executioners and the authorities who directed them. The executioners benefited by being somewhat protected from confronting the emotional and social consequences of killing someone who was not directly threatening them. The authorities benefited because men who were thus protected were more likely to carry out killing orders and remain functional doing so. Nowhere did such traditional protections come under greater challenge than within Himmler's SS and Order Police on the Eastern Front during the Second World War.

FOUR

Across the Pale

Western Russia was dry and hot in the summer of 1941, Wehrmacht officer Siegfried Knappe remembered. In the Pale of Settlement, the region an Einsatzgruppen report called "the so-called Jewish segment of Europe . . . the human reservoir of western Jewry," the swath awaited the German scythe. "The days were long and the nights were short during the summer," Knappe reminisced. "June, July, and August gave us good weather in spite of the extreme heat, and we marched endlessly across this land of boundless expanses, this land with which none of our memories were linked. Every day of marching was just like every other day." But every day was not just like every other day in the towns and villages of the Pale.

Jews called Vilnius, a city of medieval streets twenty miles southeast of Kaunas on the Neris River, "the Jerusalem of Lithuania" for its density of Jewish religious and secular institutions. Its Jewish museum— rich in books, antique Torah scrolls and works of art—preserved the original texts of the Three Privileges granted Jews by Polish kings. These were the privileges that had drawn Jews to Poland and the Pale when they suffered expulsion from western Europe in the fifteenth and sixteenth centuries. Mass killings only began in Vilnius after Einsatzkommando 9 arrived there on 2 July 1941. The Lithuanian nationalists in Vilnius had not been so eager as those in Kaunas to sign on for pogroms when the Wehrmacht took the city on 24 June. Vilnius had fallen under Polish rule from 1920 to 1939, and it still counted more Polish than ethnic Lithuanian residents. A "Committee of Lithuanian Activists," fearing it might lose control of the city to the Poles in the wake of Barbarossa, lined up with the Germans. With the approval of the military commander it seized sixty Jews and twenty Poles as hostages at the outset, ostensibly to ensure that the population would follow its orders but hoping also to link the two ethnicities in the minds of the German invaders. "In the view of the Lithuanian population in the [Vilnius] district," Stahlecker would write, summarizing the situation, "the Jewish question . . . takes second place after the Polish problem."

The SS hardly agreed. Heydrich, following developments from Berlin and improvising as he learned, issued an order on 1 July 1941 forbidding his Einsatzgruppen "to take measures against" the Polish intelligentsia "apart from cases in which there is danger in delaying the matter." The Polish inhabitants of the occupied areas, he noted, "may be expected on the basis of their experiences to be anti-Communist and anti-Jewish." Therefore "cleansing activities have to extend first of all to the Bolsheviks and the Jews . . . especially as the Poles are of great importance as elements to initiate pogroms and for obtaining information." Heydrich's order endorsing private violence was another sign that the work of the Einsatzgruppen this time around would not be decapitation, as in Poland previously, but extermination. The military administration assumed full authority over Lithuania on 2 July 1941 and immediately demoted to municipal duties the Lithuanian Committee with which it had formerly shared power.

Then Einsatzkommando 9 got to work. The Lithuanian political police were dissolved and reconstituted under the Einsatzkommando as a Lithuanian auxiliary of 150 men. The auxiliary's first task, Einsatzkommando 9 reported to Berlin, was "drawing up current lists of names of Jews in Vilnius: first the intelligentsia, political activists and wealthy Jews." The unit then carried out searches and arrests. "Fifty-four Jews were liquidated on 4 July and 93 were liquidated on 5 July," the report continues. "Sizeable property belonging to Jews was secured." Intimidating raids and elimination of Jewish leaders made easier the larger roundups that followed.

Before Barbarossa the Soviet authorities had begun constructing a fuel depot in the Baltic pinewood five miles southwest of Vilnius at a place called Ponary, close to a railroad line. Fuel tanks of various diameters were to be sunken below ground level and circular pits to receive them were being excavated in the sandy soil. With the German invasion, the excavations had been abandoned, leaving a pit sixty feet in diameter half-cleared, with a semicircular trench twenty feet deep on its perimeter shored up with planking, and another sixty-foot pit next to it fully excavated. Smaller pits pocked the woods behind the main excavations like bomb craters. This place, which a young Vilnius Jew keeping a diary would call "the great grave," was the place Einsatzkommando 9 chose for a killing site and immediately began to fill.

Two Wehrmacht drivers and a company clerk saw the early killings. All three reported watching daily columns of about four hundred Jewish prisoners marching out to Ponary from the direction of Vilnius, with armed civilians wearing armbands and carrying carbines guarding them. "They were all men," the company clerk attested, "aged between about twenty and fifty. There were no women and children. These prisoners were really quite well-dressed and most of them were carrying hand luggage such as small suitcases, parcels and bundles." The Einsatzgruppen played games of deception with their Jewish victims to make assembling them easier; the commonest, as here, was ordering them to appear for "labor duty" with minimal luggage. Victims unable to imagine the mass slaughters that the Germans were planning—who could?—credited the orders or feared to disobey them.

The Lithuanian auxiliaries led the Jewish men in groups down into the semicircular trench of the partly dug pit, which they were using as a holding area. "An elderly man stopped in front of the entrance for a moment," one of the drivers reports, "and said in good German, 'What do you want from me? I'm only a poor composer.' The two civilians standing at the entrance started pummelling him with blows so that he literally flew into the pit." When all the men had been herded into the trench, the guards standing above them on the partial excavation ordered them to strip to the waist, toss their jackets and shoes out of the trench and wrap their shirts around their heads. The guards enforced this order, the other driver says, by beating the men "with heavy truncheons and rifle butts." He also noticed that the Lithuanians rummaged among the clothes and shoes. A Pole who lived near Ponary and kept a diary commented on the vulturing. "To the Germans," this diarist wrote, "three hundred Jews means three hundred enemies of humanity. To the Lithuanians it means three hundred pairs of pants, three hundred pairs of boots." His view was myopic; the Germans looted on a far grander scale.

Now the killing proceeded. The guards led ten hooded men at a time out of the trench and lined them up by having each man hold on to the waist of the man in front of him. A guard offered a club crosswise to the first man in line and led the line across and out of the first excavation to the edge of the second. Here the eyewitnesses' stories diverge, suggesting how quickly the Einsatzkommandos adapted their techniques to improve the efficiency of their killing. One of the two drivers watched a ten-man Lithuanian firing squad shoot the ten hooded Jewish men one-on-one into the deep second pit. The other driver and the company clerk both describe seeing a light machine gun set up on the path between the two pits. When the lead guard had cleared the line, the machine gun rattled quickly and without warning, and blew the wounded or dying men over the edge. All three eyewitnesses saw a guard with a pistol finish off the wounded with *Genickschüssen*. "We stayed there for about one hour," the company clerk concludes, "and during this time some four to five groups were executed, so I myself watched the killing of about forty to fifty Jews."

Looking into the killing pit, one of the drivers estimated that some four hundred Jewish men "who had been shot the previous day were also there. They were covered with a thin sprinkling of sand. Right on top, on this layer of sand, there were a further three men and a woman who had been shot on the morning of the day in question." Since the Einsatzgruppen were not yet killing women in large numbers, the dead woman may have been a special-category victim—a teacher, a doctor, a commissar—or she may have been one of the men's wives who refused to be separated from her husband.

The drivers spoke to the Lithuanian killers. One of them, a fellow truck driver, claimed the NKVD had suspected him of spying, had tortured him and torn out his fingernails. He said "each of the guards present had had to endure the most extreme suffering"—supporting Stahlecker's report of how the Einsatzgruppen picked the collaborators for their execution detachments. The Lithuanian further claimed, however, that "a Jewish Commissar had broken into a flat, tied up a man and raped his wife before the man's very eyes," after which the commissar "had literally butchered the wife to death, cut out her heart, fried it in a pan and had then proceeded to eat it." The Wehrmacht driver who repeated this story does not say if he believed it, but a story the other driver heard, about a man's family having been locked up in a Siberia-bound train by the Bolsheviks and left to starve to death when the Germans invaded, seemed to him "highly improbable." More credible to the first driver was a report he heard from Wehrmacht comrades that "a German soldier had been shot dead from a church tower" in Vilnius and "for this another three hundred to four hundred Jews were executed in the same quarry." The retreating Soviet forces left snipers behind, which the Einsatzgruppen thought as good an excuse as any to murder Jews.

On the last day the Wehrmacht company camped in the area, one of the drivers noticed that the shooting had stopped and went to Ponary with a friend "to look at the place again." An SD* man in a gray uniform standing in the path between the two pits tried to wave the two soldiers off. "We kept going, however, and when we got close to him I said to him that there was no need to make such a fuss, as we had already seen everything." Near the SD man "there was a coach with two horses, a landau," and on the box of the coach another SD man:

> In the coach sat two very well-dressed elderly Jews. I had the impression that these were high-class or important people. I inferred this because they looked very well groomed and intelligent and

*Sicherheitsdienst, the SS security service, part of Heydrich's RSHA.

"ordinary Jews" would certainly not have been transported in a coach. The two Jews had to climb out and I saw that both were shaking dreadfully. They apparently knew what was in store for them. The SD man who had initially gestured to us to keep away was carrying a submachine gun. He made the two Jews go and stand at the edge of the pit and shot both of them in the back of the head, so that they fell in. I can still remember that one of them was carrying a towel and a soapbox, which afterwards also lay in the trench.

Had the victims bought a private death together, or had they expected a private "resettlement"? The towel and soap travel case, which the Germans usually advised their victims to take with them (to deceive them into cooperating), suggest that the couple believed they would be delivered to a camp in their landau, so they may not have known "what was in store for them" until they reached the edge of the pit and saw the strew of stiffened bodies dusted with sand. "We all said to one another," the driver concludes nervously, "what on earth would happen if we lost the war and had to pay for all this?"

"In Vilnius by 8 July," Einsatzgruppe A reported to Berlin on 13 July 1941, "the local Einsatzkommando liquidated 321 Jews. The Lithuanian special detachment . . . was instructed to take part in the liquidation of the Jews. . . . They arrested the Jews and put them into concentration camps where they were subjected the same day to special treatment. This work has now begun, and thus about 500 Jews, saboteurs among them, are liquidated daily. About 460,000 rubles in cash, as well as many valuables belonging to Jews who were subject to special treatment, were confiscated as property belonging to enemies of the Reich."

An Einsatzkommando "confiscated vast documentary materials in the local Jewish museum," the report adds, "which was a branch of the central Moscow Institute for Jewish Culture." With their haul of *pinkes* historical chronicles, antique Torah scrolls and letters of the very founder of Zionism, Theodor Herzl, the mythologizers of the Third Reich could further document Jewish perfidy.

Three hundred fifty miles south of Vilnius, Einsatzgruppe C* stabbed into Galicia, a region—fought over for centuries among Poland, Austria and the Ukraine—that was the epicenter of Hasidism, the ecstatic wing of Orthodox Judaism. Advancing through Byelorussia, Knappe may

---

*It was Einsatzgruppe B until 11 July 1941, when C in Byelorussia and B in the Ukraine exchanged letter designations to conform to their respective positions north and south.

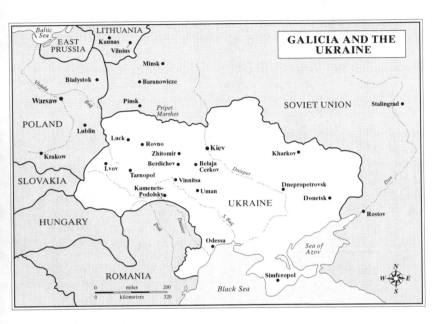

have seen, or chosen to see, an empty landscape, but an Italian war correspondent moving up through Bessarabia onto the fertile steppes of
the western Ukraine later in the summer saw carnage and squander:

> Dust and rain, dust and mud. Tomorrow the roads will be dry, the vast
> fields of sunflowers will crackle in the hot, parching wind. Then the
> mud will return. . . . This is the Russian war, the eternal Russian war,
> the Russian war of 1941. *Nichts zu machen, nichts zu machen.**
> Tomorrow the roads will be dry, then the mud will return, and
> everywhere there will be corpses, gutted houses, hordes of ragged
> prisoners with the air of sick dogs, everywhere the remains of horses
> and vehicles, the wreckage of tanks, of airplanes, of L.K.W.s,† of guns,
> the corpses of officers, NCOs and men, of women, children, old men
> and dogs, the remains of houses, villages, towns, rivers and forests.
> *Nichts zu machen, nichts zu machen.*

*Soldier slang, a verbal shrug: "Nothing to do [about it]," or, more pungently: "To hell
with it."
†*Last-Kraft-Wagen:* a heavy truck.

The rolling, temperate grasslands of the western Ukraine resemble the American prairies: black or red gypsum soils; limestone bluffs penetrated with caves; crops of wheat, rye and barley, soybeans, sunflowers; orchards in the uplands. Luck (Lutsk), eighty miles east of Lublin, marks the southern edge of the vast Pripet marshes of southern Byelorussia and the northern Ukraine that extend eastward from Lublin along the drainage of the Pripet River all the way to the Pripet's junction with the Dnieper above Kiev. One hundred twenty miles southeast of Lublin, Lvov (Lemberg), the old capital of Galicia in the foothills of the Carpathian Mountains, thrived on the historic trade route between Vienna and Kiev; its 1941 population of 370,000 included 160,000 Jews, 140,000 Poles and 70,000 Ukrainians. Eighty miles due east of Lvov on the south-flowing Seret River, Tarnopol counted 40,000 residents, including 18,000 Jews. Twenty miles farther down the Seret from Tarnopol, the small town of Trembowla, population 10,000, including 1,800 Jews, paralleled the river below an old castle ruin.

A young man in Trembowla, listening to Radio Berlin on a friend's shortwave radio on 22 June 1941, heard an important member of the Organization of Ukrainian Nationalists (OUN) demand " 'Death to Jews, death to Communists, death to Commissars,' exactly in that sequence." Thousands of young Ukrainian nationalists had defected to Nazi-occupied Poland after September 1939. Himmler had formed them into two Waffen-SS battalions, Nachtigal and Roland, which would return to plague Lvov and Tarnopol.

An advance unit of Einsatzgruppe C entered Luck on 27 June 1941 while the town was still burning. "Everything was still in wild confusion," the unit would report. "All shops had been looted by the population." In the courtyard of the fourteenth-century castle in the center of town the invaders found the piled bodies of more than a thousand Ukrainians whom the NKVD had murdered before withdrawing—all they had time to kill of the four thousand prisoners stuffed within the massive castle walls. Several days later, perhaps among the castle dead, the Wehrmacht discovered ten German soldiers the NKVD had murdered. Field Marshal Walther von Reichenau, the commander of the Sixth Army that was fighting through the area, ordered an execution of Jews equal in number to the Ukrainian dead.

By then the Einsatzgruppe had already arrested and shot several hundred Jewish citizens and a handful of looters. All of its commandos had briefly come together in Luck at the same time before fanning out across the Ukraine, among them Sonderkommando 4a, which Paul Blobel commanded. Apparently the responsibility for carrying out von

Reichenau's order fell to Sonderkommando 4a and came just when Blobel was succumbing to typhoid fever. A rangy man with red hair, a beak of a nose, a cleft chin and a permanent scowl, no stranger to violence, Blobel was a veteran of the First World War and had even won the Iron Cross, 1st Class, but fever and the execution order combined to produce what he later called "a nervous breakdown." His subordinate, SS-Obersturmführer August Häfner, returned from a journey to find "my unit . . . all running around like lost sheep. I realized something must have happened and asked what was wrong." Someone told Häfner that Blobel had collapsed and was in bed in his room:

> I went to the room. Blobel was there. He was talking confusedly. He was saying that it was not possible to shoot so many Jews and that what was needed was a plow to plow them into the ground. He had completely lost his mind. He was threatening to shoot Wehrmacht officers with his pistol. It was clear to me that he had cracked up and I asked [fellow Obersturmführer] Janssen what had happened. Janssen told me that Reichenau had issued an order. . . . No preparations to carry out this order had yet been made. . . . I had someone call a doctor. . . . When the doctor saw the condition Blobel was in he gave him an injection and instructed us to have him taken to Lublin to a hospital. While he was being examined Blobel kept on reaching for his pistol. By talking to him I managed to calm him down enough so that he did not fire.

Another officer with Sonderkommando 4a, Russian-speaking Sturmbannführer Waldemar von Radetzky, takes up the story:

> Blobel had a high temperature and was delirious. The physician was most upset about the state of health of his colleague. He made out an admission card for the field hospital in Lublin, and he treated Blobel. Blobel was taken in his car, and I went to Lublin with him the same evening, where we arrived in the morning and took him to the hospital there.

Häfner, a solid, square-jawed young officer, also accompanied Blobel to Lublin in the Opel Admiral. He remembered that they delivered their chief "to a hospital which was known as a loony bin by the enlisted men." Blobel was put in quarantine and spent the whole month of July recuperating, rejoining SK 4a at the beginning of August. His two subordinates returned to Luck the next day to find that Himmler's newly appointed Higher SS and Police Leader for the Ukraine, the coldly murderous forty-six-year-old Obergruppenführer Friedrich Jeckeln, had already arranged for Ukrainian special detachments supervised by platoons of police and infantry to shoot 1,160 Luck Jews in "retaliation."

Einsatzgruppe staff arrived in Lvov at five a.m. on 1 July 1941 and commandeered the NKVD central building for offices. A week earlier, when the NKVD still controlled Lvov, Ukrainian nationalists had staged an insurrection led by OUN commander Stepan Bandera, who had then proclaimed Ukrainian statehood on 30 June 1941 (a claim the Germans quickly quashed). The NKVD had killed three thousand of the Bandera forces; the Einsatzgruppe would report that "the prisons in Lvov were crammed with the bodies of murdered Ukrainians." There were earlier NKVD victims buried under the floors of the prison as well.

When the Germans took control of Lvov, a Jewish resident wrote in a contemporary diary, "the devil's game began":

> The Gestapo decided to make use of what had happened in the prisons under Soviet rule for the purposes of propaganda. In the presence of special commissions, Jews were made to dig out the corpses of the prison inmates. The action was shot by film operators to be shown later as evidence of the execution of innocent people by the "Jewish Bolsheviks."
>
> . . . The Germans were seizing Jews in the streets or at home and forcing them to work in prison. The arrests of Jews were also conducted by the newly created Ukrainian police. . . . The operation was over in three to four days. Every morning about a thousand Jews were brought and distributed among the three prisons. Some were ordered to break concrete and dig out corpses. Others were shot in the small inner courtyards of the prisons. . . . The "Aryan" residents of Lvov participated in this brutal show. Crowds wandered along prison corridors and courtyards, observing with satisfaction the suffering of the Jews. Here and there volunteers could be found to help the Germans in the beating of Jews. During the first days of the occupation of Lvov more than 3,000 Jews were killed in the Lvov prisons. Among them was one of the best-known and most popular rabbis of Lvov—Dr. Yehezkel Levin and his brother, the rabbi of the town of Zheshkov, Aaron Levin.

Einsatzgruppe C reported a higher number than the diarist: "Approximately 7,000 Jews were rounded up and shot by the Security Police in retaliation for the inhuman atrocities."

Felix Landau, a sergeant in one of the Einsatzkommandos, kept a diary as well. Landau had volunteered for Einsatzkommando duty when he discovered that his mistress Trude, a typist in the General Government SD office where he worked, was two-timing him with a former fiancé. His unit had pulled into Lvov at four in the afternoon on 2 July 1941 and immediately got busy. "Shortly after our arrival," he writes, "the first Jews were shot by us. As usual a few of the new officers became megalomaniacs, they really enter into the role wholeheartedly." After the murders the Einsatzkommando commandeered a military school and forced Jewish prisoners to clean the building before settling down at midnight to sleep. Landau started writing a letter to Trude the next morning "while listening to wildly sensual music" on the radio, but a killing order interrupted his composition: "*EK* with steel helmets, carbines, thirty rounds of ammunition." Without break the diary resumes: "We have just come back. Five hundred Jews were lined up ready to be shot. Beforehand we paid our respects to the murdered German airmen [casualties of the Barbarossa assault found in Lvov] and Ukrainians." He had been told at the time his unit "paid [its] respects" that the Bolsheviks had even murdered children, atrocity stories designed to motivate the men to kill. "In the children's home they were nailed to the walls." Even so, he told himself, "I have little inclination to shoot defenseless people—even if they are only Jews."

By 5 July 1941, after a night of guard duty, Landau was looking forward to his first hot meal since the unit arrived in Lvov. Given 10 Reichsmarks to buy necessities, he had bought himself a whip. "The stench of corpses is all-pervasive when you pass the burnt-out houses," he observes. "We pass the time by sleeping." That afternoon they "finished off" three hundred more "Jews and Poles." In the evening he and his buddies went into town. "There we saw things that are almost impossible to describe. We drove past a prison. You could already tell from a few streets away [by the smell] that a lot of killing had taken place here. We wanted to go in and visit it but did not have any gas masks with us so it was impossible to enter the rooms in the cellar or the cells."

On their way back to the military school they encountered injured Jews passing by who were dusted with sand. "We looked at one another. We were all thinking the same thing. These Jews must have crawled out of the graves where the executed are buried." They stopped one of the injured men and learned that Ukrainians had rounded up some eight hundred Jewish men and taken them up to the ruins of the High Castle on the hill north of the city. Landau's Einsatzkommando had been scheduled to shoot them the following day. Instead they were being released, but only after they had run a gauntlet of vengeful Wehrmacht soldiers:

> We continued going along the road. There were hundreds of Jews walking along the street with blood pouring down their faces, holes in their heads, their hands broken and their eyes hanging out of their sockets. They were covered in blood. Some of them were carrying

others who had collapsed. . . . At the entrance to the citadel there were soldiers standing guard. They were holding clubs as thick as a man's wrist and were lashing out and hitting anyone who crossed their path. The Jews were pouring out of the entrance. There were rows of Jews lying one on top of the other like pigs whimpering horribly. The Jews kept streaming out of the citadel completely covered in blood. We stopped and tried to see who was in charge of the *Kommando.* "Nobody." Someone had let the Jews go. They were just being hit out of rage and hatred.

"Nothing against that," Landau decides—"only they should not let the Jews walk about in such a state."

A similar gauntlet, but more lethal, was organized four days later in Lvov by officers of the Waffen-SS Viking division following the shooting death of the commander of one of the division's regiments. Günther Otto, a twenty-one-year-old butcher assigned to the train that carried fresh meat for the troops, described the experience in a Nuremberg Trial deposition after the war:

> The members of the meat train and the bakery company systematically rounded up all Jews who could be found based on their facial characteristics and their speech, as most of them spoke Yiddish. *Obersturmführer* Braunnagel of the bakery company and *Untersturmführer** Kochalty were in charge of rounding them up. Then a path was formed by two rows of soldiers. Most of these soldiers were from the meat train and the bakery company, but some of them were members of the 1st Mountain Hunter Division. The Jews were then forced to run down this path and while doing so the people on both sides beat them with their rifle butts and bayonets. At the end of this path stood a number of SS and Wehrmacht officers with machine pistols, with which they shot the Jews dead as soon as they had entered into the bomb crater [being used as a mass grave]. [Superior officers of the regiment] were part of this group that conducted the shootings. About fifty to sixty Jews were killed in this manner.

The Viking division "had been indoctrinated with anti-Semitic thoughts in Dachau and Heuberg" by a major and a corporal, Otto explained, "but we were never told that the anti-Semitic program went as far as extermination—only that the Jews were parasites and responsible for the war."

*Second Lieutenant.

The Wehrmacht also occupied Tarnopol on 2 July 1941 and continued to encourage its men to unmilitary murder in disproportionate reprisals. In Tarnopol as well, Einsatzkommando 4b under SS-Standartenführer Günther Herrmann, a Göttingen-educated lawyer, "inspired" (as a report called it) Bandera nationalists to pogroms. One particularly heinous inspiration was recorded in the diary of a German general, Otto Korfes, on 3 July:

> We saw trenches 5 m[eters] [16 feet] deep and 20 m [66 feet] wide. They were filled with men, women and children, mostly Jews. Every trench contained some 60–80 persons. We could hear their moans and shrieks as grenades exploded among them. On both sides of the trenches stood some 12 men dressed in civilian clothes. They were hurling grenades down the trenches. . . . Later, officers of the Gestapo told us that those men were Banderists.

These murders—allowed to include women and children, since they were set up as "spontaneous" pogroms—were ostensibly in reprisal for the mutilation of three German soldiers whose corpses had been discovered in the Tarnopol prison.

The total death count EK 4b reported when the commando finished its work in Tarnopol on 11 July 1941 was 127 executions and 600 killed in pogroms, but the relatively low numbers (compared with Luck and Lvov) obscure the shattering reverberation of each individual loss of life. A survivor, Janett Margolies, a daughter, wife and mother, testified to that loss in a postwar memoir:

> Friday, July 4, 1941, at 9:00 a.m., machine guns were posted on street corners. Death's-Head SS detachments in black uniforms appeared in the streets. Near each house a Gentile watchman pointed to who was living where. People were taken (allegedly to work) outside and shot on the spot. Mass executions took place in many parts of the city.

Among the mass executions on the night of 4 July, thirteen families in a house on Russian Street were locked inside and the house torched. Guards shot anyone who tried to escape, and neighbors who attempted to help were met with machine-gun fire.

Saturday, Margolies continues, "the Jews were ordered to bury the bodies [of the previous days' massacres] because the stench poisoned the air. In the afternoon, the massacres started again. On that day, Saturday, 5 July 1941, my father was murdered in the prison."

Many of the Jewish residents of Tarnopol had gone into hiding, believing rampaging soldiers were perpetrating the violence. On Sunday the Germans posted notices ostentatiously forbidding private violence and promising law and order. "Not suspecting anything bad, the Jews started to crawl out of their hiding places," Margolies writes. "When the Jews were back in the apartments, the Ukrainian Nationalists started to come into the houses, assuring the Jews that the killing was over and that they were now only taking people to work."

SS men forced their way into Margolies's apartment and ordered her husband and late-adolescent son out to labor duty carrying heavy ammunition boxes. Margolies followed after them in panic, trying to retrieve at least her son, until one of the guards chased her away. While she was gone, her mother "was pulled from the house and forced to carry away the dead bodies lying on the streets. Having returned from trying to help my son, I saw my mother pulling a dead body, the face all red. I ran forward to help her." Margolies was interrupted by the screams of a young woman whom two soldiers were trying to rape in the presence of the woman's two small children. "Seeing me, the Germans let the woman go and started plundering." Margolies turned back to find that her mother had disappeared. "I spotted a group of Jews with their hands up at the house where my mother was installed." She was afraid to approach too closely, so she waited nearby. "Suddenly I heard a machine-gun burst. After a few minutes the Germans left. . . . One of them said that all of them were *hin* there [gone, done for]. I understood that my mother was no longer alive."

Her despair then "was endless. Yesterday, my father, and today, my mother; my son, in the meantime, was also not around. But after one hour, I heard a voice say, 'Mama, I am here.' I threw my arms around him." Her neighbor across the hall returned. Her husband emerged from hiding.

Only two families remained in the darkened apartments. For hours they debated whether the men should obey orders to report for labor duty or go into hiding. "Our neighbor was for going. I was against it. After long arguments, it was decided that they should go." Margolies and her husband lay on their bed that night fully dressed and awake. They arose early. "I prepared something to eat, but nobody could swallow anything. My husband and son shaved. They dressed in new underwear and suits, getting ready to go."

Before they left, Margolies went out to find the place where her mother had been killed the day before:

A horrible picture appeared before my eyes. A large open pit full of dead bodies, and on top of them was my poor mother, kneeling with her face down, all stiff. From one side of the pit, some Germans took a picture with their camera. Assuming that I was not Jewish, they asked who did it. Not being able to control myself with the pain I felt, I threw it in their faces, saying: "You and yours alike!"

Margolies ran home then, "cry[ing] hysterically," and her husband and son cried with her.

Their neighbor pestered them to get going. To avoid saying goodbye, Margolies followed her husband and son to the labor muster outside the prison. She stood "among a group of Christians who were watching the show" while the men were ordered to line up and then to exercise—Nazi humor, as was labor duty itself, because Jews were supposed to be lazy and cunning at avoiding work. When her husband and son were led inside the prison, a sense of impending doom overwhelmed her. "I wanted to do something in order to save them. Wherever I went, I met indifference or helplessness." Recognizing the futility of her quest, she gave up and went home.

The endless day finally ended:

> In the evening our neighbor returned alone, without my husband and son. I understood that they were no more. I blamed my neighbor for insisting upon going to work and pulling them to their death. But what was the use? It had already happened. I started to cry, hitting my head with my fists and banging my head against the wall. I wanted to commit suicide. My neighbors were watchful. They tried to overcome my desperation with whiskey. It didn't help. Corpses, corpses.

Just then her sister-in-law arrived with the news that all the Jews in her husband's native village, including her father-in-law and brother-in-law, had been gathered, transported to the communal forest the village maintained for firewood and building materials and murdered. "My pain had no limit," Margolies writes. "I saw everything around me crumbling. I was left almost without relatives—six dead among the nearest. I stopped eating, and lit the candles for the dead souls. I didn't go outside. People started to come into the house to tell me stories that my husband and son had been seen somewhere. I ran and searched for them everywhere."

Eventually Margolies learned how her husband and son had died:

> They had been forced to carry out the Ukrainian dead bodies from the city prison to the cemetery. While my husband was working on the wagon, my son and other Jews were pulled down, chased around and beaten with wooden sticks or planks. My son allegedly cried out, "You have no right to beat and maim us. We aren't guilty. Kill us, but stop

torturing us." As a reply, he was beaten to death. My husband, seeing his son dead, lost consciousness. The Germans noticed that he stopped working, and they started to beat him murderously until he stopped moving and they later pumped a bullet into his body.

"This story broke me down again," Margolies writes. "I felt that I was on the verge of losing my mind. Day and night I saw before my eyes this terrible picture. Physically, I felt the blows." It would be ten weeks before the Tarnopol Jewish community opened a mass grave at the cemetery and Margolies identified the remains of her son and her husband and reburied them privately, "one near the other." She would come to believe "that I had a special mission to fulfill . . . to find the bodies of my dearest ones and rebury them in Israel." Her belief sustained her and she survived the war, but she never found her father's remains.

The Wehrmacht arrived in Trembowla, twenty miles south of Tarnopol, on 5 July 1941, the day Janett Margolies's father and mother were murdered. "At approximately eleven o'clock in the morning," a Jewish eyewitness remembers, "the Ukrainian population gathered in the streets to see the Germans who were arriving from the north." Three motorcycles appeared at noon. Trembowla would soon erupt in massacre, as Luck, Lvov and Tarnopol had before, but a survivor, a teenage boy in Trembowla, describes another individual loss at the very outset, of his friend Abe Briller:

> You were a frequent guest in our home. Even though [you were] much older, fully grown up when I was a teenager, we were best friends. There was something special about you. You were the incarnation of goodness. I can still see you before my eyes, a medium-sized man, somewhat plump, with two pink cheeks, eyes that shone eternally with friendliness and kindness, a face continuously covered with a smile, a willingness to be of help. . . .
> You came from a destitute family. You lost your father when yet very young. I do not remember him; maybe I never knew him or saw him. Your mother was left with fifteen children. They died one by one, of different causes, but surely the main cause was malnutrition, the eternal grinding poverty. Your mother cried until she lost all ability to cry. Of all the children only you and a brother of yours in Lvov survived. I do not know how you managed it, but you not only survived, you also educated yourself—not in school but in the dark corners of your mother's poor dwelling. You learned by yourself. You learned to write letters for people, to fill out official papers; you

learned to speak and write Polish, English, Ukrainian, Hebrew and Russian. Later you learned bookkeeping, and this became your main means of supporting yourself. . . .

It was on the first day of the triumphal entrance of the German army into Trembowla. You were by that time already married and the father of a sweet little girl. Maybe God himself envied you your new success. You were sitting at home when you heard the sudden noise of motors. Out of sheer human curiosity, you opened the door to see what all the commotion was about. A few Germans in shining uniforms and on shining new motorcycles came driving along the main road. One of them, an officer, noticed you and suddenly stopped.

"*Jude?*" he exclaimed, his hands grasping for the rifle that hung over his shoulder.

"*Ja,*" you answered, not realizing the gravity of the situation.

A sharp, short shot resounded. You fell to the ground, dead.

It is difficult to believe across the long distance of years that these early narratives of criminal brutality and slaughter chronicle only the beginning of the Einsatzgruppen Eastern campaign.

FIVE

Truehearted Heinrich I

More than concern for German and world public opinion forced the SS to escalate its mass killing cautiously. Himmler and his subordinates also needed to test Wehrmacht tolerance and contrive Wehrmacht complicity. Even more fundamentally, both the men doing the killing and the leaders ordering and directing it had to find a way to stomach it. For the killers a conditioning process was necessary to minimize the potentially disabling psychological trauma they would experience as the categories of victims expanded and the killing became harder to rationalize as defensive. For the leaders the problem was more complex.

Those leaders directly exposed to mass killing faced the same risk of disabling trauma as their men, as Paul Blobel's breakdown demonstrates. Higher-ranking leaders not directly exposed or only briefly exposed, up to and including Himmler, confronted issues of control and transformation. Men prepared to kill victims who are manifestly unthreatening—the elderly, unarmed women, small children, infants—behave differently from men prepared to kill victims such as men of military age who can be construed to be at least potentially dangerous. Men encouraged to murder unthreatening victims would not necessarily emerge from such experiences with the qualities of discipline and noblesse oblige that Himmler's kitsch vision of the SS as a new Aryan nobility required. Nor would such men necessarily follow orders with the *Kadavergehorsam*—the corpse-like conformity—that had long been the ideal of German military service and that Himmler demanded of his SS legions and rigidly enforced.

The problem that Eastern Territories Commander Johannes Blaskowitz identified in Poland in 1939 was the problem Himmler confronted as he moved to expand the categories of SS victims in the occupied East: that as a consequence of the SS's mass slaughters, "tremendous brutalization and moral depravity" might spread "rapidly among precious German manpower like an epidemic." He needed to condition the men of his Einsatzgruppen, Order Police and Waffen-SS to kill large groups of people without provocation day in and day out for weeks and months on end. At the same time, he needed to preserve them from breakdown or radical, nihilistic maleficence. He was not obviously the right man for the job. Remarkably, though he had vast experience at ordering others to kill, like Hitler he had no personal experience of killing. He idealized the SS organization he had created, investing it with a sham of noble principles. He was a martinet who imposed brutal punishments for even minor disciplinary infractions. He despised drunkenness. Ramping up the butchery in the summer of 1941, he had his squeamish hands full.

Himmler cut a sorry figure. Walter Schellenberg, the SS's counterintelligence expert, compared the mature Reichsführer's lumpish, rail-legged corpus to "a stork in a lily pond." Hermann Rauschning, recalling a young Himmler's consumptive appearance at a rural political meeting in the 1920s, before the Nazis took power, savages him as "a dirty little bit of vermin":

> The most startling grotesques are real. They are beyond invention. . . . This man, to get the right impression of him, should have been seen before he began wearing fine uniforms of black and silver—when he still went about in the plain shell of the civilian, the very type of ordinariness and commonness. A man barely of medium height, with a face that is no face. Eyes? Has he any? Whether or no, he could not look anyone in the face. He has a sleepy look. An ill-conditioned fellow. Probably with damp hands. . . .
>
> I watched him. He was nervously smoking cigarette after cigarette, throwing away each one after a few puffs. He could not stand still for a moment. He swayed from the knees. He kept shrugging his shoulders. I looked more closely at him. He was clearly not just a vulgar nobody. The man was almost on springs with suppressed passion. His hands shook. His body was tense. There was more in the man than seemed to be at first.

Both Rauschning and Schellenberg were handsome, self-assured sons of the upper middle class, which perhaps qualifies their ad hominem characterizations, but others remarked Himmler's slack butt, pigeon chest, receding chin, almost Mongolian eyes and small, feminine hands, and a Nazi Party official's assessment in 1940 nearly provoked a duel: "If I looked like Himmler," Gauleiter* Albert Forster was overheard to say, "I would not talk about race!" On the other hand, propagandist Josef Goebbels, riding with Himmler on Himmler's Swedish motorbike as he canvassed for the party, thought him "a good fellow and very intelligent;

*(Nazi Party) District Leader.

I like him." In those early days Himmler served as secretary to Lower Bavarian Gauleiter Gregor Strasser. Strasser described his secretary to his brother Otto as looking like "a half-starved shrew," but thought him "keen, I tell you, incredibly keen. He has . . . a motorbike. He is underway the whole day—from one farm to another—from one village to the next. Since I've had him our weapons have really been put into shape. . . . He's a perfect arms NCO. He visits all the secret depots."

Like everyone else who encountered the Reichsführer in full authority, Rauschning and Schellenberg also felt his menace. "The extremist and most bloodthirsty of all the revolutionaries of the Nihilist Revolution," Rauschning says, completing his portrait, "the most remarkable of the Nazi demigods." For Schellenberg, Himmler was "after Hitler, the most powerful man in the Reich, yet I could not describe him otherwise than as the archetype of the German schoolmaster. . . . He was like a schoolmaster who graded the lessons of his pupils with finicky exactitude, and for each answer would have liked to enter a mark in his classbook. His whole personality expressed bureaucratic precision, industry and loyalty." Schellenberg understood that the schoolmasterliness was a "studiously preserved façade," however, and on another occasion he was chilled by Himmler's "small, cold eyes behind the pince-nez . . . suddenly lit with sparkle like the eyes of a basilisk." ("Its hissing drove away all other serpents," the *Oxford English Dictionary* defines this mythical offspring hatched by a serpent from a cock's egg, "and . . . its breath, and even its look, was fatal.")

Heinrich Himmler was the second son of Gebhard and Anna Himmler, born in their comfortable apartment on the Hildegardstrasse in Munich on 7 October 1900. His brother Gebhard was two years older; a younger brother, Ernst, would be born in 1905.

Heinrich's paternal grandfather had been a soldier who became a police sergeant; Gebhard senior was a schoolmaster, a graduate of the University of Munich in philology. Anna, orphaned at twenty-one, brought a mercantile inheritance to the marriage. One generation up from the Bavarian peasantry, Gebhard senior was assiduous at social climbing—"laughably pushing and fawning towards the upper classes," a Gymnasium classmate of Heinrich's would remember. Gebhard's great triumph had been tutoring a Wittelsbach prince, Heinrich of Bavaria. When the former tutor named his second-born son after Prince Heinrich, the prince agreed to become the boy's godfather. The embellishments of courtierism surrounded Heinrich in his childhood—"the heavy furniture," two of his biographers catalogue, "the ancestral portraits, the collection of old coins and German antiquities." Gebhard senior, another biographer writes, "took every precaution to ensure that his sons' schooling embodied the social tone appropriate to the family's status and ambition. He recorded his assessment of the qualities and activities of the boys' teachers. He also compiled a complete list of all the students in each class, and beside each name he noted the occupation of the child's father, as if considering how to protect the family from any association which might endanger its social position."

Here already is an armature of Heinrich Himmler's life: his "caricature of a sadistic school-teacher," as the Frankfurt journalist Konrad Heiden saw him, that "conceals the man like a mask," revealed to be a hand-me-down from his father; familial antecedents in police work and social pretension; clandestine lists detailing vulnerabilities. What Himmler added was servility and malevolence—as long as others did the dirty work.

He entered the Wilhelms Gymnasium at ten, "already wearing gold-rimmed glasses on his rather sharp nose," his classmate observes, and "not infrequently [showing] a half-embarrassed, half-sardonic smile either to excuse his shortsightedness or to stress a certain superiority." His father started him keeping a diary, which the pedant schoolmaster read and corrected, denying him even the privacy of his thoughts. He struggled with gymnastics but mastered academics, doggedly maintaining himself second in his class. During summers in the country he read, swam, hiked, kayaked and took up his father's hobby of scouting medieval German stones and artifacts, from which came the SS's pretentious heraldry of runes.

At fifteen, midway through adolescence, Heinrich faltered. He recorded in his diary for the first time the nervous stomach trouble that would intermittently send him writhing to bed even at the height of his power. He began to have trouble at school. "The boy's enthusiasm for school was somewhat dampened," biographer Bradley F. Smith writes in summarizing Himmler's diary entries from 1915, "and certain subjects, mathematics in particular, became sheer drudgery. . . . His ability to please and maintain close relations with his teachers also fell off. . . . As his ability to charm his teachers diminished, he became critical of other students who tried to improve their positions by using schoolboy blandishments." Smith reports "carelessness" and "lapses in responsibility both in and out of school," after which Heinrich usually reproached himself—in a diary that his father still read. "Actually," Smith counters, "compared with most boys of his age he was a model of conscientiousness and responsibility; but his family's rigid system and his own sense of duty made every failing seem heinous." As Reichsführer, Himmler would see to it that even the small failings of others were heinously punished. Once he subjected his chauffeur to six weeks' solitary confinement without notifying the man's family—a small, cruel bureaucratic lashing of night and fog—for the crime of having caused a minor accident with an official car.

There is little direct evidence in the biographical record of Heinrich's brutalization. His friend and school classmate Karl Gebhardt confirms that Heinrich's father was "a strict schoolmaster who brought up his son with severity." But what is ubiquitous is seldom remarked, and parental discipline in this period in Germany was commonly violent, historian Aurel Ende reports:

> In the upper classes, bourgeois virtues were being taught, including discipline, punctuality, cleanliness and orderliness. The common educational method was severe corporal punishment. In contrast to the lower classes—where beatings mostly happened in rage—middle- and upper-class parents punished with what they called "complete consideration."
>
> . . . School was something children were afraid of, had to be afraid of, given the conditions which prevailed. The sadism of many teachers is remembered in nearly all autobiographies.

Schoolmaster violence persisted in Germany for years after it diminished elsewhere in Europe, a byproduct of reactionary pedagogy in response to the failed liberal revolutions of the first half of the nineteenth century. "In contrast with pedagogical theory developed in some other European countries by the early 19th century," writes historian M. J. Maynes, "law and practice in Prussia continued to rest on the maintenance of the teachers' authority through the use of corporal punishment. . . . Prussia, of course, was not all of Germany. But several other German states [including Bavaria] followed suit." A contemporary analysis of 323 newspaper reports published between 1906 and 1913 of suicides of young people aged three and a half to twenty found that "fear of punishment" or "bad treatment by parents" was mentioned for 23 percent of the boys and 16 percent of the girls. Another contemporary (1909) analysis of 807 suicides of schoolchildren up to fourteen years old identified "bad treatment by parents or teachers" or "fear of punishment" as the motives in 43 percent of the cases. Certainly Gebhard Himmler—parent and schoolmaster both—was domineering. The change in Heinrich's behavior at fifteen, like the change in Hitler's behavior in middle school, probably indicates Heinrich's passage through confused belligerency.

The Great War, which had begun in August 1914, aggrandized violent solutions to conflict and may have contributed to the change in Heinrich's behavior; like other schoolboys, he followed the battles eagerly and yearned to become a soldier. He envied his older brother Gebhard, who joined the army reserve in 1915; Heinrich was stuck in the Jugendwehr, a preliminary training program for high school students. Gebhard moved on to officer training in the Sixteenth Bavarian Infantry, service in Lorraine and a battlefield promotion to warrant officer. Only after the war had ground on for four years, in January 1918, did Heinrich also begin training as a cadet in the Eleventh Infantry. He liked soldiering but wrote home complaining of bedbugs and bad food. His mother responded with a barrage of parcels. He started smoking and asked his parents to send visiting cards so he could make the rounds of local relatives. A rumor, unfounded, that he might be dropped from training and shipped to the front panicked him: he was prepared to fight as an officer but not to die as cannon fodder in the grimy trenches.

Further training in the summer of 1918 led to a machine-gun course in the autumn and a few weeks of drilling recruits, but Germany went down to defeat and the war ended before he could be commissioned; he was discharged in December 1918 without having risked even a soldier's defensive violence. A letter to his parents in Landshut, the town forty miles northeast of Munich where they had moved for Gebhard senior's work, suggests that Himmler's vindictive, devious, paranoid adult character was beginning to coalesce. "He was unsettled by stories of attacks on officers," Smith summarizes, "which had occurred here and there, even in Bavaria, and begged his parents to send him some civilian clothes so that he would be able to travel safely." In a postscript in shorthand, however, a code to his father that his mother could not read, he added, "Now [a message] only for you. I don't know how it is in Landshut. Don't let mother go out alone at night. Not without protection. Be careful in your letters. You can't be sure. Have no fears on my account for I am sly as a fox."

Himmler had begun military training two years short of Gymnasium graduation. With other veterans he returned to school in Landshut in January 1919 to take advantage of a special six-month accelerated program. Violence continued to preoccupy him. He and his closest friend, Falk Zipperer, had begun writing poetry. Zipperer, who had served in the front lines, preferred to write about spring flowers and roguish eyes, but despite his country's defeat Himmler in his poetry almost always celebrated war. "Frenchmen, Frenchmen, oh pay close attention / For there will be no pardon for you," he wrote, threatening "bullets" that "whistle and hiss / Spreading fright and terror" and combatants "sternly hack[ing] away." His military fantasies suggest that he was prepared to try violence at least in combat, but combat continued to evade him. When it appeared that Bavarian Freikorps paramilitary units would attack the Soviet republic that had been declared in Munich in early April, he was eager to participate. His father maneuvered to delay him in school, however, and he only succeeded in joining the Landshut Freikorps a day or two before the Munich regime collapsed on 1 May 1919—too late, once again, to be blooded in battle.

This continuing failure to test his violent resolution helps explain a decision Himmler made when he finished Gymnasium in July 1919—a decision his biographers have found inexplicable: to train for a career in agriculture despite his lack of background in farming. People who succeed at violence gain a violent reputation that endorses their violent resolution. And while criminal violence is despised in civil society, military violence is often honored and respected, gilded with the heroics of accomplishment and sacrifice. Himmler's career decision, seemingly rustic and pastoral, was in fact missionary and militant. In the summer of 1919, he decided to become a *Lebensraum* pioneer: to prepare himself to colonize the East as a warrior-farmer. His most succinct statement of his intentions appears in his diary in late 1921: "If there is another campaign in the East I will go along. The East is most important for us. The West will die easily. In the East we must fight and colonize." In 1919 his plan manifested itself as an extended but unsuccessful effort to learn Russian and a decision to train as an agronomist. This choice of profession, déclassé from his family's perspective, undoubtedly disappointed his father.

Himmler's startling and seemingly disjunct decision in fact coincided with major public events. Historian Anna Bramwell lists some of them:

Securing German expansion to the East had been a red thread in German politics; during the First World War, Max Sering, for example, widely regarded as a liberal intellectual, and certainly not a Nazi supporter in later years, produced a detailed plan in 1915 to establish 250,000 German peasant settlements in Courland [an agricultural region in Russian Latvia]. Arrangements were made with Baltic landowners to give up a third of their land for this purpose after the war. The loss of what became Lithuania after 1918 ended the program. In 1917, a *Vereinigung für deutsche Siedlung und Wanderung* [Union for German Settlement and Migration] aimed at settling German peasants from the Russian interior in the Baltic lands then occupied by Germany. Dr. Stumpfe, a member of the Prussian Agricultural

Ministry, suggested "solving the German-Polish problem" by an exchange of population: Poles in Germany against Germans in what was then "Russian Poland."

A plan like Sering's began to seem possible when the Central Powers (Germany, Austria-Hungary, Bulgaria and Turkey) concluded a separate armistice with the new Bolshevik Russian government on 5 December 1917. In the peace treaty that Leon Trotsky negotiated and signed at Brest-Litovsk in March 1918, Russia recognized the independence of the Ukraine and Georgia, confirmed the independence of Finland and gave up Russian Poland (western Byelorussia) and the Baltic states to Germany and Austria-Hungary. "Massive settlements were planned in the Baltic lands for some 250,000 German farmers," Bramwell comments. In the general armistice of 11 November 1918, however, Germany was forced to renounce the Treaty of Brest-Litovsk. Russia later revoked it as well, but for some time afterward the German army continued to threaten to go back to war to enforce it. (That the war in the East had seemed to end in German victory was convincing evidence to many, including Adolf Hitler, that Germany had lost the Great War not through military defeat but through a vicious "stab in the back.")

The Freikorps paramilitaries were raised first of all for the recovery of the lost eastern frontiers. One Freikorps veteran, Ernst von Salomon, who later participated in the assassination of Walter Rathenau,* romanticized the paramilitary invasions in a notorious memoir, *The Outlaws,* that evokes at least the martial side of Himmler's belligerent rustic fantasy:

> What we wanted we did not know; but what we knew we did not want. To force a way through the prisoning wall of the world, to march over burning fields, to stamp over ruins and scattered ashes, to dash recklessly through wild forests, over blasted heaths, to push, conquer, eat our way through towards the East, to the white, hot, dark, cold land that stretched between ourselves and Asia—was that what we wanted? I do not know whether that was our desire, but that was what we did. And the search for reasons why was lost in the tumult of continuous fighting.

In Himmler's fantasy the East was the place where his personal and social insecurities would fall away and he could thrive and triumph. To mask his lack of success with women, he had announced that he

---

*The Jewish minister of reconstruction and later minister of foreign affairs for the Weimar Republic.

intended to remain a virgin until marriage. Finding an ideal partner and emigrating eastward merge in the first entry he made in his diary mentioning his plans. "For whom I work," he wrote on 11 November 1919, "at present I do not know. I work because it is my duty, because I find peace in work, and I work for my ideal of German womanhood with whom, some day, I will live my life in the East and fight my battles as a German far from beautiful Germany."

To implement his new program he planned a year or two as a *Praktikant* working on a farm and then agronomy study at the Technische Hochschule in Munich, which despite its name was the equivalent of an American engineering college. His farming *Praktikum* began in September 1919—mucking horse stalls and sheaving grain—but after only a few weeks of work he contracted paratyphoid, a milder variety of typhoid fever with similar symptoms. Three weeks in the hospital and a diagnosis of heart strain ended his *Praktikum*. He moved to Munich and enrolled at the Technische Hochschule at the end of October 1919; his first diary entry on a life in the East followed two weeks later.

Success at violent performances is only one of the many possible ways out of belligerency; otherwise all brutalized children would grow up to become violent adults. Himmler's belligerency coincided with, and was prolonged by, the Great War, which culminated in Germany's defeat and social breakdown. Those events might have demonstrated the limitations of violence as a way of resolving conflict, but the defeat seemed to many Germans to have been stolen from victory. Himmler was left as well with the private frustration of never having been tested. He could pretend to be a soldier. "Today I have put the uniform on again," he wrote unctuously on 1 December 1919 after enrolling in a reserve unit. "For me it is always the most precious clothing one can wear." Other diary entries from this period reveal the fragility of this pretense, however, and chart a new pugnaciousness that would flower in the course of time to poisonous bloom. Bradley Smith summarizes:

> In his relations with people of his own age Heinrich was self-conscious and wary of circumstances which might tear away his protective veil and show him as weak, awkward, or incapable. He assumed an outward posture of self-assurance that bordered on aggressiveness and nearly always tried to seize the initiative in conversations with his peers. Yet the difficulty of maintaining this stance gnawed away at him. He was frequently torn by self-doubt and had repeated periods of severe depression in which he despaired of himself and his future and snapped at friends and acquaintances. In the spring of 1920 his ill temper led to a long feud with his parents.

A new opportunity for violent experience arose in November 1919, when Himmler was accepted into a dueling fraternity, the Bund Apollo. Student dueling as college and university fraternities practiced it in Germany at that time was more than a sport but less than a fully violent contest. The contestants trained in protective gear. For the *Mensur* itself they used sharpened but unpointed sabers, wore padded clothing, guarded their necks with swaths of silk and their eyes with an iron frame. They slashed away standing in position inside a circle; cutting wounds to the face and head were the goal, which were then sutured without anesthesia. The contest itself and the surgical procedure that followed were therefore tests of fortitude and stoicism but only imitations of serious violence. "Unlike other one-on-one sporting contests," writes dueling historian Kevin McAleer, "the *Mensur* was a discipline in which there was neither winner nor loser. Bouts might be stopped on the basis of blood loss, and there were head-cut tallies, but everybody emerged victorious for having gamely stood the test." A 1912 student petition McAleer cites explains that "it is only required that each combatant 'stood up well,' that he betrayed no fear of the blows, of the wounds, that pain elicited no cry."

Serious dueling—dueling to the death to settle a conflict or an insult to one's honor—arose among the nobility in early modern Europe at a time when states were centralizing. In medieval days the nobility had dominated its demesnes with serious violence, enforcing decrees, claiming and defending territory and levying tribute much as present-day mafiosi do. To assert authority and collect taxes, centralizing governments had to limit such private violence. Monarchs did so in part by establishing courts that the nobility had to attend as disarmed courtiers to seek royal favor. Monarchs also outlawed violent personal contests. The duel, a formalized violent personal contest, then developed outside the law as an implicit political protest, an assertion by the nobility that while it was prepared to bend its knee to the monarch in matters of taxation and social control, it did not recognize the monarch's writ in matters of personal honor. Seventeenth-century Prussia thus interpreted duels to be "insults" to the state on two levels, McAleer writes: "The theft [by their loss of life in duels] of such citizenry as officers and officials who could render it valuable service, and the rape of justice through infringement of its sovereignty in the administration of law." The punishment for dueling varied from monarch to monarch and from century to century, but in the early days of its development the essentially treasonable practice was punished by summary execution.

Serious dueling was thus an assertion of noble status. Through all the changes that came to dueling as it spread to the officer class of the military and to the upper-middle bourgeois, the practice remained linked to higher social status—an allusion to the nobility's former violent independence from state authority. In modified form it thrived in Germany at the beginning of the twentieth century. The *Mensur* was only an imitation of serious dueling, carrying nothing like the same degree of risk, but it borrowed the reputation of its riskier counterpart. To be chosen to participate was a recognition of status, which *Mensur* scars made visible for life.

Himmler did not like watching student dueling at first. Given his weak-kneed reaction later to reviewing an Einsatzgruppen massacre staged on his behalf, the obstacle was probably squeamishness: head cuts bleed profusely. He coveted the endorsement of social status a successful duel would bring, however, and forced himself to watch and learn. He probably also thought the *Mensur* would establish his manly reputation. Dueling was so important to him that his church's disapproval of the practice precipitated his first religious crisis.

His family was Roman Catholic; up to this time—the autumn and winter of 1919—he had been a practicing Catholic, says Bradley Smith:

> He was concerned lest fraternity dueling might conflict with the teachings of the church. Since his membership in Apollo was very important to him, he was seriously troubled. A short sermon he heard on the day after Christmas 1919 . . . brought these doubts to a head: "During the sermon I had to endure an inner struggle more serious than any before. The dueling business constantly keeps cropping up. In the evening I prayed. I had, of course, earlier partly overcome it. God will continue to help me overcome my doubts."

"Only very gradually," Smith adds, "after much inner soul-searching and after reassuring talks with his father, was he able to free himself from his torment and feel completely at ease in the *Bund*." But Himmler's increasing hostility to religion dates from this time.

Overcoming religious scruples only needed sufficient rationalization; arranging a *Mensur* required a willing partner. Himmler had great difficulty finding one. Across his student years he was hardening into an aggressive, pompous, condescending prig nearly devoid of a sense of humor. A year of *Praktikum* on a farm where he was treated as a young gentleman, with easy work, a place at the family table, packages from home and a maid to clean his room bolstered his self-satisfaction without improving his character; in May 1921, for example, when his brother Gebhard was awarded an Iron Cross First Class for his war service, Himmler jealously escalated his assaults on his brother's temperament.

Back in Munich in 1922 for his final year at the Technische Hochschule he ran for pledgemaster of his fraternity and lost. "He was not very popular with his fraternity brothers," Smith reports, "some of whom quite openly expressed their lack of confidence in him. The fixity of his ideas and his continuous organizing and gossiping did nothing to break down the barriers to his social acceptance."

Facing social disapproval during this final year of school, Himmler enjoined himself to "stop talking too much" but intensified rather than modulated his right-wing radicalism. Anti-Semitism, which purported to identify hidden Jewish manipulations, was promoted in Germany as a ready explanation for almost any kind of real or perceived adversity; that year Himmler rapidly embraced anti-Semitism, began spying out Jews among fellow students and family acquaintances and made his first contacts with Captain Ernst Röhm, a Freikorps freebooter who was organizing a protective bodyguard for Hitler—which would become the Sturmabteilung, the brown-shirted SA. Only in June 1922, six weeks before he graduated, did Himmler finally find someone willing to duel him.

He fought his *Mensur* on 17 June 1922. "I certainly did not get agitated," he wrote afterward. "Stood very well and fought technically beautifully. My opponent was Herr Renner, *Alemanians* [*Bund*], he struck honest blows." Himmler took five cuts and maintained his composure during their suturing. "I really did not flinch once," he brags of the suturing. "Distl held my head in old comradeship. . . . Did not sleep especially well because the bandage was always pulling." He had proven his fortitude without proving his violent resolution.

There are references in Himmler's diary, from summer 1922, to his satisfaction with the assassination (on 24 June) of the "scoundrel" Walter Rathenau, to target practice with hand weapons and a machine gun and to an unsuccessful attempt to volunteer for a political assassination squad. So many coincidental setbacks in Himmler's pursuit of violent performances—missing war service as an officer candidate, joining the Landshut Freikorps too late to fight the Munich Soviet republic, delaying his *Mensur* with arrogant behavior he chose not to change and now again failing to convince the leader of an assassination squad that he should be given what he called in his diary "special assignments"—strongly suggest that he maneuvered across the years of his young adulthood to avoid having to risk any serious violent personal encounter while using militaristic posturing to promote a violent reputation. The *Mensur* itself was just such a sham, which explains in part why Himmler was prepared to jettison his religion if necessary to accomplish it. In the fullness of his power he would become a *Schreibtischtäter*, a desk murderer,* a physical coward willing and even eager to order others to kill. Such cowards are potentially far more destructive than the violent individuals they appoint to kill in their behalf: maintaining their fraudulent violent personal reputations requires projecting a maleficence sufficiently extreme to disguise their personal cowardice, which is made easier because in ordering blood to be shed they suffer no personal trauma, nor are they constrained by personal risk.

Himmler graduated from the Technische Hochschule in August 1922 with a degree in agronomy. His career path soon intersected Hitler's. As the developing German hyperinflation wiped out his family's assets and his own savings, he found a job researching manures for a fertilizer company in Schleissheim, a town just north of Munich that happened to be a hotbed of right-wing paramilitary activity. He joined Ernst Röhm's Reichsflagge† paramilitary group, which federated with several other groups in 1923 under an umbrella organization that Hitler controlled. In August, following Röhm, Himmler joined the Nazi Party as well. He followed Röhm into a splinter paramilitary group Röhm organized, the Reichskriegsflagge.‡ In mid-September, after quitting his manure research, he was accepted into a replacement unit of the Bavarian army, Company Werner.

Through the interactions of these various organizations, it so happened that when Hitler attempted his Beer Hall Putsch in Munich on 8–9 November 1923, Himmler carried the flag, marching with his brother Gebhard and four hundred other men of the Reichskriegsflagge to the War Ministry, where Röhm ordered them to occupy the building and surround it with a barbed-wire barricade. It was for the purpose of rescuing the Reichskriegsflagge that Hitler and two thousand fellow putschists linked arms and marched into the Odeonplatz the next day, where a firefight started with the Munich police. Hitler dislocated his shoulder diving for cover (or being dragged down by the weight of the man shot dead next to him; accounts vary). At the War Ministry Röhm was arrested, but the rank and file, including the Himmler brothers, were merely disarmed and sent home. "Toward the authorities," Smith reports of the aftermath, "Heinrich was very bitter, his mood alternating

---

*Literally, "writing table perpetrator."
†National Flag.
‡National War Flag.

between imaginary fears of his own arrest and disappointment that the government was not interested in him." He began to suspect that people were opening his mail.

Leaderless and jobless after the putsch, living with his disapproving parents, he began fantasizing again of homesteading in the East, going so far, despite his distaste for "Jewish Bolshevism," as to write the Soviet Embassy early in 1924 asking about prospects for employment in the Ukraine. His reading supported his Eastern fantasies, says Smith; besides "anti-Semitic and *völkisch* readings which became progressively more uncompromising and more extreme as the months went by," he "particularly welcomed any work that touched on German domination of other people. Rudolf Bartsch's novel about German landlords in Slavic lands [*Frans Utta und der Jäger*], for example, [Himmler] describes [in an annotated book list he maintained] as a 'wonderfully pretty and clear German story.' "

Smith identifies a voyeuristic component in Himmler's anti-Semitism. The prude who was saving himself for marriage indulged himself reading banned erotic trash, while condemning Jews as lewdly sensual. Like Hitler, he believed Jewish men seduced German girls for purposes of "race pollution." Another emerging component of Himmler's kitsch philosophy was spiritualism—he came to believe in mental telepathy and reincarnation—which allowed him to feel religious while avoiding his political conflicts with Catholicism.

Himmler found employment in Landshut as Gregor Strasser's "half-starved shrew" in June 1924. Strasser was a Landshut pharmacist before he became a Nazi Gauleiter, and the Gau office that Himmler now organized was located above the Strasser pharmacy. From that office Himmler careened around Bavaria on his Swedish motorbike, venturing farther north as his work and political campaigning expanded; it was during one of these northern forays that Rauschning watched an intense, nervous, damp-handed Himmler inciting the farmers. In a memo from this period that summarizes his political perspective, Himmler called "international Jewish capital" the farmer's "worst enemy," because it "set the townsman against the countryman." German peasantry, he argued, would be tested and strengthened by battling the Slavs:

> Particularly in the East there are, today, great masses of land available for purchase; they are now held by the great estates. The sons of farmers and farmworkers must be settled there to prevent the second and third sons of the German farmer from being forced into the towns, as has been the case hitherto. The countryman can only regain decisive influence in Germany by widespread resettlement. . . . Increase of our

peasant population is the only effective defense against the influx of the Slav working-class masses from the East. As it was six hundred years ago, the German peasant's destiny must be to preserve and increase the German people's patrimony in their holy mother earth in battle against the Slav race.

Hitler was released from Landsberg Prison in December 1924 and reestablished the Nazi Party the following February. Since the SA was still banned throughout most of Germany, he created the SS as a new palace guard that would be legal everywhere. "I told myself that I needed a bodyguard," as Hitler explained his rationale later, "even a very restricted one, but made up of men who would be enlisted unconditionally, ready even to march against their own brothers. Better a mere twenty men to a city (on condition that one could count on them absolutely) than an unreliable mass." Himmler, certainly ready to march against his own brother, joined both the SS and the SA in Bavaria, where both were legal. SS memberships were numbered consecutively; indicating his early enlistment, Himmler's personal SS number was 168. By 1925 he was SS chief in Lower Bavaria, selling subscriptions to the party newspaper and occasionally marching in parade.

When he joined the SS he started reading books on espionage and police work, including torture (which frightened him). The Soviet secret police were "almost completely Jewish," he decided against all evidence, as the Czar's secret police had been before, despite the wave of bloody pogroms they had organized and the patently fraudulent *Protocols of the Elders of Zion* they had cobbled together and loosed upon the world. Otto Strasser believed that one of Himmler's models was bloody Soviet secret police founder and commissar Felix Dzerzhinsky.

Himmler had already begun thinking about shaping the SS into a caste of noble warriors. He moved to Munich in 1926 to administer the Nazi Party's propaganda office there. He was too literal-minded to craft effective propaganda, but proximity to the party center revealed his gift for organization and for loyalty, and by 1927 he had won appointment as deputy SS leader. Full responsibility for the three-hundred-man organization came on 6 January 1929, when Hitler appointed him Reichsführer-SS; he was twenty-eight years old. "The SS will be an Order sworn to the Führer," he told Otto Strasser. "For him I could do anything. Believe me, if Hitler were to say I should shoot my mother, I would do it and be proud of his confidence." Strasser told Himmler he made him shudder. Himmler liked the acknowledgment of his potential for personal violence, however bogus, and the phrase became a running joke between them.

In 1927 in Berlin Himmler had met a sturdy nurse of Polish origin named Margarete Concerzowo. Marga, seven years his senior, shared his enthusiasm for alternative medicine and probably won him with mothering. "Size 50 knickers," Heydrich's more stylish wife would say in ridicule of the woman Himmler married in 1928—"that's all there was to her." Lina Heydrich considered Marga a "narrow-minded, humorless blonde female, always worrying about protocol; she ruled her husband and could twist him around her little finger." When they married, Marga sold the small nursing home she operated in Berlin and the Himmlers bought a modest working farm outside Munich, where they raised chickens and grew herbs for sale. Himmler's daughter, Gudrun, was born the following year, attended by a doctor who had been a medical associate of Marga's. The doctor's son, twenty-four-year-old Viktor Brack, became Himmler's driver. (Later, advanced into the Führer Chancellery of the Nazi Party* and serving as a liaison officer with the department of health, Brack would manage the Nazi euthanasia killing program and contribute to the development of the gas vans used to murder the disabled and then the Jews.)

To build the SS, Himmler sought out disaffected middle- and upper-middle-class young men, as well as sons of the former nobility. Many of them had been active in the Freikorps, which means many of them, perhaps the majority of them, already had experience with serious violence. "From 1929 onwards," writes historian Heinz Höhne, "[Freikorps men] began to stream into the SS. They came in two waves; first appeared the veterans [of the Great War] who had neither wished nor been able to reintegrate themselves into society. . . . The [Great Depression] produced a second wave of applicants for the SS. This time they were men who had managed to get a foot in the door of everyday life, but had lost their positions in the pitiless competition of a free economy. The spur which drove them into SS uniform was bankruptcy."

Himmler offered these disaffected men a vision of membership in a new nobility. The old nobility had claimed its right of inheritance by blood; Himmler's new nobility would make a similar claim, but the blood would not be restricted within families but pseudospeciated, identifying a supposedly "Nordic" (alternatively, "Aryan") race with inherited physical and moral superiorities. Its duty would be to win *Lebensraum* in the East so that Germany could eventually dominate the world—a hypertrophy of Himmler's own earlier private fantasies of making a new life

*Kanzlei des Führers, KdF.

for himself in Russia. As he explained his vision in June 1931 to an audience of SS leaders:

> For us, standing sublime above all doubt, it is the blood carrier who can make history; the Nordic race is decisive not only for Germany, but for the whole world. Should we succeed in establishing this Nordic race again from and around Germany and inducing them to become farmers, and from this seedbed producing a race of 200 million, then the world will belong to us. Should Bolshevism win, it will signify the destruction of the Nordic race ... devastation, the end of the world. ... We are called, therefore, to create a basis on which the next generation can make history.

Nazi racist visions have come to seem ridiculous, and there were many who scoffed at them even in their heyday. Nazism's similarity to a religious cult helps explain them. As religious cults do, Nazism offered impassioned followers a charismatic leader and beliefs that resonated for people whose lives had been shattered by conflict, economic hardship and loss of faith in traditional institutions. The vision that Himmler and a few like-minded colleagues assembled of a restored, superior "race" colonizing the East as soldier-farmers prepared to defend the West from the "Asiatic hordes"—meaning Slavs and Jews—gave positive valence to Nazi anti-Semitic scapegoating. It was a visionary program, modernized with pseudoscientific eugenic claptrap, that offered potential followers both high-minded goals and practical rewards. "It remains the great and decisive achievement of the *Reichsführer*," an SS propagandist wrote astutely, "that—at a time when the racial question was still regarded by the movement as a purely negative notion of anti-Semitism—he included theoretical ideas of Nazi *Weltanschauung* in his own organization of the SS and helped them to prevail."

Despite this elitist, utopian program, until Hitler became Reich Chancellor, on 30 January 1933, Himmler accepted into the SS whomever he could get, expanding the SS by that date to a membership of more than fifty thousand men. Thereafter applications rolled in and he could afford to be selective; between 1933 and 1935, with hundreds of thousands of new members, he claimed to have expelled sixty thousand, a process he called "combing out the useless material." Discussing the selection process later and changing the metaphor, he spoke of going about it "like a nursery gardener, trying to reproduce a good old strain which has been adulterated and debased; we started from the principles of plant selection and then proceeded, quite unashamedly, to weed out the men whom we did not think we could use for the buildup of the SS."

Leon Trotsky understood Nazi intentions in the East very well, alerted as he had been to German territorial aspirations in 1918, when he negotiated the Treaty of Brest-Litovsk. In September 1933, having escaped to America, he analyzed in *Harper's Magazine* a Hitler speech that purported to defend the Third Reich's pacifism:

> The assurances given by the National Socialists that they renounce "Germanization" do not signify that they renounce conquests, for one of the central and most persistent ideas in their program is the occupation of vast territories in "the East" so that a strong German peasantry may be established there. . . . The renunciation of Germanization signifies, in this connection, the principle of the privileged position of the Germanic "race" as the seignorial caste in the occupied territories. The Nazis are against assimilation but not against annexation. They prefer the extermination of the conquered "inferior" peoples to their Germanization. For the time being, fortunately, this is only a matter of hypothetical conquests.
> . . . [But] Hitler is preparing for war.

From one side of the Nazi mouth, then, a perverted idealism; from the other, territorial and exterminatory ambitions. Hitler was far more ruthless and nihilistic than Himmler, who had his gentrified middle-class pretensions to protect; the Führer sometimes ridiculed his Reichsführer's mystical elitism. But Hitler no less than Himmler dreamed of *Lebensraum*. He discussed it specifically, and hinted at mass exterminations, as early as his 1931 confidential interviews with Leipzig newspaper editor Richard Breitling (Breitling kept verbatim shorthand notes that were transcribed and authenticated after the war). Hitler told the editor:

> We propose to build a protective wall against Russian imperialism and the Slavs from Northern Norway to the Black Sea, for we must not forget that Stalin's communism is a new form of Russian imperialism. . . . If, despite our justifiable action, armed conflicts ensue because world Jewry would like to turn back the wheel of history, Jewry will be crushed by that same wheel. . . .
> The menace to western civilization was never so great. Even before we assume power we must make clear . . . that sooner or later we shall be forced to conduct a crusade against bolshevism. . . . We must already be thinking of the resettlement of millions of men from Germany and Europe. Migrations of people have always taken place. . . . We must colonize the East ruthlessly.

We intend to introduce a great resettlement policy; we do not wish to go on treading on each other's toes in Germany. In 1923 little Greece could resettle a million men. Think of the biblical deportations and the massacres of the Middle Ages . . . and remember the extermination of the Armenians. One eventually reaches the conclusion that masses of men are mere biological modeling clay.

SIX

Truehearted Heinrich II

In 1934 there was unrest in Germany. The Nazi regime had not delivered the jobs that the millions of unemployed had expected. The conservatives who had helped Hitler to the chancellorship were organizing to eject him before Hindenburg died. The German professional army—the Reichswehr—feared the growing power of Ernst Röhm's SA, almost four million strong and in Röhm's opinion a people's army to which the Reichswehr ought to be subordinated. In response to these and other challenges, Hitler ordered a purge. For the instrument of its execution he chose the SS, which was still small compared with the SA, focused on police work and therefore not a threat to the Reichswehr.

Himmler and Heydrich organized the arrests, trumping up allegations that the SA was planning a putsch. SS-Obergruppenführer Sepp Dietrich, who commanded the Leibstandarte-SS, Hitler's personal bodyguard battalion, armed two of its companies with weapons the Reichswehr provided. Early in the morning on Saturday, 30 June 1934, Hitler personally burst into Röhm's room at the Bad Wiesee resort where the SA leader and his captains had been carousing and arrested him at pistol point. Gregor Strasser was among the hundreds arrested. Firing squads rattled the neighborhood around Berlin's Lichterfelde barracks all the next day.

Hans Gisevius saw some of the Röhm Purge and survived to recall it. Gisevius was an articulate lawyer, involved throughout the war in plots against Hitler, who was maneuvering at that time to take over the Prussian state Gestapo. At Göring's palace on Saturday afternoon, with Kurt Daluege (then the federal chief of police), Gisevius encountered the execution committee itself:

> Through the door [into Göring's study] we could see Göring, Himmler, Heydrich, and little Pilli Koerner, undersecretary to Göring in his capacity as minister-president. We could see them conferring, but naturally we could not hear what was being said. Occasionally, however, we could catch a muffled sound: "Away!" or "Aha!" or "Shoot him!" For the most part we heard nothing but raucous laughter. The whole crew of them seemed to be in the best humor.

... We suddenly heard loud shouting. A police major, his face flaming, rushed out of the room, and behind him came Göring's hoarse, booming voice: "Shoot them ... take a whole company ... shoot them ... shoot them at once!" The written word cannot reproduce the undisguised blood lust, fury, vicious vengefulness, and, at the same time, the fear, the pure funk, that the scene revealed.

By then Strasser, Himmler's first patron and a figure of national prominence in the SA and the party, was already dead. Gisevius learned from an eyewitness how he died. "Strasser had been taken to the Gestapo prison around noon. By that time some hundred arrested SA leaders were crowded together in one big room." Since they had not in fact been plotting a putsch, they had no idea why they had been arrested. Time passed. An SS man arrived and called Strasser out. It made sense, says Gisevius, that "the man who had formerly been next in importance to Adolf Hitler in the Nazi Party was to be moved to an individual cell." The men gave way and Strasser was gone:

> But scarcely a minute later they heard the crack of a pistol. The SS man had shot the unsuspecting Strasser from behind and hit his main artery. A great stream of blood had spurted against the wall of the tiny cell. Apparently Strasser did not die at once. A prisoner in the adjoining cell heard him thrashing about on the cot for nearly an hour. No one paid any attention to him. At last the prisoner heard loud footsteps in the corridor and orders being shouted. The guards clicked their heels. And the prisoner recognized Heydrich's voice saying: "Isn't he dead yet? Let the swine bleed to death."

At ten o'clock that night Hitler's plane from Munich landed at Tempelhof Airport in Berlin. Gisevius was there as a spectator with his friend Arthur Nebe, the future commander of Einsatzgruppe B, who was then a Gestapo official. The sky was blood red when the plane came in, Gisevius remembered, "a piece of theatricality that no one had staged." Commands, an honor guard presenting arms, and then Göring, Himmler, Daluege and a crowd of police officers approached the plane. Hitler emerged wearing a black bow tie, a brown shirt, a leather jacket, high boots. His face was puffy from lack of sleep and unshaven, but Gisevius says, "he did not impress me as wretched, nor did he awaken sympathy. ... It was clear that the murders of his friends had cost him no effort at all. He had felt nothing; he had merely acted out his rage."

Walking toward the waiting line of cars, Hitler stopped to talk to Göring and Himmler:

> From one of his pockets Himmler took a long, tattered list. Hitler read it through, while Göring and Himmler whispered incessantly into his

ear. We could see Hitler's finger moving slowly down the sheet of paper. Now and then it paused for a moment at one of the names. . . . Suddenly Hitler tossed his head. There was so much violent emotion, so much anger in the gesture, that everyone noticed it. Nebe and I cast significant glances at one another. Undoubtedly, we thought, they were now informing him of Strasser's "suicide."

Finally they moved on. . . . Hitler was still walking with the same sluggish tread. By contrast the two blood-drenched scoundrels at his side seemed all the more lively. Both Göring and Himmler, for all the bulkiness of the one and the drabness of the other, seemed cut out of the same cloth today. Both manifested the same self-importance, loquacity, officiousness and the same sense of guilt.

We may doubt the sense of guilt, but both, Himmler especially, must have been as nervous as two tattling schoolboys colluding with the principal, afraid his wrath might next fall on them. Both men would admit that entering the Führer's presence always made them nauseous. As Göring put it, "Every time I face him, my heart falls into my trousers."

Röhm still lived. Hitler hesitated to order Röhm's murder because the saber-scarred veteran had stood with the Führer in Munich in 1923. On Sunday Himmler and Göring convinced him to have Röhm killed, but he hoped his old fellow revolutionary could be coaxed into committing suicide. Himmler gave the assignment to Theodor Eicke, his commandant at Dachau, a thick-necked pipe smoker and a fully malefic killer. Eicke drove with two deputies to Stadelheim, where Röhm was jailed, explained his purpose, left a pistol on a small table at the door of the cell and stepped out to wait. Röhm chose not to take the bait. Eicke had the pistol removed and then returned to the cell with one of his deputies, weapons at the ready, to find Röhm, a fireplug of a man, standing barechested. He started to speak to them and they shot him.

One hundred forty-two SS officers, Heydrich first among them, received promotions within the week, and on 20 July 1934 the SS won its independence from subordination to the SA. Hitler took to calling Himmler *"der treue Heinrich"*—the loyal Heinrich, truehearted Heinrich. "For us as Secret State Police and as members of the SS," truehearted Heinrich would tell his Gestapo subordinates in October, "30 June was not—as several believe—a day of victory or a day of triumph. Rather, it was the hardest day that can be visited on a soldier in his lifetime. To have to shoot one's own comrades, with whom one has stood side by side for eight or ten years in the struggle for an ideal, and who had then failed, is the bitterest thing that can happen to a man." No doubt he felt that way, though he had done none of the shooting himself.

(Heydrich expressed similar ambivalence at his dirty duties, commenting to a colleague once, "People abroad take us for bloodhounds, don't they? It is almost too hard for the individual, but we must be hard as granite.") Himmler went on to blame Röhm's fall on "Jews, Freemasons and Catholics."

Two years later, increasingly confident that he had successfully disguised his cowardice with delegated menace, Himmler would write in an SS pamphlet: "I know that there are people in Germany now who become sick when they see these black uniforms. We know the reason and we do not expect to be loved by too many." Nearly on the second anniversary of the Röhm Purge, on 17 June 1936, Hitler further rewarded Himmler by appointing him Chief of the German Police, making him responsible at thirty-five years of age for all the police functions of the Third Reich. (His full title was now Reichsführer-SS und Chef der deutschen Polizei.) He reorganized the police into two divisions, the Security Police (Sicherheitspolizei) under Heydrich and the Order Police (Ordnungspolizei) under Daluege. (The separation explains the separation of his mobile killing forces in the occupied East into Einsatzgruppen and Order Police battalions, further augmented by native auxiliaries under the authority of the Higher SS and Police Leaders whom Himmler appointed to serve as his deputies in the occupied territories.) He understood his primary police responsibility to be prevention, and was prepared to place tens of thousands of citizens who had committed no crimes under preventive arrest, a fate that in March 1937 befell several thousand felons with previous convictions, who were rounded up and incarcerated in concentration camps. The violent among this lot would serve in time as kapos—inmate orderlies—adept at brutalizing political prisoners and Jews; some of the worst would be recruited into an SS punitive battalion, SS-Sonderkommando Dirlewanger—named after its violently sadistic commander, Oskar Dirlewanger—that fought partisans, raped and tortured young women and slaughtered Jews Einsatzgruppen-style in Byelorussia beginning in 1942.

Whatever mystical brotherhood the East represented to Heinrich Himmler, to Adolf Hitler the East represented the German equivalent of the British and French colonial empires. "From the purely territorial point of view," he wrote in *Mein Kampf,* "the area of the German Reich vanishes completely as compared with that of the so-called world powers. Let no one cite England as a proof to the contrary, for England in reality is merely the great capital of the British world empire which calls nearly a quarter of the earth's surface its own." In consequence, Hitler concluded urgently, "The National Socialist movement must strive to eliminate the disproportion between our population and our area— viewing this latter as a source of food as well as a basis for power politics." At one of his table talks in the first months after Barbarossa, he drew the parallel explicitly. "The Russian space is our India," he told his staff and guests. "Like the English, we shall rule this empire with a handful of men." He went on to talk about supplying grain to all of Europe from the Ukraine. "The Crimea will give us its citrus fruits, cotton and rubber (100,000 acres of [rubber tree] plantation would be enough to ensure our independence)." In return, he added derisively, "We'll supply the Ukrainians with scarves, glass beads and everything that colonial people like." The Slavs, he claimed, were "a mass of born slaves who feel the need of a master."

This parallelism between the beckoning East and the British and French colonial empires, which most Holocaust historians have ignored, goes far to explain Hitler's exterminationist program, as Swedish historian Sven Lindqvist explains:

> In this [historical] debate no one mentions the German extermination of the Herero people in southwest Africa during Hitler's childhood. No one mentions the corresponding genocide [of indigenous peoples] by the French, the British, or the Americans. No one points out that during Hitler's childhood, a major element in the European view of mankind was the conviction that "inferior races" were by nature condemned to extinction: the true compassion of the superior races consisted in helping them on the way.

(In 1904 in German Southwest Africa—modern Namibia—disputes and misunderstandings between the colonial government, German settlers and Herero leaders led to armed conflict. German marines arrived from the coast and began lynching Herero men and slaughtering Herero women and children; letters by a Herero leader purporting to reveal a call to tribal insurrection were published in Germany and came to the attention of the Kaiser; the Kaiser sent out Lieutenant General Lothar von Trotha with full authority, in von Trotha's words, to "annihilate these masses." With troops and cannon von Trotha drove the Herero eastward into the Kalahari Desert. When the Herero offered to surrender, he issued a proclamation that has come to be known as the Vernichtungs-befehl—the Extermination Order—telling them that they were no longer German subjects, that they must leave the land and that any Herero found "within the German borders . . . with or without a gun, with or without cattle, [would] be shot." He then occupied the line of water holes at the western edge of the Kalahari and waited for the

Herero nation to die in the desert of thirst. His rationalizations for this action would echo in the rationalizations of the Third Reich: "I find it most appropriate that the nation perishes instead of infecting our soldiers and diminishing their supplies of water and food." "The exercise of violence with crass terrorism and even with gruesomeness was and is my policy. I destroy the African tribes with streams of blood and streams of money. Only following this cleansing can something new emerge, which will remain." Lindqvist concludes the story: "When the rainy season came, German patrols found skeletons lying around dry hollows, twenty-four to fifty feet deep, dug by the Hereros in vain attempts to find water. Almost the entire people—about eighty thousand human beings—died in the deserts. Only a few thousand were left, sentenced to hard labor in German concentration camps.")

Hitler was aware of the American assault on native populations through his lifelong reading and rereading of the German cowboy-western novelist Karl May (he was still reading May in his bunker years later in the war). He connected May's "Redskins" with the Russian "natives" explicitly in another of his table talks: Speaking of what he called "this Russian desert," he asserted, "We shall populate it. . . . We'll take away its character of an Asiatic steppe, we'll Europeanize it. With this object, we have undertaken the construction of roads that will lead to the southernmost point of the Crimea and to the Caucasus. These roads will be studded along their whole length with German towns, and around these towns our colonists will settle." As for "the natives":

We'll have to screen them carefully. The Jew, that destroyer, we shall drive out. As far as the population is concerned, I get a better impression in White Russia [Byelorussia] than in the Ukraine. . . .

And above all, no remorse on this subject! We're not going to play children's nurses; we're absolutely without obligation as far as these people are concerned. . . .

There's only one duty: to Germanize this country by the immigration of Germans, and to look upon the natives as Redskins. . . .

In this business I shall go straight ahead, cold-bloodedly. . . . I don't see why a German who eats a piece of bread should torment himself with the idea that the soil that produces this bread has been won by the sword. When we eat wheat from Canada, we don't think about the despoiled Indians.

Such conquest had been rationalized long before by apologists for imperialism. The British liberal philosopher Herbert Spencer had argued the case as early as 1850 in his book *Social Statics*. "The forces which are working out the great scheme of perfect happiness," Spencer wrote, "taking no account of incidental suffering, exterminate such sections of mankind as stand in their way. . . . Be he human or be he brute, the hindrance must be got rid of." Alfred Russell Wallace, Darwin's competitor, debating the extinction of the "lower" races before the London Anthropological Society in 1864, characterized the extermination of populations as a form of natural selection. He compared Europeans to their weeds: Europeans compete successfully against indigenous peoples, he argued, "just as the weeds of Europe overrun North America and Australia, extinguishing native productions by the inherent vigor of their organization, and by their greater capacity for existence and multiplication."

The Germans were latecomers to imperialist rationalization because they were late in acquiring colonies. The leading German authority on colonization at the end of the nineteenth century was geographer Friedrich Ratzel. In 1891 he faulted "the theory that this dying out [of Aborigines, American Indians, Africans and other groups] is predestined by the inner weakness of the individual race." Rather, Ratzel argued, Europeans caused the depopulation by impoverishing and killing native peoples. But Ratzel changed his tune when Germany began seeking colonial possessions. After he helped found the Pan-German League in 1891, the geographer discovered that "inferior" cultures contain inner forces of destruction that colonial domination merely releases. "Those with little culture have fundamentally passive characters," Lindqvist writes in paraphrasing Ratzel's rationalization. "They seek to endure rather than overcome the circumstances that are reducing their numbers. Contact with Europeans simply hastens an extinction already underway."

Ratzel found a formula for including the Jews in this victim-blaming rationalization in his 1897 book *Political Geography*. The Jews were hardly people of inferior culture, he conceded, but they and the Gypsies were condemned to extinction, along with "the stunted hunting people in the African interior" and "innumerable similar existences," because they were "scattered people with no land." There was no land anywhere on earth that was not occupied, Ratzel pointed out, so cultures with increasing populations that needed more land had to conquer it, turning it into uninhabited land "through killing and displacement." Given its growing population, Europe in particular needed colonies. "But it is a mistake," Lindqvist says, paraphrasing Ratzel, "to think that colonies have to be on the other side of the oceans. Border colonization is also colonization. Occupations near at hand are more easily defended and assimilated than distant ones." Hitler consulted Ratzel's *Political Geography* when he was writing *Mein Kampf.* He discusses Pan-Germanism at length in his personal and political testament; Ratzel's doctrine of border colonization echoes in sentences such as this one: "For Germany, consequently, the only possibility for carrying out a healthy territorial policy lay in the acquisition of new land in Europe itself." Such acquisition, Hitler adds, was no longer possible "by peaceful means." Ratzel influenced Hitler even more directly. It was he who coined the term and formulated the concept of *Lebensraum* in a 1904 book, *Der Lebensraum.*

Hitler's anti-Semitism was more fundamental to his attitude toward the Jews than his imperialistic, exterminationist Eastern policy—he would not, after all, seek the deaths of only the Eastern Jews—but the two agendas overlapped. The Third Reich actively worked to destroy many other groups besides the Jews. The Jews were first in line, and they were subjected to direct killing rather than slow, lethally debilitative exploitation because Hitler perceived them to be the most dangerous, "the mightiest counterpart to the Aryan" who sought no less than "destruction for the inhabitants of this planet."

Henry Friedlander, the preeminent historian of Hitler's euthanasia murder program, argues similarly from the perspective of German eugenic policy, which was yet another overlapping agenda that rationalized mass killing:

> The usual interpretation [of the Holocaust] assigns the role of racial victim exclusively to the Jews, and sees anti-Semitism as the only ideological basis for mass murder. I do not deny that anti-Semitism was a major component of Nazi ideology. I agree that the Nazis viewed the Jews as chronic enemies, and that Hitler's preoccupation with the imagined Jewish threat placed the struggle against the Jews high on the list of priorities. But I do argue that anti-Semitism was only part of a larger worldview, which divided mankind into worthy and unworthy populations. Both Nazi ideologues and race scientists believed that German blood had been polluted, and that it was the nation's primary task to purge the German gene pool. The enemies were (1) the handicapped, who were considered "degenerate," and (2) "alien races," which in Central Europe meant Jews and Gypsies, since both were considered non-European nations that could not be assimilated.

Himmler borrowed and parroted Hitler's various rationalizations and supplemented them with grandiosities of his own—his kitsch vision of colonizing the East with *Wehrbauern*, his soldier-farmers. He commissioned an entrance-hall triptych to illustrate that vision on a visit in January 1939 to Wewelsburg, the Saxon castle he was restoring as an SS leadership retreat. Writing his architect, he described the images he wanted in the triptych:

a) The attack of an SS troop in war, in which I envisage the representation of a dead or mortally wounded old SS man, who is married, to show that from death itself and despite it new life springs.

b) A field in a new land being plowed by a *Wehrbauern*, an SS man.

c) The newly-founded village with the families and numerous children.

But Himmler struggled to incorporate the repulsive duties of massacring unarmed civilians into the SS mystique. In that effort he had Prussian military tradition to draw on, with its inversion of morally reprehensible and psychologically difficult experience into a virtue, "hardness."

"Hardness" was the virtue he evoked in autumn 1940 when he spoke to his SS officers about dragging away hundreds of thousands of people in Poland "in a temperature forty degrees below zero . . . where we had to have the hardness . . . to shoot thousands of leading Poles." In other speeches during the Polish campaign he argued that the mass killings were necessary. "We must be clear about one thing," he told the Gauleiters in February 1940. "We are firmly convinced of it. I believe it exactly as I believe in God. I believe that our blood, Nordic blood, is actually the best blood on this earth. . . . In hundreds of thousands of years this Nordic blood will always be the best. Over all others, we are superior." It followed by his logic that any actions necessary to preserve and protect the superior Nordic bloodline were virtuous. Answering assertions such as Eastern Commander Blaskowitz's charge that SS mass killings in Poland would result in "tremendous brutalization and moral depravity," Himmler countered:

I can say to them: it is horrible and frightful for a German if he has to see it. That is so, and if it were not horrible and so frightful for us then, indeed, we would no longer be Germans, certainly we would not be Germans. But even though it was horrible it was necessary—and will in many cases still be necessary to carry it out. That is to say, if we now lack the nerve, then these bad nerves will affect our sons and grandsons. . . . We do not have the right to do that. . . .

An execution must always be the hardest thing for our men. And despite it, they must never become weak, but must do it with pursed lips. In the beginning it was necessary. The shock which the Poles had to have, they have had. I believe that now, for the moment, nothing will stir in West Prussia, Posen and the new provinces. It may be that the

Pole is very tough in conspiracy, all Slavs can be; it may be that it has to happen again. Then it will happen again.

There are standards here that would come back to haunt Himmler as his Einsatzgruppen increased their personal participation in killing on the Eastern front after Barbarossa: that the humanity of his men (or what was equivalent in his mind, their Germanhood) could be measured by their capacity to continue feeling horror at slaughtering unarmed civilians; that such slaughters are necessary at the beginning of an invasion to shock the invaded into submission and might be necessary again, but by implication would not be the norm.

Himmler, like Hitler, cast the entire conflict in apocalyptic terms: either the enemy would be destroyed or the German people would be. "We as a *Volk* of seventy-five million are, despite our great numbers, a minority in the world," he told a Nazi political education class in 1938. "We have very, very many against us, as you yourselves as National Socialists know very well. All capital, the whole of Jewry, the whole of freemasonry, all the democrats and philistines of the world, all the Bolshevism of the world, all the Jesuits of the world, and not least all the peoples who regret not having completely killed us off in 1918, and who make only one vow: if we once get Germany in our hands again it won't be another 1918, it will be the end." And similarly a few months later to his Gruppenführers, using language that anticipates the Holocaust:

> These forces—of which I assume the Jews to be the driving spirit, the origin of all the negatives—are clear that if Germany and Italy are not eradicated, *they* will be eradicated. This is an elementary conclusion. In Germany the Jew cannot hold out. This is a question of years. We will drive them out more and more with an unexampled ruthlessness. . . .
>
> Be clear about it, in the battle which will decide if we are defeated there will be no reservation remaining for the Germans, all will be starved out and butchered. That will face everyone, be he now an enthusiastic supporter of the Third Reich or not—it will suffice that he speaks German and has a German mother. . . .
>
> Then it is a matter of indifference if in a town one thousand have to be put down. I would do it, and I would expect you to carry it out. About that there is no doubt.

The enemy, the Jewish enemy first and foremost, was to be destroyed. How would the enemy be destroyed? They would be removed to a reservation. They would be driven into the swamps. They would be worked to death in vast projects:

- 30 January 1939: Hitler prophesies before the Reichstag:

And there is one thing that I should like to say on this memorable day—memorable, perhaps, to others beside ourselves. During my lifetime I have often made prophecies, and more often than not people have laughed at me. In my struggle for power the Jews always laughed louder when I prophesied that, one day, I should be the leader of the German State, that I should be in full control of the nation, and that then, among other things, I should find the solution to the Jewish problem. I imagine that the Jews in Germany who laughed most heartily then are now finding themselves choking on their laughter. Today I am going to make another prophecy: If the Jewish international financiers inside and outside Europe succeed in plunging the nations into another world war, the result will not be the Bolshevization of the world and thus a victory for Judaism. The result will be the extermination of the Jewish race in Europe.

- 4 September 1939: Heydrich announces to department heads that the Reichsführer-SS would soon be submitting certain proposals to the Führer that he alone could rule on because they might have international repercussions. A week later, referring to these proposals, Heydrich announces the Führer's approval to deport German Jews to Poland and farther eastward.
- 7 October 1939: Hitler appoints Himmler head of the newly formed Reich Commissariat for the Consolidation of German Nationhood, charged to create German colonies in areas from which Jews and other non-Aryan occupants ("Jews, Polacks and rabble," Hitler specifies on 18 October) have been expelled.
- 30 October 1939: Himmler promulgates a plan for a Jewish reservation eastward of Lublin into which all Jews from the formerly Polish territories incorporated into the Reich are to be expelled within four months. The area is a swamp—the western reach of the Pripet marshes—and is essentially uninhabitable. The plan fails when the large-scale transfer of populations founders that winter.
- February 1940: Himmler proposes a vast Jewish labor project. Historian Raul Hilberg: "He suggested to commander in chief of the army von Brauchitsch the construction of an enormous antitank ditch along the newly formed frontiers of the east, facing the Red Army. With the building of this line Himmler dreamed of using all the Polish Jews."
- May 1940: Himmler presents Hitler with a memorandum, "Some Thoughts Concerning the Treatment of the Foreign Peo-

ples in the East," which he notes afterward the Führer found
"very good and correct." Hitler wanted it classified Top Secret
and its distribution limited. It was important enough "as a guide-
line," Himmler added, that the Führer wanted General Government head Hans Frank to travel from his headquarters in
Krakow to Berlin to be briefed on its contents.

What were Himmler's thoughts? Significantly, they were categorically
less extreme than the reality that would follow Barbarossa. He thought
the "foreign peoples," among whom he included the Jews, should be
handled as individual groups, not as an undifferentiated mass, so that
they could be separated "into as many parts and splinters as possible."
Their leaders could be used as police officials and mayors, but in no
higher positions of authority, because it was only by splitting up "this
entire porridge of peoples of the General Government of fifteen million
and the eight million of the East Provinces" that the SS could "fish out
the racially valuable from this porridge."

By fracturing and sorting the ethnic groups, Himmler thought, by
"break[ing] them down into innumerable small splinters and particles,"
the identity of the smaller groups could be destroyed within four to five
years. Even the identity of the Ukrainians, a much larger body of people,
could be erased "over a somewhat longer period of time," and "that
which has been said about these splinter groups applies in the correspondingly larger framework to the Poles."

The Jews were a special case. "I hope to see the concept of the Jews
completely erased, possibly by means of a large emigration of the
collected Jews to Africa or else to a colony." If a reservation east of
Lublin had proven infeasible, then perhaps the Jews could be shipped
off to Africa; as Hitler would comment much later, "it is much more correct to transport [the Jews]—whom the Arabs won't have in Palestine—
to Africa and thus expose them to a climate which diminishes every
person's ability to offer resistance to us." With Hitler's approval of this
memorandum, "Africa" came to mean the island of Madagascar off the
East African coast; and as Hitler's later comment indicates, the emigration was no more perceived to be benign than the Lublin reservation
had been.

There could be no question of "fishing out the racially valuable" from
the Jews, of course. Doing so among the other ethnic groups, Himmler
thought, would involve banning education beyond a bare minimum of
four grades of elementary school, which would teach "basic addition up
to 500, how to write one's name, the lesson that it is a divine command-
ment to be obedient to the Germans and to be honest, industrious and

well-behaved. I do not consider reading necessary." Parents who wanted a better education for their children would then be allowed to apply to officials appointed by the Higher SS and Police Leaders. These officials would determine whether a child was "racially pure. . . . Should we recognize such a child as being of our blood, the parents will be informed that the child will come to Germany to go to school and will remain in Germany permanently." The parents could hand the child over or might be "required to go to Germany and become loyal citizens." The SS would essentially hold the child hostage to the parents' loyalty. The population remaining behind would constitute a "leaderless working class," supplying Germany with migrant workers and common laborers.

Himmler understood that this racial fishing policy might potentially be "cruel and tragic" from the point of view of each individual involved. In a much-debated passage, however, he wrote, "If one rejects the Bolshevist method of the physical extermination of a people from inner conviction as un-Germanic and impossible," then the method outlined in his memorandum was "the mildest and best." Since racial fishing did not apply to the Jews, who were to be "completely erased," the question of milder versus harsher racial fishing methods also did not apply to the Jews. Nevertheless, Himmler's generalization that "the . . . physical extermination of a people" was "un-Germanic and impossible" strongly implies that his own "inner conviction" had not yet prepared him to countenance the physical extermination of the Jews by direct killing. So, of course, does this chronicle of his labors to find an *Endlösung*—a Final Solution—by rooting around among the methods colonial powers had used against indigenous native populations (reservations, expulsions into inhospitable regions, leadership decapitation, harsh slave labor). Not that he felt compassion toward the Jews. But as of May 1940, the Reichsführer-SS evidently did not yet have the stomach for the direct mass murder of an entire people.

"Stomach" in Himmler's case was more than a metaphor. The stomach trouble that first appears in the record of his life in a diary entry at fifteen had continued to trouble him; it worsened as he won increasing authority. By March 1939 he suffered from abdominal spasms that came and went in response to the stresses of his work and left him writhing in pain so severe he sometimes fainted. Doctors had alleviated his pain with narcotics, but the spasms always returned. That month a masseur-*cum*-folk doctor named Felix Kersten with a gift for sympathetic intervention came to his rescue. Trained in manual therapy in Berlin by a Chinese specialist, Kersten was a ruddy, confident Buddha of Baltic German origin, a Finnish citizen (a reward for having volunteered to fight the Russians in the Finnish war of liberation of 1918) who treated the husband of Queen Wilhelmina of the Netherlands and was a member of the Dutch royal household. Upon admission to Himmler's chambers, Kersten found "a little man who gave me an alert glance from under his pince-nez; one would almost say that there was something oriental in his broad cheekbones and round face. . . . He was very worried about the severe pains he had in the region of his stomach, which sometimes lasted as long as five days and left him so exhausted that he felt afterwards as if he were convalescing after a serious illness." Over the next two weeks Kersten was able to relieve the Reichsführer-SS. When Germany occupied Holland in 1940 and the Dutch royal family took refuge in England, Himmler gave Kersten the choice of freedom tethered to service as his personal medical adviser or confinement in a concentration camp. Kersten chose tethered freedom and kept a diary.

He diagnosed Himmler accurately as a divided and cowardly man. His patient was completely subservient to Hitler:

> An unfavorable comment by Hitler on one of his measures was enough to upset him thoroughly and produce violent reactions which took the form of severe stomach pains. Simply an indication that Hitler might have a different opinion sufficed to make Himmler hesitate and postpone a decision until he had been able to make sure of Hitler's attitude. . . . Nobody who had not witnessed it would believe that a man with as much power at his disposal as Himmler had would be in such a state of fear when he was summoned to Hitler; nor would anybody believe how Himmler rejoiced if he came out of the interview successfully or, better still, received a word of praise. . . . Himmler had nothing in him to counterbalance the effect of Hitler's personality. . . .
> This weakness of his made Himmler suffer indescribably.

Comfortable around leaders, a man of personal courage, Kersten understood Himmler well:

> Fate gave him a position which he was not able to manage. There was something spasmodic in everything he did. . . . The division in his nature . . . was fundamental; his own character was weak and he preached toughness; he carried out actions which were quite foreign to his nature simply because his Führer ordered them—even the actual annihilation of human beings. . . .
> His severe stomach convulsions were not, as he supposed, simply due to a poor constitution or to overwork; they were rather the

expression of this psychic division which extended over his whole life. I soon realized that while I could bring him momentary relief and even help over longer periods, I could never achieve a fundamental cure. The basic cause of these convulsions was not removed, was indeed constantly being aggravated. It was inevitable that in times of psychic stress his physical pains should also increase.

In March and April 1941, Himmler's stomach cramps drove him to bed. Kersten found him "exhausted and twisted with pain on his chaise longue. When I came into the room he just said: 'Please help me, I can't bear any more pain.' " What provoked such misery in the Reichsführer-SS, his worst attack of the entire war?

By December 1940, historian Richard Breitman comments, Madagascar was only "a fading option." Shipping millions of Jews to the remote East African island had always depended on removing the dominant maritime power—Britain—from control of the sea lanes either by defeating the British in war or convincing them to cooperate, and neither outcome was any longer likely. When planning began for Barbarossa (which Hitler formally authorized on 18 December 1940), a new region became available to which European Jews could be evacuated. But Hitler and Himmler's vision of *Lebensraum* and *Wehrbauern* colonization required that western Russia be cleared, not populated.

Despite this inherent conflict, in SS planning the Soviet Union became the next destination for the European Jews. Eichmann reported to Himmler on 4 December 1940 that 5.8 million Jews would have to be evacuated, including the Jews of Poland. They would be evacuated, Eichmann said in euphemistic code, to "a territory yet to be determined." A week later Himmler also spoke of "Jewish emigration and thus yet more space for Poles." Looking back from late January 1941, a colleague of Eichmann's summarized what had occurred in the two preceding months:

> In conformity with the will of the Führer, at the end of the war there should be brought about a final solution of the Jewish question within the European territories ruled or controlled by Germany.
>
> The Chief of the Security Police and the Security Service [Heydrich] has already received orders from the Führer, through the Reichsführer-SS, to submit a project for a final solution. . . . The project in all its essentials has been completed. It is now with the Führer and the *Reichsmarschall* [Göring].
>
> It is certain that its execution will involve a tremendous amount of work whose success can only be guaranteed through the most painstaking preparations. This will extend to the work preceding the

wholesale deportation of the Jews as well as to the planning to the last detail of a settlement action in the territory yet to be determined.

The end of the war was not expected to be that far away; the Wehrmacht assumed, overoptimistically, that the Soviet Union could be crushed in a few months. Even at this point, Himmler was still thinking in terms of attrition of the evacuated European Jews under the harsh conditions of resettlement and forced labor rather than direct killing. Early in 1941, historian Christopher Browning reports, the Reichsführer-SS asked his former driver, Viktor Brack, now working on euthanasia murder in the Führer Chancellery, to investigate methods for mass sterilization using X rays. "Through the mixing of blood in the Polish Jews with that of the Jews of western Europe," Brack heard him say, "a much greater danger for Germany was arising than even before the war." That is, Himmler was concerned to prevent Jewish children from being conceived after the resettlement, because these children might grow up to plague the Third Reich. "Brack submitted a preliminary report on March 28, 1941," Browning writes, "which Himmler acknowledged positively on May 12. Thereafter, however, Himmler showed no further interest." Browning continues:

> The documentation for this last plan for expelling Jews into the Soviet Union is quite fragmentary and elusive in comparison to the Lublin and Madagascar Plans. [This may be] because their hearts were no longer in it—that in the minds of Hitler, Himmler and Heydrich the notion was beginning to take shape of another possibility in the future, if all went well with the imminent military campaign. Indeed, it was precisely in March 1941 that Hitler's exhortations for a war of destruction against the Soviet Union . . . were setting new parameters and expectations for Nazi racial policies.

This period when Hitler, Himmler and their subordinates wrestled with the question of what to do about the European Jews was the period of Himmler's worst attack of stomach trouble. He was sufficiently intelligent to see that the plans and conflicts were leading toward an increasingly radical program. The Führer would require the SS to carry out that program. In 1943, speaking to his Gruppenführers at Posen, he would compare the assignment—"the evacuation of the Jews," he called it, "the extermination of the Jewish people"—to another grisly assignment the Führer had laid upon the SS, the Röhm Purge:

> Just as little as we hesitated to do our duty as ordered on 30 June 1934, and place comrades who had failed us against the wall and shoot them,

just as little did we ever speak of it, and we shall never speak of it. It was a matter of course, of tact, for us, thank God, never to speak of it, never to talk of it. It made everybody shudder; yet everyone was clear in his mind that he would do it again if ordered to do so, and if it was necessary.

"It made everybody shudder": in spring 1941 Himmler was shuddering again at the thought of what his Führer was asking him and his legions to do.

Yet he would do it; he had long ago pawned his conscience at the Führer's pawnshop and he had no personal resources to redeem it. Talking to Kersten one day in late December 1940 about his *Wehrbauern* project, he said his *Wehrbauern* settlements were necessary to assure the existence of a thousand-year Reich. "We must lay the foundations for that," he went on enthusiastically, "and not allow ourselves to be put off by the difficulties which are to be encountered at the commencement of every great undertaking. Above all we must, in this as in other matters, make a start first and then see how things are going, advance step by step, do what we must, correct our mistakes and not move on to new objectives until we are quite convinced that we have found the right way."

In the summer of 1941, from Riga to Odessa, Himmler's Einsatzgruppen and Order Police had made a start; it was time to move on to new objectives.

SEVEN

Extermination

The surprise of Barbarossa devastated Josef Stalin. By 28 June 1941, after a week of continuous meetings, the Soviet dictator had succumbed to deep depression. Leaving the defense commissariat the next day with several Politburo members, he had burst out loudly, "Lenin left us a great inheritance and we, his heirs, have fucked it all up!" A Politburo delegation that tracked him down at his dacha at the beginning of July found him sitting in an armchair staring, with a strange look on his face. By the time he rallied, the Luftwaffe was bombing Moscow. Vyacheslav Molotov and Anastas Mikoyan wrote the first war speech Stalin delivered by radio to the Soviet people, on 3 July 1941. "Comrades, citizens, brothers and sisters, fighters of our Army and Navy!" he began. "I am speaking to you, my friends!" He had never spoken that way before.

Stalin described a "life-and-death struggle against [our] most perfidious enemy. . . . The enemy is cruel and merciless. He aims at grabbing our land, our wheat and oil. He wants to . . . destroy the national culture of the peoples of the Soviet Union . . . and turn them into the slaves of German princes and barons." The Soviet dictator spoke of "putting our whole production on a war footing." He called for scorched-earth withdrawals: "The enemy must not be left a single engine or a single boxcar, and not a pound of bread nor a pint of oil. The collective farms must drive away all their livestock, hand their grain reserves to the state agencies for evacuation to the rear. . . . All valuable property which cannot be evacuated, whether grain, fuel or non-ferrous metals, must be destroyed." And then he unwittingly played into Hitler's hands:

> In the occupied territories partisan units must be formed. . . . There must be diversionist groups for fighting enemy units, for spreading the partisan war everywhere, for blowing up and destroying roads and bridges and telephone and telegraph wires; for setting fire to forests, enemy stores and road convoys. In the occupied areas intolerable conditions must be created for the enemy and his accomplices, who must be persecuted and destroyed at every step.

When Hitler met with Göring and other high Reich officials at Wolf-schanze in East Prussia on 16 July 1941 to discuss Eastern policy, he referred specifically to Stalin's partisan-warfare instructions. In the notes of the meeting kept by his private secretary and Party Minister Martin Bormann, Hitler endorsed the vision he shared with Himmler of what he called "a Garden of Eden" in the East. "On principle," he said, "we have now to face the task of cutting up the giant cake according to our needs, in order to be able: first, to dominate it; second, to administer it; and third, to exploit it." He would take "all necessary measures— shootings, resettlements and so on"—to accomplish that end, a "final settlement." Stalin's partisan order, he pointed out, gave the game away: "It enables us to eradicate everyone who opposes us. . . . Naturally, the vast area must be pacified as quickly as possible; the way to do that is to shoot dead anyone who even looks at us sideways."

As far as Hitler was concerned, the Jews were implacably hostile; Stalin's partisan order gave him an excuse to murder them down to the last woman and child. (Hitler was even more specific in a meeting with Slovakian defense minister Sladko Kvaternik six days later. The Russian people were "bestial," he told Kvaternik; the only thing to be done with them was to "exterminate them," to "do away with them." The Jews were "the scourge of mankind"; Russia had become a "plague center"; "if there were no more Jews in Europe, the unity of the European states would no longer be disturbed." To this outsider Hitler still spoke of sending the Jews of Europe "to Siberia or Madagascar," but he knew full well that Madagascar was no longer an option and Siberia a cold mass grave.)

Himmler, twenty miles away at his lakeside headquarters, did not find it necessary to attend this Führer conference even though it concerned his responsibilities. He had already discussed those responsibilities with the Führer. The next day, 17 July 1941, Hitler decreed that Himmler's authority in police matters in the occupied territories was fully equiva-lent to his authority in Germany itself, thus bypassing the appointed civil authorities throughout the East. In Germany Himmler was responsible for identifying and eliminating internal enemies; from the Nazi perspec-tive, the equivalent of internal enemies in the Ostland* and the Ukraine was first of all the Jews.

The authority over the East that Hitler assigned to Himmler was fun-damental to laying the foundation for their Garden of Eden. As a result of their discussions, Himmler could prepare to turn in earnest to that work, moving beyond decapitation to extermination. That same day, 17

*That is, Estonia, Latvia, Lithuania and Byelorussia.

EINSATZGRUPPEN
KILLING SITES (SELECTED)

July 1941, the Reichsführer appointed as his deputy for *Wehrbauern* settlement the SS and Police Leader for the Lublin district, Brigadeführer Odilo Globocnik. Three days later Himmler flew to Lublin to meet with his appointee.

Globocnik was an operator, a beefy Austrian with combed-back hair and a fleshy but youthful face. Rudolf Höss, the tough-minded commandant of Auschwitz, called him "a pompous ass who only understood how to make himself look good." Globocnik was born in Trieste in 1904 into a family of minor bureaucrats of Slovenian descent who considered themselves German. Like Himmler, he missed serving in the Great War, but unlike Himmler he gained personal experience with violence in the Austrian Freikorps and the SA. He was an energetic but uneducated construction foreman, active in the Nazi Party in and around Vienna as early as 1922, anti-Semitic and fanatic. His work for the party won him appointment as a deputy Gauleiter in 1933, but because the Nazi Party was illegal in Austria, he was imprisoned four times between 1933 and 1935 for criminal party activities. Working in construction gave him easy access to explosives, which he procured and distributed; one of his convictions was for participating in a bomb attack that killed a Jewish jeweler (and probably also involved robbery). He joined the SS in 1934. His covert activity against Austria before Germany annexed it in 1938 earned him promotion to Gauleiter of Vienna, but in January 1939 his speculations in illegal foreign exchange led to his being stripped of his post and of party honors. "He made such a mess and caused such chaos," says Höss, who was jealous of Globocnik's influence, "that they had to recall him." Himmler punished the Austrian by demoting him to the rank of Unterscharführer—corporal—and assigning him to the Waffen-SS. But Globocnik was too useful—and too enthusiastic an apostle of Himmler's visions—to waste in the front lines, and in 1939 the Reichs-führer-SS pardoned him, promoted him to Brigadeführer and assigned him responsibility for Lublin province.

Himmler liked Globocnik; he called him Globus. It was Globus who had thought up the Panama Canal–scale antitank-ditch project that Himmler had proposed to von Brauchitsch in 1940. The ditch was sup-posed to serve as a military bulwark against the Red Army and put all 2.5 million Polish Jews to work. It was planned to be fifty yards wide, with its trough descending five feet below the water table. Globocnik dispatched some thirty thousand Polish Jewish prisoners to begin dig-ging it. By 1941 only eight miles had been finished; they were amateur-ishly constructed and militarily superfluous.

Himmler flew to Lublin on 20 July 1941 to tour the areas Globocnik was promoting for pilot-scale *Wehrbauern* settlements: the Lublin dis-trict itself and a picturesque valley in southeastern Poland around the old quasi-German colony of Zamosc. (Ironically, the next valley west-ward from Zamosc, the even larger valley of the San River, had been the SS's choice for a Jewish reservation centered on the town of Nisko when confining the Jews to a reservation was still being considered. As Eich-mann remembered a visit to Nisko in October 1939: "So we came finally to Nisko on the San. . . . We came to that place, saw an enormous terri-tory, a river, villages, markets, little towns, and we said to ourselves, that's the reality, and why should one not resettle the [Nisko] Poles, where indeed so many were unsettled anyway, and then give the Jews a large territory here?") Höss writes that Globocnik "promised Himmler that within one year he was going to bring in fifty thousand new [German and ethnic German] settlers as a pattern and example for the future, when huge settlements were supposed to be created farther in the East. All the necessary things, such as the cattle and the machinery, were sup-posed to be supplied by Globocnik as soon as possible." Himmler fur-ther assigned Globocnik responsibility for organizing the extermination of the Polish Jews.

After touring Zamosc on 21 July 1941, Himmler approved what he called in his action order "a major settlement area in the German colonies at Zamosc" under the umbrella of his "Quest for German Blood." Richard Breitman summarizes Globocnik's comprehensive commission:

> Himmler authorized Globocnik to carry out a geological and geographical survey of the Eastern territories as far as the Ural Mountains, to plan police strongholds scattered throughout that vast area, to construct model farms with up-to-date living quarters and equipment, to recondition existing farms, and, in a nice anthropological touch, to study ancient national costumes to be worn by German immigrants. Globocnik was allowed to recruit a staff of architects, interior decorators, contractors, drainage experts, surveyors and historians.

To support this fantastic project Himmler authorized Globocnik to establish a concentration camp for 25,000 to 50,000 prisoners in a southeastern Lublin suburb, with workshops to supply the *Wehrbauern* settlements with clothing and equipment. The camp would become Majdanek; the fact that it was sited within view of Lublin Castle in the city's blufftop medieval center indicates that it was not originally planned to be a death camp. When Höss's superior sent the Auschwitz commandant to Lublin to collect supplies from Globocnik for Majdanek, Globocnik spun out Himmler's vision to Höss as if it were his own:

> He acted incredibly important as he used Himmler's order to build new police bases [i.e., fortified *Wehrbauern* settlements] in the newly conquered areas. He developed fantasy plans for bases extending as far as the Ural Mountains. No difficulties existed as far as he was concerned. He would just dismiss any objection with a sweep of his hand. He wanted to exterminate the Jews right then and there and save only those he needed for building the police bases. . . . In the evenings by the fireplace he spoke about these ideas in his Viennese accent so casually that they seemed like harmless stories.

Exterminating the Polish and Russian Jews was the necessary counterpart, the negative *Doppelgänger*, to Hitler's and Himmler's program to colonize the East, clearing the territory just as the Kaiser's general Lothar von Trotha had cleared Namibia of the Herero. Hitler's decision in the summer of 1941 to murder the Jews of the East as partisans under cover of Stalin's partisan order answers a question that has confused Holocaust scholarship for many years: When did Hitler order the Final Solution? The answer appears to be: Progressively emboldened by military success and military challenges, he ordered direct killing (as opposed to death by privation) in two parts at two different times. The first part, for the Jews of the occupied East (meaning Poland and the Soviet Union), he ordered in July 1941. His decision followed directly from Stalin's partisan order and was a logical extension of the program formulated before Barbarossa to strip the occupied lands of food. "They deliberately and systematically planned to starve millions of Russians," the United States assistant trial counsel charged at Nuremberg. The prosecutor called the economic policy Göring's staff had formulated "a studied plan to murder millions of innocent people through starvation," a "program of premeditated murder on a scale so vast as to stagger the human imagination." The German document he cited to support his accusation acknowledged famine for "many tens of millions of people" who would "become redundant and will either die or have to emigrate to Siberia." Destroying the Soviet population by starvation, writes the German historian Christian Gerlach, proved to be impractical, and the program "was replaced in the fall of 1941 by programs for eliminating groups of specific individuals, like the millions of Soviet war prisoners who were 'incapable of work.' " The largest group to be eliminated was the Jews.

Two consecutive decisions to subject populations of Jews to direct killing, the first population the Eastern Jews, explains why, after the war, Höss remembered being told in the summer of 1941 that the Führer had ordered the Final Solution. Himmler had called him into his office in Berlin, a meeting that Breitman reliably dates during the period 13–15 July 1941, one of the few times that summer when Himmler was in the German capital. As Höss recalled the meeting:

> Contrary to [Himmler's] usual custom, his adjutant was not in the room. The *Reichsführer-SS* greeted me with the following: "The Führer has ordered the Final Solution of the Jewish question. We, the SS, have to carry out this order. The existing extermination sites in the East [e.g, Ponary, the Ninth Fort] are not in a position to carry out these intended operations on a large scale. I have therefore chosen Auschwitz for this purpose."

Himmler told Höss why he had chosen him rather than someone of higher rank—because (according to Höss) he thought Höss was the most competent person "to deal with such a difficult assignment"—and cautioned him to keep the assignment secret. Höss also remembered being told that a Sturmbannführer named Adolf Eichmann would soon visit him with details. This part of Höss's recollection is almost certainly conflated with the second, later decision also to murder the Jews of *west-*

ern Europe, because Eichmann specifically recalled going directly from *his* first briefing on the Final Solution, by Heydrich, to Lublin to meet Globocnik, who took him to see a gassing installation at a death camp that did not exist before December 1941. Höss wrote his confession in 1947. His memory of being assigned in the summer of 1941 to begin preparing to murder large numbers of (Polish) Jews at Auschwitz (up to that time a labor camp) is consistent with Himmler's actions immediately before and after his visit to Lublin and Zamosc. As Christopher Browning points out, "if the historian wants to know when the Nazi leadership decided that the mass murder of Russian Jewry was no longer a future task but rather a goal to be achieved immediately, he must ascertain when the decision was taken to commit the necessary manpower." Himmler took that decision in July 1941.

Just after the beginning of Barbarossa, on 27 June 1941, Himmler had assumed personal command of two brigades of Waffen-SS totaling some eleven thousand men serving behind the lines on the Russian front, explaining, "I need these units for other tasks." The task force staff originally organized to supervise the Einsatzgruppen—the Einsatzstab—had been absorbed into Himmler's command staff even before the beginning of Barbarossa, becoming the Kommandostab Reichsführer-SS, and the two brigades were now attached to this office. Other units—an SS cavalry brigade, a volunteer regiment and several brigades of mechanized Waffen-SS—were also attached to the Kommandostab, increasing the total force to thirty-six thousand. It answered only to Himmler, and Himmler answered only to Hitler. By the beginning of July 1941, then, Himmler had assembled a substantial private army.

On 19 July 1941, after the Hitler conference and just before he left for Lublin to meet Globocnik, Himmler assigned part of his Kommandostab army to Higher SS and Police Leader Gruppenführer Erich von dem Bach-Zelewski, responsible for Russia–Center. On 22 July 1941, after Himmler met with Globocnik, he assigned the remainder of his Kommandostab army to Obergruppenführer Friedrich Jeckeln, responsible for Russia–South. Bach-Zelewski's forces were directed to undertake what Himmler called "combing the Pripet marshes"—that is, they were supposed to flush out Jews living or taking refuge in the vast area of the Pripet marshes east of Lublin in the borderlands of Byelorussia and the Ukraine. In a radio message of 29 July 1941 Himmler made clear what they would then do with them: "Express order of the *RFSS*. All [male] Jews must be shot. Drive Jewish females into the swamps." Jeckeln's orders were even plainer: his forces were to shoot all Jews in the western Ukraine except those required for labor (which was much the same program as the one Globocnik had spun at fireside for Höss). On

23 July 1941 Himmler also reassigned at least eleven battalions of Kurt Daluege's Order Police—about 5,500 men—to the Higher SS and Police Leaders of Russia–North, –Central and –South.

These tens of thousands of SS and Order Police added to the three thousand men of the Einsatzgruppen clearly marked the expansion of the mass-killing program, but they were not yet all the forces Himmler intended to deploy. On 25 July 1941 he also ordered the rapid formation of auxiliary police units "from the reliable non-Communist elements among Ukrainians, Estonians, Latvians, Lithuanians and Byelorussians" to augment the Order Police. By the end of the year, more than thirty-three thousand men would be active in these auxiliary battalions.

Himmler flew to Kaunas on 29 July 1941 to ramp up mass killings in the Baltic states. Higher SS and Police Leader Gruppenführer Hans-Adolf Prützmann met the Reichsführer-SS and led him on a three-day tour that moved on to Riga, the major Latvian trading and industrial city built on the delta lands of the Daugava River where it enters the Bay of Riga on the Baltic Sea. Prützmann lived elegantly there in the Ritterhaus, the old Riga castle, giving popular and glittering parties that Wehrmacht generals vied to attend. Himmler inspected a Latvian auxiliary company in Riga and ordered what he called "criminal elements" to be "resettled." Then he flew south to Baranowicze, eighty-five miles southeast of Minsk in Byelorussia, to meet with Bach-Zelewski at his headquarters there. (The day after Himmler left Riga, one of Prützmann's subordinates asked Prützmann what the Reichsführer-SS meant by "resettled." "Not what you think," Prützmann told him, "they're supposed to be dispatched into the next world.")

While Himmler was moving to clear the East of Jews, Heydrich sat down with Göring in Berlin on 31 July 1941 to begin planning to move the Jews of western Europe eastward. He needed a legal order to involve the civil bureaucracy of the Third Reich—finance offices, railways and other agencies. Göring, in his capacity as Reich Marshal and chairman of the ministerial council for national defense, was the proper person to originate that legal order while preserving the Führer's deniability. Eichmann had drafted the order. Heydrich now handed it to Göring to sign—which Göring did, Heydrich told a colleague later, at the Führer's instruction. The order read:

> Complementing the task already assigned to you in the decree of 24 January 1939 to undertake by emigration or evacuation a solution of the Jewish question as advantageous as possible under the conditions of the time, I hereby charge you with making all necessary organizational, functional and material preparations for a complete solution

of the Jewish question in the German sphere of influence in Europe. In so far as the jurisdiction of other central agencies may be touched thereby, they are to be involved. I charge you furthermore with submitting to me in the near future an overall plan of the organizational, functional and material measures to be taken in preparing for the implementation of the goal of a final solution of the Jewish question.

What Himmler's wanderings meant in practical terms was already evident to the Jews of Schepetovka (Sepetivka), a middle-sized town in the western Ukraine about halfway between Lvov and Kiev, and in the Pripet marshes. If the solution was to be final, then not only men had to be killed: women and children would have to be killed as well. Himmler acknowledged the problem in a 1943 speech. "Then the question arose," he told his audience of Gauleiters: "What about the women and children? I decided to find a perfectly clear-cut solution to this too. For I did not feel justified in exterminating the men—that is, to kill them or have them killed—while allowing the avengers, in the form of their children, to grow up in the midst of our sons and grandsons." But he also acknowledged that "for the organization that had to carry out this mission, it was the most difficult that we have received to date."

This "avenger" argument was communicated to the Einsatzgruppen officers directly responsible for mass killings, as well as to their counterparts in the Order Police. When Ohlendorf was asked at his 1947 trial about murdering children, for example, he responded, "I believe that it is very simple to explain if one starts from the fact that this order did not only try to achieve a security but also a permanent security because for that reason the children were people who would grow up and surely being the children of parents who had been killed they would constitute a danger no smaller than that of their parents." ("That is the master race exactly, is it not," the exasperated prosecutor responded, "the decimation of whole races in order to remove a real or fancied threat to the German people." To which Ohlendorf countered lamely, "Mr. Prosecutor, I did not see the execution of children myself although I attended three mass executions.")

The order to murder the Jews of Schepetovka came down during the last week in July 1941 from Himmler through the commander of Police Regiment South to the commander of Reserve Police Battalion 45, a Major Franz. Franz remembered the order well, because for the first time it specifically included women and children. Reserve Police Battalion 45 carried out the order with support from the local Ukrainian militia before the end of the month. Higher SS and Police Leader Friedrich Jeckeln began personally commanding mass killings in the western

Ukraine on 28 July 1941. Whether he personally directed Battalion 45's roundup of the Schepetovka Jews is not clear from the record, but at that time or during a mopping-up operation later, a minor bureaucrat named August Meier stood beside him in Schepetovka and watched him at work:

> Jeckeln had ongoing permission to shoot Jews, one can say, at almost every location. As a result, he personally organized the executions of many thousands of Jews. I still particularly recall an *Aktion* in Schepetovka which stands out in my mind as extraordinarily gruesome. It involved about a hundred people. Women and children were among those shot. Jeckeln said: "Today we'll stack them like sardines." The Jews had to lie layer upon layer in an open grave and were then killed with neck shots from machine pistols, pistols and rifles. That meant they had to lie face down on those previously shot [whereas] in other executions they were shot standing up and fell into the grave or were dragged in. During the execution in Schepetovka I stood for some time beside Jeckeln and then managed somehow to slink away. I did not do any shooting myself. I don't know if Jeckeln did any shooting, but I don't believe so.

Jeckeln, a compact, handsome man with shrewd eyes who looked Russian, was a reliably efficient killer, cold and unapproachable. He called the method of mass killing he invented *Sardinenpackung.* As Meier describes, it involved forcing victims to lie together face down and side by side and killing them with *Genickschüssen,* then forcing the next group of victims to lie down on top of the torn, bleeding corpses of the victims who preceded them to form another layer, ignoring the victims' terror and horror in the interest of efficiently filling up the killing pit. Jeckeln's despicably cruel execution protocol destroys SS claims, during and after the war, that its executions were "correct," military-style executions of partisans. Himmler's goal was mass murder, and to achieve that goal he was willing to use less humane methods than slaughterhouses use to limit the suffering of animals killed for food. By the end of August 1941, commanding the Kommandostab SS First Brigade in the western Ukraine, Jeckeln had personally supervised the murder of more than 44,000 human beings, the largest total of Jews murdered by any of Himmler's virulent legions that month.

Between 27 July and 11 August 1941, two regiments of the SS Cavalry Brigade commanded by SS-Sturmbannführers Gunther Lombard and Bruno Magill carried out Himmler's order to "comb" the Pripet marshes, killing every Jewish man, woman and child they could find in the large area of marshes and small villages that the Einsatzgruppen had bypassed. Himmler had flown to Baranowicze to supervise the Pripet marshes operation personally, working through Bach-Zelewski, who was formally in charge. The Reichsführer-SS personally briefed the field commanders, leaving them in no doubt that "pushing the women and children into the swamps" meant killing them. Jews were to be referred to as "looters" or "partisans"; the troops were to "shoot everyone suspected of supporting the partisans," and all the villages were to be burned to the ground.

Magill filed a report on 12 August 1941 describing his regiment's previous weeks of work. The whole Pripet marshes area, he wrote, consisted of "large marshes interspersed with patches of sand, so that the ground is not very fertile. There are some better places, but others were all the poorer." The population in the area was "mainly Ukrainian; Byelorussians in second place; in third place Poles and Russians; only a very few of the latter. The Jews are mainly in the larger places, where they make up a high percentage of the population, in some cases from 50 to 80 percent, but in others as little as 25 percent." Doctors among the population tended to be Jewish; "in the towns and villages it was also noticeable that only Jewish artisans were found. There was a large number of Jewish émigrés from the Old Reich [i.e., Germany before 1938, indicating that these were refugees from Nazism] and [Austria]." When his units moved in, Magill remarks without apparent irony, "we found that, according to a Ukrainian practice, a table with a white cloth had been prepared with bread and salt that was offered to the commanders. In one case there was even a small band of musicians to welcome the troops."

"Pacification," as Magill calls the mass killing his mounted soldiers carried out, was organized by contacting the local mayors and discussing "all matters concerning the population":

> On these occasions the numbers and composition of the population, i.e., Ukrainians, Byelorussians, etc., were checked. Further, whether there were still Communists in the locality or secret members of the Red Army, or others who had been active Bolsheviks. In most cases local residents also reported that they had seen gangs or other suspicious persons. Where such individuals were still in the locality, they were detained and, after a brief interrogation, they were either released or shot.

Jews received not even a brief interrogation. "Jewish looters were shot. Only a few skilled workers employed in the Wehrmacht repair workshops were permitted to remain." Magill was prepared to take Himmler's order about women and children literally and therefore had to explain why he failed to do so: "The driving of women and children into the marshes did not have the expected success, because the marshes were not so deep that one could sink. After a depth of about a meter there was in most cases solid ground (probably sand) preventing complete sinking."

The cavalry regiment did not have to carry out its odious duties alone, Magill reported:

> The Ukrainian clergy were very cooperative and made themselves available for every *Aktion*. It was also conspicuous that, in general, the population was on good terms with the Jewish sector of the population. Nevertheless they helped energetically in rounding up the Jews. The locally recruited guards, who consisted in part of Polish police and former Polish soldiers, made a good impression. They operated energetically and took part in the fight against looters.

Two companies of Magill's regiment had in fact been diverted from the marshes to Pinsk in early August to assist an Einsatzgruppe unit preparing to murder the entire Jewish population of that southwestern Byelorussian city, more than thirty thousand people, the first large city scheduled to be rendered "free of Jews"—*Judenfrei*. "On 2 August [1941]," writes Israeli historian Yehoshua Büchler, "when the order to murder the Jews of Pinsk was transferred from SS Cavalry Brigade headquarters to units in the field, Himmler began the psychological preparation of the soldiers who were to take part in the murder. He rebuked them for their 'soft behavior,' so to speak, regarding the Jews. He demanded that the SS Cavalry kill more Jews." Using trucks to transport Jewish men to killing sites, the cavalry shot to death eight thousand men on 5 August 1941 and at least three thousand more men on 7 August 1941. Confusion between the various units, and perhaps also resistance to killing women and children directly, led to the withdrawal of the cavalry on 8 August 1941 to return to combing the marshes. As a result, writes Büchler, the larger part of the Pinsk Jewish community— about twenty thousand people, including nearly all the women and children—survived for another year. In the marsh villages, however, children caught in the roundups with their parents were shot, and women and children were included in some of the massacres.

The commander of the SS Cavalry Brigade, Standartenführer Hermann Fegelein, summarized the Pripet marshes operations in an after-*Aktion* report: the task of "imposing final peace in the area was carried out in full." His units had executed 1,000 partisans, 699 Red Army soldiers, and 14,178 "looters"—meaning Jews.

The time of Einsatzgruppen decapitations was over. On the Eastern front, wholesale murder had begun.

PART TWO

"SEVEN DEPARTMENTS OF HELL"

Even the child in the cradle must be trampled
down like a poisonous toad. . . . We are living in an
epoch of iron, during which it is necessary to sweep
with iron brooms.

HEINRICH HIMMLER, September 1941

EIGHT

Dirty Work

At the outset of the war in the East, about four million Jews lived in the western areas of the Soviet Union: 5,000 in Estonia, 95,000 in Latvia, 225,000 in Lithuania, 1,350,000 in eastern Poland, 1,908,000 in Byelorussia and the Ukraine, 300,000 in Bessarabia and 50,000 in the Crimea. Of these four million, about 1,500,000 were evacuated or escaped eastward in the first confused weeks after Barbarossa, leaving perhaps 2,500,000 to face the German onslaught. These were the millions Himmler would have to murder to carry out Hitler's order to exterminate the Eastern Jews.

In Latvia, a Sonderkommando of "natives" to do what an Einsatzgruppe functionary in Riga called the "dirty work" was already functioning when Himmler ordered auxiliary police units organized at the end of July 1941. A thirty-one-year-old blond, blue-eyed Latvian named Viktors Arajs led the Arajs commando. Arajs was an opportunist with police training and a Soviet diploma in law who had represented himself to Einsatzgruppe A commander Stahlecker as an anti-Soviet partisan when Stahlecker arrived in Riga on 1 July 1941. The next day Stahlecker appointed Arajs to organize and command an auxiliary. Arajs recruited police, soldiers and university fraternity buddies into a Sonderkommando of about three hundred men under the direct supervision and close control of SS-Sturmbannführer Rudolf Lange, who served under Stahlecker as SD tactical coordinator in Latvia.

The Arajs commando spent the summer and fall of 1941 murdering Jews. Twice a week they shot Jewish men into killing pits in Bikernieki Forest, four miles northwest of the center of Riga, executing about four thousand Jews and a thousand Communists in Bikernieki between July and September 1941. Latvian historian Andrew Ezergailis describes the commando's routine:

> The operations would start in darkness, in the very early hours of the morning. The commando members would need to leave their homes as early as 1 a.m. and depart from [commando headquarters] about 3 a.m. If the number of victims was, let us say, two hundred, the opera-

tion was finished by breakfast time. On other occasions they worked until noon and beyond. At the end of the operation, and sometimes during it, schnapps and zakuski [appetizers] were delivered. The members doing the shooting were always rewarded with alcohol in Bikernieki, but those standing watch or in the gauntlet had to wait until they returned to headquarters.

Responding to the expanded killing orders in late July 1941, the men of the Arajs commando began boarding blue Swedish-made Riga city buses and riding out into the countryside to render one Latvian town or village after another *Judenfrei*, murdering not only men now but also women and children. Stahlecker and his superiors in Berlin had not expected pogroms alone to suffice, and his "fundamental orders," in his words, had been to achieve "the most comprehensive possible elimination of the Jews." The Arajs commando's work in the countryside followed from that project, as Stahlecker went on to acknowledge: "Special detachments reinforced by selected units—in Lithuania partisan detachments, in Latvia units of the Latvian auxiliary police—therefore performed extensive executions both in the towns and in rural areas." Ezergailis estimates that Jews lived in some one hundred localities in Latvia; most were small towns or trading centers:

> The killing in the [Latvian] provinces began in late July and was almost completed by the end of September.... Some towns ... lost more than half of their population in a weekend. The murder of the provincial Jews was merciless and, unlike in the large cities, total.
>
> The smaller the Jewish community, the less chance did its Jews have of surviving the Holocaust. The establishment of the ghettos in Riga, Daugavpils, and Liepaja [to exploit Jewish labor] inadvertently saved some Jews from destruction.
>
> With some variations, the Bikernieki method was adopted in the killing of the provincial Jews. The first step towards the wholesale killing was an order to make a census. The order was issued by the district police chief, but inasmuch as it occurred everywhere, it ultimately must have come from *EK 2* headquarters in Riga. In some districts and towns a census was ordered for the whole population because the SD was also interested in apprehending Communists and in ascertaining who had fled to the Soviet Union. Although only a few of these census lists of registered Jews have been found, we can conclude that the Germans knew the number of provincial Jews very accurately. After the census, the next step was an order to the Jews to assemble at a given location, such as the market place or the syna-

gogue. In locations with a very small Jewish population the local police were ordered to transport the Jews to a larger town.

The Riga city blue bus was large enough to carry about forty men and their rifles, which was sufficient for the provincial executions. A supply officer with vodka, sausages and cigarettes always traveled on the provincial missions. When the commando arrived in a town it established a home base in an empty farmhouse or in a school building. The Germans and Arajs, if he came, traveled by passenger car.

The blue bus was observed in all corners of Latvia. . . . On some occasions the blue bus made a circuit, visiting several towns on a single trip.

Ezergailis estimates that Stahlecker's forces murdered more than twenty-three thousand provincial Jews. "In addition to Jews," he adds, "the blue-bus visits also included the execution of the mentally ill."

The methodical killing of the Jewish people in the rural areas of the East has hardly been examined in the literature of the Holocaust, probably because the Iron Curtain blocked access to documentation for almost fifty years; Ezergailis's investigation of the Arajs commando is nearly unique. But maps in Jewish museums from Riga to Odessa confirm that almost every village and town in the entire sweep of the Eastern territories has a killing site nearby.

Two thousand Jews, for example, lived in and around the small town of Tykocin, northwest of Warsaw on the road to Bialystok in eastern Poland, worshiping in a square, fortified synagogue with a turreted tower and a red mansard roof, built in 1642, more than a century after Jewish settlement began in the region. Lush farm country surrounds Tykocin: wheat fields, prosperous villages, cattle in the fields, black-and-white storks brooding wide, flat nests on the chimneys of lucky houses. Each village maintains a forest, a dense oval stand of perhaps forty acres of red-barked pines harvested for firewood and house and barn construction. Inside the forests, even in the heat of summer, the air is cool and heady with pine; wild strawberries, small and sweet, strew the forest floor. Police Battalions 309 and 316, based in Bialystok, invaded Tykocin on 5 August 1941. They drove Jewish men, women and children screaming from their homes, killed laggards in the streets, loaded the living onto trucks and jarred them down a potholed, winding dirt road past the storks and the cattle to the Lopuchowo village forest two miles southwest. In the center of the Lopuchowo forest, men dug pits, piling up the sandy yellow soil, and then Police Battalions 309 and 316, out for the morning on excursion from Bialystok, murdered the Jews of Tykocin, man, woman and child. For months the forest buzzed and stank of death.

(Twenty miles northwest of Tykocin in the village of Jedwabne, Polish villagers themselves, with German encouragement, had murdered their Jewish neighbors on 10 July 1941 by driving them into a barn and burning them alive, a massacre examined in Jan T. Gross's book *Neighbors*.)

In Daugavpils, the second-largest city in Latvia, southeast of Riga and approximately equidistant from Riga, Kaunas and Minsk, Obersturmführer Joachim Hamann of Einsatzkommando 3 directed massacres during August 1941 that ended more than nine thousand lives, with the assistance after the first week of Latvian auxiliaries and regular Daugavpils police. "The old policemen in particular fulfilled their assignments cleanly," a Daugavpils precinct chief reported proudly on 11 August 1941. ". . . During the liquidation of the Jews there was no lack of volunteers in the precinct to carry out this unpleasant task. [It] was carried out without hatred and shame, the men understanding that it would help all Christian civilization." Among the murdered were four hundred children from a Daugavpils orphanage trucked to a military training ground and shot. At a dinner party later in the war, Viktors Arajs would explain why his experienced killers often threw children up into the air to shoot them: not because of boyish exuberance, he said, but because the bullets often passed completely through the children's bodies, so that shooting children on the floor or the street risked dangerous ricochets.

On 1 August 1941 Gestapo chief Hermann Müller radioed Einsatzgruppen commanders Stahlecker, Nebe, Rasch and Ohlendorf that "the Führer is to be kept informed continually from here about the work of the *Einsatzgruppen* in the East." Müller wanted the Einsatzgruppen to send "visual materials of special interest, such as photographs," via "the speediest possible delivery." If Jews were to be murdered down to the last newborn infant, Hitler was eager to see.

Nowhere did the Wehrmacht advance more rapidly in the first months after Barbarossa than in the Ukraine, but the scale of battle on that vast, open steppe was immense. "The mass of the Red Army was battered to pieces," Alan Clark summarizes, "in a colossal 'annihilation battle' which cost the Russians nearly a million casualties." On 10 July 1941 Stalin reorganized his forces in the Ukraine under Marshall S. M. Budënny and political commissar Lieutenant General Nikita S. Khrushchev, ordering Budënny to hold Kiev at all costs. Khrushchev concentrated on dismantling and shipping eastward the Ukraine's factories and refineries, succeeding in salvaging nearly a quarter of the Soviet Union's industrial capacity. Budënny deployed more than 1.5 million soldiers on a front between Kiev and the strategic town of Uman, 120 miles due south. By mid-July Wehrmacht Panzer forces had captured two major towns eighty-five miles west of the Kiev-Uman front and paralleling it: Zhitomir, due west of Kiev, and Vinnitsa, seventy-five miles south of Zhitomir. From the Zhitomir-Vinnitsa line, while Field Marshal Walther von Reichenau's Sixth Army pushed toward Kiev, Field Marshal Ewald von Kleist's Panzer Group drove south and east around Uman in an enveloping pincer. Other Panzer Groups deployed from farther north in Byelorussia rolled down behind Kiev to encircle it and cut off its lines of supply. The Russians fought back with fierce artillery barrages and waves of suicidal frontal infantry assaults. A young Waffen-SS officer, Peter Neumann, described the result in his diary on 10 August 1941:

Everywhere [between Vinnitsa and Uman] lie tens of thousands of Russian corpses.

They have fallen on the hillsides, on the banks of the rivers, on both sides of the bridges, in the open country. They have been scythed down as they fought, by divisions, by battalions, by regiments, by sections.

Often the piles of interlaced bodies are a yard or more high, as though a machine gun has mown them down, wave after wave of them.

One has to have seen this monstrous mass of decomposing corpses to realize fully what war is like.

At certain times of day, when the sun is hot, gas dilates the ballooning, distended bellies, and then one hears the most horrible and unbelievable gurgling sounds.

Wherever we camp, we first have to spray all the carrion in the vicinity with quicklime or gasoline.

Mass death on the Eastern front was a daily reality, giving grisly cover to the feral mass murders of the Einsatzgruppen.

Einsatzgruppe C had moved into Zhitomir in mid-July, finding it heavily damaged by arson and its population reduced from ninety thousand to forty thousand, of which the group staff estimated about five thousand were Jews. By the end of July 1941 Sonderkommando 4a, Paul Blobel's commando, had shot several hundred "Jews, Communists and informants for the NKVD" in and around Zhitomir, bringing the commando's total so far in the war to 2,531 executions. Blobel had recovered from his illnesses, mental and physical, and was again directing Sonderkommando 4a operations. Perhaps because Einsatzgruppe C was operating so close to the front line, word had not yet reached it of Himmler's order to enlarge operations; in early August 1941 Blobel was still organizing public events designed to encourage pogroms. Thus on 7

August 1941 in Zhitomir Sonderkommando 4a staged the public hanging of a Jewish Soviet judge, Wolf Kieper, and his assistant, posting a
large sign accusing the judge of having murdered "1,350 ethnic Germans
and Ukrainians." A Wehrmacht truck driver hurried to the market
square that Thursday to watch the execution and found Jewish men
assembled there under SS guard:

> Round and about stood about 150 civilians watching. There were also,
> of course, members of the Wehrmacht among the onlookers. The Jews
> sat on the ground. . . . The guards asked the people standing around if
> they had any scores to settle. Thereupon more and more Ukrainians
> spoke up and accused one or other of the Jews of some misdemeanor.
> These Jews were then beaten and kicked and ill-treated where they
> were, mostly by Ukrainians. This went on for about forty-five minutes.
> Then [two] from this group were taken out and executed on a gallows.

Obersturmführer August Häfner of Sonderkommando 4a, the young
first lieutenant who had helped escort Blobel to a mental hospital earlier
in the summer, put the number of Jewish men in the square that day at
four hundred—he could tell they were Jews, he testified, "because many
of them had long beards and were wearing caftans." After the hangings
Blobel told him, "Now four hundred Jews are going to be shot." The executioners were young Waffen-SS. Both Häfner and a military judge who
watched the executions—at a killing pit on the outskirts of town—
remembered that the executioners were shaken by the experience. The
victims had been positioned facing them at the edge of the pit, and when
the young soldiers fired they had been sprayed with their victims' blood
and brains. "I also remember hearing yelling and screaming further back
among the crowd [of waiting victims]," the judge testified, "from where
each group was led for execution." The same day, 7 August 1941, Einsatzgruppe C extracted a "fee" of one hundred thousand rubles from the
Vinnitsa Jewish community—"as a contribution for residence rights," a
Ukrainian historian reports.

Blobel testified at his postwar trial that he remembered hearing the
"strict order"—meaning the Führerbefehl, the Führer's Eastern extermination order—around the time of his birthday, 13 August 1941. Erwin
Schulz of Einsatzkommando 5 confirmed the occasion, dating it around
10–12 August 1941:

> After about two weeks' stay in Berdichev the commando leaders were
> ordered to report to Zhitomir, where the staff of Dr. Rasch was
> quartered. Here Dr. Rasch informed us that *Obergruppenführer*
> Jeckeln had been there, and had reported that the *Reichsführer-SS*

had ordered us to take strict measures against the Jews. It had been determined without doubt that the Russian side had ordered to have the SS members and Party members shot.* As such measures were being taken on the Russian side, they would also have to be taken on our side. All suspected Jews were, therefore, to be shot. Consideration was to be given only when they were indispensable as workers. Women and children were to be shot also in order not to have any avengers remain.† We were horrified, and raised objections, but they were met with a remark that an order which was given had to be obeyed.

Günther Herrmann, who commanded Sonderkommando 4b, had been reproached at the meeting for not carrying out enough executions; his deputy commander, Lothar Fendler, testified that Herrmann complained afterward of having "had the feeling that they judged the efficiency of a commando according to the numbers of persons the commando executed." Blobel testified further that Rasch had quoted Jeckeln saying pointedly "that the measures against the Jewish population had to be sharper and that he disapproved of the manner in which they had been carried out until now because it was too mild." To all these professional murderers, Jeckeln's message was clear: shoot more Jews.

SS-Standartenführer Karl Jäger, based in Kaunas, began shooting more Lithuanian Jews in mid-August. Besides directing the ongoing Daugavpils executions northward in Latvia, he sent his Obersturmführer Joachim Hamann "and eight to ten reliable men from the *Einsatzkommando* . . . in cooperation with Lithuanian partisans" to the northern Lithuanian town of Rokiskis to purge a temporary concentration camp set up there that confined more than three thousand Jewish men, women and children. *Jäger* is the German word for hunter; in the notorious Jäger Report that the Einsatzkommando 3 commander filed with his superiors later in the year, he used the Rokiskis murders to brag about "the difficulties and the acutely stressful nature of the work: In Rokiskis 3,208 [*sic*] people had to be transported four and a half kilometers before they could be liquidated. In order to get this work done within twenty-four hours, over sixty of the eighty available Lithuanian partisans had to be detailed for cordon duty." In the grisly running tally Jäger offered in his report, the Rokiskis *Aktion* is listed as follows:

---

*An inflated reference to Stalin's partisan order.
†An allusion to Himmler's "revenge of the children" rationalization.

[DATE]	[PLACE]	[VICTIMS]	[TOTAL]
15–16.8.41	Rokiskis	3,200 Jews, Jewesses and J. children, 5 Lith. Comm., 1 Pole, 1 partisan	3,207

Unlike the lawyers who headed most of the Einsatzgruppen commandos, Jäger saw no need to justify executions by pretending they were punishments for crimes or partisan activity; the Rokiskis tally, listing Communists and one lone partisan separately, and indeed the entire Jäger Report, verify that Jews were murdered simply for being Jews. The Jäger Report running tally reveals that Jäger's men had been killing "Jewesses" in smaller numbers since early July 1941, but Rokiskis is the first entry that specifies Jewish children separately.

Two days later in Kaunas, where the Jewish community had recently been driven into a ghetto, Jäger's killers would achieve a lethal entrapment. William Mishell recalls the deception:

A representative of the German administration . . . ordered the [Jewish] council to recruit five hundred professionals—doctors, lawyers, engineers, and other college graduates—for work on Monday, 18 August. He explained that the people had to be intelligent and conversant in Russian and German since the work consisted of sorting and straightening out the records in the city hall of Kovno, which were left in complete disarray by the retreating Russians. The work would be indoors and three meals would be provided. He assured the council that the treatment would be proper, in order to give the men an opportunity to do a decent job. Under the starvation conditions of the ghetto, the lure of three meals a day was not to be underestimated.

The news about this new job offer quickly circulated around the ghetto. The ghetto police informed as many of the Jewish intelligentsia as possible in the hope of helping people to an easier office job. . . .

The weeks passed but no news came from the workers. Daily the families beseeched the council, but nothing authoritative could be obtained. Meanwhile some Lithuanians came to the ghetto fence and told the people who lived there that all 534 Jews had been shot the same day, 18 August, at the Fourth Fort. . . . Almost the entire intelligentsia of Jewish Kovno had thus been liquidated in one mass execution.

Either Mishell's number is an underestimate, or Jäger's number is inflated: the Einsatzkommando 3 commander lists "711 Jewish intellectuals from ghetto" in his running tally for 18 August 1941, adding, "in reprisal for sabotage action"—a rare instance of justification, typically fraudulent. Jäger also lists "689 Jews, 402 Jewesses, 1 Pole (f[emale])" executed at the Fourth Fort on the same day. Once begun, Jäger's comprehensive mass murders quickly and sickeningly expand in scope. On 22 August 1941 he reports Latvian auxiliaries under German supervision emptying a psychiatric hospital: "Mentally sick: 269 men, 227 women, 48 children, [total killed] 544." The hospital was located in Daugavpils; the patients were trucked to the small town of Aglona, thirty-five miles northwest, to be shot into killing pits. A September Einsatzgruppen report explains bizarrely that "ten males who could be regarded as partially cured were discharged by the governor of that institution, Dr. Borg, after steps for their sterilization had been taken," the discharge and sterilization indicating that the hospital patients were not Jews. Almost half the children murdered at Aglona were normal: of the forty-eight, twenty happened to have been transferred to the hospital from a children's home. Jäger's units worked relentlessly at mass murder for the rest of August:

[DATE]	[PLACE]	[VICTIMS]	[TOTAL]
23.8.41	Panevezys	1,312 Jews, 4,602 Jewesses, 1,609 Jewish children	7,523
18–22.8.41	Kreis Rasainiai	466 Jews, 440 Jewesses, 1,020 Jewish children	1,926
25.8.41	Obeliai	112 Jews, 627 Jewesses, 421 Jewish children	1,160
25–26.8.41	Seduva	230 Jews, 275 Jewesses, 159 Jewish children	664
26.8.41	Zarasai	767 Jews, 1,113 Jewesses, 1 Lith. Comm., 687 Jewish children, 1 Russ. Comm. (f)	2,569
28.8.41	Pasvalys	402 Jews, 738 Jewesses, 209 Jewish children	1,349

| 26.8.41 | Kaisiadorys | All Jews, Jewesses, and Jewish children | 1,911 |
| 27.8.41 | Prienai | All Jews, Jewesses, and Jewish children | 1,078 |

...

28.8.41	Kedainiai	710 Jews, 767 Jewesses, 599 Jewish children	2,076
29.8.41	Rumsiskis and Ziezmariai	20 Jews, 567 Jewesses, 197 Jewish children	784
29.8.41	Utena and Moletai	582 Jews, 1,731 Jewesses, 1,469 Jewish children	3,782

Even this partial tally, omitting smaller massacres, records almost twenty-five thousand people brutally murdered in one region by one Einsatzkommando with the assistance of native auxiliaries in less than one month.

Near the end of August 1941 Jeckeln perpetrated the SS's first five-figure massacre at Kamenets-Podolsky, an old fortress city anchored on limestone bluffs overlooking the Dniester River in the southwestern Ukraine.

Some thirty-five thousand Jews escaping Nazi persecution in Austria, Germany, Poland and Czechoslovakia had found refuge in Hungary in the years before Barbarossa despite the fact that Hungary was Fascist and had been the first country in Europe to adopt anti-Semitic laws. Many of these escapees had been settled in refugee camps; all had been required to register with the National Central Alien Control Office. When Hungary joined Germany in attacking the Soviet Union, its forces advanced northeast beyond the Carpathian Mountains into the Ukraine and took military control of the extensive piedmont region southwest of the Dniester. Anti-Semites in the Alien Control Office then proposed to the Hungarian General Staff a plan "to expel from Carpatho-Ruthenia all persons of dubious citizenship [i.e., alien Jews] and to hand them over to the German authorities in Eastern Galicia."

Admiral Nicholas Horthy, the man on a white horse who had overthrown the short-lived Soviet republic in Hungary in 1919 and installed a Fascist regime in its place, ruled the country as Regent. Horthy approved the expulsion plan. It was negotiated with the Gestapo. The

Hungarian council of ministers issued a decree authorizing it on 12 July 1941. A secret directive to the Alien Control Office implementing it specified that its objective was the "deportation of the recently infiltrated Polish and Russian Jews in the largest possible numbers and as fast as possible." They would be allowed to take with them three days' food, personal items they could carry and the equivalent of about three dollars in Hungarian *pengös*.

During late July and August 1941, Jews lacking Hungarian citizenship papers from the refugee camps, from Budapest and from small towns in the Carpathians were rounded up on short notice, often at night, crammed into freight cars, shipped northeast across the Carpathians to the border town of Korosmezo and turned over to the Germans, who transported them by train to Kolomiya in German-occupied Ukraine. From there the Germans marched them to temporary settlement in the area of Kamenets-Podolsky. By late August 1941 about sixteen thousand refugees had been expelled. The German military complained that it "could not cope with all these Jews," claiming they menaced Wehrmacht lines of communication. The Hungarians refused to readmit the refugees they had expelled, and they continued sending more across. The problem found its way onto the agenda of a military conference that Jeckeln attended in Vinnitsa on 25 August 1941, where its solution entered the conference record: "Near Kamenets-Podolsky the Hungarians have pushed about 11,000 [*sic*] Jews over the border. In the negotiations up to the present, it has not been possible to arrive at any measure for the return of these Jews. The Higher SS and Police Leader [i.e., Jeckeln] hopes, however, to have completed the liquidation of these Jews by 1 September 1941."

Historian Randolph Braham describes Jeckeln's subsequent *Aktion:*

> The extermination of the Jews deported from Hungary was carried out during [27–28 August 1941]. According to an eyewitness account, the deportees were told that in view of a decision to clear Kamenets-Podolsky of Jews they would have to be relocated. They were surrounded by units of the SS, their Ukrainian hirelings and a Hungarian sappers' platoon, and, together with the indigenous Jews of Kamenets-Podolsky, were compelled to march about ten miles to a series of craters created by bombings. There they were ordered to undress and brought into the crossfire of machine guns. Many of them were actually buried alive.

(Historian Richard Breitman found records of Jeckeln radio transmissions indicating that different units were involved: "His staff company did the shooting, and Police Battalion 320 cordoned off the area.")

An Einsatzgruppen report on 11 September 1941 summarized the massacre: "In Kamenets-Podolsky 23,600 Jews were shot in three days by a commando of the Higher SS and Police Leader." Of the 23,600 men, women and children murdered, Braham estimates, 14,000 to 16,000 had been refugees, the balance Ukrainian Jews from Kamenets-Podolsky. Since the decision to expand the scope of Einsatzgruppen killing was only promulgated beginning in late July, the Hungarian authorities who decided to expel "alien" Jews from Hungary may not have known that they were sending the entire population to its death. Their intentions were hardly benevolent, but they appear to have stopped short of mass murder. When the Hungarian minister of the interior learned of the Kamenets-Podolsky massacre, at least, he ordered the deportations halted; seven trainloads of potential victims already on their way were recalled.

The deaths in Kamenets-Podolsky mounted for the first time to five figures, but evil cannot be quantified. A massacre in Belaja Cerkov (Bila Cerkva) the previous week had made even the executioners tremble: fewer than one hundred died, but all the victims were children.

At Belaja Cerkov, a small town fifty miles south of Kiev on the main road to Uman, a Teilkommando* of Blobel's Sonderkommando 4a led by the young Obersturmführer August Häfner had been busy during the second half of August exterminating the Jewish population, shooting several hundred people a day into killing pits at a military firing range behind the grounds of a genetics institute. Häfner's Teilkommando included Sonderkommando men, a platoon of young Waffen-SS (perhaps the same men who had been shaken by the executions at Zhitomir) and Ukrainian auxiliaries. A Wehrmacht officer cadet who liked to stroll the institute grounds after evening mess encountered the executions by following the sounds of rifle fire back to the firing range:

> That first evening I saw some 162 people being executed.... Nine people were shot at a time while a further nine had to wait their turn. They were then led over to the grave. The people who were to be shot walked towards this grave as though they were taking part in a procession. They walked in a line, each person with his hands on the shoulders of the person in front. They went composed and quietly to their deaths. I saw only two women weep the whole time I observed such executions. I found it simply inexplicable.

*Teil means part or component.

During his time in Belaja Cerkov the officer cadet observed six such executions, on successive evenings at about six o'clock, and heard about others. He estimated he saw some eight hundred to nine hundred people killed. Only two of them were children, both boys. Evidently Häfner was not yet prepared to ask his German subordinates to murder children routinely. Instead, he had the children of his adult victims dragged away in the August heat to a house off the main road on the edge of town and locked into two rooms on the second floor without food or water, accumulating them for execution by his Ukrainian auxiliaries. Three truckloads of children went off to the firing range to be murdered on Tuesday evening, 19 August 1941. Another ninety children, many of them diapered infants, the oldest no more than seven, remained behind in the house overnight without adult supervision.

The next day around one o'clock a contingent of distressed enlisted men approached two Wehrmacht chaplains, Catholic and Protestant, in the Military Hospital Division mess. "We heard from German soldiers," the chaplains wrote in a subsequent report, "that quite a large number of children had been locked up in intolerable conditions in a house near our quarters. A Ukrainian was said to be guarding these children." In their naïveté the two chaplains suspected the incarceration to be "some arbitrary action on the part of the Ukrainians." They decided to investigate.

What they found appalled them: "About ninety children packed together into two small rooms in a filthy state. Their whimpering could be heard in the vicinity of the house. Some of the children, mainly infants, were completely exhausted and almost lifeless. There was no German guard or supervision present, only a Ukrainian guard armed with a rifle. German soldiers had free access to the house and were expressing outrage over these frightful conditions." The two chaplains went off to report the situation to the local commander. He returned to the house with them to see for himself, then bucked them up to the field commander. The field commander was unavailable. The two chaplains conferred, decided that the most senior ranking officer in the area was the commander of the 295th Infantry Division and sought out the division's Catholic and Protestant chaplains.

The four chaplains inspected the house together. The 295th Catholic chaplain described its condition in a report written the same day:

> In the courtyard in front of the house the crying and whimpering of children could be heard very loudly. Outside there were a Ukrainian militiaman keeping guard with a rifle, a number of German soldiers and several young Ukrainian girls. We immediately entered the house

unobstructed and in two rooms found some ninety (I counted them) children aged from a few months to five, six or seven years old. . . .

A large number of German soldiers, including a sanitation officer, were inspecting the conditions in which the children were being kept when we arrived. . . .

The two rooms where the children had been accommodated—there was a third empty room adjoining these two—were in a filthy state. The children lay or sat on the floor which was covered in their feces. There were flies on the legs and abdomens of most of the children, some of whom were only half dressed. Some of the bigger children (two, three, four years old) were scratching the mortar from the wall and eating it. Two men, who looked like Jews, were trying to clean the rooms. The stench was terrible. The small children, especially those who were only a few months old, were crying and whimpering continuously. The visiting soldiers were shaken, as we were, by these unbelievable conditions and expressed their outrage over them. In another room, accessible through a window in one of the children's rooms, there were a number of women and other children, apparently Jews. I did not enter this room. Locked in a further room there were some other women, among them one woman with a small child on her arm. According to the guard on duty—a Ukrainian boy aged about sixteen or seventeen, who was armed with a stick—it had not yet been established whether these women were Jews or not.

The 295th Protestant chaplain, reporting separately, adds that the children "were partly lying in their own filth, there was not a single drop of drinking water and the children were suffering greatly due to the heat."

As the chaplains left the house, some of the soldiers told the 295th Catholic chaplain "that they had their quarters in a house right next door and that since the afternoon of the previous day they had heard the children crying uninterruptedly." This chaplain's response was to ask the soldiers to make sure that no one else, locals in particular, entered the house; he was concerned for the army's reputation. A medical officer emerged then and "declared to me that water should be brought in urgently." Despite all the comings and goings, despite the soldiers' distress and expressions of outrage and the four chaplains' observations, no one seems to have thought to perform the simple kindness of giving water to the suffering children, who after all were little Jews.

The two divisional chaplains carried their story to an officer of the 295th Infantry Division general staff, Lieutenant Colonel Groscurth. By now it was four o'clock. Thirty minutes later, Groscurth in turn collected an inspection party and marched off to the house. "There were about ninety children and several women crammed into the rooms," he would write in a lengthy and indignant report. "A woman was cleaning up the farthermost room, which contained almost only babies. The other rooms were unbelievably filthy. There were rags, diapers and filth all over the place. The half-naked children were covered in flies. Almost all the children were crying or whimpering. The stink was unbearable. A German-speaking woman was claiming she was completely innocent, had never had anything to do with politics and was not Jewish."

Just then the Oberscharführer* walked in, the NCO who was in charge of the Waffen-SS platoon that was part of Häfner's Teilkommando. Groscurth asked the man what would happen to the children. "He informed me that the children's relatives had been shot and the children were also to be eliminated." Keeping his own council, Groscurth proceeded to the local commander's office and demanded an explanation. The local commander denied jurisdiction and sent Groscurth on to the field commander. "The *Feldkommandant* reported that the head of the *Sonderkommando* had been to see him, had notified him about the execution and was carrying it out with his knowledge." Groscurth asked if the Sonderkommando "had also received orders from the highest authority to eliminate children as well; I had heard nothing about this." The field commander assured him that the order was necessary and correct.

Groscurth found that hard to believe. He decided to pursue the question to the next level, which was division headquarters. He asked the field commander to seal off the area around the house while he contacted division headquarters. He knew he was treading on dangerous ground:

> I had misgivings about interrupting the measures [i.e., the execution] as I thought that the children would not be transported until evening, by which time division headquarters would have made its decision known. I was aware that suspending the measures would inevitably lead to complications with the political authorities and I wanted to avoid this if possible. However, the *Feldkommandant* stated that the transport would take place shortly. I then instructed the *Feldkommandant* to inform the head of the *Sonderkommando* that he would have to postpone the transport until a decision had been taken by headquarters.

Groscurth immediately telephoned division headquarters, which bucked him up to Sixth Army headquarters. "It took me some time to

*Sergeant First Class.

contact the operations officer there. Finally I was told that he would not be able to have a decision from the commander-in-chief until the evening." The commander in chief was von Reichenau, who had ordered the mass execution of Jews in Luck at the end of June when ten German soldiers had been found executed. Groscurth was evidently unaware of von Reichenau's enthusiasm for the Führer's *Lebensraum* policies.

Soon Häfner arrived to challenge Groscurth's moratorium. "He asked for an order in writing," Groscurth records. "I refused this, remarking that a definitive decision could be expected very shortly. He declared in a rather unmilitary tone that he would have to report these instructions to his commanding officer. He had clear orders to carry out the measure." The infantry lieutenant colonel was up to the first lieutenant's challenge: "I stated that I had to stick to my instructions and would back them with force if necessary."

At seven o'clock Groscurth reported to his divisional commander, who approved his intervention. At eight o'clock Sixth Army headquarters rang through to order the execution postponed. By then the children had been loaded into a truck parked in front of the house. The field commander had bread and water delivered to the children. The record does not reveal where they spent the night.

The next day, 21 August 1941, Blobel and Häfner sat down with army representatives, including the field commander and Groscurth, to negotiate a resolution to the Wehrmacht/SS standoff. The two Einsatz officers "admitted there had been shortcomings in the way things had been run," Groscurth writes, "and stated that a way had to be found to settle the matter quickly given the prevailing conditions." The field commander criticized the chaplains for stirring up trouble. Groscurth defended them. The field commander "declared that he considered the extermination of Jewish women and children to be pressingly urgent. . . . He was at pains to point out that as a result of the division's actions the elimination of the children had been delayed unnecessarily by twenty-four hours." Blobel agreed with him and added nastily "that it would be best if those troops who were nosing around carried out the executions themselves and the commanders who were stopping the measures took command of these troops." Groscurth restrained himself. "I quietly rejected this view without taking any position, as I wished to avoid any personal acrimony." Blobel played his trump card: von Reichenau, he claimed, "recognized the necessity of eliminating the children and wished to be informed once this had been carried out." That was still not enough for Groscurth, but when an intelligence officer at the meeting representing the Sixth Army high command confirmed Blobel's claim, the indignant infantry officer finally capitulated. "We then settled the details of how the executions were to be carried out," he writes. "They are to take place during the evening of 22 August. I did not involve myself in the details of this discussion." When von Reichenau read Groscurth's report he was livid. "It would have been far better if the report had not been written at all," he complained. The commander in chief of the German Sixth Army took particular exception to a comparison Groscurth drew between SS and Soviet policy, quoting Groscurth's words to condemn them: "The report in question contains the following sentence: 'In the case in question, measures against women and children were undertaken which in no way differ from atrocities carried out by the enemy about which the troops are continually being informed.' I have to describe this assessment as incorrect, inappropriate and impertinent in the extreme." Von Reichenau made sure Groscurth saw this rebuke: he required him to countersign it.

Häfner still had to do Blobel's dirty work. "Then Blobel ordered me to have the children executed," he testified after the war. "I asked him, 'By whom should the shooting be carried out?'" Blobel said the Waffen-SS should do it. Häfner objected: they were young men, he said; "how are we going to answer to them if we make them shoot small children?" Blobel countered, "Then use your men." Häfner said they had small children themselves. "This tug-of-war lasted about ten minutes," Häfner concludes. "... I suggested that the Ukrainian militia of the *Feldkommandant* should shoot the children." No one objected to passing on the onerous duty to the Ukrainians.

Häfner finishes the story:

> I went out to the woods alone. The Wehrmacht had already dug a grave. The children were brought along in a tractor [-drawn wagon]. I had nothing to do with this technical procedure. The Ukrainians were standing round trembling. The children were taken down from the tractor. They were lined up along the top of the grave and shot so that they fell into it. The Ukrainians did not aim at any particular part of the body. They fell into the grave. The wailing was indescribable. I shall never forget the scene throughout my life. I find it very hard to bear. I particularly remember a small fair-haired girl who took me by the hand. She too was shot later. . . . The grave was near some woods. It was not near the firing range. The execution must have taken place in the afternoon at about three-thirty or four. . . . Many children were hit four or five times before they died.

NINE

"All Jews, of All Ages"

The Wehrmacht turned over the Ostland—Estonia, Latvia, Lithuania and western Byelorussia—to German civil administration at the end of July 1941. The Reichskommissar for the Ostland, Heinrich Lohse, was a fanatical Nazi, but his first priority was restoring productivity to the regions he would now administer. He modeled his program for the urban Jews of the Ostland on the Nazi program in Poland: ghettos and forced labor rather than immediate extermination.

Stahlecker, the commander of Einsatzgruppe A, took issue with Lohse's program in a letter to Berlin dated 6 August 1941. Lohse, Stahlecker wrote, had failed to "examine the unprecedented possibility of a radical treatment of the Jewish question in the Eastern regions." He "apparently does not foresee the resettlement of the Jews ... as an immediate measure but rather sees it as a slower, later development. This will have the consequence that the Jews in the foreseeable future will remain in their present residences. . . . In view of the small number of German security and order forces, the Jews would continue their parasitical existence there and continue to play a disruptive role." In the dark mirror of Nazi paranoia, anti-Semitic hatred reflected back as Jewish malevolence; postponing extermination appeared to be a correspondingly extreme risk. But for the time being, Lohse's guidelines prevailed.

Which is not to say the Ostland Jews were protected. Lohse ordered the rural districts under his authority purged of Jews. That was the work the Arajs commando took up in Latvia. Jews in larger cities were to be marked, restricted and moved into ghettos established in neighborhoods where large numbers of Jews already lived, thus displacing the smallest possible number of Gentiles.

Ghettoization therefore loomed for the Jews of Vilnius at the beginning of September 1941. The Vilnius district commissioner, Hans Hingst, and Vilnius's Lithuanian mayor designated for the ghetto the old Jewish quarter near the center of the city. The quarter was already fully occupied. To make space available, Hingst staged what the Jews of Vilnius came to call the Great Provocation.

On the afternoon of 31 August 1941, two Lithuanian men carrying

concealed weapons entered an apartment house in the Jewish quarter that overlooked a square where German soldiers were waiting to enter a cinema. The two men fired shots inside the house and ran out shouting that Jews had fired on the square. The soldiers followed the men back into the house, dragged out two Jewish men, beat them and shot them dead.

That night Lithuanian auxiliaries arrested Jews living in the area around the square and on three nearby streets of the Jewish quarter and crowded them into the cells and courtyard of Lukiszki Prison, north near the river.

The next day Hingst had notices posted throughout the Jewish quarter claiming "shots were directed from ambush at German soldiers in Vilnius." The notices ordered all Jews except those who had valid work passes to remain confined to their homes from three o'clock that afternoon until ten o'clock the following morning. That night five more streets in the Jewish quarter were cleared of Jews.

From Lukiszki Prison these 3,700 victims went off in batches to Ponary. Men were made to march to the killing site, three miles south of the prison; women and children rode in trucks. The Jäger Report includes the Great Provocation in its callous bookkeeping:

[Date]	[Place]	[Victims]	[Total]
2.9.41	Vilnius	864 Jews, 2,019 Jewesses, 817 Jewish children	3,700

Exceptionally, Jäger cites the supposed provocation as the reason for the Vilnius "special action": "Because German soldiers [were] shot at by Jews."

Moving into the Vilnius ghetto was ordered for 6 September 1941, a Saturday. Making Jews work on the Sabbath was a Nazi joke, a deliberate expression of contempt. Yitzhak Rudashevski, a fourteen-year-old schoolboy who kept a diary of the Vilnius ghetto, felt the anxiety around him:

> The situation has become more and more strained. The Jews in our courtyard are in despair. They are transferring things to their Christian neighbors. The sad days begin of binding packages, of sleepless nights full of restless expectation about the coming day. It is the night between the fifth and the sixth of September, a beautiful, sleepless September night, a sleepless, desperate night, people like shadows. People sit in helpless, painful expectation with their bundles. Tomorrow we shall be led to the ghetto.

But Gebietskommissar Hingst soon realized that even with the Great Provocation he had not reduced the Jews of Vilnius sufficiently to crowd them into the two ghetto spaces, one larger and one smaller, that his subordinates had delimited. "The Lithuanians drive us on, do not let us rest," Rudashevski says of moving among tens of thousands of people the next day. "I think of nothing: not what I am losing, not what I have just lost, not what is in store for me. I do not see the streets before me, the people passing by. I only feel that I am terribly weary, I feel that an insult, a hurt is burning inside me. Here is the ghetto gate. I feel that I have been robbed, my freedom is being robbed from me, my home, and the familiar Vilnius streets I love so much. I have been cut off from all that is dear and precious to me." Rudashevski made it into the ghetto, but others were diverted to the prison. A woman remembered that cruel diversion:

> The march to Lukiszki was terrible. Thousands of Jews were rushed along like sheep, and beaten with rubber truncheons in the darkness of night. . . . The elderly stumbled and fell, and died; children lost their mothers, and parents lost their children. Everyone was wailing, and their cries filled the dark. We were taken to prison. Hundreds of Germans and Lithuanians opened the gate for us and, in doing so, beat the children, fathers and mothers. Many of them jeered at us and promised us death.

By the end of the action on Sunday evening, about thirty thousand people had been locked into Vilnius Ghetto No. 1, ten thousand into Ghetto No. 2 and six thousand into Lukiszki prison.

Lohse's program partly determined the fate of the people crowded into the prison. SS men confiscated money and valuables, filling the buckets they carried to the task. They made lists of the names of doctors, engineers and skilled workers. On 8 September 1941 they called out the names on their lists. Instead of sending them to Ponary to be murdered, as Jäger had done in Kaunas, they ordered them into Ghetto No. 1.

Those left behind at Lukiszki—twice as many women and children as men—were destined for Ponary. A schoolteacher, Sima Katz, the mother of three children, survived to tell the story of her encounter with what Rudashevski would call "the great grave":

> At Lukiszki we were kept outside for two days and then put into cells. We learned that the previous inmates had been sent to Ponary, but no one thought that all of them had been killed.
>
> We remained there until Thursday [11 September 1941]. At two a.m. the prison square was suddenly illuminated with floodlights. We

were put aboard trucks, fifty to sixty women in a truck. In each vehicle there were armed Lithuanian sentries. The trucks headed for Ponary. We came to an area of wooded hillocks and were dumped among them. Still, the mind would not keep pace with reality. We were arranged in rows of ten and prodded toward some spot, from which came the sound of shooting. The Lithuanians then went back for more batches of people.

Suddenly the truth hit us like an electric shock. The women broke out in piteous pleas to the sentries, offering them rings and watches. Some fell to the ground and kissed the sentries' boots, others tore their hair and clothes—to no avail. The Lithuanians pushed one group after another to the site of the slaughter. By noon, when it became clear that there was no escaping this fate, the women fell into a kind of stupor, without any pleading or resistance. When their turn came, they went hopelessly to their death.

Suddenly we saw a group of men. At their head was an aged rabbi, wrapped in his prayer shawl; passing us he called out "Comfort ye, comfort ye my people." We were seized with trembling. The women broke into moans, and even the Lithuanians took notice. One of the guards ran up and hit the rabbi with the butt of his rifle. My daughters and I were on the ground. Other women did not wait to be led away but broke from the rows and went on. The rows were broken. The women sat down and waited for a miracle to halt the massacre. I had one thought in mind: to be among the last.

Our turn came at five-thirty. The guards rounded up the remaining women. I felt my older daughter's hand in my own. . . . When I came to, I felt myself crushed by many bodies. Feet were treading on me, and the acrid smell of some chemical filled the air. I opened my eyes; a young man was sprinkling us with quicklime. I was lying in a huge common grave. I held my breath and strained my ears. Moans and sounds of dying people, and from above came the amused laughter of the Lithuanians. I wished myself dead so that I would not have to hear the sounds. Nothing mattered. It did not dawn on me that I was unhurt.

A child was whimpering a short distance away. Nothing came from above. The Lithuanians were gone. The whimper aroused me from my stupor. I crawled toward the sound. I found a three-year-old girl, unharmed. I knew that if I survived, it would be thanks to her.

I waited for darkness to fall; then, holding the child in my arms, I wriggled up to the surface and headed for the forest. Not far in the interior, I came upon five other women who had managed to survive. Our clothes were smeared with blood and burnt from the quicklime. Some of us had nothing but our underclothes on our skin.

We hid for two days in the forest. A peasant came by and was frightened out of his senses. He let out a weird shriek and fled. But he was not decent enough to come back and help us. He was sure that we were ghosts from another world.

The Jäger Report lists the massacre Sima Katz survived and another one five days later:

[Date]	[Place]	[Victims]	[Total]
12.9.41	Vilnius	993 Jews, 1,670 Jewesses, 771 Jewish children	3,334
17.9.41	Vilnius	337 Jews, 687 Jewesses, 247 Jewish children and 4 Lith. Communists	1,271

In Minsk in September 1941 Nebe, Bach-Zelewski and the commander of Rear Army Group Center organized a course of instruction in antipartisan warfare. The course was based on the premise that "wherever there is a Jew there is a partisan, and wherever there is a partisan there is a Jew." For training, participants rounded up and shot all the Jews in a Byelorussian village.

A woman in a small town near Minsk saw a young German soldier walking down the street with a year-old baby impaled on his bayonet. "The baby was still crying weakly," she would remember. "And the German was singing. He was so engrossed in what he was doing that he did not notice me."

The Final Solution in the area of the western Ukraine that included Zhitomir and Vinnitsa would not begin with ghettos. Himmler intended to establish his field headquarters in Zhitomir once the area was secure, and a forward Hitler bunker, Werwolf, was to be built north of Vinnitsa. So that the Führer might sleep peacefully, the territory for forty miles in every direction was scheduled to be made *Judenfrei*. Connected massacres under Jeckeln's authority winnowed the region throughout September 1941.

The massacres began in Berdichev, sixteen miles south of Zhitomir on the road to Vinnitsa, an industrial town of sixty thousand where half the population was Jewish. Jews in Berdichev worked at the Ilyich Leather

Curing Factory, the Progress Machine Tool Factory, the Berdichev Sugar Refinery. In smaller shops and factories they made shoes, hats, cardboard and metal products and soft slippers called *chuvyaki* known throughout the Russian-speaking world. "Thousands of Berdichev Jews," writes the Russian war correspondent Vasily Grossman, "worked as stone masons, stove builders, carpenters, jewelers, watch repairmen, opticians, bakers, barbers, porters at the railroad station, glaziers, electricians, locksmiths, plumbers, loaders. . . . [There were] dozens of senior, experienced doctors—internists, surgeons, pediatricians, obstetricians, dentists. There were bacteriologists, chemists, druggists, engineers, technicians, bookkeepers, teachers in the numerous technical schools and high schools. There were teachers of foreign languages, teachers of music, women who worked in the nurseries, kindergartens, and playgrounds."

The Wehrmacht overran Berdichev in early July 1941, when only a third of its Jewish population had been evacuated. Those left behind were crowded into a temporary ghetto in late August 1941. Jeckeln established his headquarters in Berdichev, which is probably why the large-scale September massacres in the region west of Kiev started there. While prisoners of war began digging five long killing pits on open land at the end of Brodsky Street near the Berdichev airport, Jeckeln's own staff company staged a preliminary mass killing with help from Police Battalion 45.

According to Grossman, on 4 September 1941 "the Germans and traitors who had joined their police force [i.e., Ukrainian auxiliaries] ordered 1,500 young people to leave for agricultural work. The young people made bundles of bread and food, said goodbye to their relatives and set out. On that very day they were shot. . . . The henchmen prepared the execution carefully—so carefully that none of the doomed people suspected until the very last minutes that there was a massacre in the offing." Along a railroad line near the village of Khazhin, POWs had dug two killing pits sufficiently deep that victims approaching the pit could not see the bodies of those already killed. Jeckeln numbered as victims in his report to Berlin "1,303 Jews, among them 875 Jewesses over 12 years [of age]." For justification he claimed that "on 1–2 September 1941 leaflets and inflammatory pamphlets were distributed by Jews in Berdichev," and "since the perpetrators could not be found," the victims were executed in reprisal. But Kurt Daluege had flown in to Berdichev on 4 September 1941 to meet with Jeckeln; Richard Breitman speculates that Jeckeln had probably staged the massacre of young people that day in Daluege's honor. "This execution," Grossman notes, "removed from the ghetto all the young people capable of resistance."

The mayor of Berdichev, who was German (a POW in the Great War who had stayed on in the Ukraine), and the chief of police—Reder and Koroliuk, Grossman identifies them—participated in the larger massacre in Berdichev a week and a half later. On 14 September 1941 transport planes disgorged units of a Waffen-SS regiment at the Berdichev airport. Koroliuk mobilized the city police. That night they surrounded the temporary Berdichev ghetto. The raid began at four a.m. on 15 September 1941. "Many of those who could not walk," Grossman writes— "feeble old people and cripples—were killed by the executioners on the spot. The terrible wails of women and the crying of children wakened the entire town." The Germans herded their victims into the market square at the center of the temporary ghetto.

Reder, the Berdichev mayor, stationed himself at a high point in the market square surrounded by guards and proceeded to perform a selection, sorting out about four hundred people—doctors, electricians, shoe repairmen, locksmiths, barbers, a photographer—who were allowed to collect their families before being led off into a side street to safety. Some of them had trouble finding their families in the crowded square, Grossman reports: "Witnesses tell of terrible scenes. People attempting to make themselves heard in the fear-crazed crowd shouted the names of their wives and children, and hundreds of doomed mothers stretched out their own sons and daughters to them, begging them to pass them off as their own and thus save them from death. 'You won't find your own family in this crowd anyway!' the women shouted."

The police formed the remaining twelve thousand people—those who could march—into columns and herded them down Brodsky Street toward the airport. Trucks loaded small children and the elderly. At the airport, SS men led the victims fifty yards across an open field to the pits in groups of forty and murdered them with automatic weapons while the next in line watched from the road. The shooting took all day. Grossman, who interviewed survivors at the end of the war, describes the aftermath:

> All five pits were filled to the brim, and mounds of earth were heaped above them to cover the bodies. The ground moved as if in shuddering breath. That night many dug themselves out from under these burial mounds. Fresh air penetrated the loose soil of the upper layers and lent strength to those who were only wounded, whose hearts were still beating but who had been lying unconscious. They crawled in different directions along the field, instinctively attempting to get as far away as possible from the pits. Exhausted, and streaming blood, many of them died right there in the field, a few yards from the place of execution.

Peasants driving at dawn from Romanovka to town saw that the entire field was covered with the bodies of the dead. In the morning the Germans and the police removed the bodies, killed all of those who were still breathing, and buried them again.

Uman was next, the birthplace of the Hasidic movement. German and Hungarian forces had surrounded the town in early August 1941; resistance in the Uman pocket had collapsed within two weeks. A German army officer, Oberleutnant Erwin Bingel, arrived in Uman on 15 September 1941, the day of the Berdichev massacre, commanding a company of reservists attached to the Twelfth Army. Bingel commanded reservists because he had been wounded earlier in the war and was partly disabled. His company was posted from Vinnitsa for guard duty in Uman: permanent guard duty for the railroads in the area, he was told, and temporary assignment "to surround the airport of Uman," which by special order "was to be closed the following day to all traffic, including members of the German Army."

The following day was 16 September 1941. Early in the morning Bingel's company—"strengthened by reinforcements," he says—marched to the Uman airport about a mile north of town. The men were restive, uncertain what their duty that day might involve. Bingel picketed them at the edge of the airfield. Then, in the dawn light:

> From the town, voices of a crowd of people singing Russian melodies could be heard, intimating that large masses of people were on the move and drawing near. The main streets could be seen very clearly and along them huge columns marching six abreast came by, singing all the time, approaching the confines of the airfield. We soon observed that they included not only men, but also women and children of all ages. Nobody could imagine the possible purpose of bringing this crowd of people there, and the whole affair became still more mysterious when I was given orders to withdraw my guards from the nearest posts.

Bingel moved his men back about four hundred yards, leaving a few stationed ahead of him on the main Uman-Kiev road about two hundred yards from the square in front of the airport where the people were gathering. Two long pits had been dug in the square the previous day. As the sun came up, Bingel and his men had a clear view.

Trucks followed the people crowding into the square, disgorging a field gendarmerie (military police) troop that moved off to one side. Men unloaded tables and lined them up spaced well apart. Several truckloads of Ukrainian militia arrived, men with shovels; from one

truck, driving slowly along the pit line, they unloaded at regular intervals sacks of quicklime, a powerful caustic that reacts strongly with
water.

In the meantime, in a roar of engines, transport planes had begun
landing at the airport—Bingel identifies them as Junker 52s. "Out of
these stepped several units of SS soldiers who, having fallen in, marched
up to the field gendarmerie unit, subsequently taking up positions alongside it." Bingel watched as the two units were sworn in. His interpreter
returned from mingling with the crowd. The man was Jewish, Bingel
notes, a secret the Oberleutnant kept. It seemed the crowd had come to
the airport because the Ukrainian militia had posted an order throughout the Uman area requiring "all Jews, of all ages" to report there for a
census, an order accompanied by the usual German threat that "persons
failing to comply . . . will be punished most severely."

The news that the gathering was only a census relieved Bingel and his
men—the "relatively harmless summons" allowed them to "[take] the
matter lightly," he says—but relief soon turned to horror as the Jews in
the first row were ordered forward to the tables, made to surrender their
valuables and belongings, made to undress and pile their clothes to one
side. Whereupon the troops menaced the row of naked people to the
brink of one of the pits:

> The commandos then marched in behind the line and began to
> perform the inhuman acts. . . . With automatic pistols and 0.8 pistols
> these men mowed down the line with such zealous intent that one
> could have supposed this activity to have been their lifework.
>
> Even women carrying children a fortnight to three weeks old,
> sucking at their breasts, were not spared this horrible ordeal. Nor were
> mothers spared the terrible sight of their children being gripped by
> their little legs and put to death with one stroke of a pistol butt or club,
> thereafter to be thrown on the heap of human bodies in the ditch,
> some of which were not quite dead. Not before these mothers had
> been exposed to this worst of all tortures did they receive the bullet
> that released them from this sight.
>
> The people in the first row thus having been killed in the most
> inhuman manner, those of the second row were now ordered to step
> forward. The men in this row were ordered to step out and were
> handed shovels with which to heap quicklime upon the still partly
> moving bodies in the ditch. Thereafter, they returned to the tables and
> undressed. . . .
>
> The air resounded with the cries of the children and the tortured.
> With senses numbed by what had happened, one could not help

thinking of wives and children back home who believed they had good reason to be proud of their husbands and fathers.

Two of Bingel's men in the forward posting, along the Uman-Kiev road, were sufficiently horrified to abandon their posts before their relief arrived—a capital offense under military law. The sergeant major whom Bingel had put in charge of the forward line took it upon himself to move the rest of his men back to Bingel's position. All day, relentlessly, the killing went on, row after row of human beings shot or smashed into the filling pits and dusted with quicklime glaring white in the September sun. Until the pits were full, the SS men loaded into the Junker 52s and the planes roaring off beyond the horizon, the gendarmerie and the militia marched and trucked away. "At five p.m. the square lay deserted in deadly desolation," Bingel testifies, "and only some dogs, attracted by the scent of blood in the air, were roving the site. The shots were still ringing in our ears."

Back at their quarters, Bingel's men importuned him to demand an explanation for the massacre from the town commandant. He did, and the town commandant told him "that a special, express order had been issued by Reichsführer-SS Himmler and personally signed by him." Bingel asked to see it. As he recalled it in August 1945, this is what it said:

Soldiers of the *Waffen-SS!*
In the forest of Vinnitsa, District of Kiev, six of our best officers were found assassinated, hanging on a tree.
The details are as follows:
They were found naked, with their legs pointing upward, their bodies slit open and their intestines showing.
As a result of this case, I have decided upon the following measures: As it may be taken for granted that this action was carried out by Jewish partisans, I hereby order that in the District of Kiev 10,000 Jews—irrespective of sex or age—are to die for each of the six officers mentioned above.
Even the child in the cradle must be trampled down like a poisonous toad.
May each one of you be mindful of his oath and do his duty, whatever may be demanded of you.
We are living in an epoch of iron during which it is also necessary to sweep with iron-made brooms.

Bingel puts the number murdered in Uman that day at 24,000. Ukrainian historians dispute that total, since the Jewish population of Uman prior to the German invasion had been 22,000 and another massacre of

6,000 would occur the following year. But the census order Bingel cites was issued for the entire Uman area, including outlying villages and small towns, so a total larger than the Jewish population of Uman itself is plausible. Whatever the precise number, thousands were murdered that day.

Two of Bingel's men, including the sergeant major, broke down after the massacre and had to be sent the next day to the field hospital in Lvov. Two enlisted men in Bingel's company were arrested for having taken photographs of the Uman massacre. Beyond shipping their personal possessions (in which he hid some of the photographs) home to their wives, Bingel was unable to protect them; they received one-year prison sentences, which they served in a military facility in Germany. By 19 September 1941, the third day after the Uman massacre, Bingel had to send a fifth of the men in his company on a leave of absence. "As a result of their recent experiences," he explains, "they were quite incapable of performing any duty."

That same day Blobel's Sonderkommando 4a was busy at massacre in Zhitomir. SK 4a had been systematically combing the Zhitomir region throughout September, continuing the work it had accomplished so gruesomely at Belaja Cerkov in August. A Waffen-SS division had seized Zhitomir in late July; Peter Neumann, the young SS officer, recorded the conditions there at that time in his diary:

> Zhitomir, July 28th. We occupied the town some days ago. Perhaps I am exaggerating when I call it a town, because all we have seen are miles and miles of ruins, and again ruins.
>
> Fresh orders have reached the division.
>
> In addition to People's Commissars, we are to shoot, without trial, all Jewish functionaries we find, whether civil or military.
>
> Liquidations, executions, purges. All these words, synonymous with destruction, seem completely banal and devoid of meaning once one has gotten used to them.
>
> It is a vocabulary which has become general usage, and we use such words just as we talk of swatting disagreeable insects or destroying a dangerous animal.
>
> These words however are applied to men. But men who happen to be our mortal enemies.

Once Zhitomir was secured, Blobel had suggested to the military administration that Zhitomir Jews should be confined to a restricted area. "This resulted in a quieter atmosphere," the Sonderkommando 4a commander wrote Berlin at the end of September. ". . . Simultaneously, a number of previously persistent rumors died down and it seemed as well as if Communist propaganda lost much ground." Blobel claimed

Heinrich Himmler, the son of a Bavarian schoolmaster, took command of the SS—Schutzstaffel, the Nazi Party's police and security service—at the age of twenty-nine in 1929. He dreamed of clearing Poland and Russia to make room for colonies of German soldier-farmers.

Hermann Göring, Himmler and Adolf Hitler collaborated to disarm the SA—Sturmabteilung, Hitler's first paramilitary organization—and murder its leadership in June 1934. The purge consolidated their power.

With the invasion of eastern Poland and the U.S.S.R. on 21 June 1941, Himmler unleashed the 3,000 men of his deadly Einsatzgruppen and tens of thousands of Order Police to murder Communists and Jews.

In Kaunas (Kovno), Lithuania, one of the first towns occupied by the Nazis, the SS opened the jails and encouraged local criminals and victims of Soviet repression to publicly murder Jews. The "Death-dealer of Kovno" posed for a portrait among the victims he had beaten to death with a crowbar.

Hoping at first to make their killing appear spontaneous, the Einsatzgruppen organized local auxiliaries. Here, Lithuanian paramilitary herd Jewish women toward one of the old czarist forts around Kaunas that served as prisons and killing sites.

At the Seventh Fort outside Kaunas the Lithuanian auxiliaries confined Jewish men without food or water for days before killing them with rifle and machine-gun fire.

Ponary, an unfinished Soviet fuel storage site outside Vilnius, Lithuania, became one of the most terrible mass graves of the war. From a holding area (left), men with their heads covered were lined up and driven across a walkway to another pit, where they were shot to death.

The Einsatzgruppen followed the Wehrmacht as it swept eastward across Poland and the western Soviet Union. They soon gave up trying to incite the local population to murder and began mass killing themselves. To condition their forces to killing, they limited the victims at first primarily to men.

Paul Blobel, an alchoholic former architect, commanded Sonderkommando 4a of Einsatzgruppe C. He learned to organize highly efficient massacres.

After publicly hanging a Jewish Soviet judge, Wolf Kieper, and his assistant in the western Ukrainian town of Zhitomir in August 1941 (above), Blobel organized a roundup of terrified local Jews with German soldiers looking on. The victims were driven to a killing pit on the edge of town and shot to death.

A young Obersturmführer in Blobel's Sonderkommando, August Häfner, oversaw the murder of almost one hundred infants and small children by Ukrainian auxiliaries at Belaja Cerkov, south of Kiev, in August 1941.

More than half a million Soviet soldiers died defending Kiev before the Wehrmacht won the city in September 1941. Russian high explosives burned out the central city; Einsatzgruppe C used the sabotage as an excuse to order Kiev Jews to assemble for relocation. Instead of relocation, Blobel directed a massacre at a ravine on the western edge of Kiev named Babi Yar. In two days, Blobel's few hundred men murdered more than 34,000 Jewish men, women and children, the worst single Einsatzgruppen massacre of the war. Afterward, Ukrainian workers on the floor of the ravine sorted piles of victims' clothes, which were donated to Nazi Party charities.

One of the very few victims to survive Babi Yar, Dina Mironovna Pronicheva, testified to the atrocity after the war.

Reinhard Heydrich and Himmler (second and third from left) directed Einsatzgruppen operations and received weekly reports. By October 1941, when they reviewed troops in Prague, mass killings of Jewish men, women and children were decimating Eastern Jewry.

Himmler assigned Austrian Odilo Globocnik, here reviewing troops in Lublin, Poland, the task of exterminating 2.5 million Polish Jews to make way for Himmler's SS *Wehrbauern* (soldier-farmer) settlements. Globocnik began experimenting with mass killing using explosives, quicklime or carbon monoxide from engine exhaust.

Erich von dem Bach-Zelewski (seated, left) commanded mass killing operations in Byelorussia. Himmler panicked during a mass execution Bach-Zelewski staged for his benefit. Later Bach-Zelewski himself broke down.

Friedrich Jeckeln in the Ukraine and then in Latvia, and Karl Jäger in Lithuania, Latvia and Estonia, were two of the most insidious Einsatzgruppen mass murderers. The infamous Jäger Report of 1 December 1941 credited 137,346 deaths in five months to one Einsatzkommando alone. "There are no Jews in Lithuania anymore," Jäger bragged.

On a Baltic beach northeast of Liepaja, Latvia, in December 1941, an SS sergeant photographed the massacre of almost 3,000 Liepaja Jews, most of them women and children. Forced to undress in the bitter cold and to pose for photographs, the victims were driven to a trench excavated from the deep

beach sand, faced away from
their executioners and shot from
behind. Victims who fell
wounded were then finished off
by an officer who ranged through
the trench administering
Genickschüssen (shots to the
back of the head at the base of
the skull).

On 20 January 1942 Heydrich convened a conference at this official residence on the Wannsee, a lake outside Berlin. Hitler's program to eliminate the Jews had escalated from expulsion to confinement and mortal privation. In July 1941 he had ordered the direct murder of the Eastern Jews. The Wannsee Conference implemented direct murder of the German and western European Jews as well.

Otto Ohlendorf, an economist, commanded Einsatzgruppe D, operating throughout the southern Ukraine and the Crimea. At the International Military Tribunal Nuremberg trial he admitted to 90,000 executions. He was executed for crimes against humanity in 1951.

This notorious image of a German policeman preparing to murder a Jewish mother holding a child while other victims dig their own graves was found by Polish postal workers enclosed in a German soldier's letter home. The inscription on the back read "Ukraine 1942, Jewish action, Ivangorod."

Wilhelm Kube (right), the Generalkommissar for Byelorussia, was conflicted about murdering Jews from western Europe but strewed candy into a Minsk killing pit filled with Eastern Jewish children.

Max Täubner (far right), an SS Untersturmführer in charge of an equipment repair unit, staged voluntary massacres to fulfill his resolution personally to "get rid of" 20,000 Jews.

In a final massacre in the western Ukrainian town of Vinnitsa in April 1942, an Einsatzkommando murdered the last of the region's Jews to secure the area around Adolf Hitler's forward bunker Werwolf.

At Vinnitsa in April 1942 a thousand children were torn from their parents' arms and shot to death in a separate killing pit. Mounded over with grass and marked with a small obelisk, the children's pit at Vinnitsa remains unexhumed to this day.

Hitler appointed Heydrich (center) governor of occupied Czechoslovakia. In May 1942 Heydrich was grenaded on his way into Prague by Czech patriots, and he died on 4 June. His two sons shared the front row at his funeral in Berlin with (left to right) Wilhelm Frick, Himmler, Göring and Hitler. "Is the swine dead at last?" one of his rivals asked.

By the spring of 1942, having almost rendered eastern Europe *Judenfrei,* the Einsatzgruppen turned increasingly to fighting partisans. Hitler and Himmler authorized a paramilitary unit made up of violent criminals collected from German prisons and named for Oskar Dirlewanger (right), the brutal SS professional who led it. Sonderkommando Dirlewanger murdered the populations of entire Byelorussian villages suspected of supporting partisans and burned the villages to the ground.

The growing enthusiasm for mass killing among his Ein-satzgruppen led Himmler to order his units to begin using gas vans to murder women and children. Gassing tech-nology reached its full devel-opment in death camps such as Chelmno, Treblinka, Belzec, Sobibor and Auschwitz-Birkenau. (Here, war crimes commissioners examine a mobile killing van at Chelmno in 1945.)

Himmler called the final round of SS murders of ghetto inhabitants in the fall of 1943 "Operation Harvest Festival." By then (as here, in 1942, for the Mizocz ghetto outside Rovno in the western Ukraine), most of the victims were women and children.

Hitler authorized the mass killings of the Holocaust, followed the murders in reports and photographs, and rewarded the perpetrators. Here he congratulates SS Reichsführer Himmler, "truehearted Heinrich," on Himmler's forty-third birthday, 7 October 1943.

In Poland in 1943 Himmler spoke openly to his generals and to the leaders of the Third Reich about "the extermination of the Jewish people ... a glorious page in our history." By then he was collecting books bound in human skin, and chairs and tables made from the bones of his victims.

SS mass killing descended directly to late-twentieth-century "ethnic cleansing" when Christian Serbs rationalized murdering Muslim Serbs as revenge for World War II repressions. Here, c. 1943, Himmler inspects Muslim Serbs in fezzes, the 23rd Bosnian and Croatian Waffen-SS "Kama" Division.

Assigned to exhume and burn the corpses of 1.5 million victims of Einsatzgruppen and Order Police mass killing, Paul Blobel resorted to power shovels and bone grinders and built massive funeral pyres, but still failed to eradicate the evidence of Nazi crimes.

After his capture by British forces in late May 1945 Himmler committed suicide by crushing a cyanide capsule he had hidden in his mouth. This previously unpublished photograph by British Army Major W. G. Thorpe was taken shortly after the former Reichsführer's death. He was buried in an unmarked grave.

One set of Einsatzgruppen reports was discovered after the war; it supplied damning evidence for a U.S. military trial of Einsatzgruppen leaders at Nuremberg in 1947–48. Left to right, Ohlendorf, Heinz Jost, Erich Naumann and Erwin Schulz receive their indictments in the fall of 1947. Most of the mass killers in the Einsatzgruppen and the Order Police were never brought to trial.

The Ninth Fort (right and below), outside Kaunas, Lithuania, stands today preserved as a memorial to its victims.

Fania Brancovskaja, shown here with the author at the State Museum of Vilnius Gaon Jews, escaped the Vilnius ghetto on the day in 1943 when all its remaining Jews were killed at Ponary. She and one of her sisters became anti-Nazi partisans fighting in the Lithuanian forests, the only two members of her extended family to survive the war.

that restriction without a ghetto was insufficient, however, and "the old troubles soon started again." These troubles, a familiar Einsatzgruppen litany, included "complaints ... about the insolent attitude of Jews in their workplaces," propaganda among the Ukrainians that the Red Army would soon return traced to "the Jewish district," the local militia "shot at from ambush at night and also by day" and Jews selling their belongings to fund escaping to the western Ukraine. These things happened, Blobel went on, but only rarely could the Jews responsible for them be arrested; without ghetto confinement they had "sufficient opportunities to evade arrest."

Therefore "a conference on this matter was called on 18 September 1941 with the military administration. Since all previous warnings and special measures had been unsuccessful, it was decided to liquidate the Jews of Zhitomir completely and radically."

The liquidation began as the Berdichev liquidation had begun: sixty Ukrainian militiamen surrounded and closed the Jewish district of Zhitomir during the night and at four in the morning broke down doors and drove families out of the houses and buildings where they had been crowded earlier in the month. Twelve trucks lent by the city and military administrations transported the victims to the massacre site, where a detachment of POWs had dug killing pits. The victims—a total of 5,145 men, women and children—were registered, robbed, disrobed and shot. "Fifty thousand to sixty thousand pounds of underwear, clothing, shoes, dishes, etc., that had been confiscated in the course of the action," Blobel reported to Berlin, "were handed over to the officials of the NSV* in Zhitomir for distribution. Valuables and money were conveyed to *Sonderkommando* 4a."

At the International Military Tribunal in Nuremberg in 1946, the Soviet chief counselor, L. N. Smirnov, offered into evidence a 1942 report by a German infantry officer, Major Rösler, who had commanded the 528th Infantry Regiment. Rösler had described to a superior a massacre he had witnessed in Zhitomir in the summer of 1941. He thought the massacre had occurred at the end of July, on the day his regiment arrived at the Zhitomir rest area. If so, then he may have seen the executions referred to in an Einsatzgruppen report dated 9 August 1941: "In Zhitomir about 400 Jews, mostly saboteurs and political functionaries, were liquidated during the last few days." But Rösler specifies that the victims included women and children, which points to a later event. The infantry officer may in fact have observed the 19 September 1941 Zhito-

---

*NSV: Nationalsozialistische Volkswohlfahrt: National Socialist People's Welfare, a Nazi Party welfare agency.

mir massacre and conflated it with the earlier liquidations; his description more closely matches Blobel's ugly slaughter:

> After I had moved with my staff into the staff quarters, on the
> afternoon of the day of our arrival, we heard rifle volleys nearby at
> regular intervals, followed a little later by pistol shots. I decided to find
> out what was happening and set off with my adjutant and orderly . . .
> in the direction of the rifle shots. We soon realized that a cruel spec-
> tacle was taking place; numerous soldiers and civilians were streaming
> toward the railway embankment behind which, as we were told,
> executions were being conducted. We were not able to see over the
> embankment, but at regular intervals we heard the sound of a whistle
> followed by a volley of about ten rifles, followed after awhile by pistol
> shots.
>
> When we finally climbed up onto the embankment we were com-
> pletely unprepared for the scene that confronted us. It was so abom-
> inable and cruel that we were utterly shattered and horrified. A pit
> about seven to eight meters long and perhaps four meters wide had
> been dug in the ground. The upturned earth was piled to one side of
> the pit. This earthen berm and the wall of the pit below were com-
> pletely soaked in blood. The pit itself was filled with numerous corpses
> of all ages and sexes. There were so many corpses that it was not even
> possible to estimate the depth of the pit. Behind the berm stood a
> police detachment under the command of a police officer. The uni-
> forms of the police bore traces of blood. In a wide circle around the pit
> stood scores and scores of soldiers from the units stationed in the area,
> some of them in bathing trunks, watching the proceedings. There were
> also a comparable number of civilians, including women and children.
> I approached the edge of the pit and saw something that to this day I
> have not been able to forget.
>
> Among the bodies in the pit lay an old man with a white beard, his
> hand clutching a cane. He was panting for air, so it was obvious that he
> was still alive. I ordered one of the policemen to put him out of his
> misery. The policeman smarted back, "I've already plugged him seven
> times—he'll kick off soon enough."
>
> The dead in the pit were not laid out in rows but were left where
> they happened to fall after being shot down from the ground above.
> All these people had been executed with rifle *Genickschüssen* and the
> survivors given *coups de grace* with pistol shots.
>
> I saw nothing like this spectacle either in the First World War,
> during the Civil War in Russia or in the Western campaign. I have seen
> many unpleasant things, having been a member of the *Freikorps* in

1919, but I have never seen anything like this. I cannot begin to conceive the legal basis on which these executions were carried out. Everything that is happening here seems to be absolutely incompatible with our [German] views on education and morality. Right out in the open, as if on a stage, men murder other men. I must add that, according to the accounts of the soldiers, who often see spectacles of this kind, hundreds of people are killed in this way every day.

Then it was Vinnitsa's turn. The administrative center of a large district, with a prewar population of 70,000, of whom about 36,000 were Jews, Vinnitsa had already been brutally purged in 1937 and 1938 by the NKVD. In the early summer of 1943, with unparalleled audacity, the SS would publicly exhume the victims of the NKVD killings in Vinnitsa; in three mass grave sites in an orchard, a Russian Orthodox cemetery and a public park near the town stadium, the homicide squad the SS sent from Berlin would find 9,432 bodies, of which 169 were female. With one exception, all the men had been bound, and most of the victims had been killed with shots to the head with small-caliber weapons. The victims had been "enemies of the people," not specifically Jews, and included a large number of collective farm workers and priests. The Nazi authorities would invite forensic experts from the International Commission of Foreign Medical Examiners to observe the exhumations, hoping to focus international attention on the Soviet atrocities comparable with the attention that followed the discovery earlier in 1943 of the 1940 Soviet massacre of twelve thousand Polish officers in the Katyn Forest, 125 miles west of Moscow.

Had the foreign medical examiners looked a little farther, they would have found Einsatzgruppen mass graves all over the Vinnitsa region. Already in September 1941 some 2,400 people—old men, women and children—had been shot to death at a brickworks near Nemirov, twenty-five miles southeast of Vinnitsa on the road to Uman. On 22 September 1941, the first day of the Jewish New Year, a major massacre reduced the Jews of Vinnitsa by half. The record of the Vinnitsa massacre is sparse. Erwin Bingel, stationed in the area, witnessed it "in close proximity to our quarters" and thought that it "did not lag behind that of Uman in any respect." He took two complete rolls of photographs and estimated the number of Jewish victims as 28,000.

Faina Vinokurova, the Ukrainian Jewish historian, has studied the surviving Ukrainian and German documents; she points out that a large number of Vinnitsa's 36,000 Jews were evacuated eastward at the beginning of the war. The Jews who stayed behind, she found, did so in part because they remembered that German authorities had protected Jews from pogroms after the First World War and believed that they would fare well in German hands. Her own grandfather was one who stayed behind. The Soviet government had confiscated the inn he owned and he believed the Germans would allow him to reopen it. When he made that proposal to the German authorities, he was tied to a horse and dragged through the city to his death.

On 22 September 1941 the SS used the town stadium, across from the public park where NKVD victims were buried, as a gathering and sorting center. Vinokurova estimates the death toll in the massacre that day—the massacre Bingel photographed—as around ten thousand.

The victims of these September mass killings in the Ukraine total about 42,000. There were other massacres in the region that month as well: 8,890 "Jews and Communists" in Kikorino; 22,467 in the Nikolayev area; 1,107 adults and then 561 children by Blobel's Sonderkommando 4a in Radomyshl to reduce "overcrowding"; a thousand people murdered around a well at Kachovka; 920 at Lahoysk with support from the Waffen-SS division Das Reich; the small Nevel ghetto near Minsk cleared of 640 human beings and their houses burned because "scabies broke out"; 1,025 murdered at nearby Janovichi because of "contagious disease," an operation "carried out solely by a commander and twelve men"; 2,278 from the Minsk ghetto in a "screening operation." In Lithuania, Einsatzkommando 3 proudly reported eleven districts *Judenfrei*, bringing the Jäger commando's total as of 19 September 1941, "together with Lithuanian partisans," to 46,692. And the month had not yet come to its bloody end.

TEN

Lords of Life and Death

Heinrich Himmler personally attended a mass execution in Minsk on 15 August 1941, at the end of the Pripet marshes campaign. The previous day he and some of his staff had flown in one of his command Junker 52s to Baranowicze to meet Higher SS and Police Leader Bach-Zelewski and the commander of the SS Cavalry Brigade, Hermann Fegelein. From there the group, which included Himmler's handsome chief of staff, Karl Wolff, traveled on to Minsk, where Himmler spoke to the officers and NCOs of Nebe's Einsatzgruppe B.

After the speech, according to Bach-Zelewski, "Himmler asked Nebe how many prisoners scheduled for execution he had in custody at that moment. Nebe stated a number of around one hundred. The *Reichsführer-SS* then asked if it would cause any 'special difficulties' if these prisoners were executed the next morning. He wanted to observe such a liquidation in order to get an idea of what it was like. He requested that I accompany him together with *Gruppenführer* Wolff." Wolff later claimed to know "from [Himmler's] own mouth" that the Reichsführer-SS had never seen a man killed up to that time. Himmler spent the night in Lenin House, one of the few public buildings still standing in Minsk after Wehrmacht artillery barrages and NKVD arson.

Otto Bradfisch's Einsatzkommando 8 and members of Police Battalion 9 organized the executions the next morning in a forest north of the city. Two pits had been dug in open ground. Bach-Zelewski claimed in his postwar testimony that "the criminals were without exception partisans and their helpers, among which a third to a half were Jews," but Bradfisch testified to the contrary that "the shooting of the Jews was not a matter of destroying elements that represented a threat either to the fighting troops or to the pacification of the field of operations behind the lines; it was simply a matter of destroying Jews for the sake of destroying Jews." Of the victims, whose number Bradfisch estimated as between 120 and 190, two were women—still a new category of victims in mid-August.

Bradfisch claimed to have questioned Himmler before proceeding with the executions, asking him "who was taking responsibility for the mass extermination of the Jews. . . . Himmler answered me in a fairly sharp tone that these orders had come from Hitler as the supreme Führer of the German government, and that they had the force of law." The victims were held inside the forest and brought up to the pits by truck, one group at a time, to face a twelve-man firing squad. Wolff remembered them as "ragged forms, mostly young men." Bach-Zelewski described an unforgettable confrontation between Himmler and one of the victims:

Among the Jews was a young man of perhaps twenty who was blond and blue-eyed. He was already standing in front of the rifle barrels when Himmler intervened. The barrels were lowered; Himmler approached the young man and asked several questions.
"Are you a Jew?"
"Yes."
"Are both your parents Jews?"
"Yes."
"Do you have any ancestors who were not Jews?"
"No."
The Reichsführer stamped his foot and said: "Then even I can't help you."

Bach-Zelewski's version of the massacre conflicts with Bradfisch's. Rather than a stand-up execution, Bradfisch described a *Sardinenpackung:* forcing the victims to lie face down in the pit and shooting down on them from above. Both Wolff and Bach-Zelewski remembered that Himmler was shaken by the murders. "Himmler was extremely nervous," Bach-Zelewski testified. "He couldn't stand still. His face was white as cheese, his eyes went wild and with each burst of gunfire he always looked at the ground."

When the two women were laid down to be murdered, Bach-Zelewski said, "the members of the firing squad lost their nerve" and shot badly; the two women were injured but "did not die immediately." Himmler panicked then. "*Reichsführer* Himmler jumped up and screamed at the squad commander: 'Don't torture these women! Fire! Hurry up and kill them!' "

Immediately after the massacre, Bach-Zelewski claimed, he challenged Himmler to reconsider ordering mass killings:

I said to him, "*Reichsführer,* that was only a hundred!"
"What do you mean by that?"
I answered: "Look at the men, how deeply shaken they are! Such men are finished for the rest of their lives! What kind of followers are we creating? Either neurotics or brutes!"

Himmler was visibly moved, Bach-Zelewski remembered, and impulsively called the men to assemble around him. The Higher SS and Police Leader paraphrases Himmler's speech, which he thought gave a good impression of his superior's "confusion":

> Himmler first wanted to emphasize that he demanded from the men a "repugnant" performance of their duty. He would certainly not be pleased if German men enjoyed doing such work. But it should not disturb their consciences in the slightest, because they were soldiers who were supposed to carry out every order unquestioningly.... He alone bore the responsibility before God and the Führer for that which had to happen.
>
> They surely had noticed that even he was revolted by this bloody activity and had been aroused to the depth of his soul. But he too was obeying the highest law by doing his duty and he was acting from a deep understanding of the necessity of this operation. We should observe nature: everywhere there was war, not only among human beings, but also in the animal and plant worlds. Whatever did not want to fight was destroyed.... Primitive man said that the horse is good, but the bug is bad, or wheat is good but the thistle is bad. Humans characterize that which is useful to them as good, but that which is harmful as bad. Don't bugs, rats and other vermin have a purpose in life to fulfill? But we humans are correct when we defend ourselves against vermin.

The speech as Bach-Zelewski recalled it is hardly confused; it was a speech Himmler had delivered before and would deliver again. It incorporated arguments he had formulated that he hoped would relieve his men of whatever psychological stress they might feel at shooting unarmed victims: that they were only following orders; that the responsibility was not theirs but his and the Führer's; that any repugnance they felt was cause for congratulation, since it affirmed that they were civilized; that life at every level struggled for survival (an argument borrowed from Hitler, who had borrowed it in turn from the social Darwinists and the literature of colonialism); that their victims had purposes of their own and of course wished to live, not to die, but were harmful, were comparable to vermin.

But the experience of actually watching people shot down in cold blood was not something Himmler could so easily shrug off. After the executions he and his party inspected a prisoner-of-war camp. On the way to inspect what Bach-Zelewski calls "a small mental institution close by Minsk" they drove through the ghetto that Nebe had established in the Byelorussian capital, crowded by then with more than eighty thousand Jews. According to Bach-Zelewski, the hospital held "the most severe mental patients"; Himmler ordered Nebe to "release" them—that is, to have them murdered—as soon as possible. That raised the question of how to kill them. "Himmler said that today's event had brought him to the conclusion that death by shooting was certainly not the most humane. Nebe was to think about it and submit a report based on the information he collected." Bach-Zelewski claimed Nebe asked permission to try killing the patients with dynamite. He claimed that he and Wolff both objected, saying the patients were not mere guinea pigs, but Himmler ignored their objections and authorized the experiment.

The Reichsführer-SS spent another night in Lenin House, toured a museum the next day, flew over the Pripet marshes and Pinsk, then returned to Wolfschanze and shared his experiences with Hitler over lunch.

Himmler's panic at the sight of injured women, the firing squad's loss of nerve in the first place at the prospect of having to shoot them and Nebe's concern for his troops (but not for his victims) indicate the difficulties that the SS had to overcome to perpetrate mass murder on the Eastern front during the Second World War. Hitler's executioners may have been willing, but they were not always able. More difficulties emerged as the categories of victims enlarged to include women and children and, eventually, transports of western European Jews. Himmler's response to the Einsatzgruppe execution staged for his benefit in Minsk on 15 August 1941—his "conclusion that death by shooting was certainly not the most humane"—led directly to the development of more impersonal murder technologies; Nebe experimented that autumn not only with dynamite but also with carbon monoxide gas.

The problem of impersonal killing had already been solved at pilot scale within Nazi Germany by exploiting medical technology. Handicapped children began to be killed by medical personnel in Germany in autumn 1939, a program organized secretly out of the Führer Chancellery (KdF) by Himmler's fellow agriculturalist and former driver Viktor Brack, the son of the private physician who had delivered Himmler's daughter Gudrun. In special children's wards in twenty-three state hospitals and clinics, children were killed with barbiturate or opiate overdoses in the form of pills, suppositories or, less frequently, injections. Himmler did not idly select Nebe to experiment with mass-killing techniques; the Einsatzgruppe commander had previous experience. As head of the Central Office of the Reich Detective Forces in 1939 under

Heydrich's Reich Main Security Office, he had arranged to supply Brack's child killers with untraceable supplies of the necessary drugs. The killing of handicapped adults was also organized out of the KdF beginning in autumn 1939; Brack came to manage both programs. The adult program central office took over a confiscated Jewish villa at 4 Tiergarten Strasse in Berlin, resulting in its code name Operation T4, soon abbreviated simply to T4. Murdering adults was not as simple as murdering children. The physicians who did the killing, all volunteers, initially considered using narcotic injections but rejected that slow poisoning as inhumane (more probably, it was unreliable and inconvenient). Other physicians among the killers recommended carbon monoxide, which in pure form is colorless and odorless and which in sufficient concentration is rapidly fatal. "The technology for gassing people had to be invented," notes historian Henry Friedlander. A pilot killing center was constructed in an old jail building in Brandenburg-on-the-Havel, with a gas chamber disguised as a shower room, and a successful demonstration gassing of eight male handicapped patients was conducted probably in later 1939 with several high Nazi officials and physicians present as well as Brack and Stuttgart police officer Christian Wirth, who would later work for Globocnik. "The old prison in Brandenburg on the Havel was history's first operational killing center," Friedlander concludes. T4 eventually established six adult killing centers throughout Germany and Austria, although only four operated at any one time. *Krematorien* (mobile or fixed oil-fired standard mortuary ovens) were acquired to dispose of the bodies and *Knochenmühle* (bone mills) to pulverize the burned bones. When the T4 program was paused late in August 1941, this unique technology and, perhaps more significantly, the personnel who had learned to operate it became available for mass-killing operations in the East.

In September 1941, having ordered up a chemist, Albert Widmann, from the Criminal Technology Institute in Berlin, Nebe conducted his dynamite experiment in Minsk. He justified it to his deputy, Paul Werner, with the argument that "he could not ask his troops to shoot these incurably insane people." Nebe had Widmann rig a pillbox—a reinforced-concrete machine-gun emplacement—with dynamite, lock the Russian mental patients inside and detonate the dynamite. The experiment was not a success: the dynamite destroyed both the victims and the pillbox, catapulting body parts in every direction, and the experimenters had to retrieve arms and legs from the surrounding trees.

The next day, moving to a mental hospital in Mogilev, Nebe continued experimenting. Pure carbon monoxide gas was too expensive for mass killing on the Einsatzgruppen scale; Nebe had decided to generate the gas using an automobile engine. Widmann described the procedure at his postwar trial:

> During the afternoon Nebe had the window [of a hospital room] bricked in, leaving two openings for the gas hose. . . . When we arrived, one of the hoses that I had brought was connected. It was fixed onto the exhaust of a touring car. . . . Pieces of piping stuck out of the holes made in the wall, onto which the hose could easily be fitted. . . . After five minutes Nebe came out and said that nothing appeared to have happened. After eight minutes he had been unable to detect any results and asked what should be done next. Nebe and I came to the conclusion that the car was not powerful enough. So Nebe had the second hose fitted onto a transport vehicle belonging to the regular police. It then took only another few minutes before the people were unconscious. Both vehicles were left running for about another ten minutes.

Nebe presumably communicated his results back to Himmler, and that same month, September 1941, a Reich Security Main Office department head named Walter Rauff asked the head of the RSHA transportation service to look into the possibility of remodeling a closed truck into a mobile gas chamber. The reason, Rauff later testified, was to find a way to relieve "the psychological stress felt by the men involved in the [Einsatzgruppen] shootings." Gas vans had already been used by the Lange commando in Poland in 1940, of course. Those had been charged with pure bottled carbon monoxide, but the basic idea of a mobile gas chamber would not have been new to the SS leadership. Blobel testified that Sonderkommando 4a received one of the new exhaust-charged gas vans from Einsatzgruppe C headquarters and used it to carry out an execution "in September or October 1941"; use of such a gas van is documented at Poltava, in the southern Ukraine, in November 1941.

The notorious gas chambers and crematoria of the death camps have come to typify the Holocaust, but in fact they were exceptional. The primary means of mass murder the Nazis deployed during the Second World War was firearms and lethal privation. Shooting was not less efficient than gassing, as many historians have assumed. It was harder on the shooters' nerves, and the gas vans and chambers alleviated the burden. But shooting began earlier, continued throughout the war and produced far more victims if Slavs are counted, as they must be, as well as Jews. "The Nazi regime was the most genocidal the world has ever seen," writes sociologist Michael Mann. "During its short twelve years (overwhelmingly its last four) it killed approximately twenty million unarmed persons. . . . Jews comprised only a third of the victims and their mass murder occurred well into the sequence. . . . Slavs, defined as *Untermenschen,* were the most numerous victims—3 million Poles, 7 million Soviet citizens and 3.3 million Soviet POWs." Even among Jewish victims, Daniel Goldhagen estimates, "somewhere between 40 and 50 percent" were killed "by means other than gassing, and more Germans were involved in these killings in a greater variety of contexts than in those carried out in the gas chambers."

So the Nazi hecatomb was not "modern" and "scientific," as it is frequently characterized, nor was it unique in human history. It was accomplished with the same simple equipment as the slaughters of European imperialism and, later, Asian and African civil war. State-sponsored massacre is a complex and recurring social epidemic. Understanding how its perpetrators learn to cope with its challenges is one important part of understanding how to prevent or limit further outbreaks, and no twentieth-century slaughter is better documented than the Third Reich's.

To begin with, how were perpetrators chosen? Were they "ordinary men," as Christopher Browning and, from a different perspective, Goldhagen have asserted? The question misses the point. If people only become capable of committing serious acts of violence voluntarily and without debilitating trauma by undergoing violent socialization, as Lonnie Athens's research confirms, then the right question to ask about the SS's choice of perpetrators is, Did they have previous experience with serious violence? Mann analyzed the largest sample of perpetrator biographies yet assembled, "of 1,581 men and women involved in the Nazi genocide," and concluded that "they resemble 'Real Nazis' [i.e., fanatic Nazis] more than they do 'Ordinary Germans.' " For 90 percent of Mann's sample (excluding Sudeten Germans, women and foreign ethnic Germans), "two-thirds were long-term Nazis, a third had been prewar extremists and 'careers' in violence were common. Perpetrators came disproportionately from 'core Nazi constituencies.' The more committed Nazis were of higher rank and longer experience—bringing the pressures of hierarchy and comradeship to bear on newer recruits." Of the 311 Einsatzgruppen members in Mann's sample, "only 14 had been [only] raw recruits, only 21 had been policemen and 6 had served only in the *Waffen-SS;* 76 had only been Nazi or SS members, 144 had been Nazis and policemen and 48 were Nazis and had served in a [concentration] camp or the T4 [euthanasia murder] program." Even within Police Battalion 101, the unit that was the subject of Browning's book *Ordinary Men* and that Goldhagen revisited in *Hitler's Willing Executioners* to challenge Browning's interpretation of the men's behavior, Mann found four signs . . . that things might actually have been a little out of the ordinary. First, 38% of the policemen were Nazi Party members, which was double the membership level among all German men at this time. . . . Second, the higher the rank, the higher the proportion of Nazis. . . . Third, this was a battalion whose main officers, NCOs and the more experienced lower-ranking enlisted men were career policemen: 20% had several years experience of policing, and since their average age was 39, most would have only had experience policing in a Nazi state—obviously not a training in genocide, but police work without effective limitation or regulation by the law. Fourth, the worse the complicity in genocide [as measured by postwar convictions for war crimes], the more these tendencies appeared.

And Battalion 101, Mann adds (paraphrasing a German historian), "was probably less Nazi, less steeped in violence than other police battalions formed from career policemen and volunteers and serving in Poland in 1939." The SS needed large numbers of killers on the Eastern front, Mann points out, more men than Himmler or Heydrich could personally vet as they had vetted the dossiers of the men to be assigned to the Einsatzgruppen; they "must have thought that reserve police battalions would provide relatively pliable instruments: the German police forces were already bent to the will of the Nazi state, had often killed civilians in Poland already and were likely to contain a disproportionate number of Nazis. This was not quite so ordinary a bunch of Germans."

So a higher percentage of men with previous experience with serious violence was probably recruited into Daluege's police battalions than historians searching for an explanation of their willing participation in atrocities have recognized. Indeed, a minimal qualification for police work anywhere is willingness and capacity to use serious violence at least when seriously provoked. Einsatzgruppen members, many of whom had previous experience in Poland, were even more likely to have been fully violently socialized by the time they were recruited.

They were then indoctrinated, which included violent coaching. At Pretzsch, and repeatedly later on by Einsatzgruppen commanders, Higher SS and Police Leaders and even by Himmler himself, the men were coached in their fundamental responsibility to obey orders, including violent orders. Höss, the Auschwitz commandant, though not an Einsatzgruppen officer, underwent comparable indoctrination and described it candidly after the war to the American psychologist G. M. Gilbert:

> We were all so trained to obey orders without even thinking that the thought of disobeying an order would simply never have occurred to

anybody and somebody else would have done just as well if I hadn't. . . . Himmler was so strict about little things, and executed SS men for such small offenses, that we naturally took it for granted that he was acting according to a strict code of honor. . . . You can be sure that it was not always a pleasure to see those mountains of corpses and smell the continual burning. — But Himmler had ordered it and had even explained the necessity and I really never gave much thought to whether it was wrong. It just seemed a necessity.

Of the order he received from Himmler in mid-July 1941 to prepare Auschwitz for mass killing, Höss told Gilbert:

It was always stressed that if Germany was to survive then World Jewry must be exterminated and we all accepted it as truth. That was the picture I had in my head, so, when Himmler called me to him, I just accepted it as the realization of something I had already accepted — not only I, but everybody. I took it so much for granted that even though this order, which would move the strongest and coldest nature — and at that moment this crass order to exterminate thousands of people (I did not know then how many) — even though it did frighten me momentarily — it fitted in with all that had been preached to me for years. The problem itself, the extermination of Jewry, was not new — but only that I was to be the one to carry it out, frightened me at first. But after getting the clear direct order and even an explanation with it — there was nothing left but to carry it out.

The realization by the rank and file of the Einsatzgruppen and Order Police that they were to be the ones to carry out the killings often frightened them at first as well. But as police battalion member Kurt Möbius testified at a postwar trial, the indoctrination they received helped prepare the men to push through any fright they might feel:

I would also like to say that it did not at all occur to me that these orders could be unjust. It is true that I know that it is also the duty of the police to protect the innocent, but I was then of the conviction that the Jews were not innocent but guilty. I believed the propaganda that all Jews were criminals and subhumans and that they were the cause of Germany's decline after the First World War. The thought that one should disobey or evade the order to participate in the extermination of the Jews did not therefore enter my mind at all.

The Einsatzgruppen and Order Police perpetrated their mass murders not in Germany but in territory the Wehrmacht had occupied in Poland and the Soviet Union. They operated away from home under quasi-military conditions, beyond the range of domestic public opinion and outside the bounds of domestic morality other than whatever personal morality they carried within them. No German police or judges watched over their shoulders to challenge SS authority, which they knew derived directly from the Führer, and the lands they scoured had surrendered sovereignty, and thus legal prerogative, to the invaders. The Wehrmacht looked the other way when it was not actually complicitous. The Einsatzgruppen were judge, jury and executioner all in one; anyone who even looked at them sideways, as Hitler had crowed, they could shoot.

Most of the people they were ordered to kill were different from them: came from different cultures, spoke different languages, often lived more rudely than they, dressed differently, were colored and featured differently, differently shorn (some of Himmler's SS noblemen found amusement sawing off and even burning off Jewish beards). Gendarmerie Master Fritz Jacob, writing from Kamenets-Podolsky in the summer of 1942 to a Wehrmacht lieutenant general who was a friend of his family, characterized the people he and his men were murdering this way:

> I do not know whether you too, Herr Lieutenant General, saw such frightful Jewish types in Poland. I thank my lucky stars that I've now seen this mixed race for what it is. Then if life is kind to me I'll have something to pass on to my children. Sick with venereal disease, cripples and idiots were the norm. Materialists to the last in spite of everything. Every one of them without exception said things like, "We're specialists, you're not going to shoot us, are you?" These were not human beings but ape people.

Similarly, Blobel, questioned at his Nuremberg trial by the president of the tribunal, revealed that he had eased his conscience by belittling the stoicism or realistic fatalism of Sonderkommando 4a's victims:

> JUDGE MICHAEL MUSMANNO: Did you ever have any experience with the victims being recalcitrant as they were being led to the grave, attempting to break away, or was there any demonstration or any attempted struggle?
>
> BLOBEL: I could never observe . . . that there was resistance. They were well guarded, and Eastern men get over things so very quickly and I was always surprised at that. . . . It was quite unbelievable for us Germans.
>
> MUSMANNO: You mean that they resigned themselves easily to what was awaiting them?

BLOBEL: Yes, that was the case. That was the case with these people. Human life was not as valuable as it was with us. They did not care so much. They did not know their own human value.

MUSMANNO: In other words, they went to their death quite happily?

BLOBEL: I would not say that they were happy. They knew what was going to happen to them. Of course, they were told what was going to happen to them and they were resigned to their fate and that is the strange thing about these people in the East.

Humiliation, overcrowding, starvation, fear, denial of medicines and medical care, boundless and debilitating grief widened the apparent distance between the murderers and their victims, making killing them easier.

In contrast to the moral and legal darkness that shrouded the mass killing on the Eastern front, reducing pressure on the killers, the T4 euthanasia murder program inside Germany gradually came to be exposed to public scrutiny. As a result, on 24 August 1941, after at least seventy thousand handicapped and mentally ill German citizens had been murdered, Hitler ordered the gassing program stopped (although the covert killing of German children and handicapped adults by lethal injection continued, bringing the "euthanasia" total by the end of the war to more than two hundred thousand). "Popular history and special pleading have credited the opposition by the churches with this abrogation of the killing operation," Friedlander writes. "But Hitler was probably pushed to issue his so-called stop order primarily by widespread public knowledge about the killings and far less by church opposition, an opposition that merely reflected general popular disquiet about the way euthanasia was implemented." Friedlander adds that while "the organizers of the killings could disregard the protest of the churches, they had to neutralize the [German] judiciary if they hoped to continue the killing program." Hitler had no such problem where non-Germans in occupied territory were concerned; the writ of the German judiciary did not extend so far.

Despite these efforts of ideological, social and psychological preparation, many of the men assigned to mass killing found it difficult to do. Holocaust survivors and historians have often (and understandably) greeted assertions of such difficulty with skepticism and contempt, but the evidence is sufficiently widespread and detailed to be credible. And surely any indication that slaughter is challenging and takes it toll on the slaughterers ought to be welcomed, if only as ironic justice. Dismissing perpetrators as inhuman monsters rather than human criminals positions genocidal killing beyond comprehension, beyond prevention or repair.

Blobel, continuing his exchange with Judge Musmanno, testified to the difficulty his men experienced at the beginning—testimony cankered by his continued belittling of the victims:

MUSMANNO: And did that make the job easier for you, the fact that they did not resist?

BLOBEL: In any case, the guards never met any resistance. . . . Everything went very quietly. It took time, of course, and I must say that our men who took part in these executions suffered more from nervous exhaustion than those who had to be shot.

MUSMANNO: In other words, your pity was more for the men who had to shoot than for the victims?

BLOBEL: Our men had to be cared for.

MUSMANNO: And how were they cared for? Did you have nurses along to cheer them up in this task that they had to perform? In what way were they cared for?

BLOBEL: The people had to be told before these executions about the crimes of the executees, why they had been sentenced. They were told about these facts and that the order . . . was the death sentence and that they had to carry out these orders by actually shooting these people. These men of our commandos—where did they come from? They came from all classes of the population. One was a criminologist. One had a free-lance profession. One had been a merchant. They had never shot anybody before and for these people it was something quite unusual.

MUSMANNO: And you felt very sorry for them?

BLOBEL: Yes, these people experienced a lot, psychologically.

If many of the men of the Einsatzgruppen and the Order Police were experienced killers, others were novices, as were perhaps a larger number of young Waffen-SS fresh from training. Men under command observation who have not been fully violently socialized can pull the trigger and kill when ordered to do so, but those without sufficient violent experience are likely to break down just as people break down following other traumatic social experiences for which they are unprepared.

Even among persons with violent experience, there is a sharp and commonly recognized distinction (recognized by police and military authorities and in the law, as well as in Athens's findings) between those who use violence only defensively and those who use it without provocation, instrumentally and even expressively. These three kinds of perpetrators—novice, defensive and malefic—can all be identified among Einsatzgruppen, Waffen-SS and Order Police operatives. Browning, looking at reserve police battalions, similarly identifies three types: a "significant core of eager and enthusiastic killers . . . who required no process of gradual brutalization to accustom themselves to their murderous task"; "a middle group that followed orders and complied with standard procedures but did not evince any eagerness to kill Jews"; and "a significant minority of men who did not participate in the shooting of Jews" and whose "nonparticipation was both tolerated and brushed aside as inconsequential." Einsatzgruppen members could not so easily choose not to participate, since mass killings were their primary duty. As SS members they were volunteers, however.

Obersturmführer Albert Hartl, head of the staffing section of Einsatzgruppe C under Rasch's successor Max Thomas, clearly distinguished the two extreme types (malefic and novice) in his postwar trial testimony:

> *SS-Gruppenführer* Thomas was a doctor by profession; he was very preoccupied with the psychological repercussions of the *Einsatz* on his people. From my conversations with him I know that these effects took many different forms. There were people whose participation awakened in them the most evil sadistic impulses. For example, the head of one firing squad made several hundred Jews of all ages, male and female, strip naked and run through a field into a wood. He then had them mown down with machine-gun fire. He even photographed the whole proceedings. . . . [Participation] also had the reverse effect on some of the SS men detailed to the firing squads. These men were overcome with uncontrollable fits of crying and suffered health breakdowns. Thomas once told me that a very common manifestation in members of these firing squads was temporary impotence. It also happened that one member of the *Einsatzgruppe* who had participated in mass shootings one night suddenly succumbed to a type of mental derangement and began to shoot wildly about him, killing and wounding several men*. . . . A number of SS officers and men were sent back to serve at home "on account of their great weakness."

A staff officer with Einsatzgruppe A in Riga reported similar problems. "After the first wave of shootings," the officer testified, "it emerged that the men, particularly the officers, could not cope with the demands made on them. Many abandoned themselves to alcohol, many suffered nervous breakdowns and psychological illnesses; for example we had suicides and there were cases where some men cracked up and shot wildly around them and completely lost control."

---

*Recalling Blobel's comparable berserk menacing of the men trying to control him during his early breakdown.

A German war correspondent stationed on a minesweeper in the harbor at Liepaja, Latvia, in July 1941 described witnessing a massacre and observing both extremes: "I saw SD personnel weeping because they could not cope mentally with what was going on. Then again I encountered others who kept a score sheet of how many people they had sent to their death."

With the order in late July 1941 to begin killing women and children, which made it more difficult to rationalize the killing as the defensive execution of enemy partisans, some defensive killers also broke down. Robert Barth, a member of Einsatzkommando 10b (Einsatzgruppe D), witnessed such behavior during a mass killing at Cherson, in the Ukraine, on 20 September 1941:

> About six kilometers from Cherson there was an anti-tank ditch. The Jews, among them women, children and old men, were brought up to the ditch in trucks. There they had to surrender their valuables and good clothing, then they were driven into the ditch where murder commandos had been posted to shoot the unfortunate victims. For the most part, *Waffen-SS,* regular police, Russian auxiliaries and members of the security service of the Gestapo and criminal police were employed for these shootings. Ghastly scenes took place during these shootings. Several members of the killer gangs had to be relieved, as their nerves had broken down completely. Even before they had started on their sanguinary jobs, the killer gangs were issued liquor and cigarettes before carrying out the shootings.

The SS leaders tolerated breakdown more than excess. From afar, such a distinction seems absurd: If the idea was to kill Jews, why would Himmler not welcome initiative and enthusiasm? Answering that question invokes the long history of what the sociologist Norbert Elias called "the civilizing process." European society in medieval times and earlier had been dominated by malefically violent nobles who enforced their authority with serious physical violence, which they took pleasure in and celebrated. Homicide rates in medieval Europe even among commoners, who settled their disputes privately with little local interference from the law, were twenty to fifty times as high as in modern Europe. Violence declined across seven hundred years of Western history as monarchs moved to monopolize violence in order to monopolize taxation and thereby limit the power of the nobility and as an emerging middle class sought protection in official justice from the burden of settling disputes at personal risk. Social controls over violence, primarily increasing access to courts of law, developed in parallel with changes in child-rearing practices away from physical brutalization.

The criminal justice system vividly demonstrated this transformation. When official justice began to take control it advertised its authority with public torture and executions, spectacles attended by enthusiastic crowds. As private violence declined—that is, as populations were socialized to less personally violent identities—people lost their taste for such spectacles. Punishment retreated behind institutional walls. The nature of punishment transformed as well. Michel Foucault summarizes that transformation:

> The body now [comes to serve] as an instrument or intermediary: if one intervenes upon it to imprison it, or to make it work, it is in order to deprive the individual of a liberty that is regarded both as a right and as property. The body, according to this penalty, is caught up in a system of constraints and privations, obligations and prohibitions. Physical pain, the pain of the body itself, is no longer the constituent element of the penalty. From being an art of unbearable sensations punishment has become an economy of suspended rights.

By the twentieth century in western Europe, the civilizing process had reached the point where, with the exception of small numbers of officials trained in torture, only violent criminals were prepared to use unprovoked serious violence, and such behavior (which had been normal upper-class conduct in the medieval world) was considered to be deviant and even pathological.

The Wehrmacht, for example, as Raul Hilberg points out, distinguished clearly between malefic and defensive behavior in making its men available to assist at Einsatzgruppen atrocities, and strongly censured malefic "excesses":

> There was an overall objection that was rooted in the whole psychology of the destruction process. The killing of the Jews was regarded as historical necessity. The soldier had to "understand" this. If for any reason he was instructed to help the SS and police in their task, he was expected to obey orders. However, if he killed the Jews spontaneously, voluntarily, or without instruction, merely because he wanted to kill, then he committed an abnormal act . . . dangerous to the discipline and prestige of the German army. Herein lay the crucial difference between the man who "overcame" himself to kill and one who wantonly committed atrocities. The former was regarded as a good soldier and a true Nazi; the latter was a person without self-control, who would be a danger to his community after his return home.

Himmler similarly distinguished between obedient killing and spontaneous excess, though it is not at all clear that his subordinates were equally punctilious. Barth testified, for example, that "*SS-Obersturmbannführer* Zeezen, leader of *EK* 10a, was referred to as particularly brutal. He is said to have boasted that his commando had shot the most Jews. It was also told that at one time in the course of executions of Jews when the commando ran out of ammunition the Jews were thrown alive into a well about thirty meters deep."

Ohlendorf claimed to have been especially alert to the passage of his men from defensive to malefic violence and to have attempted to prevent that maleficence from spreading through the group:

> My mission was to see to it that this general order for executions would be carried out as humanly as conditions would permit. Therefore, I gave orders for the manner of carrying out these executions. These orders had as their purpose to make it as easy as possible for the unfortunate victim and to prevent the [development of] brutality in the men [which] would lead to inevitable excesses. Thus I directed first that only so many victims should be brought to the place of execution as the execution commandos could handle. Any individual action by any individual man was forbidden. The *Einsatzkommandos* shot in a military manner only upon orders. It was strictly ordered to avoid any mistreatment; undressing was not permitted. The taking of any personal possessions was not permitted. Publicity was not permitted, and *at the very moment when it was noted that a man had experienced joy in carrying out these executions it was ordered that this man may never participate in any more executions* [emphasis added].

Besides the rationalizations incorporated into his speeches, Himmler found other ways to relieve his subordinates of their burdens so that they could continue to kill. At the early massacres in Bialystok, Browning reports, "the shooters were rewarded with an unusual treat of strawberries and cream." The Einsatzgruppe A staff officer who described breakdowns in Riga scoffed at one of Himmler's measures:

> When [these breakdowns] happened Himmler issued an order stating that any man who no longer felt able to take the psychological stresses should report to his superior officer. These men were to be released from their current duties and would be detailed for other work back home. As I recall, Himmler even had a convalescent home set up close to Berlin for such cases. This order was issued in writing; I read and filed it myself. . . . In my view this whole order was an evil trick; I do

not think I would be wrong to say it bordered on the malicious—for after all, which officer or SS man would have shown himself up in such a way? Any officer who had declared that he was too weak to do such things would have been considered unfit to be an officer.

With Hitler's authorization to expand the killing in the East to include women and children, Himmler ordered the formation of native auxiliaries that were expendable and thus could relieve his Germans of the worst of the dirty work. By November 1941, according to a German observer, Himmler had established mental hospitals and rest areas "where SS men are cared for who have broken down while executing women and children." Following his own experience of mass killing in Minsk in August 1941, the Reichsführer-SS had also begun exploring less personal methods of mass killing. August Becker, who worked on the development of gas vans, testified to the connection later in the year:

> Himmler wanted to deploy people who had become available as a result of the suspension of the euthanasia program, and who, like me, were specialists in extermination by gassing, for the large-scale gassing operations in the East which were just beginning. The reason for this was that the men in charge of the *Einsatzgruppen* in the East were increasingly complaining that the firing squads could not cope with the psychological and moral stress of the mass shootings indefinitely. I know that a number of members of these squads were themselves committed to mental asylums and for this reason a new and better method of killing had to be found. Thus in December 1941 I started working in [the RSHA, where my superior] explained the situation to me, saying that the psychological and moral stress on the firing squads was no longer bearable and that therefore the gassing program had been started.

But the complaints made Himmler impatient, caught as he was on the horns of a dilemma: How to accomplish the Führer's order to exterminate the Jews while preserving his SS men's civility, their "repugnance"; how to keep them from becoming, as Bach-Zelewski phrased it, either neurotics or brutes. His own truncated violent socialization left him concerned to find a way to exterminate an entire people while remaining within the bounds of what Foucault calls "suspended rights" (death being the ultimate suspension of rights): to orchestrate a genocide but remain "civilized." His frustration is apparent in a secret order he issued on 12 December 1941 to all his Higher SS and Police Leaders:

> Our assigned duty, to guarantee the security, peace and order of the districts entrusted to us, above all the rear area behind the German

front lines, requires that we eliminate every pocket of resistance and deliver the enemies of the German people mercilessly to their just execution.

It is the holy duty of senior leaders and commanders *personally* to ensure that none of our men who have to fulfill this burdensome duty should ever be brutalized or suffer damage to their spirit and character in doing so. This task is to be fulfilled through the strictest discipline in the execution of official duties and through comradely gatherings in the evenings of those days which have included such difficult tasks. The comradely gathering must on no account, however, end in the abuse of alcohol. It should be an evening on which—as far as possible—they sit and eat at table in the best German domestic style, and music, lectures and introductions to the beauties of German intellectual and emotional life occupy the hours.

To relieve men at the appropriate point from such difficult missions, send them on leave or transfer them to other absorbing and fulfilling tasks—possibly even to another area—I regard as important and urgent.

I wish it to be understood as well, however, that it fundamentally remains valid that it is impermissible and improper to discuss facts and related numbers or even to mention them. *Orders and duties necessary for the existence of a* Volk *must be carried out. This material is unsuited to subsequent discussion or conversation.*

In practice, Himmler's *gemütlich* evenings were drunken more often than not. "Despite the mental anguish that the killing often aroused," writes historian Konrad Kwiet of Police Battalion 322, which was active in Lithuania, "a festive atmosphere surrounded the murders. In Gargzdai, Kretinga and Palanga, coveted schnapps rations were distributed following each *Judenaktion,* and as a lasting memento group photographs were taken. Jovial and noisy gatherings often took place in the evenings, with local inns celebrating Lithuanian 'sakustas,' or prebooked and prepaid (typically with Jewish money) dinner parties.... Within the framework of *seelische Betreuung* (pastoral care), social get-togethers in the evenings as well as excursions and other forms of entertainment took place in order to wipe out the impressions of the day." In such shared experience the violent coaching, social bonding and acknowledgments of violent reputation necessary to socialize men to full maleficence could flourish.

Ultimately, men either broke down or they adjusted and adapted. They were anything but civilized. They demonstrate that the sum of violence available to a modern, "civilized" nation-state is at least as extravagant as it was in barbaric ages (as did the nineteenth-century colonialism on which Hitler modeled his policy of *Lebensraum*). But most of the killers became at least the hard-eyed men of Himmler's vision, malefic but obedient. Himmler's fantasy was not fulfilled, however; they did not remain uncorrupted. "Members of the [border police] were, with a few exceptions, quite happy to take part in shootings of Jews," a Krakow police official testified. "They had a ball! . . . Nobody failed to turn up [for such assignments]. . . . I want to repeat that people today [i.e., after the war] give a false impression when they say that the actions against the Jews were carried out unwillingly. There was great hatred against the Jews; it was revenge, and they wanted money and gold. Don't let's kid ourselves, there was always something up for grabs during the Jewish actions. Everywhere you went there was always something for the taking. The poor Jews were brought in, the rich Jews were fetched and their homes were scoured." While Himmler himself, as late as January 1942, was still dithering over whether to have a transport of Jews from western Europe shot in Riga or to "chase them into the swamp somewhere," some of his minions—how many has never been determined—opened new departments in Hitler's hell by choosing to become killers malefic to a degree unimaginable outside of genocides.

"There was, for example," writes historian Leon Poliakov, "the police constable who afterwards at Lvov used to kill Jewish children to amuse his own children; or another who used to bet that he could cut off the head of a ten-year-old boy with a single saber stroke. . . . We find the interpreter for the superintendent of police in the region of Slonim, one Metzner, using this terrible phrase in his testimony: 'The action was the work of a special SS commando that carried through the exterminations out of idealism, without using schnapps.' " In Trembowla, a survivor remembers, "the Gestapo man, Szklarek, always took part in the actions to liquidate the Jews. Once he ordered a little Jewish girl to lace her shoe, and when the child bent down, he shot her." Nor has malefic violence ever found plainer expression—and explanation—than in this testimony of SS-Hauptsturmführer Lothar Heimbach, one of Ohlendorf's supposedly proper and military killers in Einsatzgruppe D: "A man is the lord over life and death when he gets an order to shoot three hundred children—and he kills at least one hundred fifty himself."

ELEVEN

Babi Yar

Kiev fell on 19 September 1941.

"Hold it at all costs," Stalin had ordered Budënny. The dull-witted marshal had positioned more than a half million men in trenches and dugouts in its suburbs to defend it. But the Luftwaffe had dominated the air, and the Wehrmacht had beaten its way past Uman, wheeled von Kleist's Panzergruppe around from the south, wheeled Heinz Guderian's Panzergruppe down from the north and encircled the city on its bluff above the Dnieper with a deadly ring of steel. Bombs and artillery barrages had destroyed its suburbs. "The whole horizon had been lit up by flashes and fire," twelve-year-old Anatoli Kuznetsov saw from his family's house on the western outskirts of the city. Then silence had replaced the din of cannons and air-raid sirens and the boy had noticed "the men of the Red Army in their faded khaki uniforms . . . running in twos and threes through the courtyards and across the back gardens." The Wehrmacht took Kiev itself largely intact, a city twelve centuries old graced with Parisian boulevards and gilded onion-domed churches, luxurious with chestnut and linden trees glowing yellow in the gathering autumn.

Truckloads of German troops rolled into the city, columns of soldiers riding bicycles, teams of bay draft horses pulling artillery. Officers lounged at ease in open motorcars. The Germans dragooned men and women to clear away the barricades that blocked the broad avenues. They moved into the offices and hotels along the Kreshchatik, Kiev's fashionable main street, formed out of one of the many wide ravines, or *yars,* that centuries of runoff had cut down through the right bank of the Dnieper. Since the departing NKVD had blown up the power stations and water treatment plant, the Germans parked generator sets along the Kreshchatik for electricity and brought up tanker trucks filled with water from the river.

The first building to explode, on 20 September 1941, was the citadel where the Wehrmacht artillery staff was quartered. The artillery commanding general and his chief of staff were killed in the explosion. The Germans thought a delayed-action fuse had set off the explosives, but four days later the headquarters of the Wehrmacht field commander at the corner of Kreshchatik and Proreznaya exploded with such force that windows were blown out blocks away. The explosion set the building afire. As the Germans were seizing and beating anyone they happened to find in the vicinity, a second large explosion reduced the structure to rubble and dusted the Kreshchatik white. A third explosion blew up the offices across the street and started panic.

Explosions up and down the Kreshchatik continued throughout the night and intermittently for several days. The Soviets had stored crates of Molotov cocktails in the upper stories of buildings to defend the city and left them behind when they abandoned it; the explosions shattered the glass bottles and spilled jellied gasoline across the floors that ignited and poured down stairwells to fuel raging fires. "The Germans cordoned off the whole of the center of the city," Kuznetsov remembers. "But the fire was spreading: the two parallel streets, Pushkin and Mering, were already ablaze, as were the streets which crossed the Kreshchatik — Proreznaya, Institute, Karl Marx, Friedrich Engels and the Arcade. It seemed as though the whole city was being blown up."

On 17 September 1941 Paul Blobel had left behind in Zhitomir the men of the Sonderkommando 4a orderly room with the commando's kitchen and vehicle repair equipment and had marched toward Kiev with two commandos of Police Regiment South and his Ukrainian auxiliaries. His Vorkommando* of fifty men entered Kiev with the 29th Army Corps on 19 September; Blobel arrived on 24 September and the Einsatzgruppe C group staff followed the next day. Between his arrival and 28 September 1941 he reported the conditions in Kiev to Berlin, his training as an architect informing his comments:

The ensuing fire has not yet been extinguished. Fire in the center of the town. Very valuable buildings destroyed. So far, firefighting practically without effect. Demolitions by blasting being carried out to bring the fire under control. Fire in the immediate neighborhood of this office. Had to be evacuated for this reason. . . . Blasts continuing. . . . Up to now, 670 mines detected in buildings, according to a mine-laying plan which was discovered: all public buildings and squares are mined. . . . Buildings being searched most assiduously. . . . In the Lenin Museum, 1,000 pounds of dynamite discovered which were to be touched off by radio. It was repeatedly observed that fires broke out the moment buildings were taken over.

*Advance commando.

In a more extensive report a week later Blobel would acknowledge that "there exists in Kiev a Red sabotage battalion as well as numerous members of the NKVD and of the Communist Party who have orders to commit continuous acts of sabotage," but inevitably he found it convenient to blame the mining of the Kreshchatik on the Jews: "As has been proved, Jews played a preeminent part. Allegedly 150,000 Jews living here. Verification of these statements has not been possible yet. During the first action, 1,600 arrests were made and measures undertaken for the arrest of all the Jews. Execution of at least 50,000 Jews is anticipated."

Historians, crediting Blobel's claims, have presented the executions that followed in Kiev as retaliatory. The justification was nothing more than the usual window dressing; the Jews of Kiev would have been murdered anyway. Jeckeln's massacre of 23,600 refugees at Kamenets-Podolsky was a month old, and Ohlendorf's Einsatzgruppe D was busy slaughtering 22,467 "Jews and Communists" in the Nikolayev area, near Odessa, 250 miles south of Kiev, even as Blobel was radioing his report.

Anatoli Kuznetsov saw the notice, "printed on cheap gray wrapping paper," posted throughout Kiev on 28 September 1941, and checked its wording, years later, in the Central State Archives in Moscow. As a twelve-year-old it made him shudder:

> All Yids living in the city of Kiev and its vicinity are to report by 8 o'clock on the morning of Monday, 29 September 1941, at the corner of Melnikovsky and Dokhturov Streets* (near the cemetery). They are to take with them documents, money, valuables, as well as warm clothes, underwear, etc.
>
> Any Yid not carrying out this instruction and who is found elsewhere will be shot.
>
> Any civilian entering apartments evacuated by Yids and stealing property will be shot.

"This summons was posted all over town by members of the newly-organized Ukrainian militia," Blobel reported to Berlin. "At the same time it was passed around by word of mouth that all the Jews in Kiev were to be resettled."

"They started arriving while it was still dark," Kuznetsov remembers of that cold, windy Monday morning, "to be in good time to get seats in

---

*"There were no such streets in Kiev," Kuznetsov comments, ". . . whereas Melnikov and Degtyarev Streets did exist. The order had obviously been written by the Germans themselves with the help of bad translators."

the train." The ordinary Jews of Kiev believed that the Germans intended to deport them, especially since the assembly point was near the Lukyanovka railway freight yards. Word of the massacres to the west and in Poland had not reached many of them; the Soviet government had suppressed information about the Nazi treatment of the Jews during the period of the Nazi-Soviet Pact, and the confusion of war had limited communications after Barbarossa. Most of the people young Kuznetsov saw were poor, old, invalid—"sick and unfortunate," he says; many women and children walked to the assembly point unaccompanied. Able-bodied Jewish men had been drafted into the Red Army and anyone with money or influence had been evacuated eastward. People carried "bundles roughly tied together with string, worn-out cases made from plywood, woven baskets, boxes of carpenters' tools.... Some elderly women were wearing strings of onions hung around their necks like gigantic necklaces—food supplies for the journey."

"Families baked bread for the journey," Soviet journalist Lev Ozerov writes, summarizing eyewitness testimony, "sewed knapsacks, rented wagons and two-wheeled carts. Old men and women supported each other while mothers carried their babies in their arms or pushed baby carriages. People were carrying sacks, packages, suitcases, boxes." Some of them sang, moving through the streets in the brisk early morning. Russians and Ukrainians, friends and relatives, saw their neighbors off, waved from windows. "There were plenty of people on Turgenyev Street," an eyewitness told Kuznetsov, "and Artem Street was completely jammed. People with bundles, with prams, all sorts of trolleys and carts and even trucks—all standing there, then moving forward a little, then standing still again." They flowed in crowds from their neighborhoods into Melnikov Street on what had been the old Zhitomir road.

Melnikov led past a Jewish cemetery in northwest Kiev, and immediately beyond the Jewish cemetery a mile-long ravine, a yawning pit, dropped away northeastward down to the Dnieper: Babi Yar. The Einsatzgruppen had become expert at picking killing sites; Babi Yar could have swallowed the entire population of Kiev.

Babi Yar—"babushka ravine," "grandmother ravine"—ran through Kuznetsov's neighborhood and had been his childhood playground:

> The ravine was enormous, you might even say majestic: deep and wide, like a mountain gorge. If you stood on one side of it and shouted you would scarcely be heard on the other.
>
> It is situated between three districts of Kiev—Lukyanovka, Kurenyovka and Syrets—surrounded by cemeteries, woods and [garden] allotments. Down at the bottom ran a little stream with clear

water. The sides of the ravine were steep, even overhanging in places; landslides were frequent at Babi Yar.

The explosions and fires had driven Sonderkommando 4a out of its quarters in downtown Kiev. The commando had moved to a stadium near the river, then into the main NKVD building. "The police regiments of the regular police," Blobel would testify, "as well as the militia units of the Higher SS and Police Leader and of the town commandant, had marched in and were used in combating the fire, and also had to remove Russian explosives and road mines. There were thousands of mines on the roads, even in the city itself. The streets were just filled with mines." While Blobel was preoccupied with these problems, Jeckeln had planned the Babi Yar *Aktion* along the same basic lines as the Kamenets-Podolsky massacre. When the first Jews approached the Jewish cemetery on the morning of 29 September 1941, Sonderkommando 4a, two commandos of Police Regiment South and Ukrainian militia were waiting for them.

Coming up Melnikov Street after their two-mile walk from central Kiev, the victims would begin passing the long brick wall of the cemetery. "At that point," Kuznetsov writes, "there was a barbed-wire barrier across the street and anti-tank obstacles, with a passage left between them, and there were rows of Germans wearing badges on their chests as well as Ukrainian police in black uniforms with gray cuffs." A tall Ukrainian in an embroidered shirt with a Cossack mustache gave instructions. A crowd grew in the street before the barrier: people milling, talking, craning to see, children crying, dogs barking somewhere and distant bursts of machine-gun fire. Armed Ukrainians counted out thirty or forty people at a time, watched while they deposited their belongings on the growing pile at streetside and led them through the passage and farther up the street. There, Ozerov reports, "an entire office operation with desks had been set up in an open area." The headquarters staff of Einsatzgruppe C manned the desks, collecting valuables and documents. "The documents were immediately thrown to the ground," Ozerov adds, "and witnesses have testified that the square was covered with a thick layer of discarded papers, torn passports and union identification cards."

Beyond the desks waited a further gauntlet of soldiers with dogs. Kuznetsov describes it as one of the few survivors, Dina Mironovna Pronicheva, a young mother who was an actress with the Kiev Children's Theater, saw it that day:

It was very narrow—some four or five feet across. The soldiers were lined up shoulder to shoulder with their sleeves rolled up, each of them brandishing a truncheon or a club.

Blows rained down on the people as they passed through. There was no question of being able to dodge or get away. Brutal blows, immediately drawing blood, descended on their heads, backs and shoulders from left and right. The soldiers kept shouting: "*Schnell, schnell!*"* laughing happily, as if they were watching a circus act. . . . Everybody started shouting and the women began to scream. It was like a scene in a film; for one brief moment Dina caught sight of a young man she knew from her street, an intelligent, well-dressed boy, sobbing his eyes out.

She saw people falling to the ground. The dogs were immediately set on them. One man managed to pick himself up with a shout, but others remained on the ground while people pressed forward behind them and the crowd carried on, walking on the bodies and trampling them into the ground.

From this funnel into hell they debouched into an open field cordoned by Ukrainian militia—"not local people but from the western Ukraine," says Kuznetsov—piled with separated clothing. The militiamen rushed them. "Get your clothes off! Now! Hurry!" Brutally they ripped the clothes off anyone who hesitated, and kicked and beat them with brass knuckles or clubs. A truck driver named Höfer who was loading clothes saw the disrobing process. "I don't think it was even a minute from the time each Jew took off his coat before he was standing there completely naked," he testified. "Most people put up a fight when they had to undress and there was a lot of screaming and shouting." Kuznetsov thinks "all this was obviously being done so that the great mass of people should not come to their senses. There were many naked people covered in blood."

Beyond the disrobing area, Babi Yar dropped down steeply from the plateau of the green field to the sandy bed of the stream that had eroded the ravine. The Germans had cut entrances into the *yar* side canyons so the victims could descend toward the central channel, which was as wide as a two-lane road. Höfer, the truck driver, describes the killing process, an elaboration of Jeckeln's *Sardinenpackung:*

> Once undressed, the Jews were led into [Babi Yar]. Two or three narrow entrances led to this ravine through which the Jews were channeled. When they reached the bottom of the ravine they were seized by members of the *Schutzpolizei*† and made to lie down on top of Jews who had already been shot. This all happened very quickly.

---

*"Faster, faster!"
†The police battalions.

The corpses were literally in layers. A police marksman came along and shot each Jew in the neck with a submachine gun at the spot where he was lying. When the Jews reached the ravine they were so shocked by the horrifying scene that they completely lost their will. It may even have been that the Jews themselves lay down in rows to wait to be shot. . . .

The moment one Jew had been killed, the marksman would walk across the bodies of the executed Jews to the next Jew, who had meanwhile lain down, and shoot him. It went on this way uninterruptedly, with no distinction being made between men, women and children. The children were kept with their mothers and shot with them.

I only saw this scene briefly. When I got to the bottom of the ravine I was so shocked by the terrible sight that I could not bear to look for long. In the hollow I saw that there were already three rows of bodies lined up over a distance of about two hundred feet. How many layers of bodies there were on top of each other I could not see. I was so astonished and dazed by the sight of the twitching blood-smeared bodies that I could not properly register the details. . . . There was a "packer" at either entrance to the ravine. These "packers" were *Schutzpolizisten* whose job it was to lay the victim on top of the other corpses so that all the marksman had to do as he passed was fire a shot.

When the victims came along the paths to the ravine and at the last moment saw the terrible scene they cried out in terror. But at the very next moment they were already being knocked over by the "packers" and being made to lie down with the others. The next group of people could not see this terrible scene because it took place round a corner.

Höfer saw only two "marksmen" working. The level of bodies and piles of clothes suggest that he saw a late stage of the massacre. Kurt Werner, a member of Sonderkommando 4a, worked the killing floor on the first morning, even before the entrance paths had been cut, and more accurately testifies to the killing system Blobel had organized:

As soon as I arrived at the execution area I was sent down to the bottom of the ravine with some of the other men. It was not long before the first Jews were brought to us over the side of the ravine. The Jews had to lie face down on the earth by the ravine walls. There were three groups of marksmen down at the bottom of the ravine, each made up of about twelve men. Groups of Jews were sent down to each of these execution squads simultaneously. Each successive group of Jews had to lie down on top of the bodies of those that had already been shot. The marksmen stood behind the Jews and killed them with a *Genickschüss.* I still recall today the complete terror of the Jews when they first caught sight of the bodies as they reached the top edge of the ravine. Many Jews cried out in terror. It's almost impossible to imagine what nerves of steel it took to carry out that dirty work down there. It was horrible. . . .

I had to spend the whole morning down in the ravine. For some of the time I had to shoot continuously. Then I was given the job of loading submachine-gun magazines with ammunition. While I was doing that, other comrades were assigned to shooting duty. Towards midday we were called away from the ravine and in the afternoon I, with some of the others up at the top, had to lead the Jews to the ravine. While we were doing this there were other men shooting down in the ravine. The Jews were led by us up to the edge of the ravine and from there they walked down the slope on their own.

When Dina Pronicheva, whose husband was Russian, had reached the disrobing area and realized what was happening at Babi Yar she had shredded her identity card and told a Ukrainian militiaman she had been caught up by accident while seeing someone off. Her Russian name on her other papers convinced the man—she "didn't look at all Jewish," Kuznetsov says ironically or innocently—and the militiaman had moved her aside to wait among a small group of similar unfortunates. They waited all day, watching the bloodied, panicked people emerge from the gauntlet, undress and disappear into the *yar.* Pronicheva especially noticed what the Germans did when mothers tried to hold back with their children: grab the child, drag it screaming to the bluff and throw it over the edge.

At dusk an open car arrived bearing a German officer. He was tall and elegantly uniformed and carried a riding crop—Blobel? He questioned the Ukrainians about the group, a crowd by now, perhaps fifty people. Our own people, the Ukrainians explained. "Shoot the lot at once!" Pronicheva heard the officer shout. "If even one of them gets out of here and starts talking in the city, not a single Jew will turn up tomorrow."

The militiamen forced the group down into a side canyon. It opened onto Babi Yar well above the ravine floor. Pronicheva saw German soldiers at a bonfire, making coffee. She saw the carnage of bodies below. Before or after one of the soldiers began shooting—at different times she remembered the moment differently—she fell into the masses of the dead and lay still.

"All around and beneath her," Kuznetsov writes, telling her story as she told it to him, "she could hear strange submerged sounds, groaning, choking and sobbing: many of the people were not dead yet. The whole mass of bodies kept moving slightly as they settled down and were pressed tighter by the movements of the ones who were still living." Pronicheva found herself unwounded. She waited for darkness. Lights flashed down. Shots were fired. Killers walked around on the dead finishing off the wounded. The air smelled of blood and opened bodies. Later sand rained down as workers began shoveling soil to cover the bodies. Pronicheva was lying face up and the sand choked her and gritted her eyes. She scraped it away, turned over and started crawling toward the ravine wall, out of Babi Yar. She made it, survived the war, testified at war trials and went back to performing for children in puppet shows.

The *Aktion* continued through a second day. "As a result of a very clever piece of organization," Blobel bragged in a report, "[the Jews] still believed they were going to be resettled right up until the time they were executed." On the third day, as Anton Heidborn, a member of SK 4a, testified, civilians shoveled sand to cover up the last bodies and then Blobel's men dynamited the walls of that section of the ravine. "The next few days," Heidborn recalled, "were spent smoothing out banknotes belonging to the Jews that had been shot. I estimate these must have totalled millions." Truckloads of clothing were donated to the NSV "for the use of ethnic Germans" and to the Kiev city administration "for use of the needy population."

An Einsatzgruppen report on 2 October 1941 summarized the Babi Yar *Aktion* brazenly, not even bothering to justify it as retaliation:

> *Sonderkommando* 4a in collaboration with the group staff and two commandos of Police Regiment South on 29 and 30 September 1941 executed 33,771 Jews in Kiev.

Executions continued at Babi Yar every Tuesday and Friday for the next year, by which time the German administration had set up a concentration camp that backed up to the *yar*.

When Kiev fell, a German physician, Wilhelm Gustav Schüppe, was posted to the Kiev Pathological Institute assigned to destroy "life unworthy of life." His commando of about ten physicians and ten SS men dressed as medics used lethal injections to murder the disabled of the Kiev area as well as Jews, Gypsies and Turkmen.* Interrogated after the war, Schüppe estimated that in the space of six months, from September 1941 to March 1942, his commando killed more than one hundred thousand people—an average of more than five hundred per day.

---

*A Sunnite Muslim Turkic-speaking people.

"The executioners used to boast about their records," a doctor involved in similar executions at Auschwitz would testify. " 'Three in a minute,' " he said, quoting their boast. Schüppe had every reason to minimize rather than exaggerate his crimes. Since the Schüppe commando had no crematoria, the bodies were almost certainly dumped into Babi Yar. Anatoli Kuznetsov's childhood playground thus became the SS's largest single mass grave.

TWELVE

Pure Murder

"In late September [1941]," writes Wehrmacht officer Siegfried Knappe, still advancing toward Moscow, "it began to rain, and mud started to become a problem for us. Snow came in early October, but it was not cold enough for the ground to freeze and everything turned to mud. By October 8, the earth was simply a quagmire of mud. Great clumps of mud clung to our boots and every step produced a smacking suction noise." Barracking in peasant hovels, unable to bathe, many of the men picked up lice and skin infections. A corps commander reported in late October 1941 that "the health of men and horses is deteriorating due to the wretched housing facilities. . . . The men have been lying for weeks in the rain and stand in knee-deep mud. It is impossible to change wet clothing. I have seen the soldiers and spoken with them. They are hollow-eyed, pale, many of them are ill. Frostbite incidence is high."

Indifferent to the physical trial his armies were suffering, Hitler was euphoric. The collapse of Budënny's forces and the fall of Kiev had been followed within two weeks by further encirclements and victories at Vyazma, only 125 miles from Moscow, and southward at Bryansk. "In these two pockets," Alan Clark notes, "over five hundred thousand [Red Army soldiers] were pinned down for liquidation." Goebbels observed Hitler on his return to Berlin in early October 1941 and decided "he looks at his best and is in an exuberantly optimistic frame of mind. He literally exudes optimism. . . . The offensive has been surprisingly successful so far. . . . The Führer is convinced that if the weather remains halfway favorable, the Soviet army will be essentially demolished in fourteen days."

Hitler had intended to deal with the European Jews after he won the war. Göring's commission to Heydrich on 31 July 1941 to begin planning the Final Solution, an adviser to the Reich interior ministry would explain to a colleague later in the year, was supposed to lead to "an immediate and unified solution of the Jewish question in Europe after the conclusion of the war." Since Hitler thought the war was nearly over, the Final Solution was much on his mind in October 1941.

The Jews of Poland were already marked for slaughter, and Globocnik in Lublin was making progress toward developing a killing program. Ninety-two men previously under the authority of the Führer Chancellery who had organized and operated the euthanasia gassing centers in Germany that Hitler had reluctantly closed in late August were assigned to Globocnik in October 1941. At Auschwitz Höss had begun experimenting with a prussic acid insecticide powder with the brand name Zyklon,* testing it first in early September 1941 on Russian prisoners of war. In October 1941, if not earlier, Globocnik's subordinates began planning camps devoted exclusively to mass murder at Belzec, a small town southeast of Lublin, and at Chelmno, about 43 miles due east of Lublin. The euthanasia killing centers had used pure bottled carbon monoxide; the new death camps, which would require larger quantities of gas and to which Himmler begrudged only minimal funds, would borrow from gas van technology and generate carbon monoxide cheaply using large diesel engines scavenged from Russian tanks and submarines.

Even before Globocnik could clear Poland, Hitler was keen to render the Reich *Judenfrei* by moving its Jewish population eastward. On 11 October 1941 Stahlecker turned up at the private apartment of the Generalkommissar of Latvia, Otto-Heinrich Dreschler, to ask for help fulfilling the "Führer's wish" that a big concentration camp be built near Riga to hold Western Jews. Lodz, in central Poland, was another temporary destination; the first four trainloads of Jews shipped east left Vienna bound for Lodz on 16 October 1941. Though many died from starvation, writes historian Christian Gerlach, "there is no evidence from Lodz to indicate that any consideration was being given to the idea of executing the Jews who arrived from Germany." Further transports followed from Berlin, Prague, Cologne, Düsseldorf, Frankfurt, Hamburg and Luxembourg, forcefully deporting by 2 November 1941 about twenty thousand people. By moving German Jewish citizens temporarily to Lodz the SS was able to invoke a law under which they lost their citizenship and property for having taken up residence in a foreign country; maliciously, the law made no distinction between voluntary emigration and emigration at gunpoint. Himmler had persuaded the German governor of the Lodz region to accept the Jewish émigrés by promising that they would be "moved farther east next spring."

Himmler called Heydrich on 18 October 1941 and ordered an end to the "overseas emigration of Jews," closing the last escape route from Nazi-occupied Europe. A memo to that effect was circulated through the RSHA five days later. The first of twenty-two trainloads of Jews

*Cyclone.

from Germany, Austria and Czechoslovakia—each train carrying about a thousand people—began departing eastward early in November 1941. Ten trains went to Riga, five to Kaunas, seven to Minsk. By 25 October 1941 Eichmann had passed the message to the Reichskommissar Ostland, Heinrich Lohse, that "given the present state of affairs, there are no objections to getting rid of those Jews not capable of work with the Bracksian device." The "Bracksian device" was Viktor Brack's lethal gas van.

Testimony by Ohlendorf about a visit Himmler made to Nikolayev in early October 1941 also demonstrates the ramping up of killing and clearing. Einsatzgruppe D had finished its slaughters in the Nikolayev area. "In agreement with the army," Ohlendorf testified at his trial, "we had excluded from the executions a large number of Jews—the farmers." The Wehrmacht had wanted to make sure agricultural production would continue in the Ukraine, Russia's breadbasket, to sustain further campaigns. Himmler was incensed to learn that the Jewish farmers had been spared. He had never liked Ohlendorf, whom he considered arrogant, and here was another example of his insubordination. "I was reproached for this measure," Ohlendorf complained, "and [Himmler] ordered that henceforth, even against the will of the army, the executions should take place as planned." That evening Ohlendorf assembled all his available commanders. "The *Reichsführer* addressed these men and repeated the strict order to kill all those groups. . . . He added that he alone would carry the responsibility, as far as accounting to the Führer was concerned. None of the men would bear any responsibility, but he demanded the execution of this order, even though he knew how harsh these measures were." Ohlendorf claimed he pursued the matter further: "Nevertheless, after supper, I spoke to the *Reichsführer* and deplored the inhuman burden which was being imposed on the men in killing all these civilians. I didn't even get an answer."

The mistaken belief that Germany was about to defeat the Soviet Union accounts for Himmler's determination to kill even the farmers among the Jews of the East; he expected to replace them soon enough with SS *Wehrbauern*. Heydrich was developing similarly optimistic plans as he took up new responsibilities for what had been the Czech part of Czechoslovakia and was now the Reich Protectorate of Bohemia and Moravia. Hitler had made Heydrich Deputy Protector and effective authority over Bohemia and Moravia on 3 September 1941, pushing aside the ineffective former German Foreign Minister Constantin von Neurath. In Prague to meet secretly with his new administrative subordinates on 2 October 1941, Heydrich sketched out a program derived from Himmler's master plan to resettle the East.

"It is clear that we must find an entirely different way in which to treat these peoples," Heydrich told his administrators, speaking of the Czechs, "from the way used for peoples of other races, the Slavs and so on. Racial Germanics [i.e., Czechs who looked German] must be seized firmly but justly; they must be humanely led in a similar way to our own people if we want to keep them permanently in the Reich and to merge them with us." Heydrich envisioned a hierarchy of forces arrayed at the Urals to hold back the Asiatic hordes: not only *Wehrbauern* but also armies of serfs to farm and guard. He went on to allude to the Final Solution, ordering a national register compiled for the Protectorate to prepare for the deportation of its Jews and Slavs. "For those of good race who are well-intentioned towards us," he concluded, "the matter will be very simple—they will be Germanized. The others—those of inferior racial origin with hostile intentions—these people I must get rid of. There is plenty of space in the East for them."

Hitler could hardly keep his mouth shut about the Final Solution that month. "The law of existence prescribes uninterrupted killing, so that the better may live," he lectured his subordinates over lunch on 10 October 1941. When the Department of War Administration at the Quartermaster General's office complained that the "deportations of Jews" were interfering with military rail traffic, Hitler responded bluntly: "The Jewish question takes priority over all other matters." In another mealtime monologue on 21 October 1941 he bragged, "When we finally stamp out this plague, we shall have accomplished for mankind a deed whose significance our men out there on the battlefield cannot even imagine yet." And at dinner after Himmler and Heydrich met with him at Wolfschanze on 25 October 1941 he reminisced about his 1939 prophecy with a wink and a nudge to his black-uniformed minions about the rumor going around:

> From the rostrum of the Reichstag I prophesied to Jewry that if war proved inevitable, the Jew would disappear from Europe. That race of criminals has the two million dead of the World War on its conscience and now already hundreds of thousands more. Let no one tell me that we really can't ship them off to the swamps! Who's worrying about *our* people? If the rumor is going around that we have a plan to exterminate the Jews, that's all right with me. Terror is a good thing.

Handsome young SS-Untersturmführer Max Täubner was a fanatical enemy of the Jews. He kept himself trim and tanned, his dark hair shaped close to his symmetrical skull, his mouth ironic above a strong chin, a flick of contempt in his smile. A man of action, a party member since 1932 (but expelled for late payment of dues, readmitted in 1937), he had joined the SS in 1933. Yet Barbarossa had found him stuck commanding merely a Werkstattzug, a supply workshop platoon responsible for repairing SS equipment. Assigned to duty in the Ukraine with his Werkstattzug in September 1941, part of the First SS Brigade, he had resolved to "get rid of" twenty thousand Jews.

At Novograd Volynsky, sixty miles west of Zhitomir, where his platoon had arrived on 17 September 1941, Täubner had befriended the mayor, a dedicated anti-Semite. The Wehrmacht was issuing Jewesses false certificates to protect them, the mayor complained. He had more than three hundred Jews—men, women and children—locked up in a nearby prison, he added enthusiastically; might he be authorized to shoot them? Täubner realized with disgust that the Wehrmacht was afflicted with a corrosive sentimentality. It would be shameful if Ukrainians accomplished the hard duty that German officers had been too weak to perform. He told the mayor he and his platoon would undertake the executions.

Ukrainian militiamen dug the killing pit outside the town while Täubner marshaled his men. Most were willing enough. Only recruit Ernst Schumann balked. "I was deeply astonished," Schumann testified later, "that our men, as members of a workshop unit, were concerned with killing Jews." He raised the question with the Untersturmführer. "Täubner merely laughed at me and then said something to me which was frankly nothing short of outrageous. He said something to the effect that for him first came pigs, then nothing at all, and only then, far down the list, came Jews."

Täubner's men killed 319 people in Novograd Volynsky. SS-Mann Ernst Göbel complained about the way a Rottenführer named Abraham murdered children:

> There were about five of them. These were children whom I would think were aged between two and six years. The way Abraham killed the children was brutal. He got hold of some of the children by the hair, lifted them up from the ground, shot them through the back of their heads and then threw them into the grave. After a while I just could not watch this any more and I told him to stop. What I meant was he should not lift the children up by the hair, he should kill them in a more decent way.

Täubner noticed Schumann hanging back and told him to join in. Schumann asked him if he was ordering him to take part. It was not an official order, Täubner hedged, but the others were volunteering. "He said to me that I was a coward. To this I answered that I had not come to

Russia to shoot women and children. I myself had a wife and children at home." (Social shaming was a form of violent coaching common among killing squads.) Since Täubner knew he was running a rogue operation, he did not argue the point further. On 17 October 1941 Täubner's Werkstattzug arrived in the village of Sholokhovo, east of Zhitomir. Someone claimed the Jews had threatened to set fire to the agricultural collective and that two Ukrainian women had been seriously injured stepping on mines. Täubner concluded the area needed to be cleared. Murdering 191 Jewish men, women and children rendered Sholokhovo *Judenfrei*. An SS-Unterscharführer from another unit, Walter Müller, asked to participate and took it upon himself to shoot the children, Abraham-style. Täubner still had enough discipline to reproach Müller, but he did not order Müller to stop his murders.

From 22 October to 12 November 1941 Täubner and his Werkstattzug were stuck in Aleksandriya, southeast along the Dnieper about 175 miles beyond Kiev, for dreary weeks with bad weather and bad roads and nothing to do. Most of the Jews in the area had already been "resettled." Täubner put his ear to the ground and discovered that the few Jews still around intended to poison the creeks. He ordered them rounded up and delivered to him at his unit. Youth of the German labor service posted to Aleksandriya volunteered to dig a killing pit.

In the meantime there was sport with the Jews impressed for work. The Jews who cut firewood in the courtyard of the quarters took beatings for not working properly. SS-Sturmmann* Karl Ackermann got his blood up and pounded one of them with a spade. SS-Sturmmann Rudolf Wüstholz joined in and ordered two Jews to beat each other to death. To motivate them he promised that whoever survived wouldn't be executed. The men knocked each other down, but they stopped short of killing. Täubner took over. He had one man hanged and sent the other out behind the quarters to be shot.

Täubner had ten or fifteen Jewish men and women, mainly men, locked into the cellar without food, water, light or any kind of toilet. The Aleksandriya mayor came by one evening with two friends. Over schnapps Täubner organized a viewing party. He sent an advance man down with candles. He armed himself and his guests with clubs and ordered SS-Mann Heinrich Hesse and several other guards to accompany them. In the fetid cellar bearded men cowered anxiously in the flickering light. "Täubner was the first to go crazy in the cellar," Hesse testified. "He lashed out with a heavy wooden club at random at the

*Acting Corporal.

Jews lying on the ground. He poked around between the legs in the genital area of an elderly Jewess." The mayor and the others joined in. All the flailing and screaming unnerved Hesse and he backed away. Täubner saw his flinch and demanded he participate. Hesse had no weapon. "I just gave a few Jews less forceful punches or pushes with my fist," he claimed in his trial testimony.

Hesse particularly noticed one young woman in the cellar. "She was a beautiful woman," he testified, "aged between twenty and thirty." After the night visit Hesse began to worry that she would fall into the hands of the Untersturmführer. He resolved to protect her. He watched for his chance, and when it was possible to do so he went down into the cellar and ordered her out, telling her that Täubner wished to speak to her. Outside, Hesse made the woman walk in front of him, heading toward the killing pit, which still gaped empty awaiting its burden. "My only thought was that if I had to do something I should cause the person as little pain as possible. I did not want the Jewess to suffer fear of death." As she walked ahead of him, he raised his carbine and shot her suddenly in the head from behind. "I was glad to be able to shoot her," he testified, "but please don't take that to mean that I enjoyed it."

Now Täubner filled the killing pit. He encouraged his men to kill with abandon. He himself sometimes slashed victims in the face with his whip. He had SS-Sturmmann Ernst Fritsch taking photographs and took photographs himself. Between executions Täubner broke out his accordion and played "You Are Crazy, My Child" in a wild tempo. The older men especially did not agree with the way the executions were run.

Surprisingly, Täubner was brought up on charges before an SS court in 1942. It was never the business of workshop platoons to kill Jews, the court would decide:

> The accused shall not be punished because of the actions against the Jews as such. The Jews have to be exterminated and none of the Jews that were killed is any great loss. Although the accused should have recognized that the extermination of the Jews was the duty of commandos which have been set up especially for this purpose, he should be excused for considering himself to have the authority to take part in the extermination of Jewry himself. Real hatred of the Jews was the driving motivation for the accused. In the process he let himself be drawn into committing cruel actions in Aleksandriya which are unworthy of a German man and an SS officer. . . . It is not the German way to apply Bolshevik methods during the necessary extermination of the worst enemy of our people. In so doing the conduct of the accused gives rise to considerable concern. The accused

allowed his men to act with such vicious brutality that they conducted themselves under his command like a savage horde. The accused jeopardized the discipline of the men. It is hard to conceive of anything worse than this. Although the accused may have otherwise taken care of his men, by his conduct he however neglected his supervisory duty which, in the view of the SS, also means not allowing his men to become psychologically depraved.

The court also pointed out that Täubner, on leave, had the photographs taken at the executions developed at two photographic shops in southern Germany and showed them to his wife and friends. "Such pictures could pose the gravest risks to the security of the Reich if they fell into the wrong hands," the SS judges worried. The photographs were "tasteless and shameless," an "expression of an inferior character. Particularly revealing in this connection is the fact that the accused evidently took particular pleasure in a photograph of a Jewish woman who was almost completely naked." Täubner was also accused of ordering the execution of the leader of the Ukrainian militia in Aleksandriya, a manslaughter, and of inciting his wife to attempt an abortion. For all these crimes he was sentenced to a total of ten years in prison, expelled from the SS and declared unfit for service.

(Himmler would pardon Täubner late in the war and send him to the front. In the unauthorized shooting of Jews, the Reichsführer-SS discerned a difference between "executions for purely political motives" and "men acting out of self-seeking, sadistic or sexual motives.")

Sarra Gleykh kept a diary in a pink school notebook. A young Jewish woman who had fled Kharkov for Mariupol, on the Sea of Azov in the far southeastern Ukraine, where her parents lived, she worked in a telegraph office. Ilya Ehrenburg edited her diary after the war. "It is amazing," he wrote in his memoirs, "how she hurriedly and disjointedly wrote down everything from day to day." The Wehrmacht took Mariupol on 8 October 1941. "The Germans entered the town at noon," Gleykh wrote. "The town was surrendered without a fight." The Gleykh family had stayed home except for Sarra's sister Basya, who was caring for a friend who had typhoid, and her sister Fanya, who had gone to work but walked home in the afternoon after the Germans arrived. By the next day the Gleykhs were out of food and an order had already been posted requiring Jews to wear a white six-pointed star. "Jews are forbidden to change apartments," Sarra noted. "Fanya and her maid, Tanya, are bringing their things from the factory apartment to Mama's anyway."

By 10 October 1941 nine thousand people had been registered. "There have not yet been any mass repressions, but our neighbor Trievsky says that the Gestapo detachment [i.e., an Einsatzkommando] has not yet arrived and that things will change after that." Three nights later German soldiers looted the Gleykhs' apartment. "They pointed a revolver in our faces and asked where the sugar and meat were. Then they began to smash the doors of the armoire, even though it was not locked. . . . Two of them looted nonstop. They took everything—even the meat grinder. . . . In the morning we learned that looting had gone on all over town during the night. It continued during the day. . . . You can hear them from far away, since their boots make so much noise. After the Germans left, Mama cried and said: 'They don't consider us people; we're doomed.' "

On 18 October 1941 the Jews of Mariupol were required to turn in their valuables at collection points around the city. Sarra, Basya and their mother and father turned in three silver soup spoons and a ring. "After that, they did not let us leave the yard. When the entire population of the region had turned in their valuables, it was announced to us that we had to leave the city within two hours. We will have to walk to the nearest collective farm, where we will be settled. We have to take enough food and warm clothing for four days. We are to present ourselves together with our things in two hours. There will be trucks for the elderly and women with babies." Sarra recorded Solomonic regulations the conquerors promulgated that must have caused great agony: Jewish women married to Russians or Ukrainians whose husbands were in town would be allowed to remain, while those whose husbands were absent would have to leave with their children. "If a Russian woman is married to a Jew, she can choose to remain or go with her husband. The children may remain with her."

The Gleykhs' Ukrainian friends evidently knew what was coming: "The Royanovs asked Fanya to give them her grandson [Vladya]. Papa insisted that Fanya take Vladya to the Royanovs. Fanya categorically refused, cried and begged Papa not to throw her out and make her go to the Royanovs. She said: 'Without you, I'll do myself in anyway. I won't survive, so I'll go with you.' She would not give up Vladya and decided to take him with her." Fanya's maid begged her to give the boy up and promised to take care of him, "but Fanya would not even hear of this."

The Germans kept the crowds standing in the street until evening. Then "everyone was herded into a building for the night; we got a corner in the basement. It was dark, wet and dirty." The next day, 19 October 1941, was Sunday. "The Gestapo was resting," so the Gleykhs and the others were confined to the building for the day. Tanya, the maid, and friends brought food packages. Mr. Gleykh pooled his funds with two other men and bought a horse and cart. "The number of people kept increasing. . . . Vladya can't stand being here any longer, and he is begging to go home. . . . Tomorrow at seven a.m. we are to leave our last haven in town."

On 20 October 1941, Sarra wrote: "Judging by how the Germans treated those who came to say goodbye to us and brought packages, the future holds nothing good. The Germans beat all the passersby with clubs and chased them a block away from the building. The time came for Mama, Papa, Fanya and Vladya to get in the truck." The Gleykhs left first; Sarra's sister and grandnephew had not been ready to go. A little later Sarra began worrying about her parents. "It was rumored that the trucks were taking the elderly out of town to be destroyed." Fanya left by truck with Vladya. "We went on foot. The road was terrible and had been washed away by the rain. It was impossible to walk, difficult to raise a foot. If you stopped, you were struck with a club. People were beaten without regard to age." They approached the Petrovsky Agricultural Station at about two o'clock in the afternoon. It was crowded with people. Sarra searched for Fanya and her parents. "Fanya called to me. She had been searching for our parents before my arrival and had not found them. Probably they were already in the barn to which people were being taken in groups of forty or fifty." Vladya was hungry. Sarra had apples and toasted bread in her pocket to feed him. It was all she had; they had been forbidden to take food with them.

And then:

Our turn arrived, and the horrible image of a senseless, a wildly senseless and meek death was before our eyes as we set off behind the barns. The bodies of Papa and Mama were already there somewhere. By sending them by truck, I had shortened their lives by a few hours. We were herded toward the trenches which had been dug for the defense of the city. These trenches served no other function than as receptacles for the death of nine thousand Jews. We were ordered to undress to our underwear, and they searched for money and documents. Then we were herded along the edge of the ditch, but there was no longer any real edge, since the trench was filled with people for a half kilometer. Many were still alive and were begging for another bullet to finish them off. We walked over the corpses, and it seemed to me that I recognized my mother in one gray-haired woman. I rushed to her and Basya followed me, but we were driven back with clubs. At one point I thought that an old man with his brains bashed out was Papa, but I could not approach him any closer. We began to say goodbye, and we managed to kiss. . . . Fanya did not believe that this was the end: "Can it be that I will never again see the sun and the light?" she said. Her face was blue-gray, and Vladya kept asking: "Are we going to swim? Why are we undressed?" Fanya took him in her arms, since it was difficult for him to walk in the wet clay. Basya would not stop whispering: "Vladya, Vladya, why should this happen to you too? No one even knows what they have done to us." Fanya turned around and answered: "I am dying calmly with him, because I know I am not leaving him an orphan." These were Fanya's last words. I could not stand it any longer, and I held my head and began to scream in a wild voice. I seem to remember that Fanya had time to turn around and say: "Be quiet, Sarra, be quiet." At that point everything breaks off.

When I regained consciousness, it was already twilight. The bodies lying on top of me were still shuddering; the Germans were shooting them again to make doubly sure that the wounded would not be able to leave. At any rate, I understood the Germans to say that. They were afraid that there were many who had not been finished off, and they were right; there were many like that. These people were buried alive, since no one could help them even though they screamed and called for help. Somewhere above the corpses babies were crying. Most of them had been carried by their mothers and, since we were shot in the backs, they had fallen, protected by their mothers' bodies. Not wounded by the bullets, they were covered up and buried alive under the corpses.

I began to crawl out from underneath the corpses. . . . When I had crawled out, I looked around: the wounded were writhing, groaning, attempting to get up and falling again. I began to call to Fanya in the hope that she would hear me, and a man next to me ordered me to be silent. It was Grodzinsky. His mother had been killed, and he was afraid that my shouts would attract the attention of the Germans. A small group of people were resourceful enough to jump into the trench when the first shots rang out, and they were unharmed. . . . They kept pleading with me to be silent, and I begged everyone who was leaving to help me find Fanya. Grodzinsky, who was wounded in the legs and could not walk, advised me to leave. I tried to help him, but I could do nothing alone. He fell after two steps and refused to go on. He advised me to catch up with those who had left. I sat there and listened. An old woman called out in a singsong voice: "Lieutenant, Lieutenant. . . ." There was so much horror in this endlessly repeating word! From somewhere down below someone shouted: "Sir, don't kill me. . . ." By chance I overtook [an acquaintance]. She had been separated from her group. The two of us, undressed except for our slips and smeared with blood from head to toe, set off to seek refuge for the night, starting in the direction from which we could hear dogs barking. We knocked at one hut, but no one answered. Then we knocked at another, and we were driven away. At a third, we were given some rags with which to cover ourself and advised to go into the steppe. We did precisely that. In the darkness we found a haystack and sat in it until dawn. In the morning we returned to the farmstead. . . . It was not far from the trench, but on the far side. We could hear the screams of women and children until the end of the day.

After several days of wandering in the prairie steppe, moving from one haystack to another, on 24 October 1941 Sarra Gleykh found her way back to Mariupol and knocked on the Royanovs' door. "They let me in and were horrified when they learned that everyone had died. They helped me get cleaned up, fed me and put me to bed." In late November 1941 she crossed the lines to the Red Army side and found safety.

Romanian forces occupied Odessa, on the Black Sea due south of Kiev, on 16 October 1941 and announced the registration of the Jewish population the next day. Russian partisans blew up the building the Romanian command staff had made their headquarters on 23 October 1941. In retaliation, some ten thousand Jews were marched outside town the same day and murdered with machine guns. Two days later several thousand more were locked into a large barn, which was then blown up with dynamite. "On 23 and 24 October," a Russian technical editor said after the war, "no matter in which direction you looked [in Odessa] you could see gallows. There were thousands of them. At the feet of the hanged lay the bodies of those who had been tortured, mutilated and shot. Our town was a terrible sight: a town of the hanged." Odessa was quickly cleared of Jews, who were marched to concentration camps northeastward eighty miles from the harbor city along the Bug River. Across the Black Sea on the Crimean peninsula mass murder took a more inventive form. In the course of the war in the Crimea, according to the indictment of the International Military Tribunal at Nuremberg, "144,000 peaceful citizens were gathered on barges, taken out to sea and drowned."

In Dnepropetrovsk, at the eastern apex of a great triangle with Kiev and Odessa as its base, on the Dnieper where it turns and bends south, a detachment of the Higher SS and Police Leader murdered a third of the city's 30,000 Jews near a cemetery on 13 October 1941; by February 1942 only seven hundred were left.

At the other, Baltic, coast of the continent, in Estonia, more than half of that country's small population of Jews—2,500 of about 4,500—had been evacuated before the Wehrmacht rolled through in mid-August 1941. Sonderkommando 1a (Einsatzgruppe A), commanded by Martin Sandberger, a lawyer, organized Estonian militia units to augment its forces. By mid-October 1941 Sandberger was able to report to Berlin that "all male Jews over sixteen, with the exception of the appointed Jewish elders, were executed by the Estonian self-defense units under supervision of the *Sonderkommando*.... The action is still underway since the search for Jewish hideouts has not yet been completed. So far, the total number of Jews shot in Estonia is 440. When these measures are completed, about 500 to 600 Jewesses and children will still be alive." Sandberger planned to put these widows to work "farming and cutting peat" from a camp being prepared near Reval (now Tallinn, the coastal capital). "Thus the questions of feeding and financing are answered." All the villages in Estonia, Sandberger added, were now *Judenfrei*.

By October 1941, writes Latvian historian Andrew Ezergailis, the Arajs commando "had lost its function in Latvia: the Jews in the small towns had already been killed, and those of Riga, Daugavpils, and Liepaja were under the care of the *Generalkommissar* and driven into ghettos." Stahlecker, in his long, comprehensive report of 15 October 1941, lists a total of more than 30,000 Jewish men, women and children murdered in Latvia up to that date by Einsatzgruppe forces. "The Arajs commando," Ezergailis concludes, "in effect had run out of work."

Two gated, barbed-wire ghettos had been established in Kaunas's run-down Slobodka district in July 1941 for the Jews of that central Lithuanian city, a Big Ghetto that held about 27,500 people and a Little Ghetto, connected by a wooden bridge across an intervening street, that confined another 2,500. A hospital had been set up in several buildings in the Little Ghetto, with maternity, medical and surgical wards; patients with contagious diseases were housed in a separate two-story building. An orphanage had also been established in the Little Ghetto for the several hundred Jewish children whose parents had already been murdered by the Germans or in pogroms.

On 4 October 1941, the Sabbath after Yom Kippur, a detachment of Jäger's Einsatzkommando 3 under Obersturmführer Joachim Hamann began liquidating the Little Ghetto. A rabbi, Ephraim Oshry, was an eyewitness:

> Early that morning some 50 German soldiers along with around 100 Lithuanian collaborators—far more than we usually saw, which we

found terrifying—piled into the Little Ghetto and drove the people, without exception, out of their houses.

They chased people out of bed without even giving them opportunity to dress. Into the streets they drove the old and weak, the children and women and men. Using their rifle butts as clubs, they stuck people left and right. Blood gushed like water.

The Jews were chased into Sajungos Square, which had once been the horse market of Slobodka. There the Germans began to divide the Jews, similar to the way one sorts sheep for slaughter: "Right! Left!" Death! Life!

The selection lasted several hours. People who held work passes— only five thousand had been issued throughout the two ghettos—were separated from those who did not. Patients were evacuated from the medical and surgical wards. In the maternity ward, the young Kaunas attorney Avraham Tory recorded in his contemporary diary, "the Germans wanted to see the babies who had just been born. They came up to the ledge by the window on which the six babies were lying. They stood there for a while watching the babies. The eyes of one of the Germans grew misty. 'Shall we leave them?' he asked his friend. They both left the room, letting the mothers and the babies stay. This time they survived."

The orphans were not so lucky, Tory continues:

The Germans then started taking the children out of the children's home. Out of 153 children, only 12 were left in the home. They were simply overlooked. The nurses were also taken away. Those children who were in swaddling clothes* were taken out and placed on the ground in the stone-paved hospital courtyard, their tiny faces turned skyward. Soldiers of the third squad of the German Police passed between them. They stopped for a moment. Some of them kicked the babies with their boots. The babies rolled a little to the side but soon enough regained their belly-up position, their faces turned toward the sky. It was a rare spectacle of cruelty and callousness.

A heavy truck pulled up. First the children and then the nurses were thrown into it. The truck was then covered with a canvas cloth and drove off in the direction of the Ninth Fort.

The Little Ghetto Jews who had been selected were formed into columns of one hundred and marched off; the people with work passes who had been spared were sent over the bridge to the Big Ghetto. William Mishell watched the selection from the Big Ghetto. "A terrible human drama was unfolding before the eyes of the Jews on both sides of

*That is, swaddled: bundled with swaddling cloth.

the fence," he remembers. "It was clear: the people on the bad side were being taken to the Ninth Fort for a mass execution. Everybody on both sides of the street began to cry, and those on the Big Ghetto side tried desperately to catch a last glimpse of the loved ones who were being taken away." In his 1 December 1941 summary report, Jäger would list "315 Jewish men, 1,107 Jewish women, 496 Jewish children" executed at the Ninth Fort on 4 October 1941, claiming absurdly that the selection was a "punitive action because a German policeman was shot at in the ghetto."

But more were killed that day than those who marched or were trucked to the Ninth Fort. There had been sixty-seven patients, doctors and nurses in the contagious-disease hospital building that morning. An unknown number of healthy Little Ghetto residents had joined them there, thinking they might find sanctuary. At the beginning of the *Aktion* the Germans had locked the hospital gates on patients and fugitives alike. They transferred into the hospital surgical patients who had been too ill to attend the selection and then they boarded up the doors and windows. They set ten Jewish men digging a pit in the hospital courtyard. Tory describes what followed:

> Opposite the hospital building, on the other side of the fence, a fur factory called Lape was situated. From that location the hospital courtyard could be seen clearly. The factory workers there saw the ten Jews digging the pit on that day; they saw how the residents of the old people's home were lowered into it, how patients were thrown into it and then shot inside the pit; they saw how little children were thrown into the pit, as well as patients who could not stand on their feet. . . . At one p.m. smoke could be seen rising over the hospital building; later flames shot up from it. The hospital was burning. The fire burned all day and night.

Patients, staff and fugitives were thus burned alive.

If they had not understood before, the people of the Kaunas ghetto now knew that nothing protected them from death and that further *Aktionen* would follow. They began to depart from one another with a Yiddish joke, Rabbi Oshry remembers: *"Auf Wiedersehn in yenner velt"*—"See you in the next world." Later in October 1941 reports began to filter back to the ghetto of large pits being dug at the Ninth Fort by Russian prisoners of war. Optimists speculated that they were tank traps anticipating a Red Army counterattack; realists knew they were meant for mass graves.

The Black Day, as the survivors would call it, came late in the month with an order for everyone in the ghetto to show up at Democracy

Square at six o'clock on the morning of 28 October 1941 or be shot. People were to report with their families according to their work assignments: the ghetto council under one sign, the workers building a Luftwaffe airbase outside Kaunas under another, tanners, road builders, fur workers, plumbers, tinsmiths each to be identified as such. Mishell worked for the Jewish Council, and his brother-in-law worked on the airbase crew, and so crucial did his family judge the decision to be of which sign to muster under that they stayed up all night debating it, finally concluding that people working for the German military would be considered more valuable and choosing the airbase position. "No one in the ghetto closed an eye on the night of 27 October," Tory records. "Many wept bitterly, many others recited Psalms. There were also people who did the opposite: they decided to have a good time, to feast and gorge themselves on food, and use up their whole supply. Inmates whose apartments were stocked with wines and liquor drank all they could and even invited neighbors and friends to the macabre drinking party 'so as not to leave anything behind for the Germans.' "

Twenty-eight thousand people left their doors unlocked, as ordered, posted notes on the door as ordered if someone too ill to be moved lay inside and walked through the ghetto streets that morning, "very chilly," Mishell recalls, "a typical autumn day with a thin layer of snow covering the ground. It was still dark and the air was extremely damp. The last visible stars gradually disappeared as the crowd started to swell. One could see mothers with children in their arms, old people who could barely walk, small children holding the hands of their mothers, grownups supporting their elderly parents or grandparents and even invalids supported by canes. Some people who were unable to walk were carried out on stretchers." Tory describes it gravely as "a procession of mourners grieving over themselves."

Everyone stood waiting for three hours as the dawn finally broke. Tory saw then that "the ghetto fence was surrounded by machine guns and a heavy detachment of armed German policemen commanded by Captain [Alfred] Tornbaum. He also had at his disposal battalions of armed Lithuanian partisans. A crowd of curious Lithuanian spectators had gathered on the hills overlooking the ghetto. They followed the events taking place in the square with great interest, not devoid of delight, and did not leave for many hours." Beefy, brutal SS-Hauptscharführer* Helmut Rauca arrived at nine a.m. with the deputy Gestapo chief, Captain Heinrich Schmitz, Tornbaum and SA Captain Fritz Jordan.

*Master Sergeant.

Rauca in his gray-green uniform, carrying a baton, positioned himself on a mound at one end of the square and the selection began. With the flick of a black-gloved finger he directed groups and families left or right. For some time it wasn't clear which side meant life and which side death, and people sometimes asked to be moved. If the move was to the right, says Tory, "smiling sarcastically, Rauca gave his consent." Soon enough, as the sick and the elderly accumulated on the right side, which side meant death became clear. "From time to time, Rauca feasted on a sandwich . . . or enjoyed a cigarette, all the while performing his fiendish work without interruption." From time to time an assistant brought a scrap of paper bearing a tally of those sent right—they were quickly moved into the empty Little Ghetto—which indicated that Rauca had a quota to fulfill. People died waiting in the square to be sorted. As the day wore on and the tallies showed him short of his quota, Rauca sorted as much by appearance as by work pass or specialty; all five hundred of the night-shift airbase workers who, muddy and exhausted, had come directly to Democracy Square from work he sent right, but he sent the fresh day-shift workers left.

The selection dragged on through the day. "It was beginning to grow dark," Tory writes, "yet thousands of people remained standing in the square. Captain Jordan now opened another selection place; he was assisted by Captain Tornbaum." The Jewish ghetto police tried to slip people across from one side to the other and sometimes succeeded. One of them saved Mishell's brother-in-law and his wife and child that way.

It was dark when the Germans completed the selection. About ten thousand people had been transferred to the Little Ghetto, where they settled into the cold buildings for the night. The others returned home, says Tory, "hungry, thirsty, crushed, and dejected . . . most of them bereaved or orphaned, having been separated from a father, a mother, children, a brother or sister, a grandfather or a grandmother, an uncle or an aunt. A deep mourning descended on the ghetto. In every house there were now empty rooms, unoccupied beds and the belongings of those who had not returned from the selections. One third of the ghetto population had been cut down. The sick people who had remained in their homes in the morning had all disappeared. They had been transferred to the Ninth Fort during the day."

The next morning it was the turn of the ten thousand. A teenage boy escaped the ensuing slaughter and returned to Kaunas to warn the Jewish Council; Tory's summary reflects the boy's eyewitness account:

The procession, numbering some 10,000 people, and proceeding from the Little Ghetto to the Ninth Fort, lasted from dawn until noon.

Elderly people, and those who were sick, collapsed by the roadside and died. Warning shots were fired incessantly, all along the way and around the Big Ghetto. Thousands of curious Lithuanians flocked to both sides of the road to watch the spectacle, until the last of the victims was swallowed up by the Ninth Fort.

In the fort, the wretched people were immediately set upon by the Lithuanian killers, who stripped them of every valuable article—gold rings, earrings, bracelets. They forced them to strip naked, pushed them into pits which had been prepared in advance, and fired into each pit with machine guns which had been positioned there in advance. The murderers did not have time to shoot everybody in one batch before the next batch of Jews arrived. They were accorded the same treatment as those who had preceded them. They were pushed into the pit on top of the dead, the dying and those still alive from the previous group. So it continued, batch after batch, until the 10,000 men, women and children had been butchered.

Jäger listed the 29 October 1941 massacre at the Ninth Fort as "2,007 Jewish men, 2,920 Jewish women, 4,273 Jewish children," and justified it as "removal from the ghetto of surplus Jews."

While the Jews of Kaunas were undergoing selection and being murdered in batches at the Ninth Fort, Himmler was pretending to enjoy a weeklong hunting party at Schönhof, the hunting lodge of German foreign minister Joachim von Ribbentrop. The Italian foreign minister, Count Galeazzo Ciano, was the guest of honor, and Himmler's masseur Felix Kersten was a guest as well. On 26 October 1941 the party bagged 2,400 pheasants, 260 hares, 20 crows and one roebuck. "Count Ciano alone shot 620 pheasants," Kersten writes; "he's the champion. Ribbentrop shot 410 pheasants, Himmler only 95." Himmler told Kersten he had only joined the shoot because the Führer had "expressly wished me to do so." He groused about Ciano's success: "I wish the Italians in Africa had been such good shots. . . . Where there's no danger, the Italians are heroes." After dinner that evening Ciano told Kersten privately, "War will last a long time." Kersten agreed, "and Ciano remarked that we were the only ones to share this opinion. Here at Schönhof everyone is saying that the war will soon be over."

At the end of the Schönhof shoot, on the night of 28–29 October 1941, while the Kaunas ten thousand were making their beds in the cold buildings of the Little Ghetto, knowing what the morning would bring, Kersten talked with Himmler about hunting while he gave him a massage:

I said that I loved it and never felt so well as when out deer-stalking. I became quite a different person when I was in the open air stalking deer for hours on end, and continued to reap the benefit of those days out hunting for a considerable time afterwards.

Himmler replied that that was certainly the best part of hunting, but the real aim of deer-stalking, to have a shot at a wretched deer, went against the grain with him. "How can you find any pleasure, Herr Kersten, in shooting from behind cover at poor creatures browsing on the edge of a wood, innocent, defenseless and unsuspecting? Properly considered, it's pure murder."

THIRTEEN

Rumbula

As October 1941 chilled into November, the pressure on the Einsatz-gruppen and the Higher SS and Police Leaders to accelerate their massacres increased. To make room for European Jews shipped eastward, as well as for the influx of SS and German civil administration personnel, the towns, ghettos and camps of the occupied East needed to be cleared.

Slonim, for example, a town in western Byelorussia about halfway between Bialystok and Minsk, had a housing problem. Gebietskommissar* Gerhard Erren explained the difficulty in a report:

> The town of Slonim is a haphazard jumble of a few good stone buildings, quite a few serviceable wooden houses and a good many dilapidated log shacks ripe for demolition. There are no uniformly well-maintained enclosed quarters which would be suitable as areas for Germans to live in. One third of the town has been completely destroyed. As a result of this and the heavy influx of refugees [from the surrounding countryside], when I arrived Slonim was severely overpopulated and the housing situation in some places catastrophic.

Since he needed to clear an area in preparation for a "future SS base," and "operating on the premise that my colleagues need the highest standard of overall living conditions in order to maintain peak performance," Erren "saw to it from the first day that each of our men not only had decent accommodation and enough to eat but that his whole style of living embodies German culture and the prestige appropriate to it." How did he do that?

At the time of Erren's arrival about twenty-five thousand Jews were living in the Slonim area, about sixteen thousand in the town itself—some two-thirds of the total town population. Erren lacked barbed wire and sufficient guards to set up a ghetto, so he began preparations for a major *Aktion*. He expropriated property and furnishings from the Jews of Slonim to equip Wehrmacht and German civil administration buildings. He registered the entire Jewish population, noting age, gender and

*District Commissioner.

profession, and issued passes and arranged separate accommodations for "all craftsmen and workers with qualifications" so that they would not be inadvertently taken in the *Aktion*. Then he called in an extermination commando from Einsatzgruppe B and on 13 November 1941 saw to the murder of at least nine thousand and perhaps as many as eighteen thousand Jewish victims. Indicating that Erren himself was present, his driver and interpreter, Alfred Metzner, reported participating in the massacre:

> I was holding a whip or a pistol. I was loading or unloading. The men, children and mothers were pushed into the pits. Children were first beaten to death and then thrown feet [first] into the pits. . . . There were a number of filthy sadists in the extermination commando. For example, pregnant women were shot in the belly for fun and then thrown into the pits. . . . Before the execution the Jews had to undergo a body search, during which . . . anuses and sex organs were searched for valuables and jewels.

The brutal violation of searching body cavities before execution was not an Einsatzgruppen routine; it may have been an Erren innovation. Raul Hilberg says Erren used to call a meeting after the *Aktionen* he instigated (the November 1941 *Aktion* was only the first). "The meeting was the occasion for celebration, and employees of the Kommissariat who had distinguished themselves were praised." Erren's enthusiasms, Hilberg adds, earned him the nickname "Bloody *Gebietskommissar*." His driver's reference to "filthy sadists" indicates that the Einsatzgruppen killers were descending in increasing numbers into fully malefic violent expression.

"The *Judenaktion* on 13 November alleviated the [housing] situation perceptibly," Erren concluded his report. ". . . [It] rid me of unnecessary mouths to feed. The some seven thousand Jews now present in the town of Slonim have all been allocated jobs. They are working willingly because of the constant fear of death. Early next year they will be rigorously checked and sorted for a further reduction." Erren had also set up what he called "craft colleges," where he intended to make "the best of the skilled workers among the Jews . . . pass their skills on to intelligent [Gentile] apprentices . . . so that Jews will finally be dispensable in the skilled craft and trade sector and can be eliminated."

Another massacre with unusual features carried out at about the same time—mid-November 1941—in the western Polish town of Konin perhaps indicates continuing experimentation with mass-killing technology.

Theo Richmond, an English descendant of Konin Jewish émigrés, writes that Konin in czarist days was "a clean, handsome little town near the German frontier, on a river, with a wooden bridge. Nearby were meadows, orchards and forests. In winter, people skated on the river. In summer they strolled in the municipal park, where a military band played on Sunday afternoons. . . . The Jewish community was composed of pious but unfanatical Jews. Religious observance coexisted with a lively interest in secular culture. . . . There was a synagogue, a House of Study, and several small congregations. The Jewish quarter had a square, which was the heart of Jewish life in Konin."

Three thousand Konin Jews were shot into killing pits in the Kazimierz Forest outside Konin in October 1941. A larger *Aktion* in mid-November 1941 was described in detail by a Polish veterinarian, Mieczyslaw Sekiewicz, in a deposition he gave the Local Court of Konin in 1945. What is unusual is the killing method:

In the middle of November 1941, at four o'clock in the morning, Gestapo men came to my prison cell and told me to get ready for a trip. They handcuffed me and took me to a private car where I found two of my fellow prisoners, my comrades in misfortune. They were sitting in the back of the car with their hands and legs shackled together. . . . I sat down by them and the Gestapo men shackled my legs. They got into the car and drove away. . . . Past [the village of] Kazimierz Biskupi [five miles northwest of Konin], when we entered the forest, the car turned left onto a forest path. . . . [In the forest] across a clearing were two pits. The first one, nearer to the path, was about eight meters [twenty-five feet] long and six meters [twenty feet] wide and two meters [six feet] deep. Almost parallel to it at the other end of the clearing . . . there was a second pit of the same depth, six meters [twenty feet] wide and fifteen meters [fifty feet] long. Between these two pits was open space. . . . All around the clearing . . . groups of Jews were standing or sitting. . . . I cannot say how many there were, as they were standing among trees. . . .

In the crowd were women, men, children, mothers with children in their arms. Whether they were all Polish Jews I cannot say. I was told later that they came from Zagorow [a village fifteen miles southwest of Konin downriver]. Among them I recognized a tailor and a shopkeeper from Konin, but I don't know their names. The paths, the clearings, the whole forest swarmed with Germans. Besides the three of us brought from Konin there were about thirty other Poles assembled there. I don't know where they came from. On the bottom of the larger pit I saw a layer of quicklime. I don't know how thick the layer was. There was no lime in the smaller pit. The Gestapo men warned us that the forest was surrounded and closely watched, and if we attempted to escape we would be shot in the head. Then they ordered the assembled Jews to strip—first those who were standing near the large pit. They ordered the naked people to jump into the larger pit. I could not describe the wailing and the crying. Some Jews were jumping without an order—even most of them—some were resisting and they were being beaten about and pushed down. Some mothers jumped in holding their children, some were throwing their children in, others were flinging their children aside. Still others threw the children in first and then jumped in. Some were crawling at the feet of the Gestapo men kissing their boots, their rifle butts and the like. We were told to go among the standing Jews and collect clothing and shoes. I saw Gestapo men come up to where we were heaping watches, rings, jewelry, and stuff their pockets with them. Seeing that, some of us, and I among them, stopped putting anything precious in heaps, but threw watches, rings further into the forest.

Suddenly the Gestapo men ordered the Jews not to undress any more, as the pit was full. Only closely packed heads were to be seen when one looked into the pit. The Jews already stripped naked were thrown by the Gestapo men onto the heads of those already crammed in the pit. And all the while we had to collect and sort out clothing, footwear, bundles, food, eiderdowns and the like. This lasted until noon and then a truck came from the road and stopped on the path by the clearing. I noticed four vat-like containers. Then the Germans set up a small motor—it was probably a pump—connected it with hoses to one of the vats and two of them brought the hoses from the motor up to the pit. They started the motor and the two Gestapo men began to pour some liquid on the Jews. I think it was water, at any rate it looked like water. The hose was connected in turn to the other containers. Apparently, because of the slaking of the lime, people in the pit were boiling alive.* The cries were so terrible that we who were sitting by the piles of clothing began to tear pieces off to stop our ears. The crying of those boiling in the pit was joined by the wailing and lamentation of the Jews waiting for their perdition. All this lasted perhaps two hours, perhaps longer. When darkness fell we were taken along a forest path leading to the road at the edge of the forest . . . and here we were halted.

We were given coffee to drink and a quarter of a kilo of bread each.

---

*When quicklime, calcium oxide, is slaked—hydrated with water—it becomes calcium hydroxide, a powerful caustic.

Along the edge of the forest stood six or seven trucks covered with tarpaulins. We were herded into the vehicles in such a way that we were lying one next to another with our faces down so that we could not move. We were told to sleep like that. I could still hear the cries until I fell asleep, which happened rather quickly because I was so tired. The next morning the Gestapo men ordered us to cover the large pit with soil. The pit looked as if it had been dusted with a layer of earth. The human mass inside it seemed to have collapsed and dropped to the bottom. The bodies were so tightly packed that they looked as if they were standing, only the heads lolled in all directions. We did not fill the pit very thoroughly and the hands of some of the corpses were still sticking out, because trucks began to arrive and we were stopped. We were told to throw into them all the sorted-out stuff: clothing separately, footwear separately and so with other articles.

At a time when killing technologies were still under development at Auschwitz and elsewhere, this fathomless horror seems to have been an attempt—most probably, given the location, by Globocnik's subordinates—to combine killing and corpse processing into one operation: slaked lime dissolves organic matter, including human tissue, which is why the "human mass" the veterinarian saw the morning after the massacre seemed to have "collapsed and dropped to the bottom." The victims were not literally boiled alive, although the slaking process liberates a great deal of heat; they were chemically burned to death and partly dissolved by being flooded with the calcium equivalent of concentrated household bleach.

The Germans frequently used quicklime to accelerate the decomposition of corpses killed by shooting, of course, and it was often distributed layer by layer over bodies (dead or wounded and still alive) in killing pits, but the available record reveals no other instance of its having been used to kill as well as to decompose. Mercifully for later victims, the experiment did not lead to adoption of the quicklime process. Since it seems to have been effective, it probably was not adopted because the suffering of the victims was so extraordinary that it disturbed even perpetrators hardened by months of participation in mass shootings.

The veterinarian, continuing his account, also describes witnessing the results of gas-van murders, another indication that these massacres in western Poland were experimental, part of the transition developing in late 1941 from individual killing by shooting to mass-killing technologies:

In the afternoon a dark gray vehicle, looking like an ambulance, arrived in the clearing a number of times. When the back door was opened, human bodies fell out, men, women and children. They too were Jews. This gray car drove past me three times at hourly intervals. Whether it continued to come when I was taken away, I don't know. The bodies falling out of the cars were joined together, as if linked by a convulsive embrace in distorted postures, with faces bitten away. I saw one man's teeth sunk in another's jaw. Some had their noses bitten off, some their fingers. Many were holding their hands in a convulsive grip—they must have been members of the same family. These corpses we were told to separate by force. When this could not be done, we were ordered to hack them, cut off hands, legs and other parts. Then we had to put them in the smaller pit, heads to feet, packed very tightly. The severed limbs were to be put between the torsos. While I was there three layers of bodies were packed like that, and one car was not yet unloaded. . . .

The corpses brought in the gray car were, apparently, victims of gassing. One could smell the gas coming from inside the vehicle and the clothes of the dead.

And again, as at Slonim, there is indication of increasingly malefic violence, violence in the service of extreme and entirely gratuitous depravity:

I also remember that during the extermination of Jews in the forest, one of the Gestapo men snatched a small child from its mother's hands and smashed its head before her very eyes on the edge of his car. When the mother cried out, he lashed out with the body of the child so that the head hit her on her mouth and brain tissue stuck to it. Then he took something from his car—lime or Plaster of Paris—and stopped her mouth.

But given the volume of material at hand for the experiment, who can doubt that the substance the SS man stuffed into the mother's mouth to stop her screaming was quicklime?

Some eight thousand Jews were murdered at Konin in this mid-November 1941 operation.

On the twenty-fourth anniversary of the October Revolution, 6–7 November 1941 (24 October on the old-style Russian calendar), Sonderkommando 1b under Erich Ehrlinger, a lawyer, staged a contemptuous extravaganza in Minsk. "Gallows were thrown up all over Minsk," Vasily Grossman writes—"on the streets, in the parks, in the bazaars and on the outskirts of town." Some one hundred Russians and Byelorussians were hanged and left hanging; wooden signs around their necks labeled them "Partisan," "For collaborating with partisans," "Communist." But worse was reserved for the Jews of Minsk in their crowded ghetto. Early on the morning of 7 November 1941 a detachment of SS and police marched into the ghetto with a large escort of local and Lithuanian militia. They rounded up "men, women and children," writes ghetto resident Hersh Smolar, "herding them into Jubilee Square under a hail of blows and curses." Grossman says they were "ordered to put on their best clothing and to dress their children as if for a holiday. Even small babies had to be taken." The point, it seemed, was to stage a fake parade. The people crowded into Jubilee Square were ordered to line up in rows, eight wide, and handed Soviet flags, and the men in the first row were given a banner to carry:

LONG LIVE THE 24TH ANNIVERSARY
OF THE GREAT SOCIALIST OCTOBER REVOLUTION

"People began pushing, dragging their children, trying to keep their families together," Smolar recalls:

> From the *Judenrat** building nearby came groups of men in civilian clothing carrying huge movie cameras. From all angles they filmed the "demonstration," as they ordered the Jews to smile and look happy, to put their children on their shoulders and start marching. The march went along Opanski Street, where a long line of black trucks was waiting. The police ordered the Jews to climb into the trucks, which then started moving toward Tutshinka Street.

The crowds were jammed into former NKVD storehouses on Tutshinka Street without food or water. From there, across the next three days, as children and the elderly died in the thronged deprivation of the storehouse prisons, the victims were trucked to a killing site and shot into pits. Einsatzgruppe A listed 6,624 Jews shot by Sonderkommando 1b in the course of this *Aktion;* but both Grossman and Smolar (who cites "information available to the [Minsk ghetto] *Judenrat*") give twelve thousand as the number of Minsk Jews murdered in the *Oktiabrske* massacre.

Its purpose had been to make room for Reich Jews being shipped East from Germany. Seven trainloads left for Minsk on 8 November 1941. Soon afterward, writes Grossman, "German Jews began to arrive by the thousands" from Hamburg, Berlin and Frankfurt. A further massacre of seven thousand Minsk Jews on 20 November 1941 was justified on the grounds that "the plan [of 7 November 1941] had not been ful-

*Jewish Council.

filled," meaning, Grossman explains, "that a smaller number of Jews had been destroyed than was demanded by the authorities."

A detachment of Einsatzkommando 5 under SS-Obersturmbann-führer August Meier assisted by Order Police murdered "about 15,000 Jews" on the *Oktiabrske* anniversary in Rovno, in the western Ukraine. Einsatzkommando 5 was busy that month; Meier, a former business-man, also reported shooting 15 "political officials," 21 "saboteurs and looters," 414 "hostages" and "10,650 Jews" in Kiev in the first three weeks of November 1941—more victims for Babi Yar.

Himmler was frustrated with the slow pace of extermination in Latvia. Stahlecker had been more interested in moving on to help conquer Leningrad than in "cleansing" Latvia and had supervised the murder of less than half of the sixty-six thousand Latvian Jews trapped by Bar-barossa. His successor, Hans-Adolf Prützmann, the Higher SS and Police Leader for the Baltic and Byelorussia, had deferred to the deter-mination of the civilian Reichskommissar Ostland, Lohse, to confine the Riga Jews to ghettos and use them for skilled slave labor. Lohse's orders from Alfred Rosenberg, Andrew Ezergailis points out, "were to raise the productivity of the Ostland and to supply the army with daily necessities and hardware." On the other hand, Prützmann's counterpart in the Ukraine, Jeckeln, had shown ruthless initiative and efficient organiza-tion at Kamenets-Podolsky and Babi Yar. Himmler decided to solve his Latvian problem by switching Jeckeln for Prützmann, which he did on 31 October 1941.

By 5 November 1941 Jeckeln's staff had moved to Riga. The Ober-gruppenführer detoured through Berlin, where Himmler briefed him on the problem and ordered him to finish off the Riga Jews—because they were Jews, but also because Reich Jews were about to be shipped to Riga to continue clearing Germany. After the war Jeckeln reported Himmler's exact words: "Tell Lohse that it is my order, which is also the Führer's wish." Armed with Himmler's order, Jeckeln traveled on to Riga, arriving sometime after 13 November 1941. A *Führerbefehl* trumped Lohse's instructions from Alfred Rosenberg; the Reichskom-missar prudently gave way. Jeckeln took over Prützmann's quarters in the Ritterhaus and got busy.

Once moral and psychological questions have been answered, mass killing is primarily a problem of logistics. As far as Jeckeln was con-cerned, a *Führerbefehl* answered any moral question. The Higher SS and Police Leader had his own answer to the psychological question. As he told a reluctant new Einsatzgruppe commander the following year, "I have thought and considered this very carefully, and if I catch somebody who objects to this [mass killing] or breaks down, then he will also be shot." It remained, then, to organize the *Aktion,* a project to which he brought his considerable experience in the Ukraine.

The Riga ghetto was located on the east side of town. Jeckeln therefore searched southeastward of Riga for a killing site. Since the Riga area is low-lying, sandy and coastal—almost swampland—the site would have to be elevated, or the killing pits would fill up with groundwater. Jeckeln at first thought of shipping the victims to the site by railroad, so he drove toward Salaspils, where a concentration camp was under construction, along the road that paralleled the railroad line. (The camp was the one Stahlecker had told the Gebietskommissar of Latvia in October it was the "Führer's wish" to build as a way station for Reich Jews.) Six miles southeast of the Riga ghetto Jeckeln found his location: a pine forest covering a low hill situated between the railroad and the main road to Daugavpils. On the railroad side there was a small station where only local trains stopped. The station name was Rumbula, which is the name the killing site took.

Ezergailis summarizes the site preparation:

Jeckeln assigned *SS-Untersturmführer* Ernst Hemicker, a construction specialist [on his staff], to organize the digging of the pits. Hemicker, accompanied by [other staff members], drove out to Rumbula and was informed about the number of people to be killed [about twenty-five thousand]. Hemicker later testified that he was shocked by the number, but made no protestations. On November 20 or 21, 300 Russian POWs were assigned to Rumbula, where under the supervision of Germans and Latvians they dug six pits. Hemicker supervised the digging. Each pit was ten meters [33 feet] on a side and from two and a half to three meters [8 to 10 feet] deep, the size of a small house. The Russian POWs dug the pits in the shape of an inverted pyramid, lifting the dirt by stages upwards, from platform to platform. There was a walk-in ramp at one side.... The job was finished in about three days ... by approximately November 23.

Besides preparing the site, Jeckeln also had to organize personnel and transportation. Ezergailis estimates that the Higher SS and Police Leader needed about seventeen hundred men to control and guard the various locations that the *Aktion* would encompass. He ordered his personal bodyguard of ten or twelve men to do the actual killing. He tried to enlist the dozen Ritterhaus motor pool drivers as a relief execution commando, but none was willing to volunteer. For guards Jeckeln turned to Rudolf Lange, the ranking Gestapo and SD officer in Latvia, who mobilized the three hundred men of the Arajs commando as well as, says Ezergailis, "perhaps half the fifty-man Latvian guard unit of the . . . SD headquarters, plus perhaps four dozen German SD men in Riga, the remnants of Einsatzkommando 2. All together, Lange could deliver about 400 men with SD experience, meaning that most of them had taken part in killing civilians prior to November." The Order Police contributed about 140 German policemen from companies in Riga and Jelgava. Latvians also participated in the massacre. Based on his estimate of seventeen hundred positions to fill, Ezergailis concludes that the number of Latvians involved must have been about one thousand, known to have been drawn from five groups: Latvians who worked for Lange in the SD, precinct police, Riga city police, "battalion police who were being trained for military action in Russia" and some one hundred Latvian ghetto guards.

Organizing transportation was difficult. Rather than transport the Jewish victims by rail, Jeckeln decided to march them the six miles from the ghetto to Rumbula, but he still needed trucks and buses to carry personnel, small children, the sick and the elderly and to pick up the bodies of victims shot along the way. Ezergailis estimates that Jeckeln's stock of motor pool automobiles and motorcycles would have sufficed for transporting dignitaries and the killing squad, but that trucks—he needed a minimum of twenty-five—were in short supply. Jeckeln probably scavenged trucks and buses from the Latvian police organizations and the city of Riga and possibly from the Wehrmacht as well.

There was further conflict between Rosenberg and Himmler over whether or not to preserve Eastern Jews who could be exploited for labor. Ohlendorf had lost the argument with Himmler where Ukrainian farmers were concerned, but Rosenberg, with more authority, won a minor concession, at least temporarily sparing the lives of able-bodied Jewish males between the ages of sixteen and sixty. To facilitate this selection, the Germans fenced off four blocks of the Riga ghetto with barbed wire and on 28 November 1941 posted an order commanding the men to move and the people remaining in the large ghetto to prepare to be relocated. "The relocation of the Jews to be transported," as Ezergailis paraphrases it, "would begin at six o'clock on the morning of November 30; they were told that they could take a twenty-kilogram [forty-four pound] bag." Since previous selections of able-bodied men had led to their murder, the people of the ghetto feared for their men but believed they themselves were actually only being moved. "The whole ghetto was in motion like ants in an anthill," a ghetto resident, Frida Michelson, remembers. "We made and remade packages; we prepared knapsacks, selected and re-selected the more necessary clothing and food, compared lighter things against heavier. We tested the packs for each person for the weight and comfort of carrying them." About four thousand men moved into the small ghetto on 29 November 1941. Five hundred seamstresses and women with tailoring skills were also separated from the main population, housed in a Riga prison and returned later to housing near the ghetto to repair Wehrmacht uniforms.

That same day Jeckeln briefed the German commanding officers in the Ritterhaus conference hall. "He stressed that participation in the killings was a patriotic obligation," Ezergailis says in paraphrase, "and pointed out that refusal to participate was equal to the refusal to participate in a war, equal to desertion. Those HSSPF* staff members who did not have specific assignments, Jeckeln ordered to the pits as observers"—in Jeckeln's revealing words, they should "make it their obligation to be present at the executions as witnesses, so that no one is spared knowledge and complicity."

Ezergailis lists five significant factors Jeckeln had to weigh in his planning:

> 1) the killing grounds were about ten kilometers from the ghetto, a stretch that would take three hours to traverse at regular infantry pace; 2) there were only seven hours of daylight [at that time of year in northern Latvia], and even taking in the twilight hours, the killing time could be no more than eight hours; 3) the last column sent out was at 12:00 noon and would have to arrive in Rumbula around 3:00 p.m.; 4) more than 12,000 people a day would have to be transported and killed; 5) the Jews were to be driven in 1,000-person columns with the guards posted on both sides.

About three inches of snow fell in the Riga area on the night of 29 November 1941; the temperature dropped to 18 degrees Fahrenheit (it would rise into the mid-thirties during the day). A train from Berlin carrying about a thousand Jewish men, women and children arrived in Riga that Saturday evening and was left standing on a siding through the night at Skirotava station, three miles from Rumbula. Later it would prove to be a source of conflict between Jeckeln and Himmler.

A wake-up gang—German police, Arajs militiamen, Jewish ghetto police—began pounding on western ghetto doors at four a.m. on 30 November 1941. At the eastern end of the ghetto a team cut exits through the barbed wire so the columns could pass. An Arajs blue bus delivered German SD personnel. People emerged from houses with

*Höherer SS und Polizei Führer—i.e., Higher SS and Police Leader.

their bags and knapsacks. There was running, shouting, attempts to escape back into the vacated houses. Frida Michelson saw

> young women, women with infants in their arms, old women, handicapped, helped by their neighbors, young boys and girls—all marching, marching. Suddenly, in front of our window, a German SS man started firing with an automatic gun point blank into the crowd. People were mowed down by the shots and fell on the cobblestones. . . . People were trampling over those who had fallen, they were pushing forward, away from the wildly shooting SS man. Some were throwing away their packs so they could run faster. The Latvian policemen were shouting "Faster! Faster!" and lashing whips over the heads of the crowd.

Michelson was observing a Baltic German Sturmbannführer named Brasch, an accountant. He was not firing wildly. He told a Jewish ghetto policeman who had formerly been a high-ranking Latvian police official and who asked him what he was doing, "We are supposed to adhere strictly to the time schedule for moving the column to its destination, and therefore we are eliminating from the ranks everyone who could slow down the pace of the column."

The ghetto was already strewn with bodies when the first column passed through the opened wire at six a.m., picking up an escort of Latvian and German police. The blue bus loaded children and elderly. Six miles eastward at Rumbula at eight-fifteen Jeckeln had the thousand Berlin Jews shot into the pits, the first Rumbula victims. The leading column of Riga ghetto Jews arrived at Rumbula at nine. Moving a thousand people of all ages and health conditions six miles on foot in three hours had been brutal: the guards had shot people who tried to run or simply stopped to rest, and possessions and bodies had been left strewn along the road.

The system Jeckeln organized for Rumbula was adapted from the system he had used in the Ukraine, the system Blobel adapted for Babi Yar. From the road an outer gauntlet of about one hundred guards, some with dogs, funneled the victims three hundred yards across scrubland to the edge of the forest. An outer apron of another hundred guards "was to watch for escapees," Ezergailis writes. "Several machine guns were set up on the periphery, ready to stop even a massive flight." Between the road and the forest edge, with shouts and blows, the guards seized the victims' packs and bags. A wooden box positioned along the gauntlet received valuables—watches, rings, coins, jewelry. Coats came off next.

From the outer gauntlet the victims were sent forward in groups of fifty into the forest, down a narrower gauntlet manned by another hundred guards. Limiting each group to fifty may have been determined by the capacity of the clip of the Russian submachine guns the killers were using. Jeckeln's aide Paul Degenhart testified that the Russian weapons were used because they could be set on single fire and their clips held fifty bullets. With more shouts and blows the victims were forced to undress. As they approached the killing pits the gauntlet narrowed them to single file. Since three pits were being operated, the gauntlet was probably shifted from one to the next for each group of fifty, diverting the line to whichever executioner was ready to receive it. The victims descended the earthen ramp into a pit. Packers would have been stationed in the pit, as at Babi Yar, to position the victims lying down on the bodies of those who had preceded them. A *Genickschüss* by one of Jeckeln's bodyguards ended their suffering. When a killer had emptied a clip, another man replaced him and he took a break.

Jeckeln entertained guests:

> Jeckeln stood on the top of the embankment with many other high SS, SD and police officials. . . . Arajs, heavily drunk, took a more active role, working closer to the pits, overseeing his men. Jeckeln invited guests from all levels of the German hierarchy: *Reichskommissar* Ostland Lohse was there for a time, so perhaps was the *Gebietskommissar* of Latvia, Drechsler. . . . [Jeckeln] also called in police commanders from . . . other cities in the region to witness the killings. Stahlecker was called in from the Leningrad front to be present, perhaps to point out to him that he had not finished the job and to show how it must be done. . . . Although the police officials came from a long distance, Jeckeln had not invited anyone from the Wehrmacht.

Thirteen thousand Riga Jews were murdered at Rumbula that day. Thirteen thousand people in columns of one thousand each is thirteen columns marched out from Riga to Rumbula and two hundred sixty groups of fifty people moved down the gauntlet to the killing pits. If the first column arrived at nine a.m. and the last at three p.m. and if the killing continued in three pits until five p.m., an hour and a half after sundown, nine people had to be murdered in each pit every minute, three *Genickschüssen* every seven seconds. If only twelve men did the killing, as Ezergailis concludes, then each man personally murdered — pointed a submachine gun at, pulled the trigger, saw the skull tear and blood spray and the body slacken and convulse — more than one thousand human beings, most of them elderly parents and grandparents stripped to their underwear, half-naked women and children. Jeckeln's *Sardinenpackung* method was efficient because it meant bodies did not have to be moved or even rearranged, but the number of murders per man suggests another advantage as well. The back and the back of the head are relatively featureless aspects of the human body, relatively anonymous; not having to look their victims in the face as they murdered them made killing them easier. What was easier for the perpetrators, however, was harder for the victims: having to lie down on the dying and the dead and wait in fresh gore to be murdered increased their suffering.

A Wehrmacht engineer who commanded a bridge inspection company heard "curious, inexplicable gunfire and screaming" from the direction of Rumbula and followed it to its source and "saw everything," a comrade of his wrote historian Gerald Fleming many years later; "he also mentioned the brutal laughter of the SD people." The outraged engineer's subsequent report eventually reached Admiral William Canaris, the head of German military counterintelligence. Canaris took it up with Hitler himself, who responded, "You're getting soft, sir! I *have* to do it, because after me no one else will!"

Corpses had to be cleared from the streets of the Riga ghetto. That work began at about two in the afternoon. Men from the Arajs commando finished off the wounded. Twenty invalids were carried out of the ghetto hospital into the street, laid out on straw mattresses and shot in the head. Ezergailis says "sleds, wheelbarrows and horse carts" were used to transport the bodies to a cemetery where the Germans had dynamited a crater for a mass grave. One young man on the burial squad found the body of his murdered mother on the street near the cemetery and added it to his load. "The bodies were thrown into the common pit without rites or prayers," Ezergailis mourns. "The Jews of the ghetto were not allowed to visit the cemetery."

Jeckeln repeated the *Aktion* on 8 December 1941 to clear the rest of the Riga ghetto. The weeklong delay has puzzled historians. It occurred because of the conflict between Jeckeln and Himmler over the liquidation of the transport of one thousand Berlin Jews. Himmler spoke to Heydrich on the day of the first massacre, 30 November 1941, specifically excluding the transport from the *Aktion*. He made a note after the phone conversation: "Jewish transport from Berlin, no liquidation." Since the Berlin Jews had already been murdered by then, Himmler was probably responding to a call Heydrich had made prior to that date. When Himmler learned that Reich Jews had been massacred, he radioed Jeckeln and read him the riot act. He told Jeckeln he would punish "unauthorized actions or actions contrary to directives issued either by me or by the Reich Security Main Office under my authority" concerning "treatment of Jews resettled in the Ostland." In a second message the same day he ordered Jeckeln to meet with him at his headquarters in East Prussia on 4 December 1941. Jeckeln's travels account for the gap in time between the first and second Rumbula massacre.

On 8 December 1941 the remaining ten thousand Riga Jews were murdered. Frida Michelson survived by playing dead and finding herself fortuitously covered with discarded shoes. She describes going "numb with terror." She recounts being seized by "an indescribable fear . . . that bordered on loss of mind." Another survivor, Ella Medale, a twenty-eight-year-old teacher who "looked Latvian," was visited far down the gauntlet not with numbness and near loss of mind but with profound and lifesaving clarity:

> Without realizing what could occur, mechanically I took off my coat and bent to put it down when suddenly I felt a stinging pain, a blow on my back. I fell down, and for a moment my consciousness became astoundingly clear. The sense of self-preservation awakened in me and gave me an awareness: "Your life is running out! Now or never! If you don't do anything now, the grave will get you!" . . . I jumped up and ran to the next guard, who was [an Arajs man] who had guarded us frequently. He was ashen and hardly could hold the [rifle] in his hand. Apparently he was nauseated. I grabbed him by his arm and pleadingly told him: "Save me! You know that I am not a Jew!" For an answer he mumbled something incomprehensible and pointed to a group of policemen, who apparently were in charge: "Speak to the higher ups!" I rushed to them. The head executioner Arajs fastened his eyes on me. His face was disfigured, beast-like, and he swayed back and forth, horribly drunk. A shriek broke out of me: "I am not a Jew!" I trembled as in a fever. Arajs waved me away: "Here are only Jews! Today Jewish blood must flow!"

Medale survived to serve as a witness at Arajs's trial.

After the shooting stopped and Russian-speaking prisoners began shoveling earth over the dead, Michelson could hear the perpetrators, Latvian and German, from under her saving mountain of shoes:

> Suddenly I heard Latvian being spoken very close by: "Let's have a smoke."
> "A fine performance."
> "It was very efficiently organized."
> "They have experience."
> "Just leave it to the Germans; they are good at it."
> "I hope we get our cut of the booty." Pause—"The Germans have first choice."

"There is enough for everybody."

"I'm tired. I'm going home."

"Me too."

"Goodbye."

"Goodbye."

After a pause I heard German spoken: *"Was suchst du dort?"* ("What are you looking for there?")

"Ein Paar Strümpfe für meine Frau." ("A pair of stockings for my wife.")

Quiet for a while. Then, from the direction of the trench a child's cry: "Mama! Mama! Mamaaa!"

A few shots. Quiet. Killed. Then in German this smug assertion: "From our kettle nobody escapes alive."

The bridge-inspection officer whose report had reached Hitler wrote his wife a month later that German Jews had been moved into the area—into a camp and into the emptied ghetto. He could hear Swabian accents in the camp, he wrote, and Berlin accents in the ghetto. "How long will it be," he asked his wife rhetorically, "until these Jews, too, are 'resettled' to the pine forest, where I recently saw mounds of earth heaped up over five large pits, sharply sagging in the middle, and despite the cold a sickly, sweet odor lingered in the air?"

"After the killings," Ezergailis notes, "Jeckeln had told [his aide Paul] Degenhart that 22,000 rounds of ammunition had been used at Rumbula. Noting that on the two days more than 1,000 people were killed within the ghetto and on the road to Rumbula, the number adds up to just below 24,000." Adding in the trainload of victims from Berlin brings the total to twenty-five thousand.

"Although the bodies were picked up quickly," Ezergailis concludes his lamentation, "the ghetto remained in a shambles, and for days thereafter it bore the evidence of a pogrom. Broken suitcases, furniture, toys and baby carriages were all over the streets and yards. The houses were desolate, blood was splashed on the walls and in the stairwells. Days after the *Aktion,* frozen rivulets of blood were on the sidewalks and gutters. Even two months later, arriving German Jews found corpses in cellars and attics."

Jeckeln must have satisfied the Reichsführer-SS that he had not deliberately disobeyed. For his evil work liquidating the Riga ghetto he received a further promotion, to Leader of the SS Upper Section, Ostland, on 11 December 1941.

FOURTEEN

Nerves

Karl Jäger's notorious report on the murderous work of Einsatzkommando 3, issued from Kaunas on 1 December 1941, cumulates to a total
of 137,346 deaths in five months in the area assigned to one Einsatzkommando alone. "I can state today," Jäger writes in summary, "that
the goal of solving the Jewish problem in Lithuania has been reached by
Einsatzkommando 3. There are no Jews in Lithuania anymore except
the work Jews and their families, which total

in Siauliai	some 4,500
in Kaunas	some 15,000
in Vilnius	some 15,000

"I intended to kill off these work Jews and their families too," Jäger
goes on with malicious bravado, "but met with the strongest protest
from the civil administration (*Reichskommissar*) and the Wehrmacht,
which culminated in a prohibition: these Jews and their families may not
be shot dead!"

In Kaunas in the final days before he issued his report, on 25 and 29
November 1941, Jäger had overseen massacres of Reich Jews shipped
east from Berlin, Munich, Frankfurt, Vienna and Breslau, a total for the
two days of 1,869 men, 2,716 women and 327 children, all shot into the
killing pits of the Ninth Fort. Since Reich Jews shipped to Lodz had not
been immediately killed, and since Himmler vehemently protested Jeckeln's unauthorized killing of the Berlin Jews shipped to Riga, these
prompt Kaunas massacres are anomalous. Historian Christian Gerlach
notes that the Ostland section chief in the Reich Ministry for the Occupied Territories in the East met with Jäger on 22 November 1941 "and
expressed his satisfaction with the executions of Lithuanian Jews,"
which to Gerlach indicates that the Ministry for the East "was in agreement with the plan to execute the German Jews who were expected to
arrive in Kaunas." But no documents have yet emerged that reveal who
ordered these anomalous slaughters before Hitler authorized the direct
killing of Western Jews.

In his swaggering summary Jäger assesses the relative difficulties of various *Aktionen,* commenting that "the *Aktionen* in Kaunas itself, where a sufficient number of trained partisans [i.e., Lithuanian auxiliaries] was available, can best be described as parade shooting, especially if compared with *Aktionen* in the country, where the greatest difficulties had to be overcome again and again." Like Jeckeln, Jäger had required all his subordinates to participate in the massacres: "All commanders and men of my commando in Kaunas took part in the large-scale *Aktionen* in Kaunas most actively." Only one official, Jäger adds, was released from participating "because of ill health."

In a follow-up telegram in early February 1942 Jäger increased his total of Jews murdered by 75, to 136,421, added the 1,851 non-Jews his subordinates had executed and gave a breakdown of this total of 138,272 by age and gender: 48,252 men, 55,556 women and 34,464 children.

Stahlecker, in a second long report that covered the period up to 31 January 1942, similarly concluded that the work of Einsatzgruppe A in the Baltic and Byelorussian Ostland was largely finished, a point Stahlecker gruesomely dramatized with a map studded with coffins sized proportionally to the number of Jewish victims. Subsuming Jäger's tallies, the Einsatzgruppe commander gave a combined total for Latvia and Lithuania of 229,052 Jewish men, women and children liquidated, a veritable city of the dead. There were still about 128,000 Jews remaining in Byelorussia, he noted, and killing them was "fraught with certain difficulties," including the need for Jewish labor, frozen ground and shortages of fuel and transportation. These difficulties were not insurmountable; they only meant that he would need two more months to finish the job.

Frozen ground was limiting more than Einsatzgruppen murders; Russian winter had stalled the Wehrmacht just as it had stalled Napoleon in 1812. Wehrmacht officer Siegfried Knappe found it brutally unforgettable:

By December [1941], we were no more than twenty-five kilometers [16 miles] from Moscow, but the temperature was paralyzing. Heavy snow fell on December 1, and the pitiless cold became unbearable. . . .
As we approached the outermost suburbs of Moscow a paralyzing blast of cold hit us, and the temperature dropped far below zero and stayed there. Our trucks and vehicles would not start, and our horses started to die from the cold in large numbers for the first time; they would just die in the bitter cold darkness of the night, and we would find them dead the next morning. The Russians knew how to cope with this weather, but we did not; their vehicles were built and conditioned for this kind of weather, but ours were not. We all now numbly

wrapped ourselves in our blankets. Everyone felt brutalized and defeated by the cold. The sun would rise late in the morning, as harsh now in the winter winds as in the heat of August, and not one fresh footprint would be visible for as far as the human eye could see. Frostbite was taking a very heavy toll now as more and more men were sent back to the field hospitals with frozen fingers and toes. Many infantry companies were down to platoon size. On December 5, the temperature plummeted to [−22° F.]. It was almost impossible for the human body to function in such numbing cold.

But Himmler's murderous forces were nothing if not dogged. The last major massacre in Liepaja, on the western Baltic coast of Latvia, took advantage of the friability of the deep sand dunes back from the beach at Skede, ten miles north of the city. Prisoners dug a V-shaped trench twenty feet deep in the sand and notched a ledge four feet down the ditch's seaward wall, on which victims were forced to stand facing the ocean to be shot from behind. Mass killings at Skede on orders from Riga during three days in mid-December 1941 destroyed about half the Liepaja Jewish population, some three thousand men, women and children. It was not as cold on the beach as Moscow's deep freeze, but a bitter wind was biting and the Liepaja victims were required to remove all their clothes and stand naked or nearly so. Rather than *Sardinenpackung,* the Latvians and Germans who did the killing reverted to the military system of two executioners firing simultaneously at each victim. But mothers with infants were told to hold their babies over their heads; one man then shot the mother while the other shot the child. "For the corpses that did not fall into the ditch" on their own, Ezergailis notes, "there was a kicker who rolled them in." A German SD man working down in the ditch administered *Genickschüssen* to the wounded.

At Vinnitsa, in the Ukraine, where Wehrmacht engineers were building the forward Hitler bunker, Werwolf, an area forty miles around was declared *Judenfrei* in December 1941 after an October Revolution massacre of 2,580 Vinnitsa Jews. In fact, Jewish slave laborers continued to live and work in the Vinnitsa area. On 5 January 1942 the SS published an announcement in the *Vinnitsa News* ordering Jews to assemble for resettlement with luggage and a three-day supply of food. They complied, but conditions were such that the SS had to send them home; as the officer responsible for the Hitler bunker subsequently informed Berlin, the ground was frozen and it had been impossible to dig pits. Not to be thwarted in reducing the supposed risk to Hitler's security in the neighborhood of Werwolf (which he would not occupy until July 1942), the SS seized 227 Jews who lived in the village nearest the bunker, lined them up against the wall of the local NKVD prison and killed and simultaneously buried them by dynamiting the wall.

By the end of 1941 many of the men of the Einsatzgruppen, Order Police and SD and their native auxiliaries had developed fully malefic violent identities. For some that meant taking pleasure in killing; for others it meant killing when ordered to do so and drinking afterward to forget.

An SS-Scharführer* named Ribe, for example, oversaw the Minsk ghetto. Ghetto resident Hersh Smolar remembers the Scharführer's enthusiasm for viciousness:

> [Ribe] was even more sadistic than his predecessors. Jews who had escaped from Slutsk and settled in the Minsk ghetto recognized him as the murderer who had been in charge of liquidating the Slutsk ghetto. People called him "the Devil with the White Eyes." . . . Ribe never let any Jew he encountered go unscathed, regardless of age or sex. He would look at his victim with his big bulging eyes, his lips would form a smile, he would carefully aim his pistol—and never miss. It was Ribe who organized the "beauty contest" of young Jewish women, selected twelve of the youngest and prettiest, and ordered them to parade through the ghetto until they reached the Jewish cemetery. Here he forced them to undress and then shot them one by one. The last woman to be killed was Lena Neu. He took her brassiere from her and said smugly, "This will be my souvenir of the pretty Jewess."

Ribe was the SS man as beast, a familiar and all-too-common type. Not all the Third Reich's killers were so complacently socialized to violence, however. The discomfort that some of them felt certainly does not qualify as mitigation: crimes are judged by acts, not by facility. But the evidence that perpetrators exhibited a range of responses, often conflicted and even traumatic, supports Lonnie Athens's model of violent socialization and disqualifies ideology alone as the enabling mechanism for violence.

SS-Obersturmführer Karl Kretschmer of Sonderkommando 4a responded to his murderous duties with ambivalence even though he was committed to the Third Reich's anti-Semitic ideology and accepted the standard rationalizations of the Final Solution that Hitler and Himmler handed down. Kretschmer joined Sonderkommando 4a later

*Staff Sergeant.

in the war, after Blobel had been relieved and replaced by a physician, Erwin Weinmann, in January 1942, who in turn had been replaced by a former schoolteacher, Eugen Steimle, in August 1942. By then Sonderkommando 4a was working north of Stalingrad, far to the east of Kiev, but its work was the same as it had been since the beginning of Barbarossa: murdering Jews.

"The sight of the dead (including women and children) is not very cheering," Kretschmer wrote his wife soon after he arrived behind the front. "But we are fighting this war for the survival or non-survival of our people. . . . As the war is in our opinion a Jewish war, the Jews are the first to feel it. Here in Russia, wherever the German soldier is, no Jew remains. You can imagine that at first I needed some time to come to grips with this." Kretschmer counted himself lucky to be able to barter for food, a consequence of what he called "our hard work." He and his men could also choose among clothing. "We can get everything here," he told his wife. "The clothes belonged to people who are no longer alive today." He could not ship her a "Persian rug" because "the Jewish dealers are no longer alive," but he sent her canned butter, sardines, meat and tea.

All these goods were the fruits, of course, of robbery and confiscation. If the confiscation meant that Russians would die, Kretschmer told his wife, Germans would still seize the food; the Führer had given his approval. Moreover, "we have got to appear to be tough here or else we will lose the war. There is no room for pity of any kind. You women and children back home could not expect any mercy or pity if the enemy got the upper hand. For that reason we are mopping up where necessary but otherwise the Russians are willing, simple and obedient. There are no Jews here any more."

Kretschmer was traumatized by his initial exposure to mass killing. He describes his difficulties only obliquely, censoring himself not only to spare his wife but perhaps also to evade whatever censors were reading his mail. "The reveille is at six o'clock," he wrote a month after his arrival, for example, "but I always wake up earlier because up to now I have not been able to sleep more than five hours, although I sometimes go to bed early." He connected his sleep disturbance with the work he was doing: "The first few days I was tired *and could not take very much* but after that *I managed to see the night through* and was actually *the last to quit the field.*"* He found the killing sufficiently upsetting that he sought alternative duty as an administrator, an assignment, he told his wife and children, that he had been granted:

---

*Emphasis added here and below.

I have already told you about the shooting—that I could not say "no" here either [i.e., he wanted to avoid doing it but was not allowed exception or did not risk asking]. But they've more or less said they've finally found a good man to run the administrative side of things. The last one was by all accounts a coward. That's the way people are judged here. But you can trust your Daddy. He thinks about you all the time and is not shooting immoderately.

Judging men to be cowards who were unwilling to shoot unarmed victims in cold blood was a form of coercive violent coaching the group used to further the violent socialization of new members. And associating thinking about his children with "not shooting immoderately" emphasizes the difficulty Kretschmer was having accepting the group's standards. A few lines later in the same letter he responded sardonically to his wife's news of a neighbor's military assignment: "It's nice that Herr Kern is going to France. I think he would have been *too weak* for the East, *though people do change here*. People soon get used to the sight of blood, but *Blutwurst* is not very popular around here."

A few days later Kretschmer was still feeling precarious. He told his wife and children about the fine meals he enjoyed, then explained, "We have to eat and drink well because of the nature of our work. . . . *Otherwise we would crack up.* Your Papa will be very careful and *strike the right balance.* It's not very pleasant stuff. I would far rather sleep." At the end of the same letter, Kretschmer summarized the strategies he had adopted to carry him through, a combination of habituation, rationalization and denial:

If it weren't for *the stupid thoughts* [he had been having] *about what we are doing in this country,* the *Einsatz* here would be wonderful, since it has put me in a position where I can support you all very well. Since, as I already wrote to you, I consider the last *Einsatz* to be justified and indeed approve of the consequences it had, the phrase "stupid thoughts" is not strictly accurate. Rather *it is a weakness not to be able to stand the sight of dead people; the best way of overcoming it is to do it more often. Then it becomes a habit.* . . . The more one thinks about the whole business the more one comes to the conclusion that it's the only thing we can do to safeguard unconditionally the security of our people and our future. *I do not therefore want to think and write about it any further.* I would only make your heart heavy needlessly. We men here at the front will win through. Our faith in the Führer fulfills us and gives us strength to carry out our difficult and thankless task.

If he is not yet converted at this point, Kretschmer appears at least to be moving toward incorporating the values of the violent group he joined almost two months previously. To do so he had progressively blurred the distinction between defensive and offensive violence, casting his murderous work as vital for the protection of his family. Characterizing a victim group as a relentless threat to a perpetrator group is the fundamental mechanism of genocide. It allows perpetrators to interpret their violence as defensive and therefore both justified and unavoidable—in Kretschmer's words, "it's the only thing we can do."

Erich Naumann, who took over commanding Einsatzgruppe B in Byelorussia at the end of November 1941 when Nebe felt he could no longer go on, offered a variation on Kretschmer's "it's the only thing we can do" during his testimony at the postwar Einsatzgruppen trial in Nuremberg. "[The Führer order] was very harsh," Naumann told the court, "terribly harsh for the *Einsatzkommandos* and others who were involved in it. Everyone knew that it was not pleasant but was very much against one's inner feelings." Naumann insisted that he questioned the Führer order all the way up to Heydrich, who told him finally and with exasperation:

> "That is a clear Führer order. This Führer order has been issued for the security of the rear of the combating forces and of the entire army area. It can only be understood in one way, and it has to be carried out accordingly. All Jews, both male and female, all Gypsies, and all Communist officials fall under the Führer order." He repeated, "There is no discussion. The order must be carried out. The Führer issued the order for reasons of security of the army areas."

Naumann continued his testimony under questioning from the president of the court, Michael Musmanno:

> NAUMANN: These discussions concerning this order, its seriousness and its terrible burden when executing it . . . were confronted, on the other hand, with another discussion—namely, that this order had been issued by the Führer—that is to say, by the man in supreme command, the supreme head of the state. We were now faced with the problem of our personal feelings and this order. Each one of us had to make up his mind whether, during the war, we could decide according to our own personal feelings or whether we had to obey an order which was issued during the war by the supreme commander of the state. The decision was for us, as obedient soldiers, not easy, but it was clear we had to carry out the order, for the very simple reason that a soldier

during the war has to carry out orders. If every soldier only carries out an order after having considered whether he likes it or not, then there would be no more soldiers. . . .

Guilt and remorse I can only feel for crimes I personally commit. If I myself have carried out killings and cruelties then I would have to feel guilt and remorse. If I have carried out an order then I have no guilt at all, and therefore I cannot feel remorse for a guilt that does not exist.

MUSMANNO: Did you have any misgivings at that time?

NAUMANN: Yes, your Honor.

MUSMANNO: Then you did not agree with the order?

NAUMANN: Insofar as I had misgivings about the execution of this order and it was contrary to my nature to kill defenseless people.

MUSMANNO: And you believe it was wrong to kill, especially women and children?

NAUMANN: Not wrong, your Honor, because I was given the authority to do so, because there was a Führer order.

MUSMANNO: I have asked you whether you believed it was wrong at that time to shoot down women and children.

NAUMANN: No, I did not hold that opinion owing to my convictions. It was my conviction that it had to be done.

Naumann's argument that he was only obeying orders was unacceptable to the court, which sentenced him to death, but its value to him as a rationalization should not be discounted. If the highest authority of the state told him to do something, then he could convince himself he had no choice and was therefore not personally responsible. The problem with such appeals to higher authority, as psychologist Herbert C. Kelman points out, is that everyone in the chain of command, up to and including the supreme authority, may feel authorized and therefore freed of moral restraint:

According to a view that is widely held (although it has been challenged by the Nuremberg principles), the state itself is an entity that is not subject to the moral law; it is free to do anything it deems necessary to protect or promote its national interests. The central authorities, in acting for the state, are similarly not subject to moral restraints that might be operative in their personal lives. . . . According to this view, the freedom from all restraints devolves on the central decision maker [e.g., Hitler] from a higher authority, the state, of which he is merely the servant. . . . He too claims that he had no choice in that he was responding to authoritative demands. . . . The whole doctrine is, of course, extremely dangerous because of its total circularity.

But the repetition of massacre after massacre, the screams and pleadings, the faces and bodies glimpsed in their helpless final agonies that unavoidably recalled a sister, a brother, a wife, a child, an aging parent at home or the perpetrator himself, made such rationalizations difficult for some perpetrators to maintain at the edge of the killing pits, if not in the extravagant security of the Führer bunker. A few among the SS leadership succumbed. Erwin Schulz asked to be relieved of duty as commander of Einsatzkommando 5 (Einsatzgruppe C) in September 1941. In a Nuremberg affidavit he explained why: "The reasons for my [request] lay, among others, in the ever-intensified orders for the ruthless extermination of the entire Jewish population. *SS Brigadeführer* Dr. Rasch distinguished himself by particular ruthlessness. He ordered the leaders also to participate personally in the shootings. [SS-Gruppenführer Bruno] Streckenbach himself described the activity of the *Einsatzgruppen* in the East to me as murder." Schulz, like Hitler and Himmler, was prepared to organize massacres but not to participate personally.

Alfred Filbert, a lawyer who commanded Einsatzkommando 9 (Einsatzgruppe B) from June through October 1941, suffered what he later called a "nervous collapse" after organizing massacres in Grodno, Vilnius and Vitebsk and applied for a transfer to military duty in the Waffen-SS. Instead he was recalled to Berlin, charged with illegally withholding 60,000 Reichsmarks confiscated from his victims and sent home on extended unpaid leave. (He was exonerated in 1943 and assigned to the Reich Security Main Office.) A British psychiatrist, Henry V. Dicks, interviewed Filbert many years later in prison, where he was serving a life sentence for his part in murdering eleven thousand people in massacres in Lithuania and Byelorussia.

Dicks offers a rare view into the background family experiences of an Einsatzkommando leader. Filbert had been born in 1905 in Darmstadt of Protestant parents. He mentioned to Dicks several significant occasions of childhood brutalization. "In my home and family," the tall, gaunt Filbert told the psychiatrist, "we only knew command and order. I was born in military barracks. My father started as the sergeant major of the Guard of his Highness the Duke of Hesse. We had a good life then. Of course I wanted to become a soldier. After all—the Guards!" Dicks commented that the SS's rule of absolute obedience must have appealed to him. "The Kaiser demanded worse," Filbert responded—"he said 'When I order you to murder your father and mother you must obey!' The Kaiser's orders were like God's." Evidently *Kadavergehorsam*, corpse-like obedience, predated Nazism.

Protesting his sensitivity, Filbert revealed that his brother handled him violently. "I always went to great lengths to avoid anything to do with death or corpses as a child," he told Dicks. "When I was very young my brother, eighteen months older, took hold of me and held me out over the window sill. Ever since I've had a dread of heights—a feeling it draws me down."

Another memory focused on his violent subjugation by his mother during the years when his father was away at war. Dicks paraphrases Filbert's recollection:

> [Filbert] had looked up to this kind, warm-hearted father and missed him terribly as a child.... It was left to his mother to be the disciplinarian. Yes, she was too strict. [Filbert] recalls how he had a bad fall during his father's absence and lay on the ground yelling in great pain. The mother came out to him with her stick and gave him a beating for weeping. It was only after that had been done that she even looked at his leg and found that he had broken it.

("In [Filbert's] case," Dicks comments, "we are afforded a glimpse of how far back dates his sense of being surrounded by hard, unloving, even murderous figures, with his good daddy not there to save him.... I think that insofar as [Filbert] was relating a fact of his own experience, we are justified in recoiling as much from this piece of cruelty by the mother against her own child as from a typical SS man's atrocity.")

Filbert had gone to the universities of Giessen, Heidelberg and Marburg, winning his dueling scars at one of them, earning his doctorate in law in 1933. He moved up rapidly in the SS, participating with Nebe, Eichmann and others in the conference Heydrich held in 1939 to organize Einsatzgruppen for Poland. At his postwar trial the court established that Filbert had taken command of Einsatzkommando 9 with a speech to his men announcing "hard consequences for any who demurred at taking part in the destruction of Jews." He told his men that "every man must fire," including himself, "to set a good example." Dicks reports that "his bearing was described by some of his subordinates in evidence as 'ruthless,' for example in dismissing objections to the herding and stripping of women and in his lack of consideration for the youth of some of his personnel taking part. It was clear to the court that [Filbert] presented himself as the zealous as well as ferocious executor of his Führer's policies." The psychiatrist quotes the prosecution as acknowledging " 'that [Filbert] stopped the wild shooting of the Lithuanian auxiliary police, but he substituted for it the routine mechanical slaughter of the Chicago stockyards at the rate of 500 a day.' "

The court further established that Filbert had ordered a man in Einsatzkommando 9 who showed consideration for his Jewish victims to be severely punished. Filbert's history, from his childhood brutalization to his fanatic SS posturing, indicates that he was fully violently socialized. Yet he was pragmatic enough to reduce his unit's direct participation in slaughter when he saw evidence that his men were being traumatized:

> By the time the *EK* reached the Vitebsk area [Filbert] had delegated some of the shooting to a civilian militia recruited from among the local Jew haters and anti-Soviet members of the population, distinguished only by armbands, without even the semblance of "due legal process." This was shown to be due to a deterioration of morale among his own men who had to be issued with increasing rations of vodka to carry out their killing orders. Rather than shoot, they would bully the victims to jump into the pit alive, so that the local irregulars should do the final shooting for them.

And just as his men had trouble killing, so also did Filbert find it impossible to sustain the hardness Himmler demanded (but did not himself display). " 'Well,' " Filbert challenged Dicks, " 'how does a man show he cannot stand it except by his nerves giving way?' I asked if this was really how he reacted. 'Yes—a complete nervous breakdown . . . to be degraded into a hangman and murderer—nobody [i.e., the court] believes I felt it.' Myself: What were the symptoms? [Filbert:] 'Uncontrollable trembling' (*Schüttelfrost*—a word I translate as *rigor,* as in fever), 'and weeping. I did not laugh any more.' " At another point in their long conversation Filbert said of his breakdown, "I was degraded into a hangman—I began to tremble and have weeping fits—I used to be so gay."

Filbert supplies a clue to Nebe's reasons for withdrawing from command of Einsatzgruppe B in November 1941. He says Nebe, the former police officer, told him "I have looked after so many criminals, and now I have become one myself." (Nebe's driver had committed suicide, ostensibly because he was unable to bear participating in massacres, and Nebe's friend Hans Gisevius, who saw Nebe after he returned to Berlin, described him as "a mere shadow of his former self, nerves on edge and depressed.") Filbert also offered a typology of the Einsatzgruppen leaders he encountered:

> What about those in the service who could accept the extermination tasks [Dicks asked]—how do you think this was possible for them? [Filbert] says: "There were many of those others. The SS was full of desperate and bad characters." . . . He lists categories: (*a*) There were those who said: "The Führer commands, all is in order"—the

unquestioning ones; (b) another type were those whose motto was simply "In the morning we shoot . . . in the evening we feast"; (c) the third group were those, like himself, who kept aloof from these types, and he was accused of being a bad comrade . . . ; (d) yet another sort were like the young law graduate SS officer who came to him at Vilnius and said "I cannot do it" and [Filbert] had to say "Don't say that aloud!" and put him to work in the unit office.

Perhaps surprisingly, Bach-Zelewski, the Higher SS and Police Leader responsible for Russia–Center, was among those who broke down. Sometime in February 1942 he traveled to Germany and checked into the Red Cross hospital at Hohenlychen, seventy miles north of Berlin, suffering from hemorrhoids. The chief SS physician, Ernst Robert Grawitz, personally attended his case. Grawitz wrote Himmler early in March about the bad turn Bach-Zelewski's recuperation had taken. "Slow healing and prolonged pain are common in hemorrhoid operations," Grawitz wrote, but Bach-Zelewski offered additional challenges:

> It was especially noticeable, however, that the patient arrived from the eastern front for treatment suffering from a very serious state of general exhaustion, particularly nervous exhaustion. (He suffers especially from flashbacks connected with the shootings of Jews which he himself conducted and other difficult experiences in the East!) Because the psychological treatment of the patient is complex, I have personally extensively intervened and am working daily to restore his mental balance. Frau von dem Bach requested to live in the hospital and care for her husband and I have acceded to her request. I took this unusual step, which has led to unavoidable but not unbridgeable difficulties, because the psychological treatment of the patient is a significant factor in the total healing plan.

When Grawitz had asked Bach-Zelewski why he was so disturbed, the Obergruppenführer is supposed to have said, "Thank God, I'm through with it. Don't you know what's happening in Russia? The entire Jewish people . . . is being exterminated there." He wasn't through with it, however; within two months he was back in Russia supervising massacres.

Even Jäger, a hard case, eventually broke down, Jeckeln testified during his 1945 interrogation. "Jäger told me that he had become neurotic as a result of these shootings," Jeckeln said. "[He] was pensioned off and left his post for treatment."

Himmler was concerned about the effect on his subordinates of direct participation in mass killing, as his 12 December 1941 letter ordering "comradely gatherings . . . in the best German domestic style" demonstrates. But he was adamant about accomplishing the Final Solution the Führer had ordered. Heinz Jost, a lawyer and SS-Brigadeführer who took command of Einsatzgruppe A after Stahlecker was killed by Estonian partisans in late March 1942, claimed at the Nuremberg Einsatzgruppen trial to have challenged successively Jeckeln, Heydrich and Himmler with the problem of psychological casualties among the SS killing squads. When he confronted Himmler, he testified, "I was asked, 'Are you a philosopher? What is the meaning of this? What do you mean, problems? All that is concerned are our orders.' " Himmler offered an analogy: "I have given the *Handschuhbefehl,* the glove order." Jost explained to the court: "Himmler had given an order that when [an SS] superior was greeted or saluted the glove had to be removed from the hand. In the Army it was the other way around, the glove had to remain on the hand." Jost continued:

> Himmler said, "I have given this glove order. There are many who believe they do not have to bother about such an order because they don't like it. Anyone whom I meet who does not follow this order and obey it in the strictest manner, I shall punish him very severely and harshly. Even if the contents of the order are ever so ridiculous, the contents of the order don't matter, all that matters is that it is an order, and those who don't obey the glove order prove that they do not want to carry out orders of great importance. Orders cannot be discussed or debated. Orders have to be obeyed, and that principle you don't seem to have realized yet. What is your age?" he asked. I replied, "I was born in 1904." "Oh, you are one of those people who never had any military training. No one here can be an officer or a general who cannot obey, because those who don't obey orders cannot give orders either. I must think about how I can train you to do this."

Himmler trained Jost by breaking him to Unterscharführer—corporal—and sending him to the Eastern front. The episode supports Felix Kersten's unsurpassed portrait of the SS-Reichsführer, whose immense and devious labor turned the "Führer's wish" into the monstrous reality of the Holocaust:

> His eyes were extraordinarily small, and the distance between them narrow, rodent-like. If you spoke to him, these eyes would never leave your face; they would rove over your countenance, fix your eyes; and in them would be an expression of waiting, watching, stealth. His manner of reacting to things which did not meet with his approval was also not quite that expected from the jovial bourgeois [he pretended

to be]. Sometimes his disagreement was clothed in the form of a fatherly admonition, but this could suddenly change and his speech and actions would become ironic, caustic, cynical. But never, even in these expressions of disagreement and dislike, did the man himself seem to appear. . . . Never any indication of directness. Himmler, when fighting, intrigued; when battling for his so-called ideas used subterfuge, deceit—not dueling swords, but daggers in his opponent's back. His ways were the ophidian ways of the coward, weak, insincere and immeasurably cruel. . . . Himmler's mind . . . was not a twentieth century mind. His character was medieval, feudalistic, machiavellian, evil.

It bears repeating that psychological trauma incident upon carrying out criminal orders to murder large groups of unarmed noncombatants in no way mitigates the crime. Indeed, such mental conflict is indirect evidence that the men of the Einsatzgruppen were well aware that what they were doing was criminal and evil even if the highest authority of the German state had ordered it.

FIFTEEN

Final Solution

In October 1941 Stalin learned from a mole in the German Embassy in Tokyo, Richard Sorge, that the Japanese had decided to remain neutral in the German-Russian War rather than attack the Soviet Union from the east, through Mongolia, as Germany had proposed. The Japanese decided on neutrality to reserve their forces to fight the United States. Matching Sorge's information to other corroborating evidence, Stalin decided he could rely on it. He proceeded to transfer his entire Far Eastern army—some 250,000 men deploying 1,700 tanks and 1,500 aircraft—westward across Siberia to the Moscow front.

Siberian divisions began probing German forces south of Moscow as early as 18 November 1941, but the full-scale Soviet counterattack came on the night of 4–5 December 1941 all along the front. Russian winter and German overconfidence had left the Third Reich's armies ill-prepared, Panzer Group commander Heinz Guderian would argue to justify the heavy German losses that followed:

> Only he who saw the endless expanse of Russian snow during this winter of our misery, and felt the icy wind that blew across it, burying in snow every object in its path; who drove for hour after hour through that no man's land only at last to find too thin shelter, with insufficiently clothed half-starved men; and who also saw by contrast the well-fed, warmly clad and fresh Siberians, fully equipped for winter fighting; only a man who knew all that can truly judge the events which now occurred.

(A few days later Guderian recorded an outside temperature of –63°F; "many men died while performing their natural functions," he wrote gruesomely, "as a result of a congelation of the anus.")

But even with fresh divisions, Soviet strength no more than matched German numbers. "The Red Army," writes Alan Clark, ". . . had no power to achieve, nor did the weather permit, a deep penetration in the manner of the summer battles. In the few cases where the Russians succeeded in surrounding their enemy they had neither the artillery to reduce them nor sufficient strength in the air to prevent their revictualing by the Luftwaffe." Clark believes Hitler saved the day by taking personal command and refusing to allow his forces to withdraw. Moscow was spared invasion, however, and the Wehrmacht remained stalled before the Soviet capital in the worst winter in one hundred forty years.

In Hawaii the U.S. Pacific fleet lay unsuspecting at anchor in Pearl Harbor when Japanese carrier-based aircraft attacked on the morning of 7 December 1941. In two successive raids of 183 and 167 aircraft, the Japanese sank, capsized or damaged eight battleships, three light cruisers, three destroyers and four other ships, damaged or wrecked 292 aircraft and killed 2,403 American military and civilians. When President Franklin D. Roosevelt declared war on 11 December 1941 he did so against not only Japan but Germany and Italy as well.

Hitler responded the same day with a declaration of war against the United States. War against the United States as well as Great Britain and the Soviet Union meant world war to Hitler, war now enlarged to the scale of the conflict that had confirmed his anti-Semitic worldview. And world war was the catapult that would launch the consequences he had "prophesied" in his Reichstag speech of 30 January 1939:

> If the Jewish international financiers inside and outside Europe succeed in plunging the nations into another world war, the result will not be the Bolshevization of the world and thus a victory for Judaism. The result will be the extermination of the Jewish race in Europe.

What to do with the Jews in Europe—and especially in the Greater Reich itself—was the question that was supposed to be discussed at a conference of SS leaders and government ministers on the Final Solution scheduled for 9 December 1941. When Heydrich had sent out invitations on 29 November 1941 he had emphasized the importance of the conference "particularly because Jews from the Reich territory, including the Protectorate of Bohemia and Moravia, have been evacuated to the East in ongoing transports since 15 October 1941." Eichmann had organized it. "It was I who had to bustle over to Heydrich with the portfolio of invitations," he would brag in a memoir dictated from hiding in Argentina after the war. Abruptly on 8 December 1941 the conference was indefinitely postponed. New invitations went out on 8 January 1942 (Eichmann bustling over to Heydrich again), setting a new date of 20 January 1942 and explaining that the original meeting had been canceled "because of events that were announced suddenly, requiring the attention of some of the invited participants."

What were those events? The historian Christian Gerlach points to crucial meetings Hitler held in the wake of his declaration of war, meetings that appear to mark Hitler's decision to have the European Jews directly murdered rather than annihilate them through attrition in camps and ghettos in the East.

Hitler met with his Reichsleiters and Gauleiters—the leaders of National Socialism, some fifty men—in his private residence in the Führer Chancellery on 12 December 1941, the day after his declaration of war in the Reichstag. Gauleiter Josef Goebbels paraphrased in his diary part of what Hitler told his oldest and closest comrades:

> Regarding the Jewish question, the Führer is determined to clear the table. He warned the Jews that if they were to cause another world war, it would lead to their own destruction. Those were not empty words. Now the world war has come. The destruction of the Jews must be its necessary consequence. We cannot be sentimental about it. It is not for us to feel sympathy for the Jews. We should have sympathy rather with our own German people. If the German people have to sacrifice 160,000 victims in yet another campaign in the East, then those responsible for this bloody conflict will have to pay for it with their lives.

On 13 and 14 December 1941 Hitler met with key leaders of his occupation and killing operations: Philipp Bouhler, who headed the Führer Chancellery and thus the stalled euthanasia murder program; Alfred Rosenberg, Hitler's minister for the occupied Eastern territories; and at the second of the two meetings, Himmler. Rosenberg had drafted a speech earlier in December, before news of Pearl Harbor, that accused "New York Jews" of promoting "worldwide agitation against Germany" and threatened "corresponding measures against the Jews living in the East." In the Eastern territories, Rosenberg had proposed to say, "currently under the control of German armed forces, there are more than six million Jewish inhabitants. For more than a hundred years, eastern Jewry has been the source and spring of Jewish power throughout the world." In the draft speech he then threatened to "destroy . . . the springs from which the New York Jews had drawn their powers," promising "a negative elimination of these parasitic elements."

At the 14 December meeting Rosenberg gave Hitler a copy of the draft. Hitler "remarked that the text had been prepared before the Japanese declaration of war," the Ostminister noted afterward, "in circumstances that had now altered. With regard to the Jewish question, I said that my remarks about the New York Jews would perhaps have to be changed now, *after the decision.** My position was that the extermina-

---

*Emphasis added.

tion of the Jews should not be mentioned. The Führer agreed. He said they had brought the war down on us, they had started all the destruction, so it should come as no surprise if they became the first victims." Gerlach comments:

> By "the decision" Rosenberg could not have meant the entry of the United States into the war, for there is no logical connection between that event and the cessation of public threats against the Jews. Hitler's reaction indicates this as well, for he reiterates the justification for his decision to exterminate the Jews. Rosenberg certainly would have been informed immediately about such a decision, so this discussion on December 14 about the need to alter a speech that Rosenberg had written before December 7 indicates that the decision to "exterminate the Jews in Europe" must have been made after December 7 and before December 14, 1941.

Gerlach finds further evidence of a second Hitler decision on the Final Solution, this one for the European Jews, in the record of a speech Hans Frank made to his subordinates in Krakow on 16 December 1941; the speech echoes Hitler's speech to his Reichsleiters and Gauleiters on 12 December, a meeting that Frank attended:

> As for the Jews, well, I can tell you quite frankly that one way or another we have to put an end to them. The Führer once put it this way: if the combined forces of Judaism should again succeed in unleashing a world war, that would mean the end of the Jews in Europe. . . . I urge you: stand together with me . . . on this idea at least: Save your sympathy for the German people alone. Don't waste it on anyone else in the world. . . . As a veteran National Socialist I also have to say this: if the Jews in Europe should survive this war . . . then the war would be only a partial success. As far as the Jews are concerned, I would therefore be guided by the basic expectation that they are going to disappear. They have to be gotten rid of. At present I am involved in discussions aimed at having them moved away to the east. In January there is going to be an important meeting in Berlin to discuss this question [i.e., Heydrich's delayed conference]. . . . Whatever its outcome, a great Jewish emigration will commence.
> But what is going to happen to these Jews? Do you imagine there will be settlement villages for them in the Ostland? In Berlin we were told: Why are you making all this trouble for us? There is nothing we can do with them here in the Ostland or in the Reich Commissariat. Liquidate them yourselves! . . . For us too the Jews are incredibly destructive eaters. . . . Here are 3.5 million Jews that we can't shoot, we

can't poison. But there are some things we can do, and one way or another these measures will successfully lead to a liquidation. They are related to the measures under discussion with the Reich.... When and how this will all take place will be a matter for offices that we will have to establish and operate here.

Himmler met with Hitler at Wolfschanze on the afternoon of 18 December 1941. The "Jewish question" was the first subject on their agenda. Himmler had written the phrase in his notebook to remind himself to bring the subject up; during the meeting he made a note of the conclusion, which was an order from the Führer: "Jewish question / to be exterminated as partisans." Since most of the Soviet Jews within reach of the Einsatzgruppen had already been "exterminated as partisans," Gerlach argues that this December order must refer to the European Jews:

> The war situation ... created ... a kind of European fortress mentality among the Germans. The new prospect of a second front, combined with the military defeat in the Battle of Moscow, had created a rather serious situation for the German leaders. Within this more threatening context, Hitler viewed the Jews as opponents, revolutionaries, saboteurs, spies, "partisans" in his own backyard—an area that now, in light of the expected United States attack, included all of Europe.

The delusion and paranoia implicit in Hitler's assumptions have become so familiar, and led to such monumentally horrific results, that hardly anyone any longer remarks on their lunacy. They emphasize once again how much Nazism had in common with religious cults where conversion to belief, transforming the personal identities of followers, requires incorporating the interpretive framework of the leader, however objectively bizarre. The difference with Nazism was that it parasitically commandeered the full resources of a modern nation-state. A similar ideological parasitism in the Soviet Union, Soviet Communism, led to a greater number of deaths, but they were spread across a longer period of time. So also in Communist China, with even more deaths there. Parasitic infestations of ideological fanaticism, it seems, caused most of the man-made deaths of the twentieth century.

Gerlach estimates that the first large group of euthanasia murder personnel from the Führer Chancellery left for Belzec around mid-December 1941. Gas vans at Chelmno, near Lodz, had begun exterminating Polish Jews on 8 December 1941.

Heydrich soon let Eichmann in on the secret, Eichmann told his interrogator Avner Less in Israel in 1960:

[At the turn of the year 1941/42] Heydrich sent for me. I reported. He said to me: "The Führer, well, emigration is . . ." He began with a little speech. And then: "The Führer has ordered the physical extermination of the Jews." These were his words. And as though wanting to test their effect on me, he made a long pause, which was not at all his way. I can still remember that. In the first moment, I didn't grasp the implications, because he chose his words so carefully. But then I understood. I didn't say anything, what could I say? Because I'd never thought of a . . . of such a thing, of that sort of violent solution. And then he said to me: "Eichmann, go and see Globocnik in Lublin, the Führer has already given him instructions. Take a look and see how he's getting on with his program. I believe he's using Russian anti-tank trenches for exterminating the Jews." As ordered, I went to Lublin, located the headquarters of SS and Police Commander Globocnik, and reported. . . . Globocnik sent for a certain *Sturmbannführer* Höfle, who must have been a member of his staff. We went from Lublin to, I don't remember what the place was called, I get them mixed up, I couldn't say if it was Treblinka or some other place.* There were patches of woods, sort of, and the road passed through—a Polish highway. On the right side of the road there was an ordinary house, that's where the men who worked there lived. A captain of the regular [Order] police welcomed us. A few workmen were still there. The captain, which surprised me, had taken off his jacket and rolled up his sleeves, somehow he seemed to have joined in the work. They were building little wooden shacks, two, maybe three of them; they looked like two- or three-room cottages. Höfle told the police captain to explain the installation to me. And then he started in. He had a, well, let's say, a vulgar, uncultivated voice. Maybe he drank. He spoke some dialect from the southwestern corner of Germany, and he told me how he had made everything airtight. It seems they were going to hook up a Russian submarine engine and pipe the exhaust into the houses and the Jews inside would be poisoned.

I was horrified. My nerves aren't strong enough . . . I can't listen to such things . . . such things, without their affecting me. Even today, if I see someone with a deep cut, I have to look away. I could never have been a doctor. I still remember how I visualized the scene and began to tremble, as if I'd been through something, some terrible experience. The kind of thing that happens sometimes and afterward you start to shake. Then I went to Berlin and reported to . . . [Gestapo head Heinrich] Müller. . . .

*It was Belzec.

Then I was sent on to Kulm [Chelmno, west of Warsaw] in the Warthegau. I received orders from Müller to go to Litzmannstadt [Lodz] and report back to him on what was going on there. He didn't put it the same way as Heydrich . . . not as crassly. "An action against the Jews is under way there, Eichmann. Go take a look. And then report to me." I went to Gestapo headquarters in . . . Lodz . . . and there I was told. It was a special team, put in by the *Reichsführer.* And they told me exactly where this Kulm is situated. I saw the following: a room, perhaps, if I remember right, about five times as big as this one here. There were Jews in it. They had to undress, and then a sealed truck drove up. The doors were opened, it drove up to a kind of ramp. The naked Jews had to get in. Then the doors were closed and the truck drove off. . . . I don't know exactly [how many people the truck held]. The whole time it was there, I didn't look inside. I couldn't. Couldn't! What I saw and heard was enough. The screaming and . . . I was much too shaken and so on. I told Müller that in my report. He didn't get much out of it. I drove after the truck . . . and there I saw the most horrible sight I had seen in all my life. It drove up to a fairly long trench. The doors were opened and corpses were thrown out. The limbs were as supple as if they'd been alive. Just thrown in. I can still see a civilian with pliers pulling out teeth. And then I beat it. I got into my car and drove off. I didn't say another word. I sat there for hours without saying a word to my driver. I'd had enough. I was through. The only other thing I remember is that a doctor in a white smock wanted me to look through a peephole and watch the people inside the truck. I refused. I couldn't, I couldn't say another word, I had to get out of there. In Berlin I reported to *Gruppenführer* Müller. I told him the same as I've told you now. Terrible, an inferno. I can't. It's . . . I can't do it . . . I told him. . . . Müller never said anything. Never! Not about these things and not about other things.

Eichmann's descriptions document the developing transition from mobile to stationary gas chambers, which the transfer of T4 personnel to the East would accelerate. Mobile systems (killing squads or gas vans) facilitated killing victims whose communities the killers had invaded; stationary systems would facilitate killing victims shipped from large urban areas in Poland and from western Europe.

Heydrich convened the conference to discuss "the Final Solution of the Jewish Question" on 20 January 1942 at a columned official residence set amid gardens on the Wannsee, a popular public lake outside Berlin.

Present, Gerlach says, summarizing, "were five representatives from the Security Police and the SD, eight politicians and functionaries from the civil administration, and two representatives from the party, one from the party chancellery and one from the Race and Resettlement Office of the SS." Eichmann and Müller, now fully informed, were among them. "We called it the Conference of State Secretaries," Eichmann told Avner Less. It has come to be known as the Wannsee Conference.

Eichmann had organized the conference in the first place; he worked with a team of stenographers to summarize its proceedings in a protocol that survived the war. His Israeli interrogator sought his interpretation of that document's doubletalk:

LESS: I'm going to quote from your record of Heydrich's speech: "Emigration has now, with the Führer's approval, been replaced by another solution, the evacuation of the Jews to the East. The present actions, however, must be viewed as mere expedients, but they offer a source of practical experience of the utmost importance with a view to the Final Solution to come." What *does* all this mean?

EICHMANN: Since emigration was prohibited, they were to be deported to the East. This was the new—er—conception in behalf of which the conference of state secretaries was called. . . .

LESS: What is meant by "practical experience"?

EICHMANN: . . . Two months later, I was sent to see Globocnik. It is quite possible that the killing there had already begun.

LESS: I see. So you think "practical experience" refers to the killing of the Jews, which had already begun? It's true that action teams [i.e., Einsatzgruppen] were already at work at the time.

EICHMANN: They started in . . . Of course there was killing.

Eichmann was more candid about the Wannsee Conference discussions at his trial:

EICHMANN: What I know is that the gentlemen convened their session, and then in very plain terms—not in the language that I had to use in the minutes, but in absolutely blunt terms—they addressed the issue, with no mincing of words. And my memory of all of this would be doubtful, were it not for the fact that I distinctly recall saying to myself at the time: look, just look at Stuckart [Dr. Wilhelm Stuckart, State Secretary in the Ministry of the Interior], the perpetual law-abiding bureaucrat, always punctilious and fussy, and now what a different tone. The language was anything but in conformity with the legal protocol of clause and paragraph. . . . The discussion covered killing, elimination and annihilation.

But there is another, explicit admission of "killing, elimination and annihilation" hidden in plain sight in the Wannsee Conference protocol that has been consistently overlooked in historical evaluations of the document: the table prepared by SS statisticians of the distribution of Jews in Europe and the U.S.S.R. The table asserts a total Jewish population for western and eastern Europe of "over 11,000,000." The numbers for certain countries, however, are not original population totals but Einsatzgruppen numbers. Thus Estonia is listed as *"Judenfrei."* Latvia's Jewish population is counted at 3,500—in other words, the remainder of men kept alive in the Riga ghetto as "work Jews" after Rumbula. For Lithuania the number is 34,000, which corresponds closely to the 34,500 "work Jews" of Jäger's 1 December 1941 report. Bialystok, meaning essentially western Byelorussia, is counted at 400,000 and the rest of Byelorussia at the absurdly precise figure of 446,484, both numbers reflecting Einsatzgruppen depredations up to late 1941. If the Wannsee Conference protocol outlined responsibilities for the industrialized mass-killing program of the Final Solution yet to come, it also acknowledged, by deficit, responsibility for the handcrafted murder of the Final Solution already almost complete in the Ostland and the Ukraine.

The Wannsee Conference protocol thus projects 11 million Jews yet to be murdered despite the unrelenting murder that the Einsatzgruppen and Order Police had already accomplished in the East. Where did the SS statisticians find so many Jews? They did not merely confine themselves to areas that the Germans already occupied. The distribution table, which Heydrich implicitly endorsed, seemingly so factual and quantitative, can also be read as a fantasy of Nazi ambitions, a three-level document in which two of the levels are obscured: the missing hundreds of thousands already murdered in the Ostland and the Ukraine and the millions still beyond the SS's grasp. To arrive at the number 11 million, that is, the protocol included 700,000 Jews in "unoccupied France," 330,000 in England, 4,000 in Ireland, 8,000 in neutral Sweden, 18,000 in neutral Switzerland, 6,000 in friendly Fascist Spain, 55,500 in Turkey, 742,800 in friendly Fascist Hungary and 5 million more in the portion of the U.S.S.R. that the Wehrmacht was just then discovering it might not succeed in conquering even if it shed whole Wannsees of German blood. The grandiosity of the Nazi plan for the Final Solution—of Hitler and Himmler's plan—is appalling.

Much of the conference was devoted to debating the fate of special categories of Jews—"persons of mixed blood of the first degree," "persons of mixed blood of the second degree," marriages between "full Jews and persons of German blood" and between "persons of mixed blood

and persons of German blood." Resolving these category issues was a
primary reason Heydrich had called the conference in the first place.
    When it was over, Heydrich was relieved and satisfied. "Happily," he
would write a month later, "[the conference] has settled the basic outlines for the practical implementation of the Final Solution of the Jewish
question." His intention had been to establish his ultimate authority
over the Final Solution. His colleagues in the government and the party
had been more than willing to accede responsibility for the mass murder
of eleven million people to the SS. "After the conference," Eichmann
says in his memoir, "as I recall, Heydrich, Müller and your humble servant sat cozily around a fireplace. I noticed for the first time that Heydrich was smoking. Not only that, but he had a cognac. Normally he
touched nothing alcoholic. The only other time I had seen him drinking
was at an office party years before. . . . [So] we sat around peacefully
after our Wannsee Conference, not just talking shop but giving ourselves
a rest after so many taxing hours."
    Heydrich had one other satisfying duty to perform that day: approv-
ing the awarding of a decoration, the War Service Cross Second Class, to
nominees who had performed exceptional service to the state. The list
included Blobel, a physician who had experimented with poison gas
exterminations in Mogilev, three RSHA officials who had worked on
gas-van development and a number of Einsatzgruppen officers.

Himmler rewarded himself for undertaking the Final Solution in western as well as eastern Europe by expanding his program to resettle the
East with SS *Wehrbauern*. The new death camps which Globocnik was
planning and constructing in eastern Poland in the winter of 1941/42—
Belzec, Sobibor, Treblinka—had been conceived to exterminate the
Polish Jews, clearing the way for the pilot *Wehrbauern* program Himmler had assigned to Globocnik the previous summer. With an expanded
Final Solution now authorized to exterminate all the Jews of both eastern and western Europe, Himmler began practical planning toward the
full colonization of the East.
    In January 1942 he instructed the chief of his settlement-planning
department to enlarge his work from Poland alone to include the occupied territories of the East. On 31 January 1942 he wrote Oswald Pohl,
who operated the SS's Economic and Administration Main Office,
about the "absolutely huge buildings we wish to provide for the *Waffen-
SS,* General SS and police." He estimated that the concentration camp
system then just coming under Pohl's authority would have to produce
eighty percent of the materials and construction for postwar SS needs, or

else it would not be possible to provide "either decent barracks, schools, office buildings, nor houses for our SS men in the old Reich, nor will I as *Reichskommissar* for the Consolidation of German Nationhood be able to provide the giant settlements with which we make the East German."

Separate but parallel conferences in Berlin and in Prague on 4 February 1942 attempted to sort out the complicated logistics of Germanizing the occupied territories. In Berlin Rosenberg's and Himmler's representatives agreed that most of the Eastern peoples were unsuitable for *Eindeutschung* and would have to be expelled, voluntarily or forcibly, into western Siberia. The representative from Himmler's Consolidation office drew on his (or Himmler's) classical education to compare the situation to the Spartan occupation of the Peloponnesus in the eighth century B.C.: the Germans were like the Spartans; the existing middle classes in the Ostland were like the Perioeci, a Peloponnesian middle class with no voting rights; and the Russians were like the helots, indigenous peoples whom the Spartans put to work on the land as slaves. Racial sorting, the conference participants concluded, could be disguised as physical examination for a health survey. In Prague Heydrich continued the discussions he had begun in October about the *Eindeutschung* of the Protectorate of Bohemia and Moravia. Mass deportations, he told his subordinates, would also be necessary; racial sorting could be disguised as a nationwide survey for tuberculosis.

By March 1942, Hitler could tell a group of officers who had gathered to be awarded Iron Crosses, "I know exactly how far I have to go . . . so that the whole East becomes and remains German—*ur*-German. . . . We don't need to express our ideas about that now, and I will not speak about it. That [task] I have given to my Himmler and he is already accomplishing it."

What the task Hitler had given to Himmler would mean in human terms became evident when Himmler issued his master plan for the East, Plan Ost, on 27 April 1942. In anthropologist Eric Wolf's summary:

All Jews and Gypsies were to be eliminated, together with a quarter of the Russians. Thirty-one million inhabitants of Poland and the western Soviet Union were to be moved either to the General Government or to Siberia; 14 million of these were slated for eventual Germanization, while the rest were to serve the incoming ethnic German settlers from Eastern Europe and the South Tyrol. The General Government was to become a "gigantic Polish work camp," populated by [in Himmler's words] a "reservoir of manpower for unskilled labor." A document issued at the same time by the colonization division of the *Ostministerium* raised the number of people slated for removal to about 50 million but suggested that it was not enough to think in demographic and ethnic terms alone. It was important "to destroy the Russians as a people, separate and alienate them. It is essential that the majority of the people remaining on Russian territory be of a primitive, semi-European type."

The Final Solution—the systematic murder of the Jews of Europe and the Soviet Union—was intended to be only the first phase of a vast, megalomaniacal project of privation, enslavement, mass murder and colonization modeled on the historic colonization of North and South America and on nineteenth-century imperialism but modernized with pseudoscientific theories of eugenic restoration. The Einsatzgruppen and the Order Police had already far advanced the Final Solution in the East. After Hitler ordered the second phase of the Final Solution in December 1941, Western Jews began to be moved East in increasing numbers and murdered as well.

SIXTEEN

Judenfrei

While the leaders of the Third Reich debated how to organize the second phase of the Final Solution, their allies in Romania had been busy slaughtering Jewish victims in the military regions they controlled in the southwestern Ukraine. Raul Hilberg summarizes the massacres perpetrated there in late 1941 and early 1942:

> In the Golta prefecture the killings were carried out by the Romanians themselves. . . . Three primitive enclosures were organized in the district. . . . These hastily assembled concentration camps, which consisted of half-destroyed houses, stables and pigpens, held a total of 70,000 Jews, most of them from towns and hamlets, some from Odessa. Disease, especially typhus, was rampant, and food was scarce. . . .
> At Bogdanovca, the largest and most lethal camp, killings began on December 21. At first, 4,000 to 5,000 sick and infirm Jews were placed in several stables, which were covered with straw, sprinkled with gasoline, and torched. While the stables were still burning, about 43,000 Jews were marched through the woods in groups of 300 to 400 to be shot, kneeling completely naked in the icy weather on the rim of a precipice. This operation continued until December 30, with an interruption for the celebration of Christmas. During January and February 1942, about 18,000 Jews were killed in [one of the smaller enclosures]. At [the smallest enclosure] where [Lieutenant Colonel Modest Isopescu] took pleasure in tormenting and photographing his victims, 4,000 were killed.*

By January 1942 as well, some 2 million Russian prisoners of war were dead, 600,000 of whom had been shot outright, 140,000 of those by Einsatzkommandos. (By the end of the war, of more than 5.7 million Russian combatants captured, 3.3 million would be dead, most of them victims of starvation and exposure in open enclosures that the Wehrmacht murderously surrounded with electrified barbed wire while deny-

---

*In all, Romanian forces murdered some 260,000 Romanian and 100,000 Ukrainian Jews during the Second World War.

ing the enclosed prisoners food, water or shelter of any kind.) In advance and in retreat the Wehrmacht also devastated civilian communities. "Reeling under the weight of the first Soviet counteroffensive," historian Omer Bartov writes of one such episode in the winter of 1941–42, "the 18th Panzer burned all the villages it was forced to evacuate, destroyed or consumed their entire livestock, arrested and sent to the rear their adult male population, and drove the women and children out into the snow. This was common practice on the other sectors of the front as well. . . . Thus on 1 January 1942 no less than 48 villages were ordered evacuated and destroyed." In the Ukraine, in the course of the war, 230 villages would be burned to the ground and all their inhabitants murdered; in Byelorussia, 187.

Gassing of large transports of Jewish victims began in a converted farmhouse at Auschwitz-Birkenau in late January 1942. "At first, from Poland," Höss writes, recalling the origination points of the transports in postwar testimony; "that is, the General Government; from Germany; and I believe from Greece or Holland." Having seen the effects of shooting on his men (and on himself), Himmler had come to prefer gassing to other methods of mass killing, especially for women and children. Jeckeln examined the problem with him in a meeting at the end of January 1942:

> I visited Himmler in Lötzen to discuss matters to do with the organization of the Latvian SS legion. There Himmler told me that further transports would arrive in the Salaspils concentration camp [southeast of Riga beyond Rumbula] from the Reich and other countries. Himmler said that he had not yet decided how they were to be exterminated, whether to shoot them in Salaspils or to chase them off into the marshes somewhere.
>
> I pointed out that from my point of view shooting would be a simpler and quicker form of death. Himmler said he would think about it and give me orders later via Heydrich.

(Continuing his testimony, Jeckeln estimated the number of victims at Salaspils; in the end, those who did not die of disease or starvation were shot:

> Jews were brought to the Salaspils camp from Germany, France, Belgium, Holland, Czechoslovakia and other occupied countries. . . .
>
> I can give you a rough estimate. The first Jewish transports [from western Europe] arrived in Salaspils already in November 1941. In the first half of 1942 the transports came in regular succession. I think no more than three transports arrived in November 1941 but during the

next seven months, from December 1941 to June 1942, eight to twelve transports arrived each month. If one reckons on 1,000 persons for each transport, then 55,000–87,000 Jews were exterminated who had come to Salaspils from the Reich and other countries.)

Himmler made gas vans available to the Einsatzgruppen at this time. Jeckeln continued to use shooting. In February and March 1942, for example, he employed the Arajs commando to shoot some ten thousand Reich Jews into killing pits in Bikernieki Forest, about three miles due east of Riga. The Einsatzgruppen generally resisted switching to the van system, historian Ronald Headland reports:

> According to eyewitnesses, the first use of gas vans for killing Jews took place in Poltava [in the Ukraine] by *Sonderkommando* 4a in November 1941. It is also known that *Einsatzkommando* 5 received a gas van shortly before Christmas 1941 and that the other *Einsatzgruppen* received vans after the New Year. . . . The gas vans do not seem to have been used with the enthusiasm hoped for originally. They were introduced, apparently on Himmler's order, for the killing of women and children in "a more humane" fashion. In general the vans were not popular with the *Einsatzgruppen*. According to the testimony of Erich Naumann, the leader of *Einsatzgruppe* B, his *Einsatzgruppe* did not use the vans, but forwarded them on to *Einsatzgruppen* C and D. The vans kept breaking down and were not always reliable. The poor state of the roads [in the Soviet Union] limited their use and the unloading of the corpses at the burial pits presented too great a mental strain on the members of the *Einsatzkommandos*.

Ohlendorf confirmed problems with gas vans in his Nuremberg trial testimony. "An order came from Himmler that in the future women and children were to be killed only in gas vans," he testified, but "I received the report that the *Einsatzkommandos* did not willingly use the vans. . . . Because the burial of the victims was a great ordeal for [them]." Evidently gassing only reduced trauma to the perpetrators in stationary applications, where prisoners could be assigned to corpse disposal while SS supervisors kept their distance.

Himmler notified his camp administrator of the impending deportation of 150,000 Reich Jews to concentration camps on 26 January 1942, but Albert Speer, now chief of armament construction responsible for repairing the Russian railroads that the Soviets had destroyed, notified Rosenberg on the same day that Wehrmacht resupply on the Russian front would preempt all rail transport, postponing deportations until spring.

While the hecatomb of European Jews was delayed, mass murder continued in the East. SS-Obersturmbannführer Eduard Strauch, a lawyer who commanded Einsatzkommando 1b (Einsatzgruppe A), scheduled an *Aktion* against the Minsk ghetto for 2–3 March 1942. The dates coincided with the Jewish festival of Purim, which commemorates the defeat of Haman's plot to massacre the Jews—a little SS joke. Strauch wrote Bach-Zelewski in a later report that "in order to disguise the *Aktion* the [Minsk ghetto] Council of Elders was to be informed that 5,000 Jews . . . were to be resettled. These Jews were to be notified by the Council of Elders and told to get ready. Each Jew would be permitted to take along five kilograms [eleven pounds] of luggage."

The Generalkommissar for Byelorussia, a balding Gauleiter named Wilhelm Kube, was conflicted about the Final Solution (at least where it concerned the European Jews) and hostile to the SS. In December 1941 he had written his old friend Lohse, "I am certainly tough and prepared to do my part towards the solution of the Jewish question, but people from our own cultural sphere are rather different from the brutalized hordes living here." The report that Strauch sent to Bach-Zelewski accused Kube of protecting Jews. By preventing the Jews who worked for him in Minsk from going home to the ghetto on the evening before the Purim massacre, Strauch charged, Kube had given the game away.

Minsk ghetto resident Hersh Smolar, who by then was organizing a resistance movement, says his group discerned what the SS was planning when an actor among them who spoke fluent German asked whether children and old people could be included in the five-thousand-person "work detail." "The answer was cruel and unambiguous," Smolar writes: " '*Ganz egal*' (It's all the same . . .). Clearly they simply wanted five thousand Jews to murder." Smolar and his group spread the word: Find a way to save yourself:

> A night of terror fell upon the ghetto. The only people who had an encouraging word to say were the older Jews who knew that the next day, March 2nd, was Purim. They comforted each other—"perhaps another miracle would happen and our enemies would suffer the same fate as Haman. . . ." We did not know then that the [Einsatzkommando] had deliberately chosen Purim for their massacre in order to show the Jews that they had nothing left to hope for, there would be no miracle. . . .
>
> At precisely 10 a.m. the *Einsatzkommando,* assisted by groups of Lithuanian fascists and Byelorussian "Black police," began their pogrom. They invaded the ghetto near the Judenrat building and pounced brutally upon people who were trying to take refuge there.

"Where are the five thousand Jews we ordered?" The Commander dispersed the Jewish police, accompanied by squads of his own men, to go out and bring in the victims.

From Strauch's perspective the disappearance of his victims into hiding was Kube's fault:

> As a result of the betrayal no Jew appeared at the appointed time. There was nothing else to do but to round the Jews up by force. The Jews put up resistance and the men taking part in the *Aktion* had to use firearms. When matters were at their worst, just as the men were going all out to break down the resistance, the *Gauleiter* appeared.

Strauch then quoted from a file note written three days after the *Aktion* describing an agitated Kube, "accompanied by his personal adjutant and an *SS-Untersturmführer*," berating him "about the outrageous proceedings," complaining of dangerous ricochets inside and outside the ghetto from the gunfire, repeatedly using expressions such as "filthy business" and "you haven't heard the last of this." Strauch wrote that he considered himself to have been "grievously insulted" and noted that Kube "is said to have distributed sweets to Jewish children on this occasion." Smolar's description of the massacre that followed the violent roundup identifies the mysterious Untersturmführer and details Kube's bizarre act of charity, if that is what it was:

> Soon afterward came the crackling of rifles and the explosion of hand grenades. The first victims were people who could not move fast enough—the old, the sick, the infants. Then the Nazis began searching for hiding places. They would stop outside a place they suspected and the Jewish police would call out that "there was nothing to be afraid of." But no one came out. Then the grenades did their murderous work. The streets of Minsk were red with Jewish blood that day.
>
> Their next "military objective" was the Jewish Children's Home. They forced the frightened youngsters to line up and march. At the head of the line was the director of the home, a devoted mother to the orphans. Her name was Fleisher. In one arm she carried a sick child. Her other hand clutched the hand of her own young son, walking beside her. Last in line was another self-sacrificing woman, Dr. Tshermin. . . .
>
> The march of the children was halted at a freshly dug ditch at the lower end of Tatomski Street, not far from the *Judenrat* building. The air was suspiciously still, but the executioners had already taken up their "positions" around the ditch. In command was the Nazi governor of Byelorussia, *Gauleiter* Wilhelm Kube. At his side stood a tall SS

officer in a long leather coat. From the German Jews we later learned that this was Himmler's righthand man—Adolf Eichmann. At his signal the murderers began throwing the children into the ditch and covering them with sand.

The screams and cries could be heard far into the ghetto. Children stretched out their hands, pleading for their lives. *Kommissar* Kube walked alongside the ditch, tossing pieces of candy into it. . . . From the Jewish police we learned that Eichmann swore angrily when blood splattered his coat. Upon the mound of dying Jewish children the Nazis threw the dead bodies of their guardians—Director Fleisher and Doctor Tshermin.

Eichmann remembered the Purim massacre vividly, if not entirely accurately, and described it in his memoir as well as to his Israeli interrogator. The memoir version:

Later that year [*sic*] I watched my first Jewish execution. It was at Minsk, then recently [*sic*] come under German occupation. I was sent by my immediate superior, General Müller. Müller never stirred from his desk at Gestapo headquarters on the second floor of the Prinz Albrecht Strasse building, but he knew everything that went on in Europe. He liked to send me around on his behalf. I was in effect a traveling salesman for the Gestapo, just as I had once been a traveling salesman for an oil company in Austria.

Müller had heard that Jews were being shot near Minsk, and he wanted a report. I went there and showed my orders to the local SS commander. "That's a fine coincidence," he said. "Tomorrow 5,000 of them are getting theirs."

When I rode out the next morning, they had already started, so I could see only the finish. Although I was wearing a leather coat which reached almost to my ankles, it was very cold. I watched the last group of Jews undress, down to their shirts. They walked the last 100 or 200 yards—they were not driven—then they jumped into the pit. It was impressive to see them jumping into the pit without offering any resistance whatsoever. Then the men of the squad banged away into the pit with their rifles and machine pistols.

Why did that scene linger so long in my memory? Perhaps because I had children myself. And there were children in that pit. I saw a woman hold a child of a year or two into the air, pleading. At that moment all I wanted to say was, "Don't shoot, hand over the child. . . ." Then the child was hit.

I was so close that later I found bits of brains splattered on my long leather coat. My driver helped me remove them. Then we returned to Berlin.

(In a psychiatric interview before his trial in Israel in 1961, Eichmann described his response to this massacre: "Then I encapsulated myself and carried out my work. I told myself: 'Up till now [*sic*] I never killed anybody.' I created a situation for myself in which I could find a spark of inner calm. The main medicament was: I have nothing to do with it all personally. They are not my people. But my nervousness got worse. I had no rest at night. The images came back to me in the darkness.")

Frustrated by the ghetto's resistance, Strauch had Jewish workers stopped on their way into the ghetto that evening, ordered to lie down in the snow and shot. Even so, he was able to report no more than 3,412 people murdered that day.

(Kube's complaint to Heydrich in December 1941 about decorated Jewish war veterans and other "exceptions" included in the first transports of Reich Jews to Minsk elicited this response from Heydrich in March 1942, a characteristic example of Heydrich's sarcasm and contempt:

> You will agree with me that, in the third year of the war, even for the Security Police and the Security Service there are tasks which are more important for the war effort than running about pandering to the bellyaching of Jews, making time-consuming lists and distracting so many of my colleagues from other far more important duties. If I instigated an investigation into the persons on your list at all this was only in order to prove such attacks wrong once and for all in writing. I regret to have to write yet another such justification six and a half years after the enactment of the Nuremberg laws.)

The Einsatzgruppen report for March 1942 including the Minsk Purim massacre in its summary along with several other *Aktionen*, but the scale of killing had clearly changed:

> Since the Eastern territory is largely *Judenfrei* and the few remaining Jews who are required for the most urgent labor tasks have been put in ghettos, the task of the Security Police and the SD consisted here in the seizure of the Jews mostly hiding in the country. Frequently Jews were seized who had left the ghetto without permission or who did not wear the Jewish star.
> In Riga three Jews transported from the Reich to the ghetto who had escaped were captured among others and publicly hanged within the ghetto.

During larger actions against the Jews 3,412 were shot in Minsk, 302 in Wilejka, and 2,007 in Baranowicze. . . .

In the remaining territories of the Eastern front the task of the Security Police and the SD, in addition to measures against individual Jews . . . consisted in general purges of larger villages. Thus 15,000 Jews were shot in Rakov and 1,224 Jews in Artenowsk alone so that these places are *Judenfrei.*

In the Crimea 1,000 Jews and Gypsies were executed.

From the beginning of 1942 onward, the Einsatzgruppen increasingly turned to fighting Soviet partisans, as did units of the Wehrmacht and the Waffen-SS. Between January 1942 and June 1944, writes military historian French MacLean, "the Germans conducted forty-three large-scale anti-partisan operations in the occupied territory in the Soviet Union." Their greatest challenge was Byelorussia, which they never more than lightly controlled. Into that commissariat, in February 1942, came a paramilitary unit of unsurpassed viciousness and depravity: Sonderkommando Dirlewanger, Hitler and Himmler's personal creation.

Sonderkommando Dirlewanger had its beginnings in a 1940 discussion between Hitler and Himmler about poachers. Poachers were hunters, they agreed, good at tracking game; those who hunted with firearms were good shots; how wasteful, then, that the repeat offenders among them should languish in Reich prisons when there was a war on. Himmler proposed forming them into a sharpshooter company to hunt partisans and escaped Jews, and Hitler agreed. The small poacher company grew over the next year as violent criminals and SS criminal offenders were added to its number and it took up ghetto guarding in Lublin and tracking Polish partisans in the forests beyond Lvov. By then it had acquired the commander who gave it his name: Oskar Dirlewanger.

Tall, lean, with a scarred, skull-like face and a Hitler mustache, Dirlewanger had been wounded six times during his service in the First World War—shot in the foot, sabered in the chest, shrapneled in the head, shot in the hand, bayoneted in the leg, shot in the left shoulder—had gone on to fight in four different Freikorps, command an armored train and then study for and receive a doctorate in economics. He rose in the SA, but he was a drunkard and a carouser who liked young girls, and in 1934 he was sent to prison for driving while drunk, causing several accidents with injuries and repeatedly having sex in an official car with a girl under the age of consent, which in Germany at that time was fourteen. Released on parole in 1936, he rehabilitated himself by joining the ground forces of the Luftwaffe's Condor Legion in Spain during the Spanish Civil War.

After that war his sponsor in the SS, Brigadeführer Gottlob Berger, convinced Himmler to assign him to command the "poachers," which Himmler did, commissioning Dirlewanger an Obersturmführer in the Waffen-SS.

"I said to Dirlewanger," Himmler would brag in a speech late in the war, " 'Now, why not look for suitable candidates among the villains, the real criminals, in the concentration camps?' . . . The atmosphere in the regiment is often somewhat medieval in the use of corporal punishment and so on." Dirlewanger, himself a professional killer, fully malefic, organized a Sonderkommando of malefically violent criminals and kept them in line with draconian punishments. "Offenders were beaten with clubs," MacLean instances, "and some were shot without benefit of any judicial proceeding." The resulting organization was so vicious—enthusiastically extorting, raping, torturing and murdering Poles and Jews—that it even disgusted men like Globocnik, who had it transferred out of the General Government and into Byelorussia to fight partisans in February 1942.

Dirlewanger's methods were ruthless and effective, MacLean writes:

> During these anti-partisan operations, Dirlewanger frequently rounded up women and children who had been left behind in the partisan villages and marched them through minefields which protected guerrilla positions. Needless to say, this technique killed and maimed many innocent people. In another tactic, Dirlewanger would fly in a light observation aircraft over suspected Russian villages. If he received gunfire from in or near a village he would annotate the location on a map. Later, he would return in a ground action, set fire to the entire hamlet and kill all the inhabitants. On these punitive operations there were no prisoners.

A participant, Hans-Peter Klausch, described one such village burning in a postwar deposition:

> During a march—and we had driven 200 km close to Smolensk—the villages were encircled. Nobody was allowed to leave or enter. The fields were searched and the people were sent back to the village. The next morning around six a.m. all these people—it was a larger village with approximately 2,500 people—children, women, the elderly were pushed into four or five barns. Then Dirlewanger appeared with ten men, officers, etc., and said: "Shoot them all immediately." In front of the barn, he positioned four SD men with machine pistols. The barn was opened and Dirlewanger said, "Fire freely." Then there was indiscriminate shooting into the crowd of humans with the machine pistols,

without distinction whether children, women, etc., were hit. It was a most horrendous action. The [machine pistol] magazines were taken out, new ones were inserted. Then new aiming started. After that, the barn was closed again. The SD men removed straw from the roofs and set the barns on fire. This was the most horrible spectacle which I have ever seen in my life. The barns were burning brightly. Nobody could escape until the barns fell down. Meanwhile, Dirlewanger and his staff positioned themselves with the Russian rapid-fire guns about fifty meters away from the barn. Then from the barns some lightly wounded, some heavily wounded and others who had not yet been hit stormed out, burning all over their bodies. Now these bastards shot these people who tried to escape, with Dirlewanger in front, until there was nobody left. I have witnessed this example which I have described in at least four or five other cases. Each of these villages was leveled down to the ground.

Sonderkommando Dirlewanger may appear to have been busy conducting draconian antipartisan missions, but much of its assigned work in fact supplemented continued Einsatzgruppe B and Order Police *Aktionen* against Byelorussian Jews. The relative numbers of victims in its reports confirm that SK Dirlewanger was not much more than yet another of Himmler's Final Solution murder crews.

In April 1942 the remaining Jews of Vinnitsa were assembled at the local stadium for a selection. Hitler would not occupy Werwolf until mid-July, but it was time to tidy up. Tailors, shoemakers, carpenters, builders and others with letter A work permits were directed to the left and returned to the micro-concentration camps adjacent to the factories where they worked; the rest—the elderly, women and children, perhaps five thousand people—were directed to the right. These were marched or trucked by the Ukrainian auxiliaries under German supervision to the commercial nursery north of town where ten thousand had been murdered seven months before. A long grave gaped open at the nursery with planks on which to descend to the killing floor and a smiling German officer to offer the ladies a hand down. A Ukrainian killer with a machine gun sat on the rim dangling his feet into the pit, smoking a cigarette.

But ten feet from the long killing pit the Germans had opened a smaller, square pit perhaps twelve feet long and wide. As they drove the groups of victims to the long pit, they demanded the victims' children— leading the little ones, pulling the babies from their mothers' arms, shouting, shoving, beating, mothers screaming—and clubbed and shot the children separately into the separate pit while making a *Sardinenpack-ung* of the adults. Ukrainian historian Faina Vinokurova was unable to explain why the Germans killed the children separately at Vinnitsa, but two reasons suggest themselves: to keep the *Sardinenpackung* tidy, lining up the bodies of the adults; and, since children in their mothers' arms were often shielded from the bullets that killed their mothers, to make sure the little Jews were killed before the pits were covered. In the same spirit, men from the Einsatzkommando had visited the maternity hospital in Vinnitsa that morning. New Jewish mothers and Jewish women in labor had been carried away to the Pyatnychany Forest and shot. The men had packed newborn Jewish babies into two gunnysacks, like unwanted kittens, and thrown the sacks out the second-floor window.

Himmler established field headquarters up the road in Zhitomir to be near the Führer. Göring built a bunker of his own three miles from *Wer-wolf*, went about Vinnitsa in an open car and supported the local ballet.

One of the most painful questions of the Holocaust, raised first of all by the SS perpetrators themselves, has been: Why did the Jews not resist? The question, with its ugly implication that the victims deserve blame— as if they murdered themselves—has many answers. Many victims did not know what was intended for them until after they had been brought under armed guard. Able-bodied men were usually seized first, leaving women, children and the elderly more vulnerable. The path to the killing pit or the transport was a gauntlet bristling with armed men and vicious dogs, with machine guns positioned on the perimeter. Running away meant leaving family members behind. The shock of encountering the killing pits was paralyzing. Resistance is more difficult stripped naked. It was unusual for Jews to own weapons or to have experience using them. Jewish communities faced with Gentile hostility traditionally negotiated. Mass killing on the Nazi scale was incomprehensible.

The majority of these answers coalesce around the obvious truth that Jewish communities in eastern Europe were more civilized—that is, socialized more to civil methods of settling disputes, populated with fewer individuals who were personally violent—than the Germans who assaulted them. They were also more civilized than most of the Gentile societies in which they were embedded. Jews historically had not conducted pogroms against Poles, Latvians, Lithuanians, Byelorussians, Ukrainians; it had been the other way around. "Preventive attack, armed resistance, and revenge," Raul Hilberg writes, "were almost completely absent in Jewish exilic history." Hilberg implies that the tradition of civility in Jewish ghetto culture was a weakness. It was a tragedy when confronted with Nazism; even, as Hilberg calls it, a catastrophe; but historically it had been a strength. Civil society in the West evolved across seven centuries from violent medieval beginnings to the modern rule of law; the Jews of eastern and western Europe, evolving civility more rapidly than their neighbors, hardly deserve blame for falling victim to a feral collectivity dominated by violent criminals. To the contrary, their neighbors deserve blame for having stood by and allowed the Holocaust to happen in their midst, especially since Bulgaria and Denmark gave convincing demonstration that even minimal resistance to Nazi demands could save lives.

Fewer eastern European Jews evidently brutalized their children than did Gentiles, producing fewer adults prepared to use serious violence even defensively. In that sense, the Jewish civil tradition was pacifist. One significant sign of less violent methods of child-rearing is the infant mortality rate in comparable populations. In Latvia in 1931, the Jewish infant mortality rate was about half that of Germans living in Latvia and of native Latvians and a third that of Lithuanians, Poles and Russians living in Latvia, and it maintained that difference across the decade even as health conditions improved and all but the Lithuanian infant mortality rate declined.

But the most obvious indication that a difference in civility left Jewish communities unprepared to resist concerted violent assault is the belated development of armed resistance in the ghettos the SS had organized in the East. "During the catastrophe of 1933–45," Hilberg confirms, "the instances of opposition were small and few. Above all, they were, whenever and wherever they occurred, actions of last (never first) resort." Violence is not only criminal. Civilized societies authorize violent officials to wield carefully limited violence to protect their citizens against criminal and military assault. The program of violent socialization that Lonnie Athens identified in the backgrounds of violent criminals is also visited upon and available to victims of illegitimate violence. When social controls over violence fail, as they failed for the Eastern Jews during the Second World War, reverting to private violence may be the only way to survive. German violent domination of Jewish ghettos gradually brutalized the ghetto population, and Jewish violent resistance emerged, especially among the young. They staged revolts, most memorably in Warsaw in April and May 1943, or escaped the ghetto into the forests and fought as partisans. Tragically, their sacrifices came too late to save many lives.

Routine extermination of Polish Jews began at Belzec on 17 March 1942; by the middle of June, when the transports were temporarily

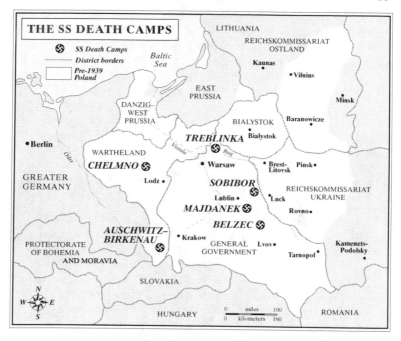

THE SS DEATH CAMPS

⊗ SS Death Camps
········· District borders
Pre-1939 Poland

LITHUANIA

REICHSKOMMISSARIAT OSTLAND

Baltic Sea

Kaunas •

• Vilnius

EAST PRUSSIA

DANZIG– WEST PRUSSIA

Minsk •

BIALYSTOK   Baranowicze •

TREBLINKA ⊗   Bialystok •

• Berlin

WARTHELAND

CHELMNO ⊗   Lodz •

• Warsaw   • Brest- Litovsk   Pinsk •

GREATER GERMANY

SOBIBOR ⊗

Lublin •   • Luck

REICHSKOMMISSARIAT UKRAINE

MAJDANEK ⊗   Rovno •

BELZEC ⊗

AUSCHWITZ– BIRKENAU ⊗   • Krakow   GENERAL   Lvov •   Kamenets- Podolsky •

PROTECTORATE OF BOHEMIA AND MORAVIA

GOVERNMENT   Tarnopol •

SLOVAKIA

N W–E S

HUNGARY

0   miles   100
0   kilometers   160

ROMANIA

stopped to build new gas chambers, about ninety-three thousand people had been murdered there. In the late spring of 1942 the transports began moving again from the Third Reich to the East. Himmler met with Hitler on 16–17 April 1942, after which he traveled to occupied Poland and ordered the removal of Reich Jews from Lodz to Chelmno. Transports left Lodz beginning on 4 May 1942, and by the middle of May more than ten thousand people had been delivered to their death. The first Vienna transport to Minsk, to a killing site on a former collective farm east of Minsk at Maly Trostinets, left on 5 May 1942; seventeen more transports followed. Construction of the death camp at Sobibor, northeast of Lublin near the Bug River, began in March 1942, and routine operation followed beginning early in May; one hundred thousand victims were gassed there in the first two months.

At least one of the desk murderers was gone. On the morning of 27 May 1942 Heydrich had been returning to Prague from his nearby summer residence in his chauffeured Mercedes when four Czech patriots, two of them dropped in by parachute from England, ambushed him along a curve in the road and grenaded his car, driving fragments of leather, horsehair and steel springs from the back seat into his spleen.

He chased his attackers and wounded one before he collapsed. Despite surgery and sulfonamide—an early antibiotic—he developed peritonitis and died of massive infection on 4 June 1942. His father had been a composer and music professor; Himmler told Lina Heydrich that in his delirium her husband had quoted a phrase from one of his father's operas: "Yes, the world is but a barrel organ, which our Lord God turns himself, and each must dance to the tune." SS-Obergruppenführer Sepp Dietrich's benediction on the Blond Beast who organized the Final Solution might be the world's: "Is the swine dead at last?"

After a state funeral in Berlin on 8 June 1942 with Hitler and Himmler prominently at hand, Himmler spoke to his Gruppenführers and department heads. "War is no matter of sentimentalities," he told them, continuing a little later:

> Even if it is so desperate—one can do no more than die. I have the conviction now—which we all have—that in the final analysis the others will die sooner than us. In the final analysis we have the thicker skull. We have the better blood, the stronger heart and the better nerves. Good, our comrade Heydrich, our friend Heydrich, is now dead, he lies under the sod. Now the whole SS—and I can assure you that if he lived he would say exactly the same—will march on with beating drums and helmets donned. And if another blow strikes us, we will march on. And if we have attacked ten times, will attack an eleventh time. So long as one man in any position, in a company, in a platoon remains who can crook a finger round a trigger, all is not lost.

He went on, a matter of sentimentalities, to evoke the future he was planning of settlements in the East, fussing over budgets but also alluding to the Final Solution:

> If we do not make the bricks here, if we do not fill up our camps with slaves—in this context I say things very plainly and very clearly— with work-slaves to build our towns, our villages, our farmsteads without regard to any losses, then after a long war we will simply not have the money to furnish the settlements so that really Germanic people can live there and take root in the first generation.
>
> I said the first great peace task is to overhaul the whole SS and police and to fuse them together. The second task is to fetch in and fuse the Germanic peoples with us. The third task is the settlement and migration of peoples in Europe which we are carrying out. The migration of the Jews will be dealt with for certain in a year: then

none will wander again. Because now the slate must be made quite clean.

In mid-July 1942 Himmler ordered the "resettlement" of the entire Jewish population of the General Government—that is, their murder—by the end of the year. Treblinka, a death camp built northeast of Warsaw beginning in late May or early June 1942 with engine-generated carbon monoxide gas chambers, began receiving transports from the former Polish capital on 22 July; by the end of August two hundred thousand people had been gassed there, with tens of thousands more to follow.

That summer saw the expansion of gassing operations at all of Globocnik's killing centers to accommodate Himmler's resettlement order. Globocnik's project to murder all the Jews of Poland had been renamed Operation Reinhard in honor of the SS's fallen hero. Höss at Auschwitz also had to expand to accommodate victims from Germany and western Europe. "In the spring of 1942," Höss recalled, "the first convoys of Jews to be exterminated arrived from Upper Silesia," but "whereas in the spring . . . only small operations were involved, the number of convoys increased during the summer, and we had to create new extermination facilities." Belzec, Sobibor and Treblinka all used carbon monoxide from engine exhaust to poison victims; Höss favored Zyklon B, the prussic acid insecticide (the letter designation B was one of several and indicated concentration), and used it exclusively at Auschwitz. Gassing was also instituted at Majdanek, outside Lublin, beginning in October 1942, using at various times either Zyklon B or pure bottled carbon monoxide.

At the same time, the Einsatzgruppen, the Order Police, Sonderkommando Dirlewanger and other SS agencies began clearing the ghettos of the Ostland and the Ukraine. Byelorussian Generalkommissar Kube, with his supposed soft spot for Reich Jews, wrote his friend and superior Lohse on 31 July 1942 detailing the carnage:

> We have liquidated [using gas vans] about 55,000 Jews in the past ten weeks. In the Minsk area the Jews have been completely eradicated, without any negative effect on the workforce. In the mainly Polish area of Lida 16,000 Jews have been liquidated, in Slonim 8,000 Jews. Our preparations for the liquidation of the Jews in the Glebokie area were disrupted when the rear army area preempted us, liquidating 10,000 Jews whom we had been due to eradicate systematically, without any prior liaison with us. . . . On 28 and 29 July about 10,000 Jews were liquidated in the city of Minsk, 6,500 of them Russian Jews—for the most part old people, women and children—and the

rest [German and Austrian] Jews unfit for work, who had mostly been sent from Vienna, Brünn, Bremen and Berlin in November of last year to Minsk on the Führer's orders.

In addition, the Slutsk area has been alleviated of several thousand Jews. The same applies for Novogrudok and Vileyka. Radical measures have yet to be taken in Baranovicze and Gantsevice. There are still some 10,000 living in the city of Baranovicze alone, of whom 9,000 will be liquidated next month.

There are 2,600 Jews from Germany left in the city of Minsk. In addition to these, there are a total of 6,000 Russian Jews and Jewesses still alive, left over from the labor units in which they were employed during the *Aktion*. . . . In all the other areas the SD and I have limited the number of Jews coming for [work assignment] to a maximum of 800 and, where possible, 500. Thus, at the conclusion of the *Aktionen* we have reported, we retain in the city of Minsk 8,600 Jews and in the other ten areas, including the Minsk area which is *Judenfrei,* some 7,000 Jews.

On 27 October 1942 Himmler ordered the destruction of the Pinsk ghetto, the last large ghetto in Byelorussia; on 1 November 1942, in an *Aktion* approaching Babi Yar in scale, 26,200 human beings were murdered at Pinsk.

Allied forces landed in North Africa on 8 November 1942. The next day in Munich Hitler felt called upon to remind his people once again of his "prophecy." Of those who had laughed at him in 1939, he said, "countless no longer laugh today; and those who still laugh today will probably not be laughing for much longer either." Soviet forces surrounded the Wehrmacht Sixth Army at Stalingrad a few weeks later and that long winter siege began. "Did Hitler begin to doubt the final victory?" asks German historian Eberhard Jäckel. "He would not admit it, but it now became obvious that the extermination of the Jews became increasingly the most important aim of the war as such; as the fortunes of war turned against Germany, the destruction of the Jews became National Socialism's gift to the world."

Hitler said as much in the will he dictated on 2 April 1945. "Although trampled underfoot," he gloated there, "the German people must try, in its helplessness, to respect the laws of racist science that we have given it. In a world whose moral order is more and more contaminated by the Jewish poison, a people immunized against it will finally regain its superiority. From this point of view, eternal gratitude will be owed to National Socialism because I exterminated the Jews in Germany and central Europe."

. . .

By the end of 1942, the Einsatzgruppen and their SS cohorts had largely fulfilled their mission. Einsatzgruppe A had murdered, according to its own reports, 249,421 Jews. Einsatzgruppe B counted 126,195, surely only a fraction of its total in Byelorussia. Einsatzgruppen C and D had murdered 363,211 between September and December 1942 alone. Adding in other agencies—the Higher SS and Police Leaders, the Wehrmacht, Sonderkommando Dirlewanger, the Romanian army and gendarmerie, Lithuanian and Ukrainian auxiliaries—and including the full period of the war, Raul Hilberg estimates that more than 1,300,000 Jewish men, women and children were murdered in the East after Barbarossa. Adding non-Jewish victims would raise the total above two million, each one a name, a person, a kin, a soul, a loss.

SEVENTEEN

"Cinders Flying in the Wind"

Outside Kiev on a day in March or April 1942—the ground was thawing but there was still snow—Obersturmbannführer and Catholic priest Albert Hartl remembered driving in the country with Paul Blobel. Hartl had been the chief of the Church Information Service in the Reich Security Main Office and would see service with Einsatzgruppe C; he was visiting Kiev because in January 1942 Heydrich had sent him on what Hartl called "a special mission to study the spiritual situation in the Soviet Union." At about the same time, Heydrich had relieved Blobel of his burdensome responsibility commanding Sonderkommando 4a; in Kiev Blobel was closing out his Sonderkommando duties pending reassignment.

Hartl hardly knew the former architect. Max Thomas, the physician who now commanded Einsatzgruppe C, had invited both men to his country estate to dine, and they had decided to ride out together on the old Zhitomir road. "That was the usual road if one wanted to leave the town for some fresh air," Hartl would testify. "It was quite beautiful as far as the landscape was concerned." Hartl was curious to observe his dinner partner. "Physically Blobel was in bad condition," he said, "and even psychologically he seemed somewhat exhausted." Thomas had used a vivid metaphor to explain Blobel's condition to Hartl: "With Blobel," the physician had told Hartl, "the film constantly tears." Hartl explained: "He meant that psychologically Blobel was entirely exhausted, to the point where he was no longer competent."

"It was evening and just getting dark," Hartl said, continuing the story to Gitta Sereny. "At one moment—we were driving past a long ravine. I noticed strange movements of the earth: clumps of earth rose into the air as if by their own propulsion—and there was smoke: it was like a low-toned volcano; as if there was burning lava just beneath the earth. Blobel laughed, made a gesture with his arm, pointing back along the road and ahead of us, all along the ravine—the ravine of Babi Yar—and said, 'Here lie my thirty thousand Jews.'" Corpse gases were bubbling up through the thawing earth. "It made a shattering impression on me at the time," Hartl said at his trial. He himself had ("or faked," Sereny interjects) a nervous breakdown a few months later. Hospitalized in Kiev, he spent six months convalescing and then was invalided out of the SS.

In mid-May 1942, shortly before Heydrich was assassinated, Blobel found himself sitting across a desk at RSHA offices in Berlin listening to the Obergruppenführer's insults. "Well, you've developed a tummy," he remembered Heydrich telling him. "You're a soft person. You've gone queer. We'll only be able to use you in a china factory." That label followed him through the years, Blobel whined at his trial. But Heydrich had a cure for Blobel's troubles. "I'll stick your nose very much deeper into it," Blobel heard him say. "You will report to *Gruppenführer* Müller."

Then the swine was dead. Heinrich Müller, the unexpressive Gestapo chief, met with Blobel at the end of June 1942 and assigned him the work Heydrich had passed along to stick his nose deeper into Einsatzgruppen mass murder:

> *Gruppenführer* Müller entrusted me with the task of removing the traces of executions carried out by the *Einsatzgruppen* in the East. My orders were to report personally to the commanders in chief of the Security Police and SD, to pass on, verbally, Müller's order and to supervise its execution. This order was top secret, and *Gruppenführer* Müller decreed that, owing to the strict secrecy of this task, no written correspondence of any kind was to be carried on.

Blobel spent a grisly summer at Chelmno investigating fuels and systems for destroying masses of corpses. The bodies of the victims murdered in the gas chambers at Chelmno had been buried in mass graves. Blobel ordered them exhumed and used them in his experiments. Höss, who had traveled there from Auschwitz in September to see what Blobel had achieved, found that he had "constructed several experimental ovens and used wood and gasoline as fuel. He tried to destroy the corpses by means of dynamiting them, too; this method was rather unsuccessful. The ashes, ground to dust in a bone mill, were thrown away in the vast forests around." Historian Shmuel Spector assesses Blobel's main achievement as "the aerodynamic arrangement of the bonfires," which alternated bodies with railroad ties; then they were doused with gasoline or other available flammable liquids. Blobel's technology was applied first in the death camps. "At the end of the summer in 1942," Spector writes, "there were serious health problems in . . . Belzec, Sobibor and Treblinka; the earth above the graves was open and noxious odors arose; leakage from the bodies also threatened the wells and the drinking water." The system was also used at Auschwitz.

Having developed an effective open-air cremation system, Blobel reported to Max Thomas in Kiev in September 1942 and verbally passed along Müller's order. Thomas, Blobel testified, "refused to carry out this [order] pending a conference with *Reichsführer* Himmler. He thought that this was a very foolish order, and this I reported to Müller after my return." With gasoline in short supply and the ground frozen, Blobel managed to delay the project through the winter and spring of 1943. That April, however, Radio Berlin announced the discovery, in a forest six miles west of Smolensk, of a mass grave containing the remains of some four thousand Polish officers, blaming the massacre on the NKVD. The Soviets denied the accusation and in turn blamed the Germans. The debate contributed to souring Allied relations, which delighted the Nazi leadership; though the forests of western Russia were crowded with Einsatzgruppen mass graves, the NKVD had in fact perpetrated the Katyn Forest massacre in 1940, before Barbarossa. But Himmler, who by the spring of 1943, with the German defeat at Stalingrad on 2 February, understood that the outcome of the war was in doubt, now demanded that Blobel get busy exhuming and cremating the remains of Einsatzgruppen butchery. "It was in May 1943," Blobel confirmed, "that I had to see Dr. Thomas again in order to report to him that the *Reichsführer-SS*, in disregard of his objection, demanded a burning of all those places on the whole Eastern Front." Himmler also gave orders, Höss adds, that "the ashes should be disposed of in such a way that no clues as to the number of cremated persons could be drawn in the future."

Blobel formed a Sonderkommando code-named 1005. Höss says "the work itself was carried out by Jewish work units, which, upon finishing their particular task, were shot. . . . Auschwitz had to furnish Jews continuously for this *Kommando* 1005." Blobel also used Russian prisoners of war and captured partisans. Burning the corpses the Einsatzgruppen had generated, he took orders from his SS superiors. "Dr. Thomas in June, July and August 1943 began with this work," Blobel testified. "According to his express wish, I had to prepare special fuels in Berlin for this purpose, fuel quotas which were to be supplied from the fuel plants in the Ukraine. That demanded constant travel from Berlin to Ukraine." Blobel described a cremation in August 1943 in a mass grave near Kiev, possibly a section of Babi Yar, although it hardly sounds deep enough. "This grave was about fifty-five meters [180 feet] long, three meters [10 feet] wide and two and a half [8 feet] deep. When the cover [of earth] had been lifted, the bodies were soaked with fuel and set on fire. It took about two days for the grave to burn down. I myself saw that the grave became red hot right down to the ground. Afterwards, the grave was filled in, and thus all traces were as good as eliminated."

In September 1943 Blobel carried Himmler's order to Jeckeln in Riga. "The Higher SS and Police Leader began burning in his own sector in October," Blobel testified. In Kaunas in autumn 1943 one of William Mishell's friends, David, had escaped the ghetto and was fighting as a partisan. The Lithuanian police captured the group of Jewish partisans and turned them over to the Gestapo. They were taken to the Ninth Fort, but rather than being murdered, they were assigned to burn bodies. David told Mishell:

We were mobilized to build a very tall enclosure around the Fort to block the view from the adjacent homes. Hundreds of trucks loaded with firewood, chemicals, gasoline, and tar were brought in and huge excavation equipment showed up at the Fort. The next week the excavation started. The excavators removed the topsoil from the entire site and huge mass graves appeared below the surface. . . . Our job was now to eradicate all traces of the mass executions. Between the prisoners of war and us, we were a group of 64 people. Except for several specialists who stayed behind in the barracks, we performed the dirty work. We were divided into three groups. One group was forced to drag the corpses out of the mass grave [using iron hooks] and put them on the ground alongside the ditch. The second group pulled the corpses across the site to a huge bonfire which could be seen all around the Fort. Here the bodies were piled in layers, a layer of wood and the layer of corpses one on top of the other, drenched with gasoline and ignited. All work was done by hand. At first we revolted, but after several good beatings we had to go on. The stench was terrible and the view was even worse: mothers with children in their arms, people with split-open heads, people naked and fully dressed one on top of the other, layer upon layer, the full depth of the trench. From the documents we found in the pockets of the dressed people, we established that these were the foreign [i.e., Reich and other European] Jews who were brought to the Fort. Most of them had documents showing that they had been recruited for "work in the East." These foreign Jews, apparently, resisted and refused to undress. From the expressions on their faces, we could tell who was killed by the bullets and who suffocated later when the bullets failed to kill him. Of course, the ones with cracked skulls needed no explanation.

Near the end of the exhumations and cremations, when the workers understood that they would be killed and burned in their turn, they managed a daring escape out through the back passages of the Ninth

Fort. The workers at Ponary and at Babi Yar, some of them, succeeded in escaping as well—at Babi Yar because one of the workers inexplicably found a key to the lock on the door of their prison block in a pocket of one of the 125,000 corpses they exhumed.

Blobel did not succeed in obliterating Einsatzgruppen massacres in the East. "According to my orders," he concluded his affidavit, "my duties should have covered the entire area in which the *Einsatzgruppen* were employed. However, owing to the [German] retreat from Russia, I did not totally carry out my orders." Many killing sites, now mounded over and overgrown with grass, some of them marked with memorial stones, many of them forlorn, have never been exhumed.

Himmler bloomed poisonously in the summer of 1942. One of his biographers, Peter Padfield, finds him "extraordinarily active," his letters and speeches "full of confidence. . . . It may be that Heydrich's departure had freed his spirit, it may be that the tasks he had won for himself in the East filled his horizons. He was at full stretch but at full power, and evidently relishing it." In a meeting at Werwolf in mid-July 1942—Himmler drove down to Vinnitsa from his field headquarters in Zhitomir—Hitler had endorsed the Reichsführer's detailed plan for clearing out the East and colonizing it with *Wehrbauern,* the *Generalplan Ost.* Felix Kersten got an excited report:

> "You won't understand how happy I am, Herr Kersten." These were Himmler's opening words. "The Führer not only listened to me, he even refrained from constant interruptions. . . . No, today he went so far as to approve my proposals, asking questions and drawing attention to important details. . . . This is the happiest day of my life. Everything I have been considering and planning on a small scale can now be realized. I shall set to at once on a large scale—and with all the vigor I can muster. You know me: once I start anything I see it through to the end, no matter how great the difficulties may be."
>
> I asked Himmler to lie down so that I could begin the treatment. He did not even listen to me, but continued: "The Germans were once a farming people and must essentially become one again. The East will help to strengthen this agricultural side of the German nation—it will become the everlasting fountain of youth for the life-blood of Germany, from which it will in turn be constantly renewed. These phrases opened my remarks to the Führer and I linked them with the idea of defending Europe's living space, which I knew lay very close to the Führer's heart. Villages inhabited by an armed peasantry will form

the basis of the settlement in the East—and will simultaneously be its defense; they will be the kernel of Europe's great defensive wall, which the Führer is to build at the victorious conclusion of the war. Germanic villages inhabited by a military peasantry and filling a belt several hundred miles wide—just imagine, Herr Kersten, what a sublime idea!

"It's the greatest piece of colonization which the world will ever have seen, linked too with a most noble and essential task, the protection of the Western world against an irruption from Asia. When he has accomplished that, the name of Adolf Hitler will be the greatest in Germanic history—and he has commissioned me to carry out the task. . . ."

Himmler fetched out his papers, maps and plans, on which I saw villages and settlements marked everywhere, small and large farms, forests, but also sites for industry, traversed by a mighty network of streets, which were again linked up with a number of arterial roads stretching across the entire country. He put this before me and explained it in detail. . . . "Cowards are born in towns, [he said], heroes in the country."

Generalplan Ost was not a fantasy. It was a grandiose but real and ongoing project. Hitler had participated in its development and given it his approval. Himmler was well along in implementing the "small scale" part of it, which was German settlement in Zamosc and the extermination of the Polish and Eastern Jews. At full scale it projected the migration to the East over a thirty-year period of 4.5 million Germans and *Volkdeutsche,* including German-Americans repatriated from overseas when America was conquered, displacing 31 million "aliens" who would be "deported" to western Siberia. "Of the Polish population," a Polish historian writes, "80 to 85 percent was to be deported, i.e., from 16 to 20.4 million; 65 percent of the population was to be deported from the 'West Ukraine' and 75 percent from Byelorussia." But first the Jews, estimated to number 5 to 6 million, would be exterminated. Himmler's order to finish murdering the entire Jewish population of the General Government by the end of 1942 followed his meeting with Hitler. Belzec, Sobibor and Treblinka were running at full tilt. "The *Reichsführer-SS* . . . has given us so much new work," Globocnik wrote Karl Wolff, "that with it now all our most secret wishes are to be fulfilled."

Secure in the Führer's approval, Himmler allowed himself a private indulgence during an Auschwitz tour on 17–18 July 1942. On the first day of the tour he thoroughly inspected the camp and watched an extermination with Zyklon-B "without comment," Höss remembered: "He just looked on in total silence." In Minsk in August 1941 with Bach-Zelewski, the botched killing of two women had panicked Himmler; now he could watch a crowd of people murdered without batting an eye and go on to an evening of *Gemütlichkeit* with Höss, the local Gauleiter and their wives, even allowing himself to smoke a few cigarettes and drink a glass of wine.

On the second day of the Auschwitz tour, however, he requested a demonstration from Höss: "In the women's camp he wanted to observe the corporal punishment of a woman who was a professional criminal and a prostitute. She had been repeatedly stealing whatever she could lay her hands on. He was mainly interested in the results corporal punishment had on her." For such beatings the women were required to bare their buttocks. How Himmler responded to watching the naked beating Höss doesn't say; he does say that the Reichsführer had long before "personally reserved the decision about corporal punishment for women." But a more elaborate exhibition of sexualized cruelty at Sobibor during an inspection in February 1943 suggests that his subordinates had noticed that Himmler had come to take pleasure in seeing women tortured.

"For this occasion," Padfield writes, "the *'Gasmeister,' SS-Oberscharführer* Erich Bauer, had selected some three hundred young and comely Jewesses; they had been fed and accommodated in the camp overnight. Now they were brought forward, ordered to strip and herded up the *'Himmelfahrtstrasse'* [the "road to heaven"] from 'Camp 2' into the gas chamber at 'Camp 3.' The door was closed and they were gassed as a special offering for the *Reichsführer*." An eyewitness, Sobibor inmate Moshe Bahir, confirms the perverse exhibition: "For Himmler's visit, several hundred young Jewish women had been brought to Sobibor from Trawniki camp. They were put into the gas chambers, destroyed, and their bodies taken to the crematoria, all in order to demonstrate to Himmler and his entourage the efficiency of the work of destroying Jews at Sobibor camp."

After the German defeat and surrender at Stalingrad on 2 February 1943, Hitler declared total war and suspended all postwar planning, which permanently stalled *Generalplan Ost.* Himmler retreated into duty. Poles continued to be expelled from Zamosc until July 1943; by then more than one hundred thousand residents had been moved out to make way for German settlers. Jews continued to be murdered in the death camps, at Auschwitz and in the East; by June 1943, Himmler noted, Hitler at Obersalzberg was declaring to him "that the evacuation [i.e., annihilation] of the Jews, regardless of the disturbances it will provoke in the next three to four months, must be ruthlessly implemented and endured to the end." Murdering the Jews had become more important than winning the war. Murdering the Jews, in Hitler's eyes, was equivalent to winning the war, even if it brought down ruin on Germany.

The brave Warsaw Ghetto uprising in April and May 1943 (during which Himmler himself at one point took control of the German forces), and uprisings at Treblinka and Sobibor in August and October 1943, determined Himmler to exterminate the 45,000 Jews remaining in the slave labor camps around Lublin: Poniatowa, Trawniki, Majdanek. After Stalingrad the Munich resistance group White Rose had distributed a leaflet invoking retribution on the German forces: "In Russia thousands fall daily. It is the time of harvest and the reaper is in full swing among the ripe corn." Now in Lublin Himmler ordered Operation Erntefest— Operation Harvest Festival—and the SS reapers gathered in the final sheaves of Eastern victims. Police and Waffen-SS conducted the massacres Einsatzgruppen-style, surrounding the camps and shooting the victims into killing pits. A Jewish underground group at Poniatowa resisted, returning the SS's fire from a barracks, but the SS torched the barracks and burned the resisters alive. By the time of Erntefest Belzec, Treblinka and Sobibor had finished their work and were closed and dismantled, the earth turned and forests planted of young trees far less numerous than the dead. Russian patrols approached the old borders of Poland, Latvia and Lithuania; the Red Army was advancing inexorably westward toward the Reich.

Himmler spoke at length to his Gruppenführers in Posen (Poznan) on 4 October 1943, the occasion of the annual SS leadership conference, frankly admitting what he and Hitler elsewhere strove to hide. He talked for three hours, reviewing the course of the war, the partisan war, the psychology of the Slavs as he understood it, the virtues of the SS man and much else. Early on, he acknowledged the privation deaths of Russian prisoners of war:

> The Russian army was driven together into great pockets, destroyed, taken prisoner. We did not then value the mass man as we do now, as raw material, as manpower. Which is not a shame in the end, if one thinks in terms of generations, but it is regrettable today due to the loss of manpower: the prisoners died by the tens of thousands or hundreds of thousands from exhaustion, from hunger.

He proclaimed German goodheartedness but with eugenic parsimony insisted it stopped at the border:

It is basically wrong for us to project our whole harmless soul and heart, all our good nature, our idealism, onto foreign peoples. . . . For the SS man, one principle must apply absolutely: we must be honest, decent, loyal and comradely to members of our own blood and to no one else. What happens to the Russians, the Czechs, is a matter of total indifference to me. Whatever is available to us in good blood of our type, we will take for ourselves, that is, we will steal their children and bring them up with us, if necessary. Whether other races live well or die of hunger is only of interest to me insofar as we need them as slaves for our culture; otherwise that doesn't interest me. Whether ten thousand Russian women collapse from exhaustion in building a tank ditch is of interest to me only insofar as the tank ditches are finished for Germany.

We will never be hard and heartless when it is not necessary; that is clear. We Germans, the only ones in the world with a decent attitude toward animals, will also adopt a decent attitude with regards to these human animals; but it is a sin against our own blood to worry about them and give them ideals, so that our sons and grandchildren will have a harder time with them. When somebody comes to me and says, "I can't build tank ditches with children or women. That's inhumane, they'll die doing it." Then I must say: "You are a murderer of your own blood, because if the tank ditches aren't built, then German soldiers will die, and they are the sons of German mothers. That is our blood." . . . Everything else is froth, a fraud against our own people, and an obstacle to earlier victory in the war.

He expressed his contempt for those among his countrymen who worried about the outcome of the war—"I always grab one out of one hundred of the defeatists . . . and lay his head between his feet; then the others will shut up for a quarter of a year"—but warned that "everyone [in occupied Europe] who is a convinced Communist is automatically against us; every Freemason, every democrat, every convinced Christian is against us."

Two hours along into his speech, Himmler spoke plainly to his Gruppenführers, as one criminal to another, about the Final Solution:

I want to mention another very difficult matter here before you in complete openness. Among ourselves, this once, it should be spoken of quite openly, but in public we will never speak of it. Just as we did not hesitate on 30 June 1934 to do our duty as ordered, to stand failed comrades up against the wall and shoot them, just as little did we ever speak of it, and we shall never speak of it. It was a discretion which, thank God, is a matter of course for us that counseled us never to discuss it among ourselves, never talk about it. It made everybody shudder; yet everyone was clear that he would do it again if ordered and if it was necessary.

I mean of course the evacuation of the Jews, the extermination of the Jewish people. It's one of those things that are easy to say. "The Jewish people will be exterminated," says every Party member, "sure, it's in our program, elimination of the Jews, extermination, can do." And then they all come along, these eighty million good Germans, and every one of them has his decent Jew. Sure, the others are swine, but this one is a first-class Jew. Of all those who talk this way, not one has seen it happen, not one has been through it. Most of you know what it means when a hundred corpses lie side by side, when five hundred lie there or when a thousand lie there. To have gone through this and— apart from cases of human weakness—to have remained decent, that has made us hard. This is a glorious page in our history, never written, which can never *be* written, but we know how tough we would have made it on ourselves if today, with the bombing raids and the suffering and deprivations of the war, we still had the Jews in every city as secret saboteurs, agitators and provocateurs. We would probably already be in the same situation as 1916 and 1917 if the Jews were still stuck fast to the body of the German *Volk*.

The riches they had we have taken from them. I have given a strict order, which *SS-Obergruppenführer* Pohl has carried out, that all these riches shall of course be turned over to the Reich. We have taken none of them for ourselves. Individuals who disobeyed will be punished according to the order I issued at the beginning: whoever takes even one mark is a dead man. A number of SS men—not very many—have violated that order, and that will be their death, without mercy. We had the moral right, we had the duty to our own people, to kill these people who wanted to kill us. But we don't have the right to enrich ourselves with even one fur, one watch, one mark, one cigarette or anything else. Just because we exterminated a bacillus, after all, we don't want to be infected by it and die. I will not allow even the smallest rotten spot to appear or to take hold. Wherever it may open, together we will cauterize it. In general, though, we can say that we have accomplished this most burdensome task out of love for our people. And we have not damaged our inner being, our soul, our character thereby.

Of course Himmler was posturing before his generals. The historical record is thick with testimony to theft and corruption at every level, to breakdown and maleficence; many of the Gruppenführers, those with any brains, must have been laughing behind their hands. Jeckeln maintained a warehouse of stolen goods in Riga; he used to sit at his desk in the Ritterhaus sorting jewelry.

The historian Peter Haidu, exploring the rhetoric of Himmler's Posen speech, observes that in speaking of seeing corpses lying side by side he makes "no mention . . . of the possible narrative role the individual subject might have played as an agent in producing the scene before his eyes. He is represented only in a passive and cognitive role: any potential narrative is elided." That is not only a rhetorical strategy, however: it's Himmler's own narcissistic perspective on the Holocaust: looking down from above, a coward ordering others to kill, almost too squeamish even to watch. He never stole a wedding ring or a cigarette, but he hardly needed to. He took from the victims on the grand scale, stealing their lives, the lives of their families, the life of their communities, their peace and their future, enlarging his power through their suffering. Signaling that tumescence, he reverted at the end of the speech to his *Wehrbauern* plans and droned on about colonizing the East "in bold strokes, without inhibition."

He managed to be marginally less dishonest two days later when he spoke in similar vein, perhaps from the same notes, to the Reichleiters and Gauleiters, burning their bridges by making sure they could not deny knowledge of the loathsome conspiracy. Speer was there, party secretary and Führer shadow Martin Bormann, new commander in chief of the navy Admiral Karl Dönitz, the leaders of the party and the Reich. Himmler repeated, a little more politely, his contemptuous remarks about good Jews and good Germans. Then, to spice his lament on the burden of duty, he bragged about killing women and children:

> I ask of you that what I say in this circle you really only hear and never speak of. We come to the question: how is it with the women and children? I have resolved even here on a completely clear solution. That is to say I do not consider myself justified in eradicating the men—so to speak killing or ordering them killed—and allowing the avengers in the shape of the children to grow up for our sons and grandsons. The difficult decision had to be taken, to cause this *Volk* to disappear from the earth. To organize the execution of this mission was the most difficult task we had hitherto. It was accomplished without—as I believe I am able to say—our men or our officers suffering injury to spirit or soul. This danger was very close. The way between the two possibilities, either to become too crude, to become heartless and no longer to respect human life, or to become weak and crack up in a nervous breakdown—the path between this Scylla and Charybdis is horribly narrow. . . .

The Jewish question in those countries occupied by us will be settled by the end of this year. Only a residue of individual Jews will remain in hiding.

This cruel, rigid, fussy pervert, bragging about mass murder and claiming he came off clean, had long since ceased to respect human life if he had ever done so. Gitta Sereny tells a story emblematic of what Himmler had become. He kept a mistress, Hedwig Potthast; with money borrowed from the party through Bormann he had built her a new house on the Berghof near Hitler and Bormann himself. One afternoon in 1944, Himmler's mistress invited Bormann's wife and Bormann's fourteen-year-old son Martin Jr. and younger daughter Eike for tea. "She gave us chocolate and cake," Martin Jr. told Sereny in 1990 at a therapy group for the children of high-ranking Nazis. After tea, Sereny writes, "Frau Potthast said she would show them something interesting, a special collection Himmler kept in what had become his special lair. She led the way up to the attic." Martin Jr. continues the story:

> When she opened the door and we flocked in, we didn't understand what the objects in that room were—until she explained, quite scientifically, you know. . . . It was tables and chairs made of parts of human bodies. There was a chair . . . the seat was a human pelvis, the legs human legs—on human feet. And then she picked up a copy of *Mein Kampf* from a pile of them—all I could think of was that my father had told me not to bother to read it as it had been outdated by events. . . . She showed us the cover—made of human skin, she said—and explained that the Dachau prisoners who produced it used the *Rückenhaut*, the skin of the back, to make it.

"He said they fled," Sereny continues, "his mother pushing them ahead of her down the stairs. 'Eike was terribly upset,' he said, 'and I was too.' It hadn't helped them much, he said, when his mother, trying to calm them, told them that their father had refused to have the book in the house when Himmler had sent him a similar copy." Someone who listened to the story at the therapy group commented, "The swine." Martin Bormann's sixty-year-old son responded, "To call those people swine is an insult to swine."

In Himmler's last days, after the Normandy invasion, after the bomb exploded in the Führer bunker in Berlin on the same day Hedwig

Potthast bore him a second child, after the Red Army had overrun Majdanek and he had unloosed Sonderkommando Dirlewanger on Warsaw when that beleaguered city had risen in revolt, the Reichsführer-SS took to his bed with stomach cramps like a Victorian neurasthenic and began negotiating an imagined new role for himself in postwar Europe. Kersten was amazed, in December 1944, to find Himmler dreaming up an agreement between England and Germany:

> Himmler said that all propaganda, particularly by way of neutral channels, would concentrate on bringing home to the English how much they had to gain from an agreement of this kind. He would talk to Goebbels and Ribbentrop about this very important matter of policy. It would not fail to make an impression in England that such a suggestion should emanate from him, who represented with his SS the factor which contributed most to order in Europe. . . .
>
> Himmler looked at me, expecting an answer. It was obvious to me that he was still swayed by ideology and was quite unaware that his reputation abroad was not that of a factor making for order, but rather that of a hangman, a murderer on a vast scale and above all else the man responsible for the abominable campaign against the Jews. No government would dare to treat with him, even if it wanted to. I hesitated a moment before telling him the brutal truth, then I let him have it, holding nothing back.
>
> It was with something more than astonishment that I heard Himmler assert that these "calumnies" spread about by enemy propaganda would have to be rectified. "The West has accepted a man like Stalin as an ally, and worse things could be said against him." Himmler put an end to the conversation, because he did not like to hear things which would not fit in with his theory.

By April 1945 Himmler was negotiating with the director of the Swedish section of the Jewish World Congress, telling Kersten, "I want to bury the hatchet between us and the Jews. If I had had my own way, many things would have been done differently." Nothing was done differently; the previous November 1944 he had ordered an end to the murders in the death camps and then reversed the order when Hitler had found out, with the brutal results—murder by forced marches to nowhere—that Daniel Goldhagen first extensively chronicled.

Later in April 1945 Speer found Himmler at Hohenlychen, the hospital north of Berlin:

> The world in which Himmler was still moving was fantastic. "Europe cannot manage without me in the future either," he commented. "It

will go on needing me as Minister of Police. After I've spent an hour with Eisenhower he'll appreciate the fact. They'll soon realize that they're dependent on me—or they'll have a hopeless chaos on their hands." He spoke of his contacts with Count Bernadotte, which involved transfer of the concentration camps to the International Red Cross. . . . Earlier, they had always talked about liquidating all political prisoners before the end. Now Himmler was trying to strike some private bargains with the victors. . . .

Finally, Himmler after all held out a faint prospect of my becoming a minister in his government. For my part, with some sarcasm I offered him my plane so he could pay a farewell visit to Hitler. But Himmler waved that aside. He had no time for that now, he said. Unemotionally, he explained: "Now I must prepare my new government. And besides, my person is too important for the future of Germany for me to risk the flight."

When Hitler heard that Himmler had been negotiating with the Allies, he ordered truehearted Heinrich's arrest as a traitor and expelled him from the Nazi Party and all his offices.

American and Soviet troops linked up at Torgau on the Elbe on 25 April 1945. Five days later, having married Eva Braun and dictated his final testament, Hitler committed suicide by shooting himself with a Walther pistol in the right temple while biting into a cyanide capsule. An orderly, Hermann Karnau, recalled the aftermath:

> I was commanded by an SS officer to leave my station. . . . I did so and went into the officers' club. After half an hour I returned. The entrance to the Führer bunker was locked. I went back and tried to get in through the emergency exit, the one which led to the garden of the Reich Chancellery. As I reached the corner between the tall sentry-post bunker and the Führer bunker proper, when I was up there, I suddenly saw what looked like a petrol rag being thrown. In front of me lay Adolf Hitler on his back and Eva Braun on her belly. I definitely established that it was he. I went back and informed my comrade Hilger Poppen, who however didn't believe me. Half an hour later I returned to the spot. I could no longer recognize him because he was pretty charred. I spoke to Erich Mansfeld, who was at this time on sentry duty in the tower, who also confirmed: There lies Adolf Hitler. He is burning. I left this place . . . and by the staircase met *Sturmbannführer* Schedle, who confirmed that the Chief was burning behind the house in the garden of the Reich Chancellery. At about 1300 [one p.m.] I was at this spot again. . . . I saw that Hitler and Eva Braun by now had burnt to the point that the skeletal structure could

clearly be seen. Whether during the period from 1800 to 2000 [six to eight p.m.] gasoline was poured over the remains once more, I don't know, but when I was there again at 2000, cinders were already flying in the wind.

Germany surrendered unconditionally on 7 May 1945. Himmler lay low in Flensburg, on the Danish border, with Potthast, their two children, Ohlendorf and several former subordinates. He tried to move by car to Bavaria on 10 May 1945, disguised as Sturmscharführer Heinrich Hitzinger of the Geheime Feldpolizei—the Secret Military Police, a branch of the Gestapo—with his mustache shaved off and a black patch over his left eye. The group made little progress in the confusion of Russian and British troop movements, refugees and damaged roads and bridges, and on 20 May 1945 Himmler and two adjutants, all three now in civilian clothing, were arrested at a British checkpoint between Hamburg and Bremen. They were driven to a British POW camp, ending up three days later at an interrogation center near Lüneburg, where Himmler identified himself and was recognized and searched. Two small brass cases turned up in his clothes, one holding a glass capsule, the other empty. His guard assumed the capsules contained cyanide and that one must be in his mouth and began watching him closely.

The officer in charge, Captain Tom Selvester, remembered that strange day with Himmler waiting for an interrogation officer to arrive:

> He behaved perfectly correctly, and gave me the impression that he realized things had caught up with him. He was quite prepared to talk, and indeed at times appeared almost jovial. He looked ill when I first saw him, but improved tremendously after a meal and a wash. . . . He was in my custody for approximately eight hours, and during that time, whilst not being interrogated, asked repeatedly about the whereabouts of his "Adjutants," appearing genuinely worried over their welfare.

Colonel Michael Murphy, the interrogation officer, arrived at eight in the evening and moved Himmler roughly by car to an interrogation center at British Second Army headquarters outside Lüneburg. There a doctor, C. J. L. Wells, saw him stripped, gave him a thorough body search and finally tried to examine his mouth. "Wells saw a small black knob protruding between a gap in [Himmler's] teeth on the lower righthand side," Padfield says—the cyanide capsule's rubber stopper. He asked Himmler to move to a light. Himmler did, made to open his mouth, but as Wells reached in to remove the capsule Himmler jerked away and crushed it, releasing a lethal dose of cyanide.

Himmler died at 11:04 p.m., 23 May 1945. In the next days British Army pathologists took a death mask and performed an autopsy, reserving a slice or two of brain. On 26 May 1945 a four-man British guard unit trucked Himmler's corpse to Lüneburg Heath and buried it in an unmarked grave. It was no killing pit, but it would do.

EPILOGUE

Twenty-four commanders and officers of Einsatzgruppen organizations were brought to trial in Germany by the U.S. military government after the war.* The Einsatzgruppen trial, *United States of America v. Otto Ohlendorf et al.*, was the ninth of twelve war-crimes trials before U.S. military tribunals held at Nuremberg following the well-known Trial of the Major War Criminals conducted there before the International Military Tribunal (IMT) beginning in late 1945. *Otto Ohlendorf et al.* was heard by a panel of three judges from 15 September 1947 to 10 April 1948 with Judge Michael Musmanno presiding.

According to the chief prosecutor, Benjamin Ferencz, no trial of the Einsatzgruppen had originally been planned. The Einsatzgruppen reports—one set, the only set that survived the war—had been scooped up among two tons of documents found on the fourth floor of Gestapo headquarters in Berlin in September 1945. They escaped prosecutor attention for more than a year; a thousand tons of documents captured throughout Germany had to be sorted. The Einsatzgruppen figured into the IMT Nuremberg trial—Ohlendorf notoriously admitted in open court that his Einsatzgruppe D had murdered 90,000 people—but the full range and scale of Einsatzgruppen activity did not emerge.

Ferencz, a tough, smart, compact graduate of the Hell's Kitchen district of Manhattan and Harvard Law School, chief of the Berlin branch of the Office of Chief of Counsel for War Crimes, remembers seeing the Einsatzgruppen reports for the first time in late 1946 or early 1947. Having participated in the liberation of Buchenwald, Mauthausen and Dachau as a sergeant in George Patton's Third Army, he was horrified by the extent of Einsatzgruppen atrocity. He carried the three folders of reports to Telford Taylor, the chief prosecutor at the IMT Nuremberg trial and chief of counsel for war crimes for the subsequent Nuremberg

---

*They were Otto Ohlendorf (EG D); Heinz Jost (EG A); Erich Naumann (EG B); Otto Rasch (EG C); Erwin Schulz (EK 5); Franz Six (Vorkommando Moskau); Paul Blobel (SK 4a); Walter Blume (SK 7a); Martin Sandberger (SK 1a); Willy Seibert (EG D); Eugen Steimle (SK 7a, SK 4a); Ernst Biberstein (EK 6); Werner Braune (EK 11b); Walter Hänsch (SK 4b); Gustav Nosske (EK 12); Adolf Ott (SK 7b); Eduard Strauch (EK 2); Emil Haussmann (EK 12); Woldemar Klingelhöfer (SK 7b, Vorkommando Moskau); Lothar Fendler (SK 4b); Waldemar von Radetzky (SK 4a); Felix Rühl (SK 10b); Heinz Schubert (EG D); and Matthias Graf (EK 6).

trials. Taylor agreed that the crimes of the Einsatzgruppen were appalling but pointed out that the trials he was preparing (intended to reveal the criminal participation of a representative cross section of German institutions, including medicine, the law, industry and government ministries) had already been scheduled and budgeted. Ferencz insisted that at least the leaders of the Einsatzgruppen had to be brought to trial. Whereupon Taylor appointed twenty-seven-year-old Ferencz, who had never tried a criminal case before, to organize *Otto Ohlendorf et al.* and to serve as chief prosecutor.

Ferencz was up to the challenge. Brilliantly, he introduced the Einsatzgruppen reports as evidence in the first two days of the trial, authenticated them and rested his case. The remainder of the trial consisted of defense presentations and incisive cross-examination. Two defendants escaped conviction. Otto Rasch arrived in Nuremberg with such severe Parkinson's disease and associated dementia that his trial had to be severed from the case; he died on 1 November 1948. Emil Haussmann, an SS-Sturmbannführer with Einsatzkommando 12, committed suicide. All twenty-two other defendants were convicted on at least one of the three counts of indictment (crimes against humanity, conventional war crimes, membership in an illegal organization). Fourteen were sentenced to death by hanging, two to life imprisonment, the remaining six to lesser sentences. After the trial Ohlendorf, one of those sentenced to death, told Ferencz, "The Jews in America will suffer for what you have done to me." (Ferencz, one Jew in America, went on to a successful legal career in partnership with Taylor and became in the fullness of time one of the founding organizers of the International Criminal Court.)

All defendants except Gustav Nosske applied to the U.S. military governor of the American sector of occupied Germany, General Lucius Clay, for clemency, but Clay confirmed all their sentences in 1949. In January 1951 U.S. High Commissioner John J. McCloy confirmed some sentences but reduced others, including ten of the fourteen death sentences. On 7 June 1951 Blobel, Werner Braune, Erich Naumann and Ohlendorf were hanged at Landsberg Prison. By 1958 all surviving defendants had been freed. Four other Einsatzgruppen leaders were sentenced to death and executed after trials conducted by other nations.

The West German Central Prosecution Office of Nazi War Criminals initiated proceedings against more than one hundred Einsatzgruppen members, but between 1945 and 1992, West German courts convicted and punished only 472 defendants in total for involvement in the persecution and murder of Jews. It follows that most Einsatzgruppen, Order Police, Totenkopf, Waffen-SS and other SS members who perpetrated mass murder in the East during the Second World War were neither indicted nor convicted but have lived out their lives in freedom, unpunished, a liberty they summarily denied their victims.

The fate of other SS leaders involved in SS and Einsatzgruppen atrocities: Otto Bradfisch (Einsatzkommando 8), who conducted the 15 August 1941 *Aktion* in Minsk that upset Himmler, was sentenced in 1961 to thirteen years, subsequently commuted to six years. Kurt Daluege, the head of the Order Police, was executed in Czechoslovakia in 1946. Oskar Dirlewanger was beaten to death by guards at the Altshauser Detention Center on 7 June 1945. Adolf Eichmann was brought to trial in Israel in 1960 and hanged in 1962. Hans Frank, the head of the General Government, was sentenced to death at the IMT Nuremberg trial and hanged on 16 October 1946. Odilo Globocnik committed suicide in a British prisoner-of-war camp on 31 May 1945.

August Häfner (Einsatzkommando 4a), who murdered the children at Belaja Cerkov, was sentenced in 1973 to eight years. Joachim Hamann (Einsatzkommando 3), who supervised the Arajs commando and supplied the victims for Karl Jäger's charts, died on 13 July 1945. Albert Hartl (EG C), who saw the corpse gases bubbling at Babi Yar, was never tried. Rudolf Höss, the commandant of Auschwitz, was executed in Poland in 1947. Jäger, facing trial in West Germany, committed suicide in his cell at the Hohenasperg detention center on 22 June 1959. Friedrich Jeckeln was executed in the USSR in 1946. Wilhelm Kube, the Generalkommissar for Byelorussia, was assassinated in 1943. Heinrich Lohse, the Reichskommissar Ostland, was sentenced by a German denazification court to ten years in prison but released because of ill health in 1951. Heinrich Müller, the head of the Gestapo, disappeared. Arthur Nebe, implicated in the 20 July 1944 plot against Hitler, was executed by the SS on 2 March 1945. Alfred Rosenberg, convicted in the IMT Nuremberg trial, was hanged in 1946. Franz Walther Stahlecker died of wounds inflicted by Estonian partisans on 23 March 1942. Bruno Streckenbach was a prisoner of war in the USSR until 1955; he died in Hamburg in 1977. Max Thomas, commander of Einsatzgruppe C, committed suicide in 1945.

Erich von dem Bach-Zelewski managed to evade incarceration until late in life. He testified for the prosecution at IMT Nuremberg, denouncing Himmler and his fellow Higher SS and Police Leaders. In 1951 he was convicted in a Munich denazification trial and sentenced to ten years' "special labor" but he did not report to prison and was not picked up; he worked as a night watchman during those years and lived at home. In 1951 he also identified himself to an American prosecutor as the person who had supplied Hermann Göring, awaiting hanging at Nuremberg, with the cyanide capsule with which Göring cheated the hangman. Bach-Zelewski was never prosecuted for murdering Jews, but in 1961 he was tried for his part in a Röhm Purge murder and sentenced to four and a half years. ("I was Hitler's man to the end," he testified boastfully in that forum. ". . . I am still convinced Hitler was innocent.") Indicted again in 1962 for the 1933 murder of six Communists, he was sentenced to life in prison. He died in a German prison hospital in 1972.

The Einsatzgruppen mass killings were the direct predecessors of the so-called ethnic cleansing that bloodied the former Yugoslavia five decades later. Murder makes for long memories: Christian Serbs shot Muslim Serb men into mass graves in the recent war in Serbia; in 1941 Muslim Serbs had massacred Christians. Short on manpower, Himmler in 1943 approved the formation of Muslim SS divisions. The SS "Handschar" Division appeared in Yugoslavia in October 1943, writes historian Gerald Reitlinger:

> It consisted of 20,000 Bosnian Muslims, the so-called "Mujos." A further Muslim SS division, recruited in the Balkan countries in 1944 and known as the 23rd SS division "Kama," was never brought to completion. These Muslims were traditional enemies of the Christian Serbs, and in 1941 their religious zeal had urged them to join in the massacres of Serbs, which were carried out by the Ustashe, the militia of the Croat leader Ante Pavelic. As pillage was followed by discipline, the energy of the Mujos was canalized into the *Waffen-SS*. The Mujos were organized on the lines of the Bosnian regiments of the old imperial Austrian army, with officers and even NCOs of German race, but they wore the Turkish fez with their SS runes and, in contrast with the "six godless SS divisions" of 1941, each battalion had a chaplain or Imam.

The history of the Einsatzgruppen supports a few general observations. The fundamental reason the Holocaust became possible—a reason that links it to other mass-killing regimes and other genocides—was that social, economic and political breakdown brought disorder that allowed Hitler and his criminal subordinates, a surprising number of them actual murderers, to parasitize and dominate the government of Germany, sweeping aside checks and balances (the essence of stable government) that would have limited their absolute power, coopting the police, coopting the bureaucracy, the military and the judiciary. Soviet Russia under Stalin and Communist China under Mao Zedong saw parallel developments with similarly lethal consequences totaling millions of privation deaths and murders. Without robust checks and balances, a leader's appetite for domination—death being the ultimate domination—can become insatiable, since everyone without exception is potentially a threat to his power.

External checks also faltered. For the Nazis, the Jews were a nation unto themselves, but for the rest of the world the European and Eastern Jews were people of specific nationalities, citizens of other states, non-citizens of their own. In response to Franklin Roosevelt's call for a conference at Evian in July 1938, Hitler sneered, "We, on our part, are ready to put all these criminals at the disposal of these countries, for all I care, even on luxury ships." Germany was not prepared to allow Jews to emigrate with more than the clothes on their backs, however, and few countries that sent delegates to the Evian Conference were willing to admit impoverished immigrants. "As we have no real racial problem," Australia announced, "we are not desirous of importing one." Peru wanted no doctors or lawyers. Canada wanted only farmers. France was already saturated. The nations of Central America disdained "traders or intellectuals." The United States grandly agreed to begin—in 1938!—accepting its full legal annual quota for Germany and Austria of 27,370 immigrants. The Jewish victims—someone else's citizens and thus someone else's problem—fell into the anarchic interstices of the nation-state system. "We see," a German newspaper editorialized smugly, "that . . . no state is prepared to fight the cultural disgrace of central Europe by accepting a few thousand Jews. Thus the conference serves to justify Germany's policy against Jewry."

Even the victims inadvertently sent the wrong signals, offering a civil response to violent challenge when the violent consider a civil response to be cowardice and an open door to exploitation. Yehuda Bauer, the Israeli historian and former director of Holocaust research at Yad Vashem, underlines the normative regularity of the Jewish response:

> The Germans did not know, until sometime in 1941, what they would do with the Jews: the decision to murder them was not taken until then. If the Germans did not know, the Jews cannot be expected to have known either. Their problem, as they saw it, was how to survive an occupation that would end one day. . . . That meant, to use Isaiah Trunk's terminology, not "collaboration," but "cooperation"—that is, yielding to the demands of the conqueror while trying to evade the worst excesses; cooperation did not mean agreement with the conqueror's policies or war aims, and it was based on the assumption that the Germans would ultimately be defeated. . . .

Once it began to dawn upon the Jewish populations of Europe that the Germans had decided to murder them, the reaction was flight, hiding, armed resistance on the part of a small minority who were able to obtain weapons, attempts to seek employment that would be essential to the Germans, and a despairing but often dignified acceptance of inevitable death. Psychologically, Jewish responses to knowledge of impending destruction were no different from similar responses of other groups. Russian or Polish peasants on the point of execution by German troops, French resistance fighters caught and sentenced to death, Serb villagers confronting Croat or German murderers—people facing inescapable destruction behave in much the same way. The range of reactions extends from numbed fear and hysterical crying to heroic defiance. We value the latter, which was indeed quite widespread. But the other kinds of response are no less human, no less understandable or worthy of empathy.

The Germans like Eichmann and Blobel, who expressed wonder at seeing Jewish victims willingly jumping into killing pits, came from a nation whose sons, like the sons of other European nations, had followed orders to charge over the top of the trenches during the First World War and run directly into machine-gun fire. When there are (for whatever complex reasons of patriotism, military discipline or mortal threat) no other reasonable choices, people do what they are told. Did not Eichmann and Blobel walk unaided to the gallows when their time came? They at least deserved their deaths.

The Great War set the stage for the Holocaust. The foul trenches ("the long grave already dug," the English poet John Masefield called them), the no-man's-lands of barbed wire, the piles of rotting corpses, the muddy, denuded landscape prefigured the killing pits and the concentration and death camps of the Third Reich. Hitler spent four years as a runner on the front lines in that war. He found himself in war, but he too broke down at the end of it, to forge a new identity on a vision of apocalyptic revenge.

Bauer argues plausibly that anti-Semitism was the organizing principle of Nazism:

In the Nazi case ... the persecution of the Jews was pure, abstract antisemitic ideology in the context of biological racism, and it became a central factor in Hitler's war against the world. In the minds of the Nazi elite, the main enemies of Germany—the Soviet Union, France, the United States, Britain—were controlled by the Jews. The proof of Jewish control of a country lay in the very fact that it turned against Germany. After all, World War II was started by Germany not for any economic or military reasons—nobody threatened Germany in 1939, and the economy had risen from the depth of the world economic crisis to almost full employment and prosperity. The desire to expand to the east and control Europe was motivated by a phantasmagoric racial-biological ideology in which the enemy was controlled by Jews; therefore, the Jews were, from the Nazi point of view, the main enemy. The war was indeed a "war against the Jews."

But it is one thing to rage rhetorically against a people from the safety of a beer-hall stage, quite another to face the daily dreadfulness of murdering them. One place Holocaust historians seem not to have looked for models of the killing process is the history and anthropology of the slaughtering of animals for food. The parallels are compelling.

The French anthropologist Noëlie Vialles examines slaughtering in her book *Animal to Edible*. She remarks on the parallels "between the mass slaughter of animals and equally large-scale exterminations of human beings," because she heard such analogies "expressed on a number of occasions, inside abattoirs themselves." She found that modern slaughtering is carefully arranged to dilute responsibility for the actual killing by dividing the killing into stunning (with a hammer or a bolt gun), one man's job, and then bleeding (by cutting the throat), another man's job—two separate functions, usually performed out of sight of each other in two separate rooms, neither one of which can be said to cause the animal's death. "We are left," Vialles writes, "without any 'real' killing at all, nor do we have any one person who 'really' kills; by separating the jobs, you completely dilute the responsibilities and any feelings of guilt, however vague and held in check." She compares this dilution arrangement to the one rifle loaded with a blank in a firing squad, "so that each person is able to believe, as he pulls the trigger, that he is not killing, or at least no one can be absolutely certain of having committed a fatal action." The use of multiple executioners in the early Einsatzgruppen massacres served a similar function.

But as the range of Einsatzgruppen killing widened, the killing took on a different character. This too was prefigured in the history of slaughtering, Vialles writes:

> Back in the days when slaughtering was done in the middle of towns, the butchers who worked and lived on terms of familiarity with blood were already credited with possessing a violent and brutal character. Whatever their means and whatever their skill, "master butchers live by slitting the throats of animals and will always, even if it is only metaphorically, have blood under their fingernails." Moving abattoirs

out of towns undoubtedly contributed towards relieving butchers of images of bloody brutality, but only the more effectively to transfer those images to the men who henceforth did nothing but slaughtering. Blood not only spattered their clothing; it appeared to impart a moral stain as well, either in terms of the sight of blood making men bloodthirsty or in terms of their sanguinary occupation attracting already "sanguine" temperaments.

The solution was to industrialize slaughtering. Fundamentally, of course, the industrialization of the slaughter of food animals concerned efficiency and therefore profit. But it also served to reduce the psychological disturbance the workers felt, Vialles argues:

> It is a thought-provoking fact that the first industrial production lines were in fact slaughter lines in the Chicago abattoirs. . . . We know the effects of job fragmentation in terms of lowering awareness levels, and its application to slaughtering is probably no accident. Each man is able, as he performs a task that has been reduced to a small number of movements, to overlook the significance of those movements. Slaughterers often stress that once you "get used to it" you "stop taking any notice," you "do it as you would anything else." The thought vacuum and the lack of identification with one's job that are elsewhere experienced as distressing features of production-line work, here constitute on the contrary a prerequisite for "getting used to it."

The movement for "humane" methods of slaughter, another driving force behind modern industrial slaughtering technologies, did not originate among butchers but among middle-class English men and women repelled by the implications of the mass killing of animals. "The 1835 [English] law against cruelty to animals," a British historian notes, "announced its intention of reducing both the suffering of dumb creatures and 'demoralization of the people.' . . . The S.P.C.A. (Society for the Prevention of Cruelty to Animals) may thus be regarded as another middle-class movement aimed at civilizing the lower classes." Moving butchering out of sight paralleled moving public executions out of sight, another stage in the civilizing process that had been ongoing since medieval times.

Himmler's was just such a middle-class sensibility, coupled grotesquely with the eager viciousness of a desk murderer. Pressing his organization to find a more "humane" method of slaughtering Jews, he extracted from it a solution similar to (perhaps modeled on?) the solution animal processors had evolved. For Himmler as for the English middle-class reformers (in Vialles's words):

The logic of the industrial abattoir not only satisfies the specific techno-economic demands of the industry concerned; it also satisfies the demands of modern sensitivities in that it meets and readily takes account of considerations relating to the humane treatment of animals as well as our obscure desire for our meat to be obtained without bloodshed, for slaughtermen to be "just like other workers" and for abattoirs to be "just like other factories."

Himmler also wanted his victims killed without bloodshed and his SS men to be just like other workers, which is the fundamental reason he switched the method of killing from Einsatzgruppen executions to gas vans and gas chambers. The difference between killing animals and killing human beings is not merely a matter of degree, however, whatever animal rightists believe. Himmler knew his project was fundamentally futile, or he would not have bragged ad nauseam about the "duty" of mass execution making his SS men "hard."

The last word belongs to a victim who survived, Israel Goldfliess of little Trembowla in the western Ukraine, where the Seret River runs beside the town, writing his sister and brother-in-law in mid-May 1944:

Seven weeks have passed since the Red Army liberated us. What I have to tell you is not vain talk but the naked truth. To my sorrow, a pitiful few lived to see the liberation. It is with great difficulty that I write to you—my precious treasures, the only people still alive in my whole world. I did not know how it would be possible to hold a pen in my hand and write about what happened to us. I am indeed able to inform you of the good news that your brother is one of the few survivors, or, more accurately, one of the few miserable individuals who was fated to live through the torment of Hitler's Seven Departments of Hell and remain alive. But when I remember all our suffering—the terrible shocking tragedy!—it is so awful, savage, dreadful that there is no prophet or writer who ever described, even in his imagination at its richest, such a horrible reality.

Killing sites await memorials all over eastern Europe.

NOTES

I EASTWARD FROM PRETZSCH

3 **Polish service, Russian preference:** Krausnick (1981), p. 122.
Pretzsch assignments: Krausnick (1981), p. 122.
Handpicked leaders: Krausnick (1981), p. 122.
4 **Order Police battalion:** Büchler (1989), p. 457.
Destination England: according to Lothar Fendler, Nuremberg War Crimes Trials (1978) (hereafter EG Trial Tr.), p. 3995.
"The last act": Speer (1970), p. 162.
"The idea of treating war": quoted in Fest (1970), p. 57, from Frank (1953).
5 **Field marshal recollection:** quoted in Reitlinger (1957), pp. 124–25.
Polish campaign Einsatzgruppen: Höhne (1969), p. 297.
Streckenbach: Höhne (1969), p. 297.
Hitler's card indexes: Bromberg (1983), p. 93.
"As a group leader": Moczarski (1981), p. 106.
6 **531 towns, etc.:** Lucas (1986), p. 3.
"The first victims": quoted in Lucas (1986), p. 3.
Wagner/Heydrich agreement: Hilberg (1985), p. 191.
Heydrich letter to Einsatzgruppen commanders: IMT IV, p. 119ff.
Eichmann: Von Lang (1982), pp. 92–93.
7 **Wloclawek incident:** Krausnick et al. (1968), pp. 51–52.
Polish leadership: quoted in Padfield (1990), p. 273.
SS killings of the disabled preceded euthanasia: Friedlander (1995), p. 136.
"In front of the pit": quoted in Friedlander (1995), p. 137.
8 **Tiegenhof, Chelm:** Friedlander (1995), p. 137.
"After killing handicapped": Friedlander (1995), p. 139.
"Little by little": Von Lang (1982), p. 159.
Expulsions from western Poland: Burring (1994), p. 69, citing *Das politische Tagebuch Alfred Rosenberg,* ed., H. G. Seraphim (Munich: Deutscher Tasenbuch Verlag, 1964), p. 99.
"I had to set up guidelines": Von Lang (1982), p. 102.
"What a pleasure": quoted in Browning (2), p. 7.
9 **"where, in a temperature":** quoted in Padfield (1990), p. 288.
"your hair stand up": Gilbert (1947), p. 63.
One hundred mass executions, six thousand lives: Lucas (1986), pp. 8–9.
"It is wholly misguided": adapted from translations in Klee et al. (1988), pp. 4–5, and Bartov (1992), pp. 65–66.

10   **"Obviously it is possible":** quoted in Padfield (1990), p. 287.
      "may I kindly": Padfield (1990), p. 287.
11   **"I will in no way":** Padfield (1990), pp. 287–88.
      "Executions of all": quoted in Manvell and Fränkel (1965), p. 85.
      "With wagging pince-nez": quoted in Padfield (1990), p. 288.
      "a war assignment": Waldemar von Radetzky, EG Trial Tr., p. 4142.
      "putting down resistance": quoted in Klee et al. (1988), p. 81.
12   **"terrain exercises":** quoted in Reitlinger (1957), p. 182.
      Brief military training: Lothar Fendler, EG Trial Tr., p. 3993.
      When EG learned of assignment: according to Lothar Fendler, EG Trial Tr., p. 3995.
      EG A 990 people: Hilberg (1985), p. 289.
13   **"had 180 vehicles":** Ohlendorf, EG Trial Tr., p. 672.
      MacLean conclusions: MacLean (1999), p. 14.
14   **Hitler himself dictated:** Krausnik et al. (1968), p. 60. Directive No. 21: IMT, PS-447.
      "authorized within the frame": quoted in Headland (1992), p. 137.
      "clash between two ideologies": quoted in Förster (1989), p. 498; Noakes and Pridham (1998), vol. 3, pp. 1086–87.
15   **"Out of eighty":** Clark (1965), p. 34.
      "This is the first time": Schellenberg (1956), p. 196.
      "bearers of the Jewish-Bolshevik worldview": quoted in Förster, "Operation Barbarossa as an Ideological War," in Cesarani (1994), p. 91.
      Commissar Order: see Lozowick (1989), p. 476.
16   **Keitel's conclusions:** quoted in Fleming (1984), p. 34.
      "The fight which would soon": EG Trial Tr., p. 934.
      Schulz testimony denying prewar announcement of Führer Order: Other EG leaders on trial, of course, did make such a claim, but there is good evidence that they were lying. For a full discussion, see Alfred Streim, "The Tasks of the SS Einsatzgruppen," in Marrus (1989), vol. 2, p. 436 ff.
      Four categories: from Heydrich's 2 July 1941 minute to the Higher SS and Police Leaders, which "summarized" the "basic instructions" that he had already issued to the Einsatzgruppen. Quoted in Krausnik et al. (1968), pp. 62–63.
17   **"any purges":** also from Heydrich's 2 July 1941 minute, quoted in Krausnik et al. (1968), pp. 62–63.
      Lange on "execution of all Jews": Noakes and Pridham (1998), vol. 3, p. 1093.
      "a knightly Order": quoted in Padfield (1990), p. 139.
      three-day meeting in June: Browning (2), p. 23, n. 72.
      "It is a question of existence": quoted in Browning (2), p. 23.
18   **"On that day":** Erwin Schulz testimony, EG Trial Tr., p. 1068.

2   VICIOUS CIRCLES

20   **"eliminationist anti-Semitism":** Goldhagen (1996), p. 48.
21   **"People must be motivated":** Goldhagen (1996), p. 24.
      "a radical break": Goldhagen (1996), p. 28.
23   **"Harsh military discipline":** Bartov (1992), p. 59.
      Stangl on Austrian police academy: Sereny (1974), p. 28.
      Belligerency: Athens (1992), p. 57ff.
24   **The belligerent subject resolves to resort to violence:** Athens (1992), p. 60.
25   **Mixed populations of pacifist and marginally violent:** cf. Athens (1998).
      Stage four: virulency: Athens (1992), p. 72ff.
27   **"Within the ranks":** Bartov (1992), p. 61.
28   **Nearly thirty percent militaristic:** Merkl (1980), p. 109ff.
      Ballerstedt assault: Bromberg (1983), p. 89; Payne (1973), p. 160.
      Victor on Hitler: Victor (1998), p. 55.
      Middle-class morality: cf. Victor (1998), pp. 55–56.
29   **"Everyone who knew Hitler":** Rauschning (1940), p. 17.
      Alois's qualities: Smith (1967), p. 26; Jetzinger (1958), p. 51; Bromberg (1983), p. 32.
      William Patrick Hitler's and Brigid Hitler's testimony: Langer (1942–43), quoted in Bromberg (1983), pp. 32–33.
      Paula Hitler told John Toland: quoted in Miller (1990a), p. 153.
30   **"Hitler repeatedly talked":** Speer (1970), p. 124.
      Alois Jr. and Adolf unconscious: for Alois Jr., Toland (1976), p. 9; for Adolf, Miller (1990b), p. 97, and Victor (1998), p. 29.
      Teachers' labels: quoted in Bromberg (1983), p. 45.
      Middle school teacher's testimony: Eduard Huemer, quoted in Redlich (1998), p. 16.
      "It was not long": quoted in Toland (1976), p. 13.
      Kubizek on Hitler's orations and anti-Semitism: quoted in Toland (1976), p. 20; Fleming (1984), p. 4.
      "In Vienna I learnt": Calic (1971), p. 67.
      "This pathological, evil-smelling world": Fest (1970), pp. 8–9.
31   **"At that time I formed":** quoted in Jäckel (1972), pp. 108–9.
      "To me, those hours": Hitler (1927, 1971), pp. 161–63.
      "The orders he carried": Gilbert (1950), p. 35.
32   **"Thus it went on":** quoted in Maser (1971), p. 96.
      "distinguishing the broad outlines": Hitler (1927, 1971), p. 203.
      "the greatest villainy": Hitler (1927, 1971), p. 202.
      "The old gentleman": Hitler (1927, 1971), p. 204.
33   **"Do you know":** Calic (1971), p. 39.
      "As I lay there": quoted in Victor (1998), p. 136.

33   **"At its roots":** Fest (1970), p. 71.
       "World War I brought": Wolf (1999), pp. 219–20.
34   **"It is nonsense":** Merkl (1980), p. 13.
       "foreign influences": Hitler in a February 1915 letter, quoted in Jäckel
       (1972), p. 117.
       "a racial tuberculosis": quoted in Fest (1970), p. 16.
       "The effects of the inflation": Bramwell (1985), pp. 34–35.
       "welcomed the misery": Bromberg (1983), p. 94.
       Hanging all the Jews: Fleming (1984), p. 28–29.
35   **"Experience teaches us":** quoted in Victor (1998), p. 133.
       "Suddenly the opposition": Girard (1978), p. 24.
       "The revolution of 1918": Jäckel (1981), p. 52.
       Hitler's idea of a war against the Soviet Union: Jäckel (1981), p. 32.
       "four new aspects": Jäckel (1981), p. 53.
36   **"had now turned into their extinction":** Jäckel (1981), p. 57.
       "Associates of Hitler": Victor (1998), p. 80.
       "The final aim of our policy": quoted in Krausnik et al. (1968), p. 34.
       "Out with them": quoted in Krausnik et al. (1968), p. 34.
37   **Evian:** cf. Morse (1968), p. 199ff; Feingold (1970), p. 22ff.
       "We are going to destroy": quoted in Krausnik et al. (1968), p. 44.

3   BARBAROSSA

38   **"the crack of rifle shots":** Knappe and Brusaw (1992), p. 180.
       "Polish civilians": Knappe and Brusaw (1992), p. 181.
       "people were fleeing": Smolar (1989), p. 4.
       Actions in the border towns: cf. Kwiet (1998).
       Small advance detachment: according to Stahlecker Report, Gitelman
       (1997), p. 265.
39   **Lithuanian irregulars:** Stahlecker Report, quoted in Klee et al. (1988), p. 26.
       Bakers' company accounts: Klee et al. (1988), pp. 32–35.
41   **Colonel's testimony:** Klee et al. (1988), p. 28ff.
       Military photographer's testimony: Klee et al. (1988), p. 31ff.
42   **Vainilavicius testimony:** Baranauskas (1970), pp. 194–95.
       Stahlecker Report: in variant translations in Klee et al. (1988), p. 24ff, and
       Gitelman (1997), p. 265ff.
       Klimaitis and Zigonys: OSR USSR No. 12, Arad et al. (1989), p. 7.
       "long columns": Klee et al. (1988), p. 29.
43   **EK 1b report:** OSR USSR No. 8, Arad et al. (1989), p. 1.
       "utterly ridiculous": Mishell (1988), p. 27.
       "heavy masonry walls": Mishell (1988), p. 38.
44   **Seventh Fort survivor:** Mishell (1988), p. 38ff.
45   **fifteen hundred people:** MacQueen (1996), p. 47, n. 43.
       "The women were immediately": Mishell (1988), p. 44.

45 **"It was thought a good idea":** quoted in Klee et al. (1988), p. 24.
   "The attempts at self-cleansing": quoted in Longerich (1997), p. 263.
   Early pogroms: The Stahlecker Report speaks specifically of "Klimatis" [*sic*] "starting a pogrom with the aid of instructions given him by a small advance detachment [of EG A] operating in Kovno." Gitelman (1997), p. 265.

46 **"When Lithuanian and Latvian":** Gitelman (1997), p. 266.
   Lithuanian NKVD numbers: MacQueen (1996), p. 33.
   Lithuanian deportations: MacQueen (1996), p. 34.
   "Our conversation": Mishell (1988), p. 10.
   Ukrainian NKVD executions: Boshyk (1986), p. 43.
   "It was not only": Boshyk (1986), p. 11.

47 **"Jews were paraded":** Himka (1997), p. 174.
   "The Security Police": Gitelman (1997), p. 265.
   "the good coffee": quoted in Padfield (1990), p. 339.
   Augustowo and Grodno: Breitman (1991), p. 170.
   Bialystok raid: Kwiet (1993), p. 82ff; Browning (2000), p. 120ff.

48 **Himmler unhappy with death toll:** Angrick (1994), p. 334.
   Montua order: Kwiet (1993), p. 84.

49 **Blume testimony:** EG Trial Tr., p. 1778ff.

4   ACROSS THE PALE

53 **"the so-called Jewish segment":** OSR USSR No. 33, Arad et al. (1989), p. 47.
   "The days were long": Knappe and Brusaw (1992), p. 194.
   "the Jerusalem of Lithuania," Jewish museum: Kostanian (1996), p. 4.
   Jewish and Polish hostages: Arad (1982), p. 47.
   Stahlecker on Lithuanian view: Stahlecker Report, p. 112, quoted in Arad (1982), p. 49.

54 **Heydrich 1 July 1941 order:** Arad (1982), p. 46, n. 7; OSR USSR No. 10, Arad et al. (1989), p. 2.
   150-man MP unit; "the auxiliary's first task": OSR USSR No. 17, 21, Arad et al. (1989), p. 15, p. 22.
   "Fifty-four Jews": OSR USSR No. 17, Arad et al. (1989), p. 15.
   "the great grave": Rudashevski (1973), p. 41.

55 **Ponary eyewitness testimony:** Klee et al. (1988), pp. 38–45.
   "To the Germans": quoted in MacQueen (1996), p. 36.

57 **"In Vilnius by 8 July":** OSR USSR No. 21, Arad et al. (1989), pp. 22–23.

58 **"Dust and rain":** Malaparte (1957), p. 159.

59 **"Death to Jews":** Sabrin (1991), p. 7.
   "wild confusion" in Luck: OSR USSR No. 24, Arad et al. (1989), p. 31.
   Number of Ukrainians imprisoned and killed: OSR USSR No. 24, Arad et al. (1989), pp. 31–32.

59   **several hundred Jewish citizens:** OSR USSR No. 24, Arad et al. (1989), pp. 31–32.
60   **"nervous breakdown":** EG Trial Tr., p. 1524.
        Häfner testimony: Klee et al. (1988), pp. 111–12.
        Von Radetzky testimony: EG Trial Tr., p. 4162.
        1,160 Luck Jews: OSR USSR No. 24, Arad et al. (1989), p. 32.
61   **EG arrival in Lvov:** OSR USSR No. 10, Arad et al. (1989), p. 2.
        Insurrection: OSR USSR No. 10, Arad et al. (1989), p. 3; Bandera proclamation: Sabrin (1991), p. 5.
        "the prisons in Lvov": OSR USSR No. 24, Arad et al. (1989), p. 31.
        Lvov Jewish resident's diary: Gitelman (1997), pp. 278–80.
        "7,000 Jews": OSR USSR No. 24, Arad et al. (1989), p. 31.
62   **Landau diary:** Klee et al. (1988), p. 88 ff.
63   **Otto testimony:** IMT NO-4434.
64   **"inspired":** OSR USSR No. 19, Arad et al. (1989), p. 19.
        "We saw trenches": Sabrin (1991), p. 53.
        Three German corpses: Hilberg (1985), p. 311.
        Margolies testimony: Sabrin (1991), p. 61ff.
        House burning on Russian Street: Sabrin (1991), p. 270.
66   **A Trembowla Jewish eyewitness:** Joseph Einleger, Sabrin (1991), p. 132ff.
67   **Briller narrative:** Sabrin (1991), pp. 283–84.

5   TRUEHEARTED HEINRICH I

70   **"stork in a lily pond":** Schellenberg (1956), p. 317.
        Rauschning re. Himmler: Rauschning (1942), pp. 266–67.
        "If I looked like Himmler": quoted in Padfield (1990), p. 297.
        "a good fellow": quoted in Manvell and Fränkel (1965), pp. 16–17.
71   **Strasser on Himmler:** quoted in Padfield (1990), p. 80.
        "after Hitler": Schellenberg (1956), p. 52.
        "small, cold eyes": Schellenberg (1956), p. 295.
        "laughably pushing": George Hallgarten, quoted in Padfield (1990), p. 20.
        "the heavy furniture": Manvell and Fraenkel (1965), p. 1.
        "took every precaution": Smith (1971), p. 25.
72   **"caricature of a sadistic school-teacher":** Heiden (1944), p. 244.
        "already wearing gold-rimmed glasses": quoted in Padfield (1990), p. 24.
        "The boy's enthusiasm": Smith (1971), pp. 41–42.
        Chauffeur incident: Padfield (1990), p. 138.
73   **"a strict schoolmaster":** quoted in Reitlinger (1957), p. 15.
        "In the upper classes": Ende (1979/80), pp. 252, 256.
        "In contrast with pedagogical theory": Maynes (1996), pp. 152–53.
        Suicide studies: Baartman (1994), pp. 853–54.
74   **"He was unsettled":** Smith (1971), pp. 59–60.

74 **Poetry:** Smith (1971), pp. 62–63.
75 **"If there is another campaign":** quoted in Höhne (1969), p. 37.
"Securing German expansion": Bramwell (1985), p. 132.
76 **"What we wanted":** Salomon (1930), p. 65.
77 **"For whom I work":** quoted in Padfield (1990), p. 13. That this is the first entry re Himmler's emigration plans is confirmed in Angress and Smith (1959), p. 210, n. 15.
"Today I have": Smith (1971), p. 78.
"In his relations with people": Smith (1971), pp. 79–80.
78 **"Unlike other one-on-one":** McAleer (1994), p. 141.
Early modern Europe: for an extended discussion of these developments, cf. Elias (1994/1939).
"insults" to the state: McAleer (1994), p. 29.
79 **"He was concerned":** Smith (1971), p. 87.
"Only very gradually": Smith (1971), p. 88.
80 **"He was not very popular":** Smith (1971), p. 113.
"stop talking": quoted in Smith (1971), p. 117.
"special assignments": quoted in Smith (1971), p. 126.
81 **"Toward the authorities":** Smith (1971), p. 137.
82 **"anti-Semitic and** *völkisch***":** Smith (1971), p. 141.
Himmler's sexuality and spiritualism: Smith (1971), pp. 143–45.
Himmler's 1924 memo: quoted in Höhne (1969), p. 46.
83 **"I told myself":** quoted in Höhne (1969), p. 23.
"almost completely Jewish": quoted in Padfield (1990), p. 90.
caste of noble warriors: cf. Padfield (1990), p. 90; Smith (1971), p. 170.
"For [Hitler] I could do anything": quoted in Padfield (1990), p. 99.
84 **"Size 50 knickers":** quoted in Höhne (1969), p. 164.
"From 1929 onwards": Höhne (1969), p. 56.
85 **"For us, standing sublime":** quoted in Padfield (1990), p. 101.
"It remains the great": quoted in Frischauer (1953), p. 32.
More than fifty thousand men: Fest (1970), p. 122.
Sixty thousand, "combing out": Höhne (1969), p. 144; quoting Himmler, Reitlinger (1957), pp. 72–73.
"like a nursery gardener": quoted in Höhne (1969), p. 52.
86 **"The assurances given":** Trotsky (1933), pp. 71–73.
"We propose to build": Calic (1971), pp. 72–81.

6 TRUEHEARTED HEINRICH II

88 **"Through the door":** Gisevius (1947), p. 152.
89 **"Strasser had been taken":** Gisevius (1947), p. 158.
"a piece of theatricality": Gisevius (1947), p. 160.
"From one of his pockets": Gisevius (1947), p. 161.
90 **"Every time I face him":** quoted in Fest (1970), p. 75.

90 **Röhm's murder:** Kershaw (1998), p. 516.
  "For us as Secret State Police": quoted in Padfield (1990), pp. 162–63.
91 **"People abroad take us":** quoted in Höhne (1969), p. 166.
  "I know that there are people": quoted in IMT 4, p. 230.
  "From the purely territorial": Hitler (1927), p. 644.
92 **"The National Socialist movement":** Hitler (1927), p. 646.
  Table-talk discussion: Hitler (1953), pp. 28–29.
  "In this debate": Lindqvist (1992), p. 10.
  German-Herero war: see Gewald (1999).
  "annihilate these masses": quoted in Gewald (1999), p. 171.
  Vernichtungsbefehl: Gewald (1999), pp. 172–73.
93 **"I find it most appropriate":** Gewald (1999), p. 173.
  "The exercise of violence": Gewald (1999), p. 174.
  "When the rainy season came": Lindqvist (1992), p. 149.
  "We'll have to screen": Hitler (1953), pp. 56–57.
  "The forces which are working": quoted in Lindqvist (1992), p. 8.
94 **"just as the weeds":** quoted in Lindqvist (1992), p. 132.
  "the theory that this dying out": quoted in Lindqvist (1992), p. 144.
  "Those with little culture": Lindqvist (1992), p. 145.
  "the stunted hunting people": quoted in Lindqvist (1992), p. 145.
  "But it is a mistake": Lindqvist (1992), p. 146.
95 **"For Germany, consequently":** Hitler (1927), p. 139.
  "the mightiest counterpart": Hitler (1927), p. 308, p. 65.
  "The usual interpretation": Friedlander (1994a), p. 496.
96 **"a) The attack of an SS troop":** quoted in Padfield (1990), p. 248.
  "We must be clear": quoted in Padfield (1990), p. 289.
  "I can say to them": quoted in Padfield (1990), p. 290.
97 **"We as a *Volk*":** quoted in Padfield (1990), pp. 223–24.
  "These forces": quoted in Padfield (1990), pp. 238–39.
98 **"And there is one thing":** quoted in Krausnik et al. (1968), pp. 44–45, and Gerlach (1998), p. 784.
  "Jews, Polacks and rabble": quoted in Browning (2000), p. 7.
  "He suggested to commander-in-chief": Hilberg (1985), p. 252.
  Himmler's May 1940 memorandum: reproduced in German with a preface and Himmler's note in Himmler (1940). Translated by Michael Schmelzle.
  "It is much more correct": Picker (1976), p. 340.
101 **"An unfavorable comment":** Kersten (1957), pp. 300–301.
  "Fate gave him a position": Kersten (1957), p. 306.
102 **"exhausted and twisted":** Kersten (1957), p. 174.
  His worst attack: cf. Kersten (1957), p. 267.
  "a fading option": Breitman, p. 78, in Cesarani (1994).
  Eichmann report: cited in Browning (2000), p. 19.
  "Jewish emigration": quoted in Browning (2000), p. 19.
  "In conformity with the will": quoted in Browning (2000), p. 20.
103 **Brack and X rays:** discussed in Browning (2000), p. 21.

103 **"The documentation for this last plan"**: Browning (2000), p. 21.
104 **"We must lay the foundations"**: Kersten (1957), p. 71.

7 EXTERMINATION

105 **"Lenin left us"**: quoted in Volkogonov (1991), p. 409.
Stalin 3 July 1941 speech: quoted in Werth (1964), p. 162ff.
106 **Hitler 16 July 1941 conference**: 221-L, IMT vol. 38, pp. 86–94; IMT vol. 4, pp. 10–11.
Hitler to Kvaternik: quoted in Kershaw (2000), p. 470.
107 **Globocnik biography**: cf. Pucher (1997), Höss (1992), p. 253ff; Reitlinger (1987), p. 245ff.
"a pompous ass": Höss (1992), p. 253.
108 **"He made such a mess"**: Höss (1992), p. 256.
Globocnik antitank ditch: Pucher (1997), p. 83.
"So we came finally": quoted in Pucher (1997), p. 71.
"promised Himmler": Höss (1992), pp. 255–56.
109 **"major settlement area"**: quoted in Pucher (1997), p. 94.
"Himmler authorized Globocnik": Breitman (1991), p. 186.
"He acted incredibly important": Höss (1992), p. 253.
110 **"They deliberately"**: IMT, vol. 4, p. 4.
"a studied plan": IMT, vol. 4, p. 9.
"many tens of millions": quoted in IMT, vol. 4, p. 9.
"was replaced in the fall": Gerlach (1998), p. 812.
Breitman dates Höss meeting: Breitman (1991), p. 189.
As Höss recalled: Höss (1992), p. 27ff.
111 **"if the historian"**: Browning in Cesarani (1994), p. 139.
"I need these units": quoted in Büchler (1989), p. 459.
Himmler's private army: Büchler (1989), p. 460.
"combing the Pripet marshes": quoted in Büchler (1989), p. 460.
"Express order": quoted in Breitman (1998), p. 60.
112 **23 July 1941 Order Police transfers**: Browning in Cesarani (1994), p. 140.
"from the reliable non-Communist": quoted in Breitman (1998), p. 52.
more than 33,000 men by the end of 1941: Browning (1992), p. 106.
Prützmann's parties: cf. Bach-Zelewski (1946).
"Not what you think": IMT 3839-PS.
Final Solution needed legal order: cf. Krausnik et al. (1968), p. 176.
Eichmann drafted the order: Kershaw (2000), p. 471.
"Complementing the task": quoted in Breitman (1991), pp. 192–93.
113 **"Then the question arose"**: quoted in Fleming (1984), p. 57.
"I believe that it is very simple": Ohlendorf testimony, EG Trial Tr., p. 661.
Police Battalion 45: Browning (1992), p. 107ff.
114 **"Jeckeln had ongoing permission"**: Wilhelm (1991), p. 231.

114   **Sardinenpackung:** see Ezergailis (1996), p. 148.
    More than 44,000 murders: Büchler (1989), p. 462.
115   **"shoot everyone suspected":** Browning (1992), p. 106.
    Magill report: excerpted in Gitelman (1997), pp. 270–71.
116   **"On 2 August":** Büchler (1989), p. 461.
    Children caught in roundups, women and children: Browning (1992), p. 107.
    Fegelein report: Büchler (1989), pp. 460–61.

8   DIRTY WORK

119   **Jewish population totals:** Headland (1992), p. 83.
    "dirty work": Walter Münch, quoted in Ezergailis (1996), p. 173.
    Arajs commando: cf. Ezergailis (1996), p. 173ff.
    Bikernieki totals: Ezergailis (1996), p. 190.
    "The operations would start": Ezergailis (1996), p. 190–91.
120   **"fundamental orders":** Gitelman (1997), p. 265.
    Stahlecker's 15 October 1941 report: extracts in English in *Nazi Conspiracy and Aggression,* v. 6, p. 978ff.
    "The killing in the [Latvian]": Ezergailis (1996), p. 225.
121   **"The Riga city blue bus":** Ezergailis (1996), p. 191.
    Number of provincial Jews murdered: Ezergailis (1996), p. 225.
    "In addition to Jews": Ezergailis (1996), p. 191.
    Tykocin: cf. Wisniewski (1998). I visited Tykocin and the Lopuchowo killing site in the summer of 2001.
122   **"The old policemen":** quoted in Ezergailis (1996), p. 277.
    Throwing children into the air: Ezergailis (1996), p. 197, n. 34.
    Müller request: quoted in Fleming (1984), pp. 109–10.
    "The mass of the Red Army": Clark (1965), p. 129.
123   **"Everywhere [between Vinnitsa and Uman]":** Neumann (1959), p. 134.
    About 5,000 Jews in Zhitomir: OSR USSR No. 37, Arad et al. (1989), p. 55.
    SK 4a statistics: Arad et al. (1989), p. 56.
124   **"1,350 ethnic Germans":** cf. photograph, Klee et al. (1988), p. 109.
    "Round and about": Klee et al. (1988), pp. 109–10.
    "I also remember": Klee et al. (1988), p. 116.
    Fine of one hundred thousand rubles: Faina Vinokurova.
    "After about two weeks' stay": EG Trial Tr., pp. 954–55.
125   **"had the feeling":** EG Trial Tr., p. 4035.
    "it was too mild": EG Trial Tr., pp. 1537–38.
    Jäger Report: full text in Klee et al. (1988), p. 46ff.
    Rokiskis concentration camp setting: McQueen in Gitelman (1997), p. 100.
126   **"A representative":** Mishell (1988), pp. 64–67.

126 **"711 Jewish intellectuals":** Jäger Report, sheet 2.
127 **"22 August 41":** Jäger Report, sheet 3.
"ten males": OSR USSR No. 88, Arad et al. (1989), p. 138.
Twenty of forty-eight children: USSR-41, National Archives Record Group (hereafter NA RG) 895, roll 11.
128 **Kamenets-Podolsky massacre:** see Hilberg (1985), p. 811ff; Braham (1973).
"to expel from Carpatho-Ruthenia": quoted in Braham (1973), p. 137.
129 **"deportation of the":** quoted in Braham (1973), p. 138.
Sixteen thousand refugees: one estimate from a postwar trial; another trial estimated 18,500. Braham (1973), p. 140, n. 16.
"could not cope": quoted in Braham (1973), p. 140.
"Near Kamenets-Podolsky": quoted in Hilberg (1985), p. 812.
"The extermination of the Jews": Braham (1973), p. 141.
"His staff company": Breitman (1998), p. 64.
130 **"In Kamenets-Podolsky 23,600 Jews":** OSR USSR No. 80, Arad et al. (1989), p. 129.
Braham estimates: Braham (1973), p. 141.
Belaja Cerkov massacre: cf. Klee et al. (1988), p. 137ff; Lozowick (1989), p. 477.
"That first evening": Klee et al. (1988), p. 140.
131 **Chaplains' report:** Klee et al. (1988), p. 151ff.
295th Catholic chaplain's report: Klee et al. (1988), p. 141ff.
132 **295th Protestant chaplain's report:** Klee et al. (1988), p. 144.
133 **Lieutenant Colonel Groscurth report:** Klee et al. (1988), p. 145ff.
135 **Von Reichenau statement:** Klee et al. (1988), pp. 152–53.
Häfner testimony: Klee et al. (1988), p. 153ff.

9 "ALL JEWS, OF ALL AGES"

136 **Lohse:** see Arad (1982), p. 8off.
Stahlecker letter: Appendix 1, Ezergailis (1996), p. 378ff.
Hingst notice: Arad (1982), pp. 102–3.
137 **"The situation has become":** Rudashevski (1973), p. 31.
138 **"The Lithuanians drive us":** Rudashevski (1973), p. 32.
"The march to Lukiszki": quoted in Arad (1982), p. 113.
Ghetto and prison numbers: Arad (1982), p. 113.
"At Lukiszki we were kept outside": quoted in Lazar (1985), p. 29ff.
140 **Antipartisan warfare course:** Streit in Cesarani (1994), p. 117, n. 44.
"The baby was still crying": Ehrenburg and Grossman (1980), p. 203.
141 **"Thousands of Berdichev Jews":** Ehrenburg and Grossman (1981), p. 13.
Jeckeln's own staff company: cf. Breitman (1998), p. 65.
"the Germans and traitors": Ehrenburg and Grossman (1981), p. 17.
Breitman speculates: Breitman (1988).

141 **"This execution":** Ehrenburg and Grossman (1981), pp. 17–18.
142 **"Many of those":** Ehrenburg and Grossman (1981), p. 18.
"Witnesses tell": Ehrenburg and Grossman (1981), p. 19.
"All five pits": Ehrenburg and Grossman (1981), pp. 20–21.
143 **Bingel testimony:** Bingel (1959).
146 **"Zhitomir, July 28th":** Neumann (1959), p. 131.
Blobel report to Berlin: OSR USSR No. 106, Arad et al. (1989), p. 174; NO-3140, NA RG 895, roll 11.
147 **18 September 1941:** Arad et al. (1989), p. 174, has "September 10, 1941," but close inspection of a microfilm copy of the original German document confirms the later date.
5,145: Most sources give 3,145, but close inspection of a microfilm copy of the original German document (OSR USSR No. 106) confirms the larger number.
EG report of 9 August 1941: USSR OSR No. 47, Arad et al. (1989), p. 79.
148 **Rösler report:** cf. Klee et al. (1988), pp. 117–19; Hilberg (1985), p. 323–24; Levin (1968), p. 260ff; IMT v. 7, p. 533ff.
149 **Vinnitsa NKVD killings:** cf. Ihor Kamenetsky, ed. *The Tragedy of Vinnytsia* (Toronto: Ukrainian Historical Association, 1989).
Nemirov brickworks massacre: Faina Vinokurova.
Bingel Vinnitsa testimony: Bingel (1959), p. 309.
Vinokurova on Vinnitsa: interview, Vinnitsa, 23 June 2001.
150 **Kikorino:** OSR USSR No. 89, Arad et al. (1989), p. 142.
Nikolayev area: OSR USSR No. 101, Arad et al. (1989), p. 168.
Radomyshl: OSR USSR No. 88, Arad et al. (1989), pp. 139–40.
Kachovka: Klee et al. (1988), p. 61.
Lahoysk: OSR USSR No. 92, Arad et al. (1989), p. 152.
Nevel: OSR USSR No. 92, Arad et al. (1989), p. 152.
Janovichi: OSR USSR No. 92, Arad et al. (1989), p. 152.
Minsk: OSR USSR No. 92, Arad et al. (1989), p. 152.
Lithuania: OSR USSR No. 88, Arad et al. (1989), p. 138.

10   LORDS OF LIFE AND DEATH

151 **Bach-Zelewski version of 15 August 1941 execution:** *Aufbau* (1946).
"from [Himmler's] own mouth": quoted in Padfield (1990), p. 342.
"the shooting of the Jews": quoted in Fleming (1984), p. 50, n. 1.
"who was taking": quoted in Fleming (1984), p. 51.
152 **"ragged forms":** quoted in Padfield (1990), p. 342.
154 **Himmler's post-Minsk itinerary:** Breitman (1998), p. 62.
Killing handicapped children: cf. Friedlander (1995), p. 39ff.
155 **"The technology for gassing":** Friedlander (1995), p. 87.
"The old prison": Friedlander (1995), p. 88.
"he could not ask his troops": quoted in Friedlander (1995), p. 141.
Nebe dynamite experiment: Friedlander (1995), p. 141ff.

156 **Widmann testimony:** quoted in Kogon et al. (1993), pp. 52–53.
"the psychological stress": quoted in Kogon et al. (1993), p. 53.
Blobel gas van testimony, Poltava gas van: Kogon et al. (1993), p. 60.
"Jews comprised only": Mann (2000), pp. 331–32.
157 **"somewhere between 40 and 50 percent":** Goldhagen (1996), p. 523, n. 4.
"ordinary men": cf Browning (1992); Goldhagen (1996).
Mann analysis: Mann (2000).
158 **"We were all so trained":** Gilbert (1947), p. 260.
159 **"It was always stressed":** Gilbert (1947), p. 268–69.
"I would also like to say": quoted in Goldhagen (1996), p. 179.
160 **"I do not know whether":** quoted in Klee et al. (1988), pp. 158–59.
Musmanno-Blobel exchange: EG Trial Tr., pp. 1682–83.
161 **"Popular history":** Friedlander (1995), p. 111.
"the organizers of the killings": Friedlander (1995), p. 116.
162 **Musmanno-Blobel exchange:** EG Trial Tr., pp. 1683–85.
Browning three types: Browning (2000), pp. 166–67.
163 **Hartl testimony:** Klee et al. (1988), pp. 83–85.
"After the first wave": Klee et al. (1988), pp. 81–82.
164 **"I saw SD personnel":** Klee et al. (1988), p. 129.
Barth testimony: NO-3663.
"the civilizing process": cf. Elias (1994); Rhodes (1999), p. 214ff, reviews these issues more fully.
165 **"The body now [comes to serve]":** Michel Foucault, *Discipline and Punish* (Pantheon, 1977), p. 11.
"There was an overall objection": Hilberg (1985), pp. 326–27.
166 **Ohlendorf testimony:** EG Trial Tr., p. 524.
"the shooters were rewarded": Browning (2000), p. 122.
"When these breakdowns happened": Klee et al. (1988), pp. 81–82.
"where SS men are cared for": Helmuth von Moltke, quoted in Cesarani (1994), p. 116, n. 27.
167 **Becker testimony:** Klee et al. (1988), pp. 68–69.
"Our assigned duty": HH an alle Höheren SS- und Polizeiführer, 12.12.1941, Latvian State Archives P-83/80. My translation.
168 **"Despite the mental anguish":** Kwiet (1998), p. 20.
169 **"Members of the [border police]":** Klee et al. (1988), p. 76.
"chase them into the swamp": quoted in Fleming (1984), p. 96.
"There was, for example": Poliakov (1954), p. 131.
"the Gestapo man": Sabrin (1991), p. 219.
"A man is the lord": quoted in MacLean (1999), p. 7.

II   BABI YAR

170 **"Hold it at all costs":** quoted in Clark (1965), p. 136.
"The whole horizon": Anatoli (1970), p. 21.

171   **"The Germans cordoned off":** Anatoli (1970).
        Blobel movements: EG Trial Tr. 1; OSR USSR No. 106, NA RG 895, roll 11.
        "The ensuing fire": OSR USSR No. 97, Arad et al. (1989), p. 164. Arad
        gives "8000, pounds," but OSR USSR No. 106, NA RG 895, roll 11, has
        "about one thousand pounds." Eight thousand pounds of explosives
        would be difficult to conceal.

172   **"there exists in Kiev":** OSR USSR No. 106, NA RG 895, roll 11.
        "As has been proved": OSR USSR No. 97, Arad et al. (1989), p. 164; IMT
        NO-3145 evidence summary.
        "Jews and Communists": OSR USSR No. 101, Arad et al. (1989), p. 168.
        "printed on cheap gray," notice text: Anatoli (1970), pp. 90–91.
        "This summons": OSR USSR No. 106, Arad et al. (1989), p. 173 (transla-
        tion modified).
        "They started arriving": Anatoli (1970), p. 93.
        "There were no such streets": Anatoli (1970), p. 92.

173   **"Families baked bread":** Ehrenburg and Grossman (1981), pp. 6–7.
        "There were plenty": Anatoli (1970), p. 100.
        "The ravine was enormous": Anatoli (1970), p. 15.

174   **"The police regiments":** Blobel testimony, EG Trial Tr., p. 1569.
        Coming up Melnikov Street: this reconstruction is based on information
        in Anatoli (1970), p. 99ff; Ehrenburg and Grossman (1981), p. 3ff; Gitel-
        man (1997), pp. 275–78; Klee et al. (1988), pp. 63–68; and interviews with
        members of the Kyiv Jewish Council, Kyiv, June 2000.
        "At that point": Anatoli (1970), p. 101.
        "an entire office operation": Ehrenburg and Grossman (1981), p. 7.
        "The documents were": Ehrenburg and Grossman (1981), p. 7.

175   **Höfer testimony:** Klee et al. (1988), p. 63ff.
176   **Werner testimony:** Klee et al. (1988), pp. 66–67.
178   **"As a result of":** OSR USSR No. 128, quoted in Klee et al. (1988), p. 68,
        and in Noakes and Pridham (1988), p. 1095.
        Heidborn testimony: Klee et al. (1988), pp. 67–68.
        Clothing donations: OSR USSR No. 106, NA RG 895, roll 11.
        2 October 1941 report: IMT NO-3137.
        Executions every Tuesday and Friday: interview with Kyiv Jewish Coun-
        cil, June 2000.
        Schüppe: Friedlander (1995), p. 142.

179   **"The executioners used to boast":** quoted in Padfield (1990), p. 345.

12   PURE MURDER

180   **"In late September":** Knappe and Brusaw (1992), p. 198.
        "the health of men and horses": quoted in Bartov (1992), p. 18.
        "In these two pockets": Clark (1965), p. 155.
        "he looks at his best": quoted in Browning (2000), p. 38.

180 **"an immediate and unified":** Walter Labs, paraphrasing an oral report from Werner Feldscher, quoted in Gerlach (1998), p. 779.
181 **Transfer of ninety-two men:** see Arad (1987), p. 17.
   Belzec and Chelmno planning: Arad (1987), pp. 23–25.
   Stahlecker visit: Hilberg (1985), p. 351.
   Four trainloads to Lodz: Burrin (1989), p. 127.
   "there is no evidence": Gerlach (1998), p. 766.
   Loss of citizenship and property: Friedlander (1995), p. 288.
   "moved farther east": quoted in Friedlander (1995), p. 288.
   "overseas emigration": RSHA memo: Burrin (1989), p. 129.
   Twenty-two trainloads: Friedlander (1995), p. 289.
182 **"given the present state":** Dr. Erhard Wetzel to Heinrich Lohse, quoted in Fleming (1984), p. 71.
   "I was reproached": EG Trial Tr., p. 526.
183 **"It is clear":** quoted in Manvell and Fraenkel (1965), pp. 125–26.
   "The law of existence": quoted in Fleming (1984), p. 27.
   "The Jewish question": quoted in Fleming (1984), p. 31.
   "When we finally stamp out": quoted in Fleming (1984), p. 2.
   "From the rostrum": Hitler (1953), p. 72. Translation revised.
   Täubner: see Klee et al. (1988), pp. 196–207.
184 **Schumann testimony:** Klee et al. (1988), p. 204.
   Göbel testimony: Klee et al. (1988), p. 197.
186 **Hesse testimony:** Klee et al. (1988), p. 199, p. 201.
187 **"executions for purely political":** Klee et al. (1988), p. 205.
   "It is amazing": Ehrenburg and Grossman (1981), p. 70n.
   Sarra Gleykh diary: Ehrenburg and Grossman (1981), pp. 70–76.
191 **Romanian forces occupied Odessa:** Ehrenburg and Grossman (1981), p. 78.
   "On 23 and 24 October": Ehrenburg and Grossman (1981), pp. 79–80.
   "144,000 peaceful citizens": quoted in Tenenbaum (1955), p. 55.
   Dnepropetrovsk: Orbach (1976), p. 37; Hilberg (1985), p. 372; OSR USSR No. 135, Arad et al. (1989), p. 242.
192 **Sandberger report to Berlin:** OSR USSR No. 111, Arad et al. (1989), p. 184.
   Stahlecker Report: L-180, *Nazi Conspiracy and Aggression,* v. 6, p. 992.
   "The Arajs commando": Ezergailis (1996), p. 185.
   "Early that morning": quoted in Ephraim Oshry, *The Annihilation of Lithuanian Jewry* (Judaica Press, 1995), p. 49.
193 **"the Germans wanted to see":** Tory (1990), p. 41.
   "The Germans then started": Tory (1990), p. 41.
   Columns of one hundred, Ninth Fort: Mishell (1988), p. 84.
   "A terrible human drama": Mishell (1988), p. 84.
194 **Jäger Report:** Ezergailis (1996), p. 385.
   "Opposite the hospital building": Tory (1990), p. 42.
   Reports of pits at Ninth Fort: Tory (1990), p. 46.

194	**Optimists speculated:** Littman (1998), p. 88.
195	**"No one in the ghetto":** Tory (1990), p. 48.
	"very chilly": Mishell (1988), p. 90.
	"a procession of mourners": Tory (1990), p. 49.
	"the ghetto fence": Tory (1990), p. 50.
196	**"smiling sarcastically":** Tory (1990), p. 51.
	"From time to time": Tory (1990), p. 52.
	Mishell's family saved: Mishell (1988), p. 91.
	"hungry, thirsty, crushed": Tory (1990), p. 55.
	"The procession, numbering": Tory (1990), p. 58.
197	**Jäger 29 October 1941 listing:** Ezergailis (1996), p. 385.
	Shooting party at Schönhof: Kersten (1957), p. 112ff.

13   RUMBULA

199	**Erren report:** Klee et al. (1988), pp. 178–79.
200	**Metzner testimony:** Klee et al. (1988), p. 179.
	"The meeting was the occasion": Hilberg (1985), pp. 380–81.
201	**"A clean, handsome little town":** Richmond (1995), p. 3.
	Deposition of Polish veterinarian: Richmond (1995), p. 478ff; Central Commission (1982), p. 60ff. I have merged these two variant translations.
204	**Eight thousand Konin Jews:** Richmond (1995), p. 530, n. 70.1, citing Polish sources.
	"Gallows were thrown up": Ehrenburg and Grossman (1981), p. 152.
205	**"men, women and children":** Smolar (1989), p. 41.
	"ordered to put on": Ehrenburg and Grossman (1981), p. 152.
	Banner: quoted in Smolar (1989), p. 41.
	"People began pushing": Smolar (1989), p. 41.
	6,624 Jews in Minsk: OSR USSR No. 140, Arad et al. (1989), p. 246.
	"information available": Smolar (1989), p. 42.
	"German Jews began": Ehrenburg and Grossman (1981), pp. 154–55.
206	**"about 15,000 Jews":** OSR USSR No. 142, Arad et al. (1989), p. 252.
	Kiev numbers: OSR USSR No. 142, Arad et al. (1989), p. 252.
	Latvia/Rumbula: This discussion, dates, etc., generally follows Ezergailis (1996), p. 239ff.
	Lohse's orders: Ezergailis (1996), p. 239.
	Jeckeln in Riga: This account follows Ezergailis's thorough investigation; see Ezergailis (1996), p. 239ff.
	"Tell Lohse": quoted in Fleming (1984), p. 76.
207	**"I have thought":** quoted by Heinz Jost, EG Trial Tr., p. 1162.
	"Jeckeln assigned": Ezergailis (1996), pp. 241–42.
	Bodyguard and motor pool: Ezergailis (1996), p. 242.
208	**"perhaps half":** Ezergailis (1996), p. 243.
	"battalion police": Ezergailis (1996), p. 246.
	Ezergailis estimates: Ezergailis (1996), p. 242ff.

208 **"The relocation of the Jews":** Ezergailis (1996), p. 247.
"We made and remade": Ezergailis (1996), p. 248.
209 **"He stressed that":** Ezergailis (1996), p. 244. Jeckeln's words ibid, my translation.
"1) the killing grounds": Ezergailis (1996), p. 241.
Weather, Berlin train: Fleming (1984), pp. 79–80; Ezergailis (1996), p. 253.
210 **"young women, women":** quoted in Ezergailis (1996), p. 250.
"We are supposed": quoted in Ehrenburg and Grossman (1981), p. 312.
"An outer apron": Ezergailis (1996), p. 253.
211 **Russian submachine guns:** Ezergailis (1996), p. 241.
"Jeckeln stood on the top": Ezergailis (1996), p. 254.
212 **"curious, inexplicable gunfire":** quoted in Fleming (1984), p. 81.
"You're getting soft": quoted in Fleming (1984), p. 85.
"sleds, wheelbarrows": Ezergailis (1996), p. 255.
"Jewish transport from Berlin": quoted in Gerlach (1998), p. 765.
Himmler-Jeckeln radio messages: quoted and discussed in Gerlach (1998), p. 766.
213 **Michelson narrative:** Michelson (1979), p. 85ff.
"Without realizing": quoted in Ezergailis (1996), p. 259.
"Suddenly I heard": Michelson (1979), pp. 91–92.
214 **"How long will it be":** quoted in Fleming (1984), p. 86.
"After the killings": Ezergailis (1996), p. 261.
"Although the bodies": Ezergailis (1996), p. 255.
Jeckeln 11 December 1941 promotion: Fleming (1984), p. 98, n. 5.

14   NERVES

215 **Jäger Report:** Appendix A, Ezergailis (1996), p. 381ff.
"and expressed his satisfaction": Gerlach (1998), p. 768.
216 **Jäger follow-up telegram:** Fleming (1984), p. 98.
Second Stahlecker Report: see Headland (1992), p. 153ff.
"By December [1941]": Knappe and Brusaw (1992), p. 203–5.
217 **Liepaja massacre:** see Ezergailis (1996), p. 293ff.
2,580 Jews in Vinnitsa: summary report for Nemirov District quoted in Weiner (1999), p. 332.
218 **Vinnitsa wall dynamiting:** interview with Faina Vinokurova, Vinnitsa, June 2000.
"[Ribe] was even more sadistic": Smolar (1989), p. 46.
219 **Kretschmer correspondence:** Klee et al. (1988), p. 163ff.
221 **"[The Führer order] was very harsh":** EG Trial Tr., p. 855.
"That is a clear": EG Trial Tr., p. 852.
Naumann testimony: EG Trial Tr., pp. 856–98.
222 **"According to a view":** Kelman (1973), pp. 45–46.
223 **"The reasons for my [request]":** IMT NO-3841.
Dicks and Filbert: cf. Dicks (1972), p. 204ff.

223   **"In my home and family"**: Dicks (1972), p. 209.
224   **"[Filbert] had looked up to"**: Dicks (1972), p. 220.
       "In [Filbert's] case": Dicks (1972), p. 226.
       "hard consequences": Dicks (1972), p. 206.
225   **"By the time the *EK*"**: Dicks (1972), p. 207.
       "how does a man show": Dicks (1972), pp. 213–14.
       "I was degraded": Dicks (1972), p. 212.
       "I have looked after": Dicks (1972), p. 211.
       "a mere shadow": quoted in Höhne (1969), p. 363.
       "What about those": Dicks (1972), p. 215.
226   **Grawitz wrote Himmler:** 4 March 1942 letter reproduced in Bartoszewski (1961), pp. 97–99.
       "Thank God, I'm through": Höhne (1969), p. 363.
       Within two months: see Klee et al. (1988), p. 121.
       "Jäger told me": Fleming (1984), p. 98.
227   **Jost testimony:** EG Trial Tr., pp. 1150–87.
       "His eyes were extraordinarily small": quoted in Breitman (1991), pp. 5–6.

15   FINAL SOLUTION

229   **"Only he who saw"**: quoted in Clark (1965), p. 175.
       –63°; "many men died": Clark (1965), p. 181.
       "The Red Army . . . had no power": Clark (1965), p. 183.
230   **140 years:** Clark (1965), p. 187.
       "If the Jewish international": quoted in Krausnik et al. (1968), p. 45, and Gerlach (1998), p. 784.
       "particularly because Jews": quoted in Gerlach (1998), p. 772.
       "It was I": Eichmann (1960), p. 23ff.
       "because of events": quoted in Gerlach (1998), p. 793.
231   **"Regarding the Jewish question"**: quoted in Gerlach (1998), p. 785.
       Rosenberg draft speech: quoted in Gerlach (1998), p. 784, n. 112.
       "remarked that the text": PS-1517 (IMT vol. 27, p. 270), quoted in Gerlach (1998), p. 783.
232   **"By 'the decision' "**: Gerlach (1998), pp. 783–84.
       "As for the Jews, well": quoted in Gerlach (1998), p. 790.
233   **"Jewish question"**: quoted in Gerlach (1998), p. 780.
       "The war situation": Gerlach (1998), pp. 786–87.
       Belzec departure: Gerlach (1998), p. 782.
       Gas vans at Chelmno: Gerlach (1998), p. 763.
234   **"[At the turn of the year 1941/42]"**: quoted from German edition of Eichmann interrogation (*Ich, Adolf Eichmann,* Leoni am Starnberger See, Germany, Druffel-Verlag, 1980, p. 17) in Arad (1987), p. 26. The German version and the version in Von Lang (1982) (see next note) appear to be variant versions Eichmann told.

234   **"Heydrich sent for me":** Von Lang (1982), pp. 75–78.
236   **"were five representatives":** Gerlach (1998), p. 794.
       "We called it the Conference": Von Lang (1982), p. 91.
       Wannsee Protocol: IMT NG-2586.
       "LESS: I'm going to quote": Von Lang (1982), pp. 90–91.
       "EICHMANN: What I know is": quoted in Fleming (1984), pp. 91–92.
238   **"Happily":** quoted in Gerlach (1998), p. 797.
       "After the conference": Eichmann (1960), p. 23ff.
       War Service Cross nominees: cf. Gerlach (1998), p. 797.
       January 1942 planning enlargement: Padfield (1990), p. 363.
       Himmler to Pohl: quoted in Padfield (1990), pp. 362–63.
239   **Berlin 4 February 1942 conference:** Padfield (1990), p. 363ff.
       Prague 4 February 1942 conference: Manvell and Fraenkel (1965), p. 127.
       "I know exactly": quoted in Breitman (1991), pp. 234–35.
       "All Jews and Gypsies": Wolf (1999), p. 264.

16   *JUDENFREI*

241   **"In the Golta prefecture":** Hilberg (1985), p. 374–75; Romanian totals: Bauer (2001), p. 50.
       Russian POWs: Bartov (1992), p. 83.
242   **"Reeling under the weight":** Bartov (1992), p. 81.
       "At first, from Poland": quoted in Mendelsohn (1982), pp. 70–71.
       Jeckeln testimony: Noakes and Pridham (1988), pp. 1121–22.
243   **Bikernieki Forest massacres:** Ezergailis (1996), p. 191.
       "According to eyewitnesses": Headland (1992), p. 58.
       "An order came from Himmler": IMT, v. 4, pp. 322–23.
       Himmler announcement, Speer countermand: Gerlach (1998), pp. 803–4.
244   **"in order to disguise":** Klee et al. (1988), p. 188.
       "I am certainly tough": quoted in Noakes and Pridham (1988), p. 1123.
       "The answer was cruel": Smolar (1989), p. 72.
       "A night of terror": Smolar (1989), p. 73.
245   **"As a result of the betrayal":** Klee et al. (1988), p. 189.
       "Soon afterward came the crackling": Smolar (1989), pp. 73–74.
246   **"Later that year":** Eichmann (1960), p. 102.
247   **"Then I encapsulated myself":** Kulcsar et al. (1966), p. 39.
       "You will agree with me": quoted in Klee et al. (1988), pp. 186–87.
       "Since the Eastern territory": Activity and Situation Report No. 11 (PS-3876), NA RG 895, roll 11.
248   **"the Germans conducted":** MacLean (1998), p. 69.
       SK Dirlewanger beginnings: cf. MacLean (1998), p. 42ff.
249   **"I said to Dirlewanger":** quoted in MacLean (1998), p. 15.
       "Offenders were beaten": MacLean (1998), p. 13.
       "During these anti-partisan": MacLean (1998), p. 73.

249   **"During a march":** quoted in MacLean (1998), p. 133–34.
251   **"Preventive attack":** Hilberg (1985), p. 22.
252   **Latvian infant mortality rates:** cf. Table 3a. 5, "Infant Mortality per 100 Children Born," Ezergailis (1996), p. 397.
       "During the catastrophe": Hilberg (1985), p. 23.
253   **Himmler-Hitler meeting, renewal of transports:** Browning (2000), p. 55.
       Sobibor victims: Sereny (1974), p. 114.
       Details of Heydrich assassination: Höhne (1969), pp. 494–95.
254   **"Yes, the world is but":** quoted in Padfield (1990), p. 380.
       "Is the swine dead": quoted in Deschner (1981), p. 9.
       "War is no matter of sentimentalities": quoted in Padfield (1990), pp. 383–85.
255   **Himmler ordered General Government "resettlement":** Padfield (1990), p. 396.
       Treblinka numbers: Table 3, Arad (1987), p. 392.
       "In the spring": quoted in Kogon et al. (1993), pp. 148–49.
       Gassing at Majdanek: cf. Kogon et al. (1993), p. 174ff.
       "We have liquidated": Klee et al. (1988), pp. 180–81.
256   **"countless no longer laugh":** quoted in Padfield (1990), p. 408.
       "Did Hitler begin to doubt": Jäckel (1972), p. 64.
       "Although trampled underfoot": quoted in Kogon et al. (1993), p. 216.
257   **Einsatzgruppen numbers:** Hilberg (1985), p. 390; Headland (1992), p. 105.

17   "CINDERS FLYING IN THE WIND"

258   **"It made a shattering":** EG Trial Tr., p. 2900.
       "a special mission": EG Trial Tr., p. 2866.
       "That was the usual road": EG Trial Tr., pp. 2895, 2898.
       "Physically Blobel": EG Trial Tr., p. 2896.
       "It was evening": quoted in Sereny (1974), pp. 97–98.
       "or faked": Sereny (1974), p. 98.
259   **Blobel-Heydrich meeting:** EG Trial Tr., p. 1618.
       "*Gruppenführer* Müller": IMT, NO-3947.
       "constructed several experimental": Höss affidavit, NA 895, roll 11, NO-4498.
       "the aerodynamic arrangement": Spector (1990), p. 159.
       "At the end of the summer": Spector (1990), p. 161.
260   **"refused to carry out":** EG Trial Tr., pp. 1617–18.
       "It was in May": EG Trial Tr., p. 1618.
       "the ashes should be": NA RG 895, roll 11, NO-4498.
       "the work itself": NA RG 895, roll 11, NO-4498.
       "Dr. Thomas in June": EG Trial Tr., p. 1619.
261   **"The Higher SS":** EG Trial Tr., p. 1619.
       "We were mobilized": Mishell (1988), p. 197.
262   **"According to my orders":** IMT, NO-3947.

262   **"extraordinarily active"**: Padfield (1990), p. 400.
      "You won't understand": Kersten (1956), pp. 132–35.
263   **"Of the Polish population"**: Madajczyk (1962), p. 392.
      "resettlement" by 31 December 1942: Padfield (1990), p. 396.
      "The *Reichsführer-SS*": quoted in Breitman (1991), p. 238.
      "without comment": Höss (1992), p. 287.
264   **Beating of prostitute**: Höss (1992), p. 289.
      "For this occasion": Padfield (1990), pp. 416–17.
      "For Himmler's visit": Moshe Bahir in Novitch (1980), p. 156.
      "that the evacuation": quoted in Fleming (1984), pp. 20–21.
265   **"determined Himmler"**: cf Arad (1987), p. 365ff.
      "In Russia thousands": quoted in Padfield (1990), p. 429.
      4 October 1943 Himmler speech: IMT, PS-1919.
268   **Jeckeln sorting jewelry**: Hilberg (1985), p. 361, n. 75.
      "no mention": Peter Haidu, "The Dialectics of Unspeakability: Language, Silence, and the Narratives of Desubjectification," in Saul Friedlander, ed., *Probing the Limits of Representation* (Harvard University Press, 1992), p. 286.
      "I ask of you": quoted in Padfield (1990), p. 469.
269   **Sereny story**: Sereny (1995), p. 309ff.
270   **"Himmler said that"**: Kersten (1957), pp. 238–39.
      "I want to bury": Kersten (1957), p. 286.
      "The world in which Himmler": Speer (1970), pp. 486–87.
271   **Hitler ordering Himmler's arrest and expulsion**: Padfield (1990), pp. 597–98.
      "I was commanded by": quoted in Fest (1970), p. 324, n. 40.
272   **"He behaved perfectly correctly"**: quoted in Breitman (1991), p. 8.
      Himmler's death: Breitman (1991), p. 7ff; Padfield (1990), p. 608ff.

EPILOGUE

274   **Ferencz information**: interview with Benjamin B. Ferencz, New Rochelle, New York, 15 September 2000.
275   **Four other EG leaders executed**: MacLean (1999), p. 142.
      More than one hundred EG members: Arad et al. (1989), p. xvi.; 472 defendants: de Mildt (1996), p. 21.
276   **Dirlewanger death**: MacLean (1998), p. 226.
277   **"I was Hitler's man"**: quoted in Bartoszewski (1961), p. 57.
      "It consisted of 20,000": Reitlinger (1957), p. 199.
278   **"We, on our part"**: quoted in Morse (1968), p. 204.
      "As we have": quoted in Morse (1968), p. 212.
      German newspaper editorial: quoted in Morse (1968), p. 214.
      "The Germans did not know": Bauer (2001), pp. 25–27.
      Hitler in the war: cf. Victor (1998), pp. 55–56.
      "In the Nazi case": Bauer (2001), p. 28.

280   **"between the mass slaughter":** Vialles (1994), p. 31.

"We are left": Vialles (1994), p. 45.

"so that each person": Vialles (1994), p. 46.

"Back in the days": Vialles (1994), p. 76.

281   **"It is a thought-provoking":** Vialles (1994), p. 51.

"The 1835 [English] law": quoted in Vialles (1994), p. 122.

282   **"The logic of the industrial":** Vialles (1994), p. 65.

"Seven weeks have passed": Sabrin (1991), p. 121.

BIBLIOGRAPHY

Abel, Theodore Fred. 1938. *Why Hitler Came into Power: An Answer Based on the Original Life Stories of Six Hundred of His Followers.* New York: Prentice-Hall.

Aly, Götz. 1999. *"Final Solution": Nazi Population Policy and the Murder of the European Jews.* London: Arnold.

Aly, Götz, Peter Chroust and Christian Pross. 1994. *Cleansing the Fatherland: Nazi Medicine and Racial Hygiene.* Baltimore: Johns Hopkins University Press.

Anatoli (Kuznetsov), A. 1970. *Babi Yar: A Document in the Form of a Novel.* (D. Floyd, trans.) New York: Farrar, Straus and Giroux.

Angress, Werner T., and Bradley F. Smith. 1959. "Diaries of Heinrich Himmler's Early Years." *Journal of Modern History* 31(3): 206–24.

Angrick, Andrej, Martina Voigt et al. 1994. "Da Hätte Man Schon ein Tagebuch Führen Müssen": Das Polizeibatallion 322 und die Judenmorde . . ." In H. Grabitz et al. (eds.), *Die Normalität des Verbrechens.* Berlin: Edition Hentrich.

Arad, Yitzhak. 1982. *Ghetto in Flames: The Struggle and Destruction of the Jews in Vilna in the Holocaust.* New York: Holocaust Library.

———. 1987. *Belzec, Sobibor, Treblinka: The Operation Reinhard Death Camps.* Bloomington: Indiana University Press.

———, ed. 1990. *The Pictorial History of the Holocaust.* New York: Macmillan.

Arad, Yitzhak, Shmuel Krakowski and Shmuel Spector, eds. 1989. *The Einsatzgruppen Reports: Selections from the Dispatches of the Nazi Death Squads' Campaign Against the Jews July 1941–January 1943.* New York: Holocaust Library.

Arendt, Hannah. 1965. *Eichmann in Jerusalem.* New York: Viking.

———. 1973. *The Origins of Totalitarianism.* New York: Harcourt Brace Jovanovich.

Athens, Lonnie H. 1992. *The Creation of Dangerous Violent Criminals.* Urbana: University of Illinois Press.

———. 1994. "The Self as a Soliloquy." *Sociological Quarterly* 35(3): 521–32.

———. 1995. "Dramatic Self-Change." *Sociological Quarterly* 36(3): 571–86.

———. 1997. *Violent Criminal Acts and Actors Revisited.* Urbana: University of Illinois Press.

———. 1998. "Dominance, Ghettos and Violent Crime." *Sociological Quarterly* 39(4): 673–91.

Baartman, Herman. 1994. "Child Suicide and Harsh Punishment in Germany at the Turn of the Last Century." *Paedagogica Historica* 30(3): 849–64.

Bach-Zelewski, Erich von dem. 1946, 23, 30 August; 6 September. "Leben eines SS-Generals: aus den Nürnberger Geständnissen des Generals der Waffen-SS Erich von dem Bach-Zelewski." *Aufbau Nachrichtenblatt des German-Jewish Club* 12.

Baranauskas, B., and K. Ruksenas. 1970. *Documents Accuse.* Vilnius: Gintaras.

Bartoszewski, Wladyslaw. 1961. *Erich von dem Bach.* Warsaw: Wydawnictwo Zachodnie.

Bartov, Omer. 1985. *The Eastern Front, 1941–45: German Troops and the Barbarisation of Warfare.* Basingstoke, Hampshire: Macmillan / St. Antony's College, Oxford.

———. 1992. *Hitler's Army: Soldiers, Nazis, and War in the Third Reich.* New York: Oxford University Press.

———. 1996. *Murder in Our Midst: The Holocaust, Industrial Killing, and Representation.* New York: Oxford University Press.

Bauer, Yehuda. 2001. *Rethinking the Holocaust.* New Haven, Conn.: Yale University Press.

Bauman, Zygmunt. 1989. *Modernity and the Holocaust.* Ithaca, N.Y.: Cornell University Press.

Baur, Erwin, Eugene Fischer, and Fritz Lenz. 1931. *Human Heredity.* (E. and C. Paul, trans.) New York: Macmillan.

Bezwinska, Jadwiga, and Danuta Czech, eds. 1978. *KL Auschwitz Seen by the SS: Höss, Broad, Kremer.* Oswiecimiu (Poland): Panstwowe Muzeum.

Bingel, Erwin. 1959. "The Extermination of Two Ukrainian Jewish Communities: Testimony of a German Army Officer." In S. Esh (ed.), *Yad Vashem Studies on the European Jewish Catastrophe and Resistance III* (pp. 303–20). Jerusalem: Yad Vashem.

Binion, Rudolph. 1976. *Hitler Among the Germans.* New York: Elsevier.

Blumer, Herbert. 1978. "Social Unrest and Collective Protest." *Studies in Symbolic Interaction* 1: 1–54.

Borowski, Tadeusz. 1959. *This Way for the Gas, Ladies and Gentlemen.* New York: Penguin.

Boshyk, Yury, ed. 1986. *Ukraine during World War II: History and Its Aftermath: A Symposium.* Edmonton: Canadian Institute of Ukrainian Studies.

Braham, Randolph L. 1973. "The Kamenets Podolsk and Délvidék Massacres: Prelude to the Holocaust in Hungary." In L. Rothkirchen (ed.), *Yad Vashem Studies on the European Jewish Catastrophe and Resistance IX* (pp. 133–56). Jerusalem: Yad Vashem.

Bramwell, Anna. 1985. *Blood and Soil: Richard Walther Darré and Hitler's "Green Party."* Abbotsbrook (U.K.): Kensal Press.

Breitman, Richard. 1991. *The Architect of Genocide: Himmler and the Final Solution.* New York: Alfred A. Knopf.

———. 1994. "Plans for the Final Solution in Early 1941." *German Studies Review,* 17(3): 483–94.

———. 1998. *Official Secrets: What the Nazis Planned, What the British and Americans Knew.* New York: Hill & Wang.

Bromberg, Norbert, and Verna Volz Small. 1983. *Hitler's Psychopathology.* New York: International Universities Press.

Browning, Christopher R. 1985. *Fateful Months: Essays on the Emergence of the Final Solution.* New York: Holmes & Meier.

———. 1990. *The Path to Genocide: Essays on Launching the Final Solution.* Cambridge: Cambridge University Press.

———. 1992. *Ordinary Men: Reserve Police Battalion 101 and the Final Solution in Poland.* New York: HarperCollins.

———. 2000. *Nazi Policy, Jewish Workers, German Killers.* New York: Cambridge University Press.

Büchler, Yehoshua. 1989. "Kommandostab Reichsführer-SS: Himmler's Personal Murder Brigades in 1941." In M. R. Marrus (ed.), *3. The "Final Solution": The Implementation of Mass Murder* (vol. 2). Westport, Conn.: Meckler.

Buloff, Joseph. 1991. *From the Old Marketplace.* Cambridge, Mass.: Harvard University Press.

Burke, Kenneth. 1941, 1967. "The Rhetoric of Hitler's 'Battle.' " *The Philosophy of Literary Form: Studies in Symbolic Action.* Baton Rouge: Louisiana State University Press.

Burleigh, Michael. 2000. *The Third Reich: A New History.* New York: Hill & Wang.

Burrin, Philippe. 1994. *Hitler and the Jews: The Genesis of the Holocaust.* London: Edward Arnold.

Byron, Robert. 1987. "Nuremberg, 1938: The Final Rally." *Spectator* I: 19–23 (22 Aug.); II: 20–23 (29 Aug.).

Calic, Edouard. 1971. *Unmasked: Two Confidential Interviews with Hitler in 1931.* London: Chatto & Windus.

———. 1985. *Reinhard Heydrich: The Chilling Story of the Man Who Masterminded the Nazi Death Camps.* New York: Morrow.

Carr, William. 1978. *Hitler: A Study in Personality and Politics.* London: Edward Arnold.

Cecil, Robert. 1975. *Hitler's Decision to Invade Russia, 1941.* London: Davis-Poynter.

Celan, Paul. 1988. *Poems of Paul Celan.* (M. Hamburger, trans.) New York: Perseus.

Central Commission for Investigation of German Crimes in Poland. 1982. *German Crimes in Poland.* New York: Howard Fertig.

Cesarani, David, ed. 1994. *The Final Solution: Origins and Implementation.* London: Routledge.

Clark, Alan. 1965. *Barbarossa: The Russian-German Conflict.* New York: Quill.

Clendinnen, Inga. 1999. *Reading the Holocaust.* Cambridge: Cambridge University Press.

Conot, Robert E. 1983. *Justice at Nuremberg.* New York: Carroll & Graf.

Corni, Gustavo. 1990. *Hitler and the Peasants: Agrarian Policy of the Third Reich, 1930–1939.* New York: Berg.

Crankshaw, Edward. 1956. *Gestapo: Instrument of Tyranny.* New York: Da Capo Press.

Dallin, Alexander. 1957. *German Rule in Russia, 1941–1945: A Study of Occupation.* New York: St. Martin's Press.

Davidson, Eugene. 1977. *The Making of Adolf Hitler.* New York: Macmillan.

Dean, Martin. 1996. "The German *Gendarmerie,* the Ukrainian *Schutzmannschaft* and the 'Second Wave' of Jewish Killings in Occupied Ukraine: German Policing at the Local Level in the Zhitomir Region, 1941–1944." *German History* 14(2): 168–92.

DeGaulle, Charles. 1941 (1934). *The Army of the Future.* Philadelphia: J. B. Lippincott.

deMause, Lloyd, ed. 1974. *The History of Childhood.* Northvale, N.J.: Jason Aronson.

deMildt, Dick. 1996. *In the Name of the People: Perpetrators of Genocide in the Reflection of Their Post-War Prosecution in Western Germany.* The Hague: Martinus Nijhoff.

Des Pres, Terrence. 1969. "Excremental Assault." In J. K. Roth and Michael Berenbaum (eds.), *Holocaust: Religious and Philosophical Implications.* New York: Paragon House.

Deschner, Gunther. 1981. *Heydrich: The Pursuit of Total Power.* London: Orbis.

Deuerlein, Ernst, ed. 1968. *Der Aufstieg der NSDAP in Augenzeugenberichten (The Rise of the Nazi Party in Eyewitness Reports).* Düsseldorf: Karl Rauch Verlag.

Dicks, Henry Victor. 1972. *Licensed Mass Murder: A Socio-Psychological Study of Some SS Killers.* New York: Basic Books.

Dietrich, Otto. 1955. *Hitler.* Chicago: Henry Regnery.

Dimsdale, Joel E., ed. 1980. *Survivors, Victims, and Perpetrators: Essays on the Nazi Holocaust.* Washington, D.C.: Hemisphere.

Dobroszycki, Lucjan, ed. 1984. *The Chronicle of the Lodz Ghetto 1941–1944.* New Haven, Conn.: Yale University Press.

Donat, Alexander, ed. 1979. *The Death Camp Treblinka: A Documentary.* New York: Holocaust Library.

Dornberger, Walter. 1954. *V-2.* New York: Viking Press.

Ehrenburg, Ilya, and Vasily Grossman, eds. 1981. *The Black Book: The Ruthless Murder of Jews by German-Fascist Invaders Throughout the Temporarily-Occupied Regions of the Soviet Union and in the Death Camps of Poland During the War of 1941–1945.* New York: Holocaust Publications.

Eichmann, Adolf. 22 and 28 November 1960. "Eichmann's Own Story." *Life* 49: 20–24, 101–12; 146–60.

————. 1980. *Ich, Adolf Eichmann: ein historischer Zeugenbericht.* Leoni am Starnberger See, Germany: Druffel-Verlag.

Elias, Norbert. 1994(1939). *The Civilizing Process.* (E. Jephcott, trans.) Oxford: Blackwell.

Elliot, Gil. 1972. *Twentieth Century Book of the Dead.* New York: Charles Scribner's Sons.

Ellis, John. 1976. *Eye-Deep in Hell: Trench Warfare in World War I.* Baltimore: Johns Hopkins University Press.

Ende, Aurel. 1979/80. "Battering and Neglect: Children in Germany, 1860–1978." *Journal of Psychohistory* 7: 249–79.

Ezergailis, Andrew. 1996. *The Holocaust in Latvia 1941–1944.* Riga: The Historical Institute of Latvia.

Feingold, Henry L. 1970. *The Politics of Rescue: The Roosevelt Administration and the Holocaust, 1938–1945.* New Brunswick, N.J.: Rutgers University Press.

Fest, Joachim C. 1970. *The Face of the Third Reich.* New York: Pantheon.

———. 1974. *Hitler.* New York: Vintage.

Fischer, Klaus P. 1995. *Nazi Germany: A New History.* New York: Continuum.

Fleming, Gerald. 1984. *Hitler and the Final Solution.* Berkeley: University of California Press.

Flood, Charles Bracelen. 1989. *Hitler: The Path to Power.* Boston: Houghton Mifflin.

Forché, Carolyn, ed. 1993. *Against Forgetting: Twentieth-Century Poetry of Witness.* New York: W. W. Norton.

Förster, Jürgen. 1989. "The Wehrmacht and the War of Extermination Against the Soviet Union." In M. R. Marrus (ed.),*3. The "Final Solution": The Implementation of Mass Murder* (vol. 2, pp. 492–519). Westport, Conn.: Meckler.

Fox, John P. 1990. "Adolf Hitler's Imperatives for War in September 1939: An Assessment of the Jewish Factor." *Holocaust Studies Annual,* 135–54.

Friedlander, Henry. 1994a. "Step by Step: The Expansion of Murder, 1939–1941." *German Studies Review* 17(3): 495–507.

———. 1994b. The T4 killers: Berlin, Lublin, San Sabba. In H. Grabitz et al. (eds.), *Die Normalität des Verbrechens: Bilanz und Perspektiven der Forschung zu den nationalsozialistischen Gerwaltverbrechen.* Berlin: Edition Hentrich.

———. 1995. *The Origins of Nazi Genocide: From Euthanasia to the Final Solution.* Chapel Hill: University of North Carolina Press.

Friedlander, Henry, and Sybil Milton, eds. 1989–93. *Archives of the Holocaust: An International Collection of Selected Documents.* New York: Garland.

Friedländer, Saul. 1969. *Kurt Gerstein: The Ambiguity of Good.* New York: Alfred A. Knopf.

———. 1984. *Reflections of Nazism: An Essay on Kitsch and Death.* New York: Harper & Row.

Friedrich, Ernst. 1924 (1987). *War Against War.* Seattle: Real Comet Press.

Frischauer, Willi. 1953. *Himmler: The Evil Genius of the Third Reich.* London: Odhams Press.

Furet, François, ed. 1989. *Unanswered Questions: Nazi Germany and the Genocide of the Jews.* New York: Schocken.

Fussell, Paul. 1975. *The Great War and Modern Memory.* New York: Oxford University Press.

Gabriel, Richard A. 1988. *The Painful Field: The Psychiatric Dimension of Modern War.* New York: Greenwood Press.

Gafencu, Grigore. 1948. *Last Days of Europe.* (Reprint ed.) n.p.: Archon Books.

Garrard, John, and Carol Garrard. 1996. *The Bones of Berdichev: The Life and Fate of Vasily Grossman.* New York: Free Press.

Gay, Peter. 1993. *The Cultivation of Hatred.* New York: W. W. Norton.

Genoud, François, ed. 1960. *The Testament of Adolf Hitler: The Hitler-Bormann Documents February–April 1945.* London: Cassell.

Gerlach, Christian. 1998. "The Wannsee Conference, the Fate of German Jews, and Hitler's Decision in Principle to Exterminate All European Jews." *Journal of Modern History* 70(4): 759–812.

Gewald, Jan-Bart. 1999. *Herero Heroes: A Socio-Political History of the Herero of Namibia 1890–1923.* Oxford: James Currey.

Gilbert, G. M. 1947. *Nuremberg Diary.* New York: Da Capo Press.

———. 1950. *The Psychology of Dictatorship: Based on an Examination of the Leaders of Nazi Germany.* New York: Ronald Press.

Gilbert, Martin. 1985. *The Holocaust: A History of the Jews of Europe During the Second World War.* New York: Henry Holt.

Girard, René. 1987. *Things Hidden Since the Foundation of the World.* Stanford: Stanford University Press.

Gisevius, Hans Bernd. 1947 (1998). *To the Bitter End: An Insider's Account of the Plot to Kill Hitler, 1933–1944.* New York: Da Capo Press.

Gitelman, Zvi, ed. 1997. *Bitter Legacy: Confronting the Holocaust in the USSR.* Bloomington: Indiana University Press.

Glass, James M. 1997. *"Life Unworthy of Life": Racial Phobia and Mass Murder in Hitler's Germany.* New York: Basic Books.

Glicksman, William. 1978. "Violence and Terror: The Nazi-German Conception of Killing and Murder." In M. H. Livingston (ed.), *International Terrorism in the Contemporary World.* Westport, Conn.: Greenwood Press.

Goldhagen, Daniel Jonah. 1996. *Hitler's Willing Executioners: Ordinary Germans and the Holocaust.* New York: Alfred A. Knopf.

Graber, G. S. 1980. *The Life and Times of Reinhard Heydrich.* New York: McKay.

Grabitz, Helge, Klaus Bästlein and Johannes Tuchel, eds. 1994. *Die Normalität des Verbrechens.* Berlin: Edition Hentrich.

Gross, Jan T. 2001. *Neighbors: The Destruction of the Jewish Community in Jedwabne, Poland.* Princeton, N.J.: Princeton University Press.

Gross, John. 1998. "A Nice Pleasant Youth." (Review of Ron Rosenbaum, *Explaining Hitler.* Random House, 1998.) *New York Review of Books,* 17 Dec. 1998, 12–17.

Grzesinski, Albert C. 1939. *Inside Germany.* New York: E. P. Dutton.

Guérin, Daniel. 1994. *The Brown Plague: Travels in Late Weimar and Early Nazi Germany.* Durham, N.C.: Duke University Press.

Gumbel, E. J. 1962. *Vom Fememord zur Reichskanzlei.* Heidelberg: Verlag Lambert Schneider.

Gutman, Israel, ed. 1990. *Encyclopedia of the Holocaust.* New York: Macmillan.

Hackett, David A., ed. 1995. *The Buchenwald Report.* Boulder, Colo.: Westview Press.

Haffter, Carl. 1968. "The Changeling: History and Psychodynamics of Attitudes to Handicapped Children in European Folklore." *Journal of the History of the Behavioral Sciences* 4(1): 55–61.

Hamann, Brigitte. 1999. *Hitler's Vienna: A Dictator's Apprenticeship.* New York: Oxford University Press.

Hanfstaengl, Ernst. 1957. *Hitler: The Missing Years.* New York: Arcade.

Hawkins, Mike. 1997. *Social Darwinism in European and American Thought, 1860–1945: Nature as Model and Nature as Threat.* New York: Cambridge University Press.

Headland, Ronald. 1992. *Messages of Murder: A Study of the Reports of the Einsatzgruppen of the Security Police and the Security Service, 1941–1943.* Rutherford, N.J.: Fairleigh Dickinson University Press.

———. 1999. "The *Einsatzgruppen:* The Question of Their Initial Operations." *Holocaust and Genocide Studies* 4(4): 401–12.

Heiber, H. 1968. *Reichsführer: Briefe an und von Himmler.* Stuttgart: Deutsche Verlags Anstalt.

Heiden, Konrad. 1944. *Der Führer: Hitler's Rise to Power.* Boston: Houghton Mifflin.

Heller, Celia S. 1977. *On the Edge of Destruction.* New York: Columbia University Press.

Hilberg, Raul, ed. 1971. *Documents of Destruction: Germany and Jewry, 1933–1945.* Chicago: Quadrangle Books.

———. 1985. *The Destruction of the European Jews.* (Revised ed.) New York: Holmes & Meier.

———. 1992. *Perpetrators, Victims, Bystanders.* New York: HarperPerennial.

Himka, John-Paul. 1997. "Ukrainian Collaboration in the Extermination of the Jews During the Second World War: Sorting Out the Long-Term and Conjunctural Factors." *Studies in Contemporary Jewry* 13: 170–89.

Himmler, Heinrich. 1940 (1957). "Denkschrift Himmlers über die Behandlung der Fremdvölkischen im Osten (Mai 1940)." *Vierteljahrshefte für Zeitgeschichte* 5: 194–98.

———. 1974. *Geheimreden, 1933 bis 1945.* Frankfurt am Main: Propyläen Verlag.

Hitler, Adolf. 1927 (1971). *Mein Kampf.* Boston: Houghton Mifflin.

———. 1942. *The Speeches of Adolf Hitler, April 1922–August 1939: An English Translation of Representative Passages Arranged Under Subjects and Edited by Norman H. Baynes.* New York: Oxford University Press.

———. 1953. *Hitler's Secret Conversations 1941–1944.* New York: Farrar, Straus and Young.

Hochschild, Adam. 1998. *King Leopold's Ghost: A Story of Greed, Terror and Heroism in Colonial Africa.* Boston: Houghton Mifflin.

Höhne, Heinz. 1969. *The Order of the Death's Head: The Story of Hitler's S.S.* New York: Coward-McCann.

Höss, Rudolf (Steven Paskully, ed.). 1992. *Death Dealer: The Memoirs of the SS Kommandant at Auschwitz.* Buffalo, N.Y.: Prometheus Books.

Huckel, Oliver. 1914. *Rienzi: A Dramatic Poem by Richard Wagner Freely Translated in Poetic Narrative Form.* New York: Thomas Y. Crowell.

IMT. 1947. *Trial of the Major War Criminals Before the International Military Tribunal, Nuremberg, 14 November 1945–1 October 1946.* Nuremberg: International Military Tribunal.

———. 1949. *Trials of War Criminals Before the Nuernberg Military Tribunals Under Control Council Law No. 10* (vol. IV). Washington, D.C.: U.S. Government Printing Office.

Jäckel, Eberhard. 1972, 1981. *Hitler's World View: A Blueprint for Power.* Cambridge, Mass.: Harvard University Press.

Joffroy, Pierre. 1971. *A Spy for God: The Ordeal of Kurt Gerstein.* New York: Harcourt Brace Jovanovich.

Jünger, Ernst. 1929. *The Storm of Steel: From the Diary of a German Storm-Troop Officer on the Western Front.* (Reprint ed.) New York: Howard Fertig.

Karski, Jan. 1944. *Story of a Secret State.* Boston: Houghton Mifflin.

Katz, Fred E. 1993. *Ordinary People and Extraordinary Evil: A Report on the Beguilings of Evil.* Albany: State University of New York Press.

Keegan, John. 1989. *The Second World War.* New York: Penguin.

———. 1999. *The First World War.* New York: Alfred A. Knopf.

Kelly, Alfred. 1981. *The Descent of Darwin: The Popularization of Darwinism in Germany, 1860–1914.* Chapel Hill: University of North Carolina Press.

Kelman, Herbert C. 1973. "Violence Without Moral Restraint: Reflections on the Dehumanization of Victims and Victimizers." *Journal of Social Issues* 29(4): 25–61.

Kershaw, Ian. 1998. *Hitler 1889–1936: Hubris.* New York: W. W. Norton.

———. 2000. *Hitler 1936–1945: Nemesis.* New York: W. W. Norton.

Kersten, Felix. 1957. *The Kersten Memoirs 1940–1945.* New York: Macmillan.

Klarsfeld, Serge, ed. 1985. *Documents Concerning the Destruction of the Jews of Grodno 1941–1944.* New York: Beate Klarsfeld Foundation.

Klee, Ernst, and Willi Dressen, eds. 1989. *"Gott mit Uns": der Deutsche Vernichtungskrieg im Osten 1939–1945.* Frankfurt am Main: S. Fischer.

Klee, Ernst, Willi Dressen and Volker Riess, eds. 1988. *"The Good Old Days": The Holocaust as Seen by Its Perpetrators and Bystanders.* New York: Free Press.

Klein, George. 1994. *The Atheist and the Holy City: Encounters and Reflections.* Cambridge, Mass.: MIT Press.

Klemperer, Victor. 2000. *The Language of the Third Reich: LTI—Lingua Tertii Imperii, a Philologist's Notebook.* (M. Brady, trans.) London: Athlone Press.

Knappe, Siegfried, and Ted Brusaw. 1992. *Soldat: Reflections of a German Soldier 1936–1949.* New York: Orion.

Kogon, Eugen. 1950. *The Theory and Practice of Hell.* New York: Berkley.

Kogon, Eugen, Hermann Langbein and Adalbert Rückerl, eds. 1993. *Nazi Mass Murder: A Documentary History of the Use of Poison Gas.* New Haven, Conn.: Yale University Press.

Kostanian, Rachel. 1996. *The Jewish State Museum of Lithuania.* Vilnius: Jewish State Museum.

Krasilshchik, S., ed. 1985. *World War II: Dispatches from the Soviet Front.* New York: Sphinx Press.

Krausnick, Helmut, Hans Buchheim, Martin Broszat and Hans-Adolf Jacobsen. 1968. *Anatomy of the SS State.* New York: Walker.

Kubizek, August. 1954. *The Young Hitler I Knew.* Boston: Houghton Mifflin.

Kulcsar, I. S., Shoshanna Kulcsar and Lipot Szondi. 1966. "Adolf Eichmann and the Third Reich." In R. Slovenko (ed.), *Crime, Law and Corrections.* Springfield, Il.: Charles C. Thomas.

Kwiet, Konrad. 1993. "From the Diary of a Killing Unit." In J. Milfull (ed.), *Why Germany?: National Socialist Anti-Semitism and the European Context.* Providence, R.I.: Berg.

———. 1998. "Rehearsing for Murder: The Beginning of the Final Solution in Lithuania in June 1941." *Holocaust and Genocide Studies* 12: 3–26.

Langer, Lawrence L. 1991. *Holocaust Testimonies: The Ruins of Memory.* New Haven, Conn.: Yale University Press.

Langer, W. C. 1972. *The Mind of Adolf Hitler: The Secret Wartime Report.* New York: Basic Books.

Lanzmann, Claude. 1985. *Shoah: An Oral History of the Holocaust.* New York: Pantheon.

Laqueur, Walter, ed. 1976. *Fascism: A Reader's Guide.* Berkeley: University of California Press.

Lazar, Chaim. 1985. *Destruction and Resistance.* New York: Shengold.

Lepre, George. 1997. *Himmler's Bosnian Division: The Waffen-SS Handschar Division 1943–1945.* Atglen, Pa.: Schiffer Military History.

Levin, Dov. 1985. *Fighting Back: Lithuanian Jewry's Armed Resistance to the Nazis, 1941–1945.* New York: Holmes & Meier.

Lifton, Robert Jay. 1986. *The Nazi Doctors: Medical Killing and the Psychology of Genocide.* New York: Basic Books.

Lifton, Robert Jay, and Eric Markusen. 1990. *The Genocidal Mentality: Nazi Holocaust and Nuclear Threat.* New York: Basic Books.

Lindqvist, Sven. 1992. *"Exterminate All the Brutes."* New York: New Press.

Littman, Sol. 1998. *War Criminal on Trial: Rauca of Kaunas.* Toronto: Key Porter.

Lochner, Louis P. 1943. *What About Germany?* London: Hodder and Stoughton.

Loewenberg, Peter. 1971. "The Unsuccessful Adolescence of Heinrich Himmler." *American Historical Review* 76(3): 612–41.

Longerich, Peter. 1997. "From Mass Murder to the 'Final Solution': The Shooting of Jewish Civilians During the First Months of the Eastern Campaign Within the Context of Nazi Jewish Genocide." In B. Wegner (ed.), *From Peace to War: Germany, Soviet Russia and the World, 1939–1941* (pp. 253–75). Providence, R.I.: Berghahn Books.

Löns, Hermann. 1996. *Der Wehrwolf.* Hannover: Adolf Sponholtz Verlag.

Lozowick, Yaacov. 1989. "Rollbahn Mord: The Early Activities of Einsatzgruppe C." In Marrus (ed.) 1989.

Lukacs, John. 1997. *The Hitler of History.* New York: Alfred A. Knopf.

Lukas, Richard C. 1986. *The Forgotten Holocaust: The Poles Under German Occupation.* Lexington: University Press of Kentucky.

McAleer, Kevin. 1994. *Dueling: The Cult of Honor in Fin-de-Siècle Germany.* Princeton, N.J.: Princeton University Press.

MacLean, French. 1998. *The Cruel Hunters: SS-Sonderkommando Dirlewanger, Hitler's Most Notorious Anti-Partisan Unit.* Atglen, Pa.: Schiffer Military History.

————. 1999. *The Field Men: The SS Officers Who Led the Einsatzkommandos— the Nazi Mobile Killing Units.* Atglen, Pa.: Schiffer Military History.

MacMillan, Ian. 1991. *Orbit of Darkness.* San Diego: Harcourt Brace Jovanovich.

MacQueen, Michael. 1996. "The Context of Mass Destruction: Agents and Pre-requisites of the Holocaust in Lithuania." *Holocaust and Genocide Studies* 2: 27–48.

Madajczyk, Czeslaw. 1962. "Generalplan Ost." *Polish Western Affairs* 3(2): 391–442.

Malaparte, Curzio. 1957. *The Volga Rises in Europe.* London: Alvin Redman.

Mann, Michael. 2000. "Were the Perpetrators of Genocide 'Ordinary Men' or 'Real Nazis'?: Results from Fifteen Hundred Biographies." *Holocaust and Genocide Studies* 14(3): 331–66.

Manvell, Roger, and Heinrich Fränkel. 1965. *Heinrich Himmler.* London: Heine-mann.

Markusen, Eric, and David Kopf. 1995. *The Holocaust and Strategic Bombing: Genocide and Total War in the Twentieth Century.* Boulder, Colo.: Westview.

Marrus, Michael R., ed. 1989. *3. The "Final Solution": The Implementation of Mass Murder* (vol. 2). Westport, Conn.: Meckler.

Marszalek, Jozef. 1986. *Majdanek: The Concentration Camp in Lublin.* Warsaw: Interpress.

Maser, Werner. 1971. *Hitler: Legend, Myth and Reality.* New York: Harper & Row.

————. 1973. *Hitler's Letters and Notes.* New York: Harper & Row.

Mayer, Arno J. 1988. *Why Did the Heavens Not Darken?: The Final Solution in History.* New York: Pantheon.

Mayhew, Henry. 1864. *German Life and Manners as Seen in Saxony at the Pres-ent Day.* London: William H. Allen.

Maynes, M. J. 1996. "Childhood Memories, Political Visions, and Working-Class Formation in Imperial Germany: Some Comparative Observations." In G. Eley (ed.), *Society, Culture, and the State in Germany, 1870–1930.* Ann Arbor: University of Michigan Press.

Mend, Hans. 1931. *Adolf Hitler im Felde, 1914–1918.* Diessen vor München: J. C. Huber.

Mendelsohn, John, ed. 1982. *The Holocaust: Selected Documents in Eighteen Volumes.* New York: Garland.

Merkl, Peter H. 1975. *Political Violence Under the Swastika: 581 Early Nazis.* Princeton, N.J.: Princeton University Press.

———. 1980. *The Making of a Stormtrooper.* Princeton, N.J.: Princeton University Press.

Michelson, Frida. 1979. *I Survived Rumbuli.* New York: Holocaust Library.

Milfull, John, ed. 1993. *Why Germany?: National Socialist Anti-Semitism and the European Context.* Providence, R.I.: Berg.

Miller, Alice. 1990a. *For Your Own Good: Hidden Cruelty in Child-Rearing and the Roots of Violence.* New York: Farrar Straus and Giroux.

———. 1990b. "Adolf Hitler's Childhood: From Hidden to Manifest Horror." In R. S. Gottlieb (ed.), *Thinking the Unthinkable: Meanings of the Holocaust* (pp. 88–106). New York: Paulist Press.

Miller, Emanuel. 1940. *Neuroses in War.* New York: Macmillan.

Miller, Richard Lawrence. 1995. *Nazi Justiz: Law of the Holocaust.* Westport, Conn.: Praeger.

Mishell, William W. 1988. *Kaddish for Kovno: Life and Death in a Lithuanian Ghetto 1941–1945.* Chicago: Chicago Review Press.

Morse, Arthur D. 1968. *While Six Million Died: A Chronicle of American Apathy.* New York: Random House.

Mosse, George L. 1964. *The Crisis of German Ideology: Intellectual Origins of the Third Reich.* New York: Grosset & Dunlap.

———, ed. 1966. *Nazi Culture: Intellectual, Cultural and Social Life in the Third Reich.* New York: Grosset & Dunlap.

———. 1978. *Toward the Final Solution: A History of European Racism.* New York: H. Fertig.

———. 1990. *Fallen Soldiers: Reshaping the Memory of the World Wars.* New York: Oxford University Press.

Müller, Filip. 1979. *Eyewitness Auschwitz: Three Years in the Gas Chambers.* New York: Stein and Day.

Neumann, Peter. 1959. *The Black March: The Personal Story of an SS Man.* New York: William Sloan Associates.

Noakes, J., and G. Pridham, eds. 1983–98. *Nazism, 1919–1945: A Documentary Reader.* Exeter, Devon: University of Exeter.

Novitch, Miriam, ed. 1980. *Sobibor: Martyrdom and Revolt.* New York: Holocaust Library.

Nuremberg War Crimes Trials. 1978. *Records of Case 9:* United States v. Otto Ohlendorf et al., *September 15, 1947–April 10, 1948.* (Microfilm.) Washington, D.C.: National Archives and Records Service.

Orbach, Wila. 1976. "The Destruction of the Jews in the Nazi-Occupied Territories of the USSR." *Soviet Jewish Affairs* 6(2): 14–51.

Padfield, Peter. 1990. *Himmler: Reichsführer-SS.* New York: Henry Holt.

Pawelczynska, Anna. 1979. *Values and Violence in Auschwitz: A Sociological Analysis.* Berkeley: University of California Press.

Payne, Robert. 1973. *The Life and Death of Adolf Hitler.* New York: Praeger.

Perechodnik, Calel. 1996. *Am I a Murderer?* Boulder, Colo: Westview Press.

Pick, Daniel. 1993. *War Machine: The Rationalisation of Slaughter in the Modern Age.* New Haven, Conn.: Yale University Press.

Picker, Henry, ed. 1976. *Hitlers Tischgespräche im Führerhauptquartier.* Stuttgart: Seewald Verlag.

Poliakov, Leon. 1954. *Harvest of Hate: The Nazi Program for the Destruction of the Jews.* Syracuse, N.Y.: Syracuse University Press.

Prawdin, Michael (Michael Charol). 1940. *The Mongol Empire: Its Rise and Legacy.* New York: Free Press.

Press, Bernhard. 1988. *Judenmord in Riga 1941–1945: ein Mensch ist dann erst tot, wenn auch die Erinnerung an ihn gestorben ist (Talmud).* Berlin: B. Pres.

———. 1992. *Judenmord in Lettland: 1941–1945.* Berlin: Metropol-Verlag.

Pucher, Siegfried J. 1997. *"In der Bewegung führend tätig": Odilio Globocnik— Kämpfer für den "Anschluss," Vollstrecker des Holocaust.* Klagenfurt, Germany: Drava.

Rashke, Richard L. 1982. *Escape from Sobibor.* Boston: Houghton Mifflin.

Rauschning, Hermann. 1940. *The Voice of Destruction.* New York: Putnam.

———. 1942. *Makers of Destruction: Meetings and Talks in Revolutionary Germany.* London: Eyre & Spottiswoode.

Redlich, Fritz. 1999. *Hitler: Diagnosis of a Destructive Prophet.* New York: Oxford University Press.

Reitlinger, Gerald. 1957. *The SS, Alibi of a Nation, 1922–1945.* New York: Da Capo Press.

———. 1987 (1968). *The Final Solution: The Attempt to Exterminate the Jews of Europe 1939–1945.* Northvale, N.J.: Jason Aronson.

Rhodes, Richard. 1999. *Why They Kill: The Discoveries of a Maverick Criminologist.* New York: Alfred A. Knopf.

Richmond, Theo. 1995. *Konin: A Quest.* New York: Vintage.

Rosenbaum, Ron. 1998. *Explaining Hitler: The Search for the Origins of His Evil.* New York: Random House.

Rosenberg, Alfred. 1982. *The Myth of the Twentieth Century: An Evaluation of the Spiritual-Intellectual Confrontations of Our Age.* Torrance, Calif.: Noontide Press.

Rudashevski, Yitzhak. 1973. *The Diary of the Vilna Ghetto, June 1941–April 1943.* Israel: Ghetto Fighters' House.

Sabrin, B. F., ed. 1991. *Alliance for Murder: The Nazi-Ukrainian Nationalist Partnership in Genocide.* New York: Sarpedon.

Salomon, Ernst von. 1930 (1983). *The Outlaws.* Millwood, N.Y.: Kraus Reprint.

Scarry, Elaine. 1985. *The Body in Pain: The Making and Unmaking of the World.* New York: Oxford University Press.

Schellenberg, Walter. 1956. *The Labyrinth: Memoirs.* New York: Harper & Brothers.

Schleunes, Karl A. 1970. *The Twisted Road to Auschwitz: Nazi Policy Toward German Jews, 1933–1939.* Urbana: University of Illinois Press.

Schorske, Carl E. 1979. *Fin-de-Siècle Vienna: Politics and Culture.* New York: Vintage.

Schulze, Hagen. 1998. *Germany: A New History.* Cambridge, Mass.: Harvard University Press.

Schwarzwäller, Wulf. 1989. *The Unknown Hitler: His Private Life and Fortune.* Don Mills, Ontario: Stoddart.

Sereny, Gitta. 1974. *Into That Darkness: An Examination of Conscience.* New York: Vintage.

———. 1995. *Albert Speer: His Battle with Truth.* New York: Vintage.

Shirer, William L. 1940. *Berlin Diary: The Journal of a Foreign Correspondent 1934–1941.* New York: Galahad Books.

———. 1960. *The Rise and Fall of the Third Reich.* New York: Simon & Schuster.

Shneidman, N. N. 1998. *Jerusalem of Lithuania: The Rise and Fall of Jewish Vilnius.* Oakville, Ontario: Mosaic Press.

Smith, Bradley F. 1967. *Adolf Hitler: His Family, Childhood and Youth.* Stanford, Calif.: Hoover Institution Press.

———. 1971. *Heinrich Himmler: A Nazi in the Making, 1900–1926.* Stanford, Calif.: Hoover Institution Press.

Smith, Bradley F., and Agnes F. Peterson, eds. 1974. *Heinrich Himmler: Geheimreden 1933 bis 1945.* Frankfurt am Main: Propyläen Verlad.

Smolar, Hersh. 1989. *The Minsk Ghetto: Soviet-Jewish Partisans Against the Nazis.* New York: Holocaust Library.

Smolen, Kazimierz, ed. 1967. *From the History of KL-Auschwitz.* Oswiecimiu, Poland: Panstwowe Muzeum.

Sofsky, Wolfgang. 1993. *The Order of Terror: The Concentration Camp.* Princeton, N.J.: Princeton University Press.

Spector, Shmuel. 1990. "*Aktion* 1005—Effacing the Murder of Millions." *Holocaust and Genocide Studies* 5: 157–73.

Speer, Albert. 1970. *Inside the Third Reich.* New York: Simon & Schuster.

———. 1981. *Infiltration.* New York: Macmillan.

Spencer, Herbert. 1892. *Social Statics.* New York: D. Appleton.

Staub, Ervin. 1989. *The Roots of Evil: The Origins of Genocide and Other Group Violence.* Cambridge: Cambridge University Press.

Stein, George H. 1966. *The Waffen SS: Hitler's Elite Guard at War, 1939–1945.* Ithaca, N.Y.: Cornell University Press.

Steinberg, Paul. 2000. *Speak You Also: A Survivor's Reckoning.* New York: Henry Holt.

Stierlin, Helm. 1976. *Adolf Hitler: A Family Perspective.* New York: The Psychohistory Press.

Stone, Dan. 1999. "Modernity and Violence: Theoretical Reflections on the Einsatzgruppen." *Journal of Genocide Research* 1(3): 367–78.

Streim, Alfred. 1989. "The Tasks of the SS Einsatzgruppen." In Marrus (1989).

Sutin, Jack and Rochelle. 1995. *Jack and Rochelle: A Holocaust Story of Love and Resistance.* Saint Paul, Minn.: Graywolf Press.

Swank, Roy L., and Walter E. Marchand. 1946. "Combat Neuroses." *Archives of Neurology and Psychiatry* 55: 236–47.

Sydnor, Charles W. 1977. *Soldiers of Destruction: The SS Death's Head Division, 1933–1945.* Princeton, N.J.: Princeton University Press.

Tacitus. 1948. *Tacitus on Britain and Germany: A Translation of the "Agricola" and the "Germania."* (H. Mattingly, trans.) Baltimore: Penguin.

Taylor, Telford. 1992. *The Anatomy of the Nuremberg Trials: A Personal Memoir.* New York: Alfred A. Knopf.

Tec, Nechama. 1987. *When Light Pierced the Darkness: Christian Rescue of Jews in Nazi-Occupied Poland.* New York: Oxford University Press.

———. 1990. *In the Lion's Den: The Life of Oswald Rufeisen.* New York: Oxford University Press.

Tenenbaum, Joseph. 1955. "The Einsatzgruppen." *Jewish Social Studies* 17: 43–64.

Theweleit, Klaus. 1987. *Male Fantasies.* Minneapolis: University of Minnesota Press.

Toland, John. 1965. *The Last 100 Days.* New York: Random House.

———. 1976. *Adolf Hitler.* New York: Anchor.

Tory, Avraham. 1990. *Surviving the Holocaust: The Kovno Ghetto Diary.* Cambridge, Mass.: Harvard University Press.

Trotsky, Leon. 1933 (rep. 1999), September (rep. July). "What Hitler Wants." *Harper's,* 70–73.

Turner, Henry Ashby, Jr., ed. 1985. *Hitler—Memoirs of a Confidant.* New Haven, Conn.: Yale University Press.

United States Holocaust Memorial Museum. 1996. *Historical Atlas of the Holocaust.* New York: Macmillan.

U.S. Office of Chief of Counsel for the Prosecution of Axis Criminality, ed. 1946. *Nazi Conspiracy and Aggression.* Washington, D.C.: U.S. Government Printing Office.

Vialles, Noëlie. 1994. *Animal to Edible.* Paris: Cambridge University Press (Editions de la Maison des Sciences de L'homme).

Victor, George. 1998. *Hitler: The Pathology of Evil.* Washington, D.C.: Brassey's.

Vinberg, Fyodor. 1934. *The Protocols of the Elders of Zion.* (V. E. Marsden, trans.). N.p.

Volkogonov, Dmitri. 1991. *Stalin.* New York: Grove Weidenfeld.

von Lang, Jochen. 1979. *The Secretary: Martin Bormann: The Man Who Manipulated Hitler.* New York: Random House.

———, ed. 1982. *Eichmann Interrogated: Transcripts from the Archives of the Israeli Police.* New York: Farrar, Straus and Giroux.

Wachtel, Curt. 1941. *Chemical Warfare.* Brooklyn, N.Y.: Chemical Publishing Company.

Wagner, Ludwig Anton. 1942. *Hitler, Man of Strife.* New York: W. W. Norton.

Waite, Robert G. L. 1977. *The Psychopathic God: Adolf Hitler.* New York: Da Capo Press.

Warlimont, Walter. 1962. *Inside Hitler's Headquarters.* New York: Frederick A. Praeger.

Weinberg, Gerhard L. 1996. "Germany's War for World Conquest and the Extermination of the Jews." *Holocaust and Genocide Studies* 10(2): 119–33.

———. 1997. *Crossing the Line in Nazi Genocide: On Becoming and Being a Professional Killer.* (Occasional paper.) Burlington: Center for Holocaust Studies at the University of Vermont.

Werth, Alexander. 1964. *Russia at War 1941–1945.* New York: E. P. Dutton.

Winternitz, M. C., ed. 1920. *Collected Studies on the Pathology of War Gas Poisoning.* New Haven, Conn.: Yale University Press.

Wisniewski, Tomasz. 1998. *Jewish Bialystok and Surroundings in Eastern Poland: A Guide for Yesterday and Today.* Ipswich, Mass.: Ipswich Press.

Wolf, Eric R. 1999. *Envisioning Power: Ideologies of Dominance and Crisis.* Berkeley: University of California Press.

Yahil, L. 1989. "Madagascar—Phantom of a Solution for the Jewish Question." In Marrus (1989).

ACKNOWLEDGMENTS

Several people facilitated travel through Eastern Europe visiting killing sites. Kassie Kulikowska guided and translated in Poland, Auste Tamulynaite in Lithuania. Fania Brancovskaja, a Vilnius ghetto survivor and former anti-Nazi partisan who lost all but one member of her extended family to the SS killers, showed me the ghetto environs, the Jewish Museum and Ponary. Halyna Hyrn indefatigably located witnesses and scholars in Ukraine, organized travel and interviews and translated. Faina Vinokurova, vice director of the State Archive of Vinnitsa Oblast, generously shared her scholarship in Vinnitsa. Yuri Orechwa introduced me to Stanislav Shushkevich, who welcomed me to Belarus and guided me to NKVD and SS killing sites in Minsk and eastward, after which Irena Shushkevich restored us with food and conversation.

Ben and Gertrude Ferencz in New Rochelle brought the Einsatzgruppen trial alive. Michael Schmelzle at Yale elegantly translated several crucial documents. Eric Markusen lent me hard-to-find books from his own genocide research collection. Helen Haversat transcribed difficult interviews. Judy Cohen at the United States Holocaust Memorial Museum helped me with photo research. I benefited from conversations with Lonnie Athens, Harvey Goldblatt, George Klein, Grazina Miniotaite, Laurie Pearlman, Ron Rosenbaum and Ervin Staub. Morton L. Janklow and Anne Sibbald ably represented me. Jon Segal's editing made it a better book. Ida Giragossian put the pieces together. Ginger Rhodes, as always, walked beside me down every dark road and into every dark wood.

330

Index

Jews *(cont.)*
 exterminations and, xi–xii, 9–10,
  47–52, 59–64, 67, 69–70, 93–4,
  96–100, 103–4, 106, 108–16,
  119–31, 133–4, 136–57, 159,
  163–9, 172–97, 199–228, 231–48,
  250–1, 253, 255–61, 263–5,
  267–70, 276–9, 281–2
 in Galicia, 57, 59–68
 German Eastern expansionism
  and, 239, 263
 ghettoization of, 6, 120, 136–8,
  141–2, 150, 192–7, 205–10, 212,
  214, 218, 237, 244–7, 251–2, 256,
  261, 265
 in Hungary, 128–9
 imperialist apologists on, 94
 in Latvia, 17, 119–22, 125, 127, 136,
  182, 192, 206–17, 237, 242–3, 247,
  251–2
 in Lithuania, xi, 38–46, 53–7,
  119–20, 125–7, 136–40, 150, 168,
  182, 192–7, 215–16, 223–4, 226,
  237, 251–2, 257, 261–2
 and mandate of Einsatzgruppen,
  14–17
 in Pale of Settlement, 53–7, 59–68
 in Poland, 6–10, 16, 37, 47–8, 53,
  98–9, 102–3, 108, 119, 121–2,
  128–9, 136, 173, 180–1, 200–4, 215,
  233–6, 238, 242, 251–3, 255, 263–5
 proposed sterilization of, 103
 racial fishing policy and, 99–100
 resistance of, 244–5, 251–2, 265, 279
 in response to impending destruction, 278–9
 Röhm Purge and, 91
 in rural areas, 120–1
 Soviet evacuation murders and, 47
 suicides among, 25
 in Ukraine, xi–xii, 46, 59–68,
  111–16, 119, 123–5, 128–35,
  140–50, 164, 169, 172–9, 182,
  184–91, 206–8, 210–11, 217–18,
  237–8, 241, 243, 248, 250–1, 255–8,
  276
 see also anti-Semitism; Final Solution

Jordan, Fritz, 195–6
Jost, Heinz, 227, 274*n*

Kalusch, Hans-Peter, 249–50
Kamenets-Podolsky, 128–30, 160, 172,
 174, 206
Karnau, Hermann, 271–2
Katyn, Katyn Forest, xi, 149, 260
Katz, Sima, 138–40
Kaunas, 53, 112, 122, 125–7, 261
 Barbarossa and, 38–45
 Black Day in, 194–6
 Jews in, 39–46, 126–7, 138, 182,
  192–7, 215–16
Kazimierz Forest, 201–4
Keitel, Wilhelm, 14, 16
Kersten, Felix, 100–2, 104, 197, 227–8,
 262–3, 270
Kiev, 46, 59, 113, 130, 143, 170–80, 185,
 191, 219, 258–60
 Babi Yar executions and, 173–9
 Barbarossa and, 12, 122–3
 crematoria and, 260
 explosions in, 170–1
 fall of, 170–2, 174, 178, 180
 Jews in, xi, 145, 172–9, 206
Kleist, Ewald von, 123, 170
Knappe, Siegfried, 38, 180
 and Pale of Settlement, 53, 57–8
 and stalling of Wehrmacht, 216–17
Konin, 200–2
Krakow, 169, 232
Kretschmer, Karl, 218–21
Kube, Wilhelm, 244–7, 255–6, 276
Kuznetsov, Anatoli, 170–5, 177, 179

Landau, Felix, 61–3
Lange, Rudolf, 17, 119, 207–8
Latvia, Latvians, 12, 75, 164, 181–2,
 261, 265
 exterminations in, 17, 112, 119–22,
  125, 127, 206–14, 216–17, 237,
  242–3, 247
 Jews in, 17, 119–22, 125, 127, 136,
  182, 192, 206–17, 237, 242–3, 247,
  251–2
 pogroms in, 46, 119–21, 192, 214
 Soviet prisoner executions in, 46

PERMISSIONS ACKNOWLEDGMENTS

Grateful acknowledgment is made to the following for permission to reprint previously published material:

Andrew Ezergailis: Excerpts from *The Holocaust in Latvia 1941–1944* by Andrew Ezergailis (Riga: The Historical Institute of Latvia, 1996). Reprinted by permission of the author.

The Free Press and Penguin Books Ltd.: Excerpts from *The Good Old Days: The Holocaust as Seen by Its Perpetrators and Bystanders,* edited by Ernst Klee, Willi Dressen, and Volker Riess, translated by Deborah Burnstone. Copyright © 1988 by S. Verlag GmbH. Translation copyright © 1991 by Deborah Burnstone. Rights outside of the United States from *Those Were the Days: The Holocaust Through the Eyes of the Perpetrators and Bystanders* administered by Penguin Books Ltd., London. Reprinted by permission of The Free Press, a division of Simon & Schuster, Inc., and Penguin Books Ltd.

Harvard University Press: Excerpts from *Surviving the Holocaust: The Kovno Ghetto Diary* by Avraham Tory, edited by Martin Gilbert, translated by Jerzy Michaelowicz, with textual and historical notes by Dina Porat (Cambridge, Mass.: Harvard University Press.) Copyright © 1990 by the President and Fellows of Harvard College. Reprinted by permission of Harvard University Press.

David Higham Associates: Excerpts from *The Kersten Memoirs 1940–1945* by Felix Kersten, translated by Constance Fitzgibbon (London: Hutchinson UK, 1957). Reprinted by permission of David Higham Associates.

Mrs. Chaia Lazar: Excerpts from *Destruction and Resistance* by Chaim Lazar, translated from Hebrew by Galia Eden Barship (Shengold Publishers, 1985). Reprinted by permission of Mrs. Chaia Lazar.

Mrs. William Mishell: Excerpts from *Kaddish for Kovno* by William Mishell (Chicago Review Press, 1988). Reprinted by permission of Mrs. William Mishell.

Peter Padfield: Excerpts from *Himmler* by Peter Padfield. Copyright © 1990 by Peter Padfield. Reprinted by permission of the author.

Pantheon Books, Theo Richmond and The Random House Group Limited: Excerpts from *Konin: A Quest* by Theo Richmond (New York: Pantheon Books and London: Jonathan Cape). Copyright © 1995 by Theo Richmond. Reprinted by permission of Pantheon Books, a division of Random House, Inc., Theo Richmond and The Random House Group Limited.

Time, Inc.: Excerpts from "Eichmann's Own Story: Part I & II" by Adolf Eichmann (*Life,* November 21 & 28, 1960). Copyright © 1960 by Time Inc. Reprinted by permission of Time Inc.

The University of Chicago Press and Christian Gerlach: Excerpts from "The Wannsee Conference, the Fate of German Jews, and Hitler's Decision to Exterminate All European Jews" by Christian Gerlach (*Journal of Modern History* 70:4, December 1998, pp. 759–812). Reprinted by permission of the University of Chicago Press and the author.

PHOTOGRAPHIC CREDITS

Page numbers below refer to photographic insert following text page 146.

Page 1: top and bottom, Bundesarchiv.

Page 2: top and bottom, Zentrale Stelle der Landesjustizverwaltungen, courtesy of USHMM Photo Archives.

Page 3: top left and right, Yad Vashem Photo Archives, courtesy of USHMM Photo Archives; bottom, U.S. National Archives, courtesy of USHMM Photo Archives.

Page 4: inset, Courtesy of USHMM Photo Archives; top and bottom, Main Commission for the Prosecution of the Crimes against the Polish Nation, courtesy of USHMM Photo Archives.

Page 5: top right, Hessisches Hauptstaatsarchiv Wiesbaden, Bundesrepublik Deutschland; bottom, Babi Yar Society, courtesy of USHMM Photo Archives.

Page 6: top, Bundesarchiv; bottom, Main Commission for the Prosecution of the Crimes against the Polish Nation, courtesy of USHMM Photo Archives.

Page 7: top, © Bildarchiv Preussischer Kulturbesitz, Berlin 2001; bottom right, Berlin Document Center.

Pages 8 and 9 (all): Zentrale Stelle der Landesjustizverwaltungen, courtesy of USHMM Photo Archives.

Page 10: top, Ullstein Bild; center, Berlin Document Center; bottom, Jerzy Tomaszewski, courtesy of USHMM Photo Archives.

Page 11: center, Library of Congress, courtesy of USHMM Photo Archives; bottom, © 2000 by Richard Rhodes.

Page 12: top, Czechoslovak News Agency; center, William Gallagher, courtesy of USHMM Photo Archives; bottom, Bundesarchiv.

Page 13: top, YIVO Institute for Jewish Research, courtesy of USHMM Photo Archives; center and bottom, Main Commission for the Prosecution of the Crimes against the Polish Nation, courtesy of USHMM Photo Archives.

Page 14: bottom, YIVO Institute for Jewish Research, courtesy of USHMM Photo Archives.

Page 15: center, Stephen Davis; bottom, U.S. National Archives, courtesy of USHMM Photo Archives.

Page 16 (all): © 2000 by Richard Rhodes.

Printed in the United States
by Baker & Taylor Publisher Services